Foundations of Comparative Politics

This authoritative new introductory textbook  theories and issues involved in the study of c Focusing on democratic government, it covers the field, from constitutional design and institutions through mass and elite politics, groups, parties, the media and governments to policy making and implementation. The final chapter considers the future of the state and democracy in a globalising world. The authors draw on experiences and examples from around the world, and the book includes an extensive supporting apparatus for students and teachers, including briefings, controversies, fact files, key terms, guides to further reading and related websites. Each chapter ends with a section dealing with major theoretical approaches to the subject. The aim is to give students a clear and comprehensive account of comparative politics and government at the start of the twenty-first century.

KEN NEWTON is Professor of Comparative Politics at the University of Southampton, UK. He previously taught at the University of Essex, and was Director of the European Consortium for Political Research. Among his publications is the successful textbook, *The New British Politics* (Longmans, 3rd edn., 2003).

JAN W. VAN DETH is Professor of Political Science and International Comparative Social Research at the University of Mannheim, Germany and was Director of the Mannheim Centre for European Social Research (MZES). His main research areas are political culture (especially social capital and citizenship), social change and comparative research methods.

The companion website for this textbook is at www.cambridge.org/newton. It includes live links and PowerPoint slides for each chapter, plus electronic versions of the glossary and fact files.

CAMBRIDGE TEXTBOOKS IN COMPARATIVE POLITICS

Series Editors:
Jan W. van Deth, *Universität Mannheim, Germany*
Ken Newton, *University of Southampton, United Kingdom*

Comparative research is central to the study of politics. This series
offers accessible but sophisticated materials for students of
comparative politics at the introductory level and beyond. It comprises
an authoritative introductory textbook, *Foundations of Comparative
Politics*, accompanied by volumes devoted to the politics of individual
countries, and an introduction to methodology in comparative
politics. The books share a common structure and approach, allowing
teachers to choose combinations of volumes to suit their particular
course. Attractively designed and accessibly written, this series
provides an up-to-date and flexible teaching resource.

Foundations of Comparative Politics

Democracies of the Modern World

KEN NEWTON and JAN W. VAN DETH

CAMBRIDGE UNIVERSITY PRESS

CAMBRIDGE UNIVERSITY PRESS
Cambridge, New York, Melbourne, Madrid, Cape Town, Singapore, São Paulo

Cambridge University Press
The Edinburgh Building, Cambridge, CB2 8RU, UK

Published in the United States of America by Cambridge University Press, New York

www.cambridge.org
Information on this title:www.cambridge.org/9780521536202

© Ken Newton, Jan W. van Deth 2005

This publication is in copyright. Subject to statutory exception
and to the provisions of relevant collective licensing agreements,
no reproduction of any part may take place without
the written permission of Cambridge University Press.

First published 2005
Third printing 2007

Printed in the United Kingdom at the University Press, Cambridge

A catalogue record for this publication is available from the British Library

Library of Congress Cataloguing in publication data

ISBN 978-0-521-82931-1 hardback
ISBN 978-0-521-53620-2 paperback

Cambridge University Press has no responsibility for the persistence or accuracy
of URLs for external or third-party internet websites referred to in this publication,
and does not guarantee that any content on such websites is, or will remain,
accurate or approppriate.

This book is dedicated to Konstanza and Joke

Contents

Contents

Acknowledgements

This book is the result of our discussions and contacts with many people at various places in the last few years. Ken Newton would like to thank the Wissenschaftszentrum Berlin for time spent there researching and writing early drafts of chapters. Wolfgang Zapf and Roland Habich made this possible with a kind invitation to join their group as a visitor. Tom Cusack, Jan Delhey, Wolf-Dieter Eberwein, Dieter Fuchs, Rick Hofferbert, Ron Inglehart, Max Kaase, Hans-Dieter Klingemann, Christiane Neumann, Marion Obermaier and Edeltraud Roller all combined to make the visits both delightful and productive.

Ken Newton would also like to thank colleagues at the University of Southampton who have provided friendship and intellectual stimulation in the past few years. Though they don't know it, some of the ideas in this book were first tried out over our sandwiches and a great many cups of really bad coffee at lunch time. Sadly, most of the most brilliant theories and insights were shot down in flames in these discussions, by colleagues who based their criticism on no more than acute intelligence, hard information, a thorough knowledge of the subject and a sharp eye for a weak argument. Special thanks are due to Fritz and Mocha and Mocha Metzeler who, with habitual kindness and generosity, made the Mulina available for work on this book, and for rest and recuperation afterwards.

Jan van Deth would like to thank his collaborators at the University of Mannheim and the Mannheim Zentrum für Europäische Sozialforschung (MZES) for similar friendship and intellectual stimulation. In Mannheim, too, many ideas were shot down with good arguments based on an excellent knowledge of the subject matter of comparative politics and a firm grasp of its methods.

Finally, we would like to thank Jana Jughard for preparing the final version of the manuscript.

Ken Newton and Jan W. van Deth
August 2004

Briefings

Fact files

Controversies

Tables

Figures

Abbreviations and acronyms

AfDB	African Development Bank
ASEAN	Association of South East Asian Nations
AV	Alternative Vote
Benelux	Belgium Netherlands, Luxembourg Economic Union
CA	Consumer Association
CBA	Cost-benefit analysis
CEO	Chief executive officer
CIS	Confederation of Independent States
CND	Campaign for Nuclear Disarmament
CoR	Committee of the Regions (EU)
DARS	Democratic Arab Republic of the Sahara
DGB	Deutscher Gewerkschaftsbund (trade union association, Germany)
EAPC	Euro-Atlantic Partnership Council
ECHR	European Court of Human Rights
ECJ	European Court of Justice
ENA	*Ecole Nationale d'Administration*
EP	European Parliament
ESA	European Space Agency
ETUC	European Trade Union Confederation
EU	European Union
FBI	Federal Bureau of Investigation (USA)
GATT	General Agreement on Tariffs and Trade
GM	Genetically modified
IBRD	International Bank for Reconstruction and Development (World Bank)
ICJ	International Court of Justice
IDA	International Development Association
IISS	International Institute for Strategic Studies
ILO	International Labour Organisation
IMF	International Monetary Fund
IOC	International Olympic Committee
IOM	International Organisation for Migration
IPU	Inter-Parliamentary Union
IT	Information technology

JV	Joint venture
MCW	Minimum connected winning (coalition)
MITI	Ministry of International Trade and Industry (Japan)
MMP	Mixed-member proportional voting system
MNC	Multi-national corporation
MWC	Minimum winning coalition
NAFTA	North American Free Trade Association
NASA	National Aeronautics and Space Administration (USA)
NATO	North Atlantic Treaty Organisation
NGO	Non-governmental organisation
OAU	Organisation of African Unity
OECD	Organisation for Economic Cooperation and Development
OFCOM	Office of Communications (UK)
OPEC	Organisation of Petroleum Exporting Countries
OSCE	Organisation for Security and Cooperation in Europe
PAC	Political Action Committee (USA)
PPP	Purchasing power parity
PR	Proportional representation
R&D	Research and Development
SB	Second ballot (voting system)
SES	Socio-economic status
SMSP	Single member, simple plurality voting system
SNTV	Single non-transferable vote
STV	Single transferable vote
TI	Transparency International
TNC	Transnational Corporation
UK	United Kingdom
UN	United Nations
UNHCR	UN High Commission for Refugees
UNITAR	UN Institute for Training and Research
USA	United States
USSR	Union of Soviet Socialist Republics (Soviet Union)
WDIs	World Development Indicators
WEU	Western European Union
WHO	World Health Organisation
WTO	World Trade Organisation

Key terms and concepts

As key terms and concepts are introduced in the book, they are briefly defined in the margin of the text. Rather longer definitions, sometimes with qualifications and examples, are given in the Glossary at the end of the book and a fully searchable, electronic version is available on the companion website.

PART I

The state: origins and development

It was already late at night on 4 August 1789 when the French National Assembly continued its debates. The situation was disastrous. A new wave of social unrest, upheaval and looting had swept the country and people were near starvation in many cities. The problems seemed insoluble and the three classes – nobility, clergy and bourgeoisie – were fighting each other and the king. If no reconciliation could be reached soon, the country would collapse into chaos and civil war. Instead of dealing with these burning problems directly, the Assembly argued about a list of principles that should be used as a guideline and benchmark for political activities. On 26 August 1789, the 'Declaration of the Rights of Man and of the Citizen' was proclaimed. It sought to smash the ancient institutions and end privilege. From that moment on, the power of the state was to be based on the consent of its citizens and the protection of individual rights.

Until the National Assembly declared these principles, France was ruled by the king and his royal clique. The heated debates in August 1789 mark the rise of a new type of government and politics. Political power was no longer based on some 'natural order', God's will, or long-established rights of the nobility. As a citizen, every person had basic and equal rights, and the state was the property of its own citizenry. This double recognition indicated a radical break with previous thinking. Power, government, politics, the state – all these had existed long before the Declaration was proclaimed, but in August 1789 the Assembly knocked down many conventional ideas and replaced them by new interpretations consciously focusing on the crucial position of 'the people'. In this way, the much older idea of the state was given a radically new interpretation.

We start our treatment of comparative politics in this volume with an overview of the historical development of the 'state concept' as well as the actual establishment of states around the world. Part I consists of two chapters. Chapter 1 examines the emergence of the state, its main characteristics, and its spread and variety in the latter half of the twentieth century. As will become clear, states are the most important agencies for the organisation of political power. In chapter 2, we will take a closer look at democratic states and welfare states as they originated in the last two centuries.

At the outset, you should note five important features of this book:

1. It is restricted to the functioning of *democratic states* of the world and to the ways in which they meet the needs and demands of their citizens.
2. It emphasises the *close links and correspondence* between government and politics, on the one hand, and the social and economic conditions of wider society, on the other.
3. It pays attention to the *political relevance* of organisations such as the European Union, Greenpeace or Microsoft, but it considers the state as the most important agency for the organisation of political power.
4. It emphasises the nature of government and politics as being essentially concerned with *power* – that is, with the capacity to make people do things that they do not want to do.
5. It shows how, despite enormous variation in the detail of government and politics in different states, the democratic countries of the world tend to fall into a *small number of types*, and to follow a rather *limited number of patterns*. This is very good news indeed for those studying comparative politics: they would otherwise be overwhelmed by a mass of detail about different countries.

1 The development of the modern state

Watch any newsflash or open any newspaper and you will see headlines such as 'France and Britain agree on migration', 'Reforms in Costa Rica problematic', 'US presents new plan for the Middle East', or 'Germany objects to Dutch tomatoes'. These phrases are shorthand. They refer to an agreement among French and British diplomats to check all passports of passengers from Paris to London, or to an initiative of the German minister for agricultural affairs to reduce the import of watery vegetables. Messages such as these are the alpha and omega of politics and current affairs. And states are always at the centre.

Indeed, the study of states and the similarities and differences in their political institutions and forms of government are at the centre of the study of comparative government. Even fashionable debates about the 'withering away' of the state in an era of globalisation are possible only if we are clear about the concept of the state to start with. Nor can we understand the politics of the European Union, a form of political organisation that is above and beyond individual states, unless we understand what states are and what they do. This does not mean that states are the only things that matter, nor does it mean that 'the state' is a perfectly clear and straightforward concept. But it does mean that the centrality of states in the modern world cannot be neglected, and that the 'state concept' is one of the most important building blocks of comparative politics. Virtually every spot on earth belongs to some state. The starting point of our account of comparative government and politics is therefore the nature of the modern state. And the starting point of our account of the state is a pragmatic approach to the question: *How do we recognise a state when we see one*?

In this introduction, we shall deal with the emergence of the state and the state concept. In spite of the common use of the term, it is not easy to discern states from other organisations and institutes.

The five major topics in this chapter are:

- What is a state?
- Territory, people and sovereignty
- The rise of the modern state
- Catalysts: warfare and capitalism
- Growth after 1945.

Declaration of the Rights of Man

The seventeen articles, describing the purpose of the state and the rights of individual citizens, proclaimed by the French National Assembly in August 1789. A similar list had been proclaimed in the USA thirteen years earlier, in 1776.

■ What is a state?

The state is only one of many different ways of organising government. In the eighteenth century, when the French Assembly issued its '**Declaration of the Rights of Man and of the Citizen**' (see briefing 1.1), states were not widely spread across the globe. Other forms of political organisation such as city-states, empires, princedoms and tribes were much more widespread. The state is a relatively recent political invention. Today, however, the whole world is divided into states, and the concept of the state has triumphed as a form of political organisation. With the exception of the high seas and Antarctica, every place on earth belongs to a state (see figure 1.1). Several areas are disputed among states and wars over territory are waged, but in general there is no quarrel about the fact that states are the main actors in these disputes.

Though states are universal, they still present a puzzle. Philosophers, politicians, jurists and political scientists have argued about them for centuries. It goes without saying that France, Denmark, Uruguay, or South Africa are states: all are independent political entities and each of them is recognised by the others as a state. You can find them on maps, their representatives meet in

---

Briefing 1.1

First three articles of the 'Declaration of the Rights of Man and of the Citizen' (Paris, 1789)

1. Men are born and remain free and equal in rights. Social distinctions may be founded only upon the general good.
2. The aim of all political association is the preservation of the natural and imprescriptible[1] rights of man. These rights are liberty, property, security, and resistance to oppression.
3. The principle of all sovereignty resides essentially in the nation. No body nor individual may exercise any authority which does not proceed directly from the nation.

(www.yale.edu)

[1] 'Imprescriptible' means self-evident and obvious, and not derived from or dependent upon any external authority.

Figure 1.1: States of the world, 2004

Source: http://www.lib.utexas.edu/maps/world_maps/world_pol2004.pdf.

New York or Paris and you hear their national anthems on various occasions. Still, seven key difficulties can arise when we try to characterise states in general terms:

- States vary hugely, ranging from France under Louis XIV to the most modern democracies. They range from India and Canada, to Denmark and New Zealand, and from Stalin's Soviet Union to Germany under Hitler. How can we put such a diverse collection of political phenomena into the same box labelled 'states'?
- Some forms of government look like states in some respects, but they are not actually states. The European Union and the Russian Federation perform many state-like functions, but are they the same as states such as Argentina, Latvia, or Taiwan?
- The Vatican, Luxembourg, Monaco and San Marino look like states in some respects, but they are not the same as their neighbours, France and Italy.
- States are certainly not the only political actors in the world. The political impact of organisations such as the IMF, Al Quaida and Microsoft are obvious. Why should we focus on states instead of these powerful organisations?
- Some states have been recognised for centuries, but others, such as Israel and Palestine, are highly disputed. Is the latter a state simply because it calls itself one?
- Even for undisputed states such as France it is not easy to reach agreement about the exact date of its beginning. Was it in 1789? Or should we go back to the Treaty of Verdun in 843? Did states exist in Africa or Asia before European colonisers drew borders, almost haphazardly, through these continents? Were Babylon or Ancient Rome states as we understand them today?
- The term 'state' is quite close to other but different terms, such as country, nation, political system, nation-state and empire. To make things even more complicated, these terms are often confused or loosely used as synonyms.

We do not get a clear picture of what is meant by the term 'state' by simply looking at the different ways it is used (or misused) today. We have to be more systematic, and we can do this by following in the footsteps of the Greek **Aristotle** philosopher Aristotle. He began with the question: What distinguishes a state **(384–322 bc)** from other forms of social life? In the opening sentences of book I of his *Politics*, Aristotle remarks:

> Every state is a community of some kind, and every community is established with a view to some good ... But, if all communities aim at some good, the state or political community, which is the highest of all, and which embraces all the rest, aims, and in greater degree than any other, at the highest good.
>
> *(Louise R. Loomis, ed., Aristotle: On Man in the Universe, Roslyn, NY: Black, 1943: 249)*

This characterisation contains a number of important assertions. First of all, a state is not some abstract construct, but a variant of human social life (a 'community'). It is, furthermore, not just any variant of social life, but the most important one ('the highest of all') and it can also be called a 'political community'. Finally, all other communities are included in the state because it 'embraces all the rest'. Modern states still claim to be the dominant force, just as Aristotle noted. In order to obtain and keep its place as the highest and most encompassing 'community', a state must be in charge: that is, it must be more powerful than any of the 'communities' it incorporates. This characterisation immediately suggests that power is vital for any discussion of states and politics. And yet even this focus on power, important though it is in defining the state, is not sufficient. States also have other characteristics to do with territory, people and sovereignty (controversy 1.1).

Controversy 1.1

What is a state?

1. Do we have a clear idea about the state?

What is a (or the) nation? No satisfactory criterion can be discovered for deciding which of the many human collectivities should be labelled in this way. (Eric Hobsbawm, *Nations and Nationalism since 1780*, Cambridge: Cambridge University Press, 1990: 5)

As a concept the State has been somewhat overlooked in the political theory and research of the last century, especially in the Anglo-Saxon world, and still creates a good deal of confusion and uncertainty.

(David Robertson, *The Penguin Dictionary of Politics*, Harmondsworth: Penguin, 1985: 308)

2. Is the rise of states self-evident?

Of the many theories addressing the problem of state origins, the simplest denies that there is any problem to solve. Aristotle considered states the natural condition of human society, requiring no explanation. His error was understandable, because all societies which with he would have been acquainted – Greek societies of the fourth century B.C. – were states. However, we now know that, as of A.D. 1492, much of the world was instead organised into chiefdoms, tribes, or bands. State formation does demand an explanation.

(Jared Diamond, *Guns, Germs, and Steel*, New York: Norton, 1999: 283)

3. Where do states come from?

If we now ask, where the state comes from, the answer is that it is the product of a long and arduous struggle in which the class which occupies what is for the time the key positions in the process of production gets the upper hand over its rivals and fashions a state which will enforce that set of property relations which is in its own interest. In other words any particular state is the child of the class or classes in society which benefit from the particular set of property relations which it is the state's obligation to enforce . . . the state power must be monopolised by the class or classes which are the chief beneficiaries.

(Paul M. Sweezy, *The Theory of Capitalist Development*, New York: Monthly Review Press, 1942: 242–3)

■ Territory, people and sovereignty

States collect taxes, offer protection against crime, provide schools and highways, wage wars, control the opening hours of shops and promote economic growth. They erect police stations and Inland Revenue offices, municipal swimming pools and embassies abroad, mints and hospitals and they employ fire fighters and soldiers. Some states improve the living conditions of their citizens and provide services for the young and old, the sick and disabled, and the poor and unemployed. But it is not difficult to find examples of states that behave quite differently – ranging from the protection of illegal money deposited in Swiss banks to war and the genocidal killing of innocent millions for 'reason of state'. How, then, do we recognise a state if virtually anything can and has been done by them?

In spite of confusion and continuing debate about the 'nature' of the state, it seems to be rather easy to recognise a **state**. Almost every state call itself a 'state' and emphasises its uniqueness by having a national anthem, a flag, a coat of arms, a national currency, a national capital and a head of state. States are acknowledged by other states as 'states', and they exchange ambassadors. These are, however, the symbols of statehood. At the heart of the matter lie three core features of the state:

State
The organisation that issues and enforces binding rules for the people within a territory.

Territory
Terrain or geographical area.

- A state entails a **territory** *that it considers to be its own*. This area can be as huge as Canada or India, as small as The Netherlands or Switzerland, or even as tiny as Slovenia and Tuvalu. It can be an island or a continent (or, in the case of Australia, both), and its borders may have been undisputed and secure for centuries or constantly challenged. To the territory of a state belongs the air space above it as well as its coastal waters. The only restraint on the territorial aspect of the state is that it has to be more or less enduring; an ice floe – even one as large as France or Uruguay – does not count. Sometimes the label 'territorial state' is used to underline the importance of this geographical feature. Less precisely, we commonly use the term '**country**'.

Country
An imprecise synonym or short-hand term for state or nation-state.

People
A group of people whose common consciousness and identity makes them a collective entity.

- A state entails a **people**, that is, *persons living together*. Here, too, numbers are irrelevant (think of China, India, the Palau Islands and Iceland). To be a people, the individuals concerned must have something in common, but exactly what they must share to be called 'a people' – language, religion, a common history, a culture – is a highly contested matter. Minorities who do not speak the same language, or share the same religion or culture can be found in almost every state in the world. For instance, 30 per cent of the citizens of Latvia are Russians. For the moment, we shall stick to the requirement that any state requires a population, and say nothing about minimum numbers or what they have in common. In other words a deserted island may be part of a state, but it cannot itself be a state. Equally, not all individuals are citizens of a state. As the number of exiles, migrants, and asylum seekers increases, so the problem of the stateless becomes ever more acute (briefing 1.2).

Briefing 1.2

Not every human being is a citizen . . .

Citizens are protected and supported by the state. They can usually get a passport, a licence to drive a car, admission to elementary education, a job, or assistance if they are unemployed or ill. Yet quite a number of citizens are forced to leave the state they were born in, because they are refugees, exiles, or asylum seekers. Those of us lucky enough to be secure in our citizenship are likely to take it for granted, but its great importance in our lives can be seen in the plight of those who are deprived of citizen rights – no residency rights, no working rights, no passport, no welfare services, no driving licence and perhaps no bank account. More and more people are in this situation as the number of migrants, exiles and asylum seekers grows. Which state should provide a stateless person with a passport, work rights, or unemployment support? Many are very reluctant to take in citizens of other states and offer them the same rights as their own citizens.

   In 1950, the UN created the High Commission for Refugees (UNHCR), a special organisation to deal with exiles and refugees. Its main aim was to find new places to live for about 400,000 people who had been forced to leave the place they lived in Europe after the Second World War. Initially, UNHCR was founded for three years, but in 2002 it was working harder than ever, faced with the problem of about 20 million people forced to live in exile spread over more than 120 countries. (www.unhcr.ch)

- A state is *sovereign*; that is, it holds the highest power and, in principle, *can act with complete freedom and independence*: it has **sovereignty**. Aristotle had something like this in mind with his remark that the state is a community 'which is the highest of all, and which embraces all the rest'. Sovereignty is a claim to ultimate authority and power. Usually, two types are distinguished: (i) *internal* **sovereignty**, meaning that within its own territory every state can act as it wishes and is independent of other powers and (ii) *external* sovereignty, referring to the fact that the state is recognised as a state by other states. Sovereignty means that a state is independent and not under the authority of another state or 'community'. Here, we must distinguish between *power* and *sovereignty*: the USA and Luxembourg are, legally speaking, equal as sovereign states, though the USA is vastly more powerful. States are also sovereign in principle, as we noted above. This does not necessarily mean that they are free to do whatever they want, because all sorts of factors may limit their powers – other states, the global economy, even the weather. Moreover, states may voluntarily limit their power by signing international agreements, although if they are sovereign states they may also decide to revoke these agreements if circumstances change. Briefing 1.3 gives an example of how state sovereignty may be conditioned or limited by international agreements.

Sovereignty
The highest power that gives the state freedom of action within its own territory.

  Each state is characterised by these three features; each claims sovereign power over its people and its territory. More specifically, we can speak of a state as an organisation that issues and enforces rules for a territorially defined area that are binding for people in that area. Sovereignty does not mean that

---

Briefing 1.3

Sovereignty: (un)limited power?

By definition, sovereignty means unlimited power. But states can and do accept restrictions on their sovereignty, for instance by binding their own exercise of power by constitutional rules. An example of a restriction on the basis of an international agreement is Article 33 of the 'Geneva Convention relating to the Status of Refugees' of 1951 which stipulates that:

No Contracting State shall expel or return ('refouler')[1] a refugee in any manner whatsoever to the frontiers of territories where his life or freedom would be threatened on account of his race, nationality, membership of a particular social group or political opinion.' (www.unhchr.ch)

[1] By 'refouler' is meant to expel or return a refugee.

---

the state is above the law. Indeed, most states bind their sovereign power by subjecting them to the rules of a constitution (see chapter 3).

Straightforward as this definition of a state may seem to be, there are still complications. Some regions in the south of Italy are, in effect, controlled by the Mafia in a state-like manner. Multi-national companies (MNCs) such as Nike or Shell, and organisations such as the IMF, are also hugely powerful. Did the states of The Netherlands and Belgium disappear when they were occupied by Germany in the 1940s? What about the Baltic states that were overrun by the Soviet Union in the 1930s?

In order to deal with those complications, the notion of the state is further specified by looking more closely at sovereignty. The German social scientist **Max Weber** Max Weber did this stressing, first of all, that the abstract term 'sovereignty' **(1864–1920)** meant that the state possessed the monopoly of the use of physical force. Only if the state controlled the use of physical force could it impose its rules and realise its claims as the most important 'community'. Weber moved one crucial step further. In his view, the control of physical force was not sufficient for statehood. Also required was a 'monopoly' that was accepted as right – **Legitimacy** a monopoly that was not only legal, but also has **legitimacy**. The Weberian The condition of definition of the state, then, consists of four elements:

being in
accordance with
the norms and
values of the
people.
'Legitimate
power' is
accepted
because it is
seen as right.

- Weber accepts the *three conventional characteristics* of a state – territory, people, sovereignty.
- He specifies the meaning of 'sovereignty' by referring to the distinction between 'legal' and 'legitimate'. It is not sufficient to base physical force upon the law (legality). In addition there must be a legitimate use of physical force; that is, the use of physical force by the state must be *accepted by its people*.
- The use of physical force alone, therefore, does not distinguish between states and other organisations. Organisations such as Microsoft, the World Bank, the IMF, the Mafia and the European Union are powerful, and may be more important for many people than, say, the state of Latvia or Iceland.

Some of these organisations use physical force, but none of them claims the *monopoly of the legitimate use of this force* over its people as states do.

- Finally, Weber points to the fact that some *actor* or *institution* must monopolise the legitimate use of physical force if the state is to avoid the danger of anarchy and lawlessness.

We can see these elements in Max Weber's definition of the state:

> A compulsory political organisation with continuous operations will be called a 'state' insofar as its administrative staff successfully uphold the claim to the *monopoly* of the *legitimate* use of physical force in the enforcement of its order.
>
> (Max Weber, Economy and Society: An Outline of Interpretative Sociology, *eds. Guenther Roth and Claus Wittich,* New York: Bedminster Press 1968: 54; emphasis in the original)

Can we recognise a state if we see one with the help of Weber's characterisation? Most of the time it will not be too difficult to grasp that a trade agreement by Chile and Argentina will involve two states, or that Poland's application for EU membership is an act of state. Similarly, traffic regulations are enforced by the police in the name of their state, as are invitations to participate in public elections. All these are based on the claim of a monopoly of the legitimate use of physical force over people living in a specific area – and so all are acts of state.

We mentioned earlier that other terms are sometimes used in place of 'state'. Most usually, states are referred to as 'countries'. At the beginning of the third millennium, the world is divided into slightly fewer than 200 states or countries. The phrase '**nation**' is also used as a synonym for 'state', so we now turn to this concept, and the even more confusing concept of the **nation-state**.

Nation-state
A state based on the acceptance of a common culture, a common history and a common fate, irrespective of whatever political, social and economic differences may exist between the members of the nation-state.

▪ The rise of the modern state

The modern state emerged in medieval Europe, between about 1100 and the sixteenth century. In that period, territorially based rulers claimed independence and created their own administrations and armies. At the same time, the idea of sovereign power was developed. However, each state has its own unique historical patterns in its progress towards modern statehood, and none follows quite the same path. Any discussion of state formation and the development of states must therefore start from a two-fold assertion: (i) the state concept is inextricably bound up with European history and Western political theory, and (ii) there is no uniform or general law that governs the appearance, or disappearance, of states.

▪ *Historical origins and development*

States originate in many different ways and their development follows no single pathway. There are three general patterns, however:

Fact file 1.1

The Treaty of Westphalia (1648)

The first decades of the seventeenth century were characterised by a series of wars between Spain, France, Sweden, Bavaria, The Netherlands, Denmark and countries in central Europe, known as the *Thirty Years War* (1618–48). It destroyed about 2,000 castles, 1,600 cities and more than 18,000 villages across Europe. The population of the war-torn area declined about 50 per cent in rural areas, and up to 30 per cent in urban regions. This changed the economic, demographic and political landscape in Europe profoundly and eventually led to a settlement that, in effect, created the state system of the modern world.

In a situation of continual wars and conflicts, it slowly became clear that a solution could be based on a 'package deal' between different sides. In 1648, delegates from the warring factions met in the cities of Osnabrück and Münster in Westphalia to negotiate an all-encompassing peace treaty. The final set of agreements is called the *Treaty of Westphalia* or the *Peace of Westphalia*. It had very important consequences for the division of power – and therefore for the development of states – in Europe. The agreements recognised the rights of states and their sovereignty, settled the religious disputes in Europe and provided solutions for a number of territorial claims. Most important, the Treaty established a system of states, and of diplomatic relations between them, that has lasted more or less intact until the present day.

Treaty of Westphalia (1648)

- *Transformation*   First, states arose on the basis of the *gradual transformation of existing independent political units* – mostly medieval monarchies. Major examples were Britain and France, whose independence goes back to the Middle Ages and whose development as states took several centuries. In Europe the Treaty of Westphalia signalled the final triumph of the state as a form of political organisation, as well as settling the borders of many states (see fact file 1.1).
- *Unification*   Second, some states arose by the *unification of independent but dispersed political units*. This process was mainly concentrated in the nineteenth century and major examples were Germany and Italy.
- *Secession*   Finally, states arose from the *secession or break-up of independent political units* – mostly empires or large heterogeneous states – into one or more states. The break-up of the Austro-Hungarian Empire and the Ottoman Empire after the First World War are examples. More recently, Czechoslovakia was split into two independent states: the Czech Republic and Slovakia.

Most new states today, such as those born out of the collapse of the Soviet Union and Yugoslavia, are the product of secession. Few states are now the result of successful attempts to unify formerly divided or dispersed independent units.

■ *State formation and nation building*

One of the best-known efforts to account for the different historical paths taken by the modern states of Europe is presented by the Norwegian political scientist Stein Rokkan. In his view, the formation of modern states proceeded in several phases, which are closely linked to basic societal conflicts ('**cleavages**'). Rokkan also distinguished between *state formation* and *nation building*. The first concerns the creation of state institutions, especially an army, a bureaucracy, and a system of **government**. The second involves welding the population of the state into a single 'people' with a shared sense of belonging that often comes from a common language, religion, education, historical heritage and culture.

Rokkan discerned four stages in the development of the modern state. The first two are generated by powerful elites who attempt to consolidate their power and territorial independence. The second two are of a quite different nature and concern the internal restructuring of established states.

The four stages are:

- State formation
- Nation building
- Mass democracies
- Welfare states.

State formation: penetration

In the first phase, elites took the initiative for the *unification of a given territory*, usually the elites of major urban centres who consolidated their control over peripheral and rural areas. Territorial consolidation was achieved mainly by economic and military means. In order to control these territories and secure their compliance, institutions were built to provide internal order and deal with disputes (police and courts), to provide external security (armed forces and diplomatic services), to extract resources (taxes and tolls) and to improve communications (roads and bridges), often for military reasons. Clear demarcation of territory was crucially important. Broadly speaking, the period of state formation in Europe started in the high Middle Ages and lasted until the foundations of the west European state system were enshrined in the Treaty of Westphalia (see fact file 1.1).

Nation building: standardisation

During the second phase of nation building the main concerns were *cultural issues* of a common language, religious differences and compulsory education. The aim was to create feelings of a common identity and a sense of allegiance to the political system among the often disparate populations of the new states. A common, standardised language was spread by compulsory education for every child. Military conscription for young men strengthened feelings of identity with the nation. The central idea of the nation-state is the acceptance of a common culture, a common history and a common fate, irrespective of any social and economic differences between people. If the historical roots of this common fate were not self-evident – and usually they were not – national myths about shared experiences and historical destinies were often created

Stein Rokkan (1921–79)

Cleavages
Cleavages are deep and persistent differences in society where (1) objective social differences (class, religion, race, language, or region) are aligned with (2) subjective awareness of these differences (different cultures, ideologies and orientations).

Government
A government executes the monopoly on the legitimate use of physical force within a state. Securing internal and external sovereignty of the state are major tasks of any government.

and spread through the school system. In order to heighten national identity, 'system symbols' – such as a national hymn, national flag and national
heroes – were emphasised. By developing this sense of 'belonging', elites tried
to transform their states into nation-states.

Mass democracies: equalisation

Although the nation-state is now the 'property' of its citizenry it was elites,
not masses, who originally created and ruled it. In the third phase the masses
conquered the right to *participate in governmental decision making*, and hence
democratic states (or democracies) were created. Political parties were founded
to link citizens with elites in assemblies and parliaments. Less visible – but certainly not less significant – was the institutionalisation of opposition parties:
gradually these political systems accepted the idea that peaceful opposition
to the government was legitimate, and even the idea of peaceful change of
groups or parties in government. The idea of the alternation of parties in government was associated with the belief in the principle of the legitimacy of
popularly elected government. Hence universal adult suffrage was introduced
at a fairly early stage, although women usually had to wait much longer to
vote. In mass democracies, political power is legitimated by mass participation
and elections. The earliest mass democracies arose in Europe towards the end
of the nineteenth century.

Welfare states: redistribution

The last phase in the development of the territorial state is the explicit endorse-
ment of policies to strengthen economic solidarity between different parts of
the population. Public welfare services were created to support the young and
old, the sick and disabled, and the unemployed and poor. Progressive taxation
and state contributions facilitate the transfer of resources from the wealthier
to the less fortunate parts of the population. **Welfare states**, characterised by
redistribution and equality of opportunity, were created, particularly in north-
western Europe after the Second World War.

Welfare states
Democracies
that accept
responsibility for
the well-being of
their citizens,
particularly by
redistributing
resources and
providing
services for the
young, old, sick,
disabled and
unemployed.

Few states went through these four stages from the medieval period to the
third millennium in a more or less regular and ordered way (France and Britain
are exceptional). In many cases, the order of the four stages was interrupted by
revolution, war or foreign occupation (as for Germany) and it is not easy to say
when some phases started or how long they lasted. When, for example, did Italy
become a welfare state? In some instances, phases overlapped or coincided.
Spain combined the last two phases after its transition to democracy in the
1970s. Some phases are very long for some states, but hardly discernible for
others.

In other words, the history of each state is too complex and diverse to be covered by a simple, uniform scheme. Rokkan's four phases help us understand the
process of state and nation building not because each state follows exactly the
same pattern but because we can compare and understand how they developed

by describing how each deviates from, or conforms to, the general pattern. In spite of their differences, however, the early developments of almost all states were in the early stages driven by two fundamental and enormously powerful forces: *warfare* and *capitalism*.

■ Catalysts: warfare and capitalism

The initial phase of the state building process in Europe, as we have seen, is focused on securing the compliance of territories with the wishes of centralising elites. Military might was important in this process. Military technology changed in the late medieval period, replacing the heavy cavalry with massed infantry and, later, with artillery and guns. Small private armies with an obligation to a feudal lord were replaced by large standing armies serving the state. The rights and powers of local landowners and of the nobility were replaced by centralised state power and resources. At the same time, the need to wage war against internal and external enemies functioned as catalysts for state formation, because only states were able to organise and pay for the large armies and the wars they fought. War was a normal state of affairs for the emerging states of the sixteenth and seventeenth centuries: great powers such as Spain, France, England, and The Netherlands were very frequently at war during this period. Persistent involvement in wars can thus be seen as the primary factor behind the emergence of the modern state: 'The long revolution in military affairs and the incessant struggle for hegemony and counter hegemony forged the high-capacity states of Europe' (Spruyt 2002).

The rise of capitalism in the eighteenth and nineteenth century also facilitated the emergence of the modern state. The capitalist mode of production brings together two important factors – labour and capital – for the creation of goods that can be sold at a profit. But this production process depends on the availability of a secure infrastructure; that is, investment and profit depend on *social and physical security and stability*. The infrastructure necessary for capitalism and profit includes not just roads, bridges, harbours, canals and railways but also educational and health facilities, as well as police to protect property and a legal system regulating contracts and commercial disputes. Some of these can be produced only by a central power, while others require central regulation and control.

Hendrik Spruyt, 'The origins, development, and possible decline of the modern state', *Annual Review of Political Science,* **5, 2002: 136**

Capitalism, then, requires an agency capable of the following four tasks:

- To secure investments
- To provide social and physical infrastructures
- To control and regulate conflicts between capitalists and other classes
- To protect the interests of capitalists and other classes against competition from abroad.

The obvious institution to perform these functions is the state with its territorial boundary and its claim to monopolise the legitimate use of physical force. No other institution can perform the functions as effectively. As one observer remarks: 'If the state had not existed prior to capitalism, it would have been necessary for capitalism to invent it' (Johnston 1993).

Was the state created to wage war and promote capitalism? In large part, yes, but this interpretation is too simple for the complex, difficult and varied process of state formation. Warfare and capitalism are certainly very important factors in the formation of states and the development of states in Europe. Yet none of these factors accounts for the initial rise of independent territorial units and the idea of sovereignty. The demands of war and profit certainly strengthen the formation of territorially defined political units that became known as states, but equally they were also important catalysts rather than direct causes of state formation.

Ronald J. Johnston, The rise and decline of the corporate-welfare state: a comparative analysis in global context', in Peter J. Taylor (ed.), *Political Geography of the Twentieth Century*, London: Belhaven Press, 1993: 121

■ Growth after 1945

From Europe, the idea of the modern state rapidly spread over the world, but it was not until the second half of the twentieth century that the number of states suddenly increased. After the First and Second World War, states founded special organisations to deal with relations among themselves, especially with regard to international conflicts. Some observers even looked forward to the creation of a single 'world state'. The League of Nations was created in 1919, but not all those eligible applied for membership and the organisation remained rather weak. After the Second World War a new organisation of states was set up: the United Nations (UN). UN membership is an unambiguous sign of internationally recognised statehood, and virtually all states have joined. Only the Vatican, Sahara (DARS) and Taiwan are not members of the UN, although they can be considered states. For a long time Switzerland declined membership to underline its international neutrality, but it applied for admission in 2003.

The spread of states over the world is illustrated by the steady growth of UN membership. Figure 1.2 shows the increase from about fifty states in 1945 to 191 in 2004. Three stages of growth are evident:

- A first occurs in the *second half of the 1950s*, when a first wave of decolonisation (e.g. Ghana, Morocco, Tunisia, Libya, Laos) took place. In addition, the recognition of 'spheres of influence' for the USA and the Soviet Union (USSR) allowed a number of states (e.g. Albania, Austria, Finland, Japan, Romania) to become UN members.
- Decolonisation also marks the second wave of the spread of states, which started in the *early 1960s* (including Algeria, Gabon, Senegal, Chad) and lasted until well into the 1970s (Surinam, Mozambique, Vietnam). By 1980, more than 155 states were UN members.
- The last rapid increase took place *after 1989*, when the collapse of the Soviet Union and the end of communist rule in central and eastern Europe caused

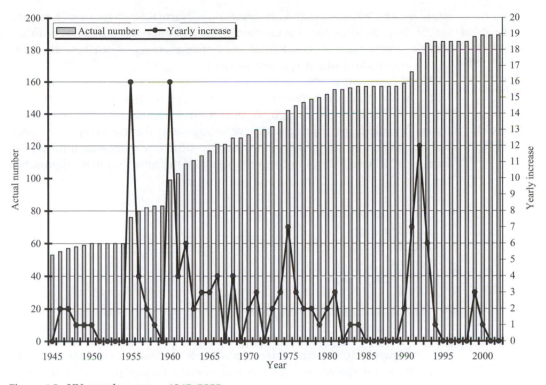

Figure 1.2: UN member states, 1945–2002
Source: Der Fischer Weltalmanach (Frankfurt/M.: Fischer, various years).

a fresh wave of nation-state creation in places such as Hungary, Latvia, Lithuania and Poland. The spread of states, however, continued in the 1990s because of the foundation of new ones (including Bosnia-Herzegovina, the Czech Republic, Slovakia) and to the search for recognition among existing countries, such as Kiribati and Tonga.

Occasionally states disappear. This was the case with the unification of East and West Germany in 1990 and North and South Yemen in the same year. Attempts to obtain independence by regional or ethnic separatist movements in some parts of the world probably mean that states will continue to increase in number in the coming decades.

**Plato
(427–347 BC)**

■ State theories

The state has fascinated political theorists since the rise of the Greek city-state and the writings of Aristotle and Plato more than 2,400 years ago. Modern theories fall into two very broad categories. First, there are **normative political theories**. These are based on values and judgements about how the world

Normative political theories
Theories about how the world should be or ought to be.

should be, and what governments *ought to do*. Normative theories of the state are discussed in some detail in chapter 13. Second, there are **empirical political theories**, completely different from normative theories, about how the state *actually operates* and why it *operates that way*.

Empirical political theories
Theories that try to understand how the political world actually works and why it works that way.

We shall present a systematic overview of empirical theories of the state based on the relations between states and societies at the end of chapter 2. For the moment, it is enough to note that political scientists, historians and philosophers have presented a very large and diverse array of theoretical approaches to the state and its origin, which is surpassed only by the number of different states in the world. Four of the most common approaches are:

- Constitutional
- Ethical and moral
- Conflict
- Pluralist

■ *Constitutional approaches*

According to these theories, the state is established by some *agreement or social contract* between citizens and rulers that defines the major functions and tasks of the state and the powers of its rulers. Social contract theorists know very well that there never was an actual 'contract' of this kind, but they conduct a sort of mental experiment in order to understand what sorts of agreements between citizens and rulers are necessary to establish an ordered and stable state. The main concern of these theories is the question of how the *legitimacy* of the state is established.

■ *Ethical and moral approaches*

The starting point of these theories is how we can organise society so that individuals can live together as *peacefully and satisfactorily* as possible. Some take the view that society consists of individuals who should be as free as possible to do what they wish. Others view society as a collective entity that should ensure the collective well-being and welfare of its individual citizens. A variant of such views is the religious theories that argue that the state should establish the rule of God on earth, or else ensure that the state conducts its affairs according to God's intentions and rules.

■ *Conflict approaches*

These theories stress the conflicting nature of interests and values in society and see the state as a device to exercise the *power necessary to regulate these conflicts.* Marxist theories are one version of this approach. They emphasise the unavoidable struggle between different classes and their incompatible economic interests, and claim that the state is nothing other than an instrument by which property owners maintain their power over the great mass of the working class. As we have already seen, capitalism and state building were closely connected, and from this it can also be argued that the state is the means by which capitalists control other classes in society in order to secure their own interests. Feminist theories of the state are similar in some respects to class theories, but instead of seeing the world in terms of classes they see it as divided between male and female interests. Feminists argue that the state has been used by men to control women, and that it should now become the battle ground for women's liberation.

■ *Pluralist approaches*

Like conflict approaches, pluralist theories see the state as the main instrument for the regulation of conflict and the reconciliation of competing interests. But rather than arguing that the state is the instrument of the ruling class, pluralists see it as a kind of referee that uses its legitimate authority (force if necessary) to make sure that the *interests of all groups are treated reasonably fairly.* The state is a battle ground for many competing groups, not an instrument of class control and oppression.

This does not exhaust the main theories of the state, nor the many variations on each of the main approaches, and you will inevitably encounter other theories and other variations. It will be helpful to ask four questions about any new theory in order to get an idea of its main content and concerns:

1. Is the theory a *normative* one that deals with the ideals and goals of the state, or is it an *empirical* theory that tries to describe and understand the nature and organisation of the state – the way in which the state actually operates as opposed to how it should operate?
2. Does the theory start from *individual rights and duties* and the importance of preserving them (in which case it is probably an individualist one)? Or does it start from the *mutual obligations and interdependence* of citizens (in which case it is probably a collectivist one)?
3. Does the theory emphasise the *laws and the formal structure* of institutions of the state (in which case it is likely to have its roots in organisational or constitutional approaches)?
4. Does the theory concentrate on the *competing interests* of classes, ethnic groups, or men and women (in which case it is likely to be a conflict theory), or does it emphasise the capacity of the state to *reconcile and integrate* the interests of different social groups (in which case it is likely to belong to the pluralist family)?

■ Summary

This chapter has dealt with the difficulties of characterising and defining states, and with the historical development of modern states. It argues that:

- States developed in Europe in the late medieval period and gradually spread over the rest of the world. With the exception of Antarctica and the high seas, every spot on earth belongs to one of the 191 states that exist today.
- States arise out of the transformation of existing political units, from the unification of different political units and as a result of the secession of political units that become independent. Historically, the creation of each state has followed a unique path, but warfare and capitalism have played a major role in most cases.
- States are characterised by three features: territory, people and sovereignty.
- An important aspect of state's power is that it should not only be legal, but also legitimate; that is, the use of power should be in accordance with the norms and values of its citizens. The term 'legitimacy' is especially used by Max Weber in his definition of the state.
- Although the decline of the state has been predicted, even the death of the state in a global world, the number of states in the world is still rising.

Further reading

Discussions about the state and its development can be found in overviews by Patrick Dunleavy and Brendan O'Leary, *Theories of the State: The Politics of Liberal Democracy* (Basingstoke: Macmillan, 1987) and Andrew Vincent, *Theories of the State* (Oxford: Blackwell, 1987). A concise overview of the same subject matter is presented by Graeme Gill, *The Nature and Development of the Modern State* (Basingstoke: Palgrave, 2003). The development of the concept of the state is summarised by Alexander d'Entrèves in his contribution on this topic to the *Dictionary of the History of Ideas* (New York: Scribners, 1973). A very detailed historical description of government and politics is presented by Samuel E. Finer in his monumental three-volume publication *The History of Government* (Oxford: Oxford University Press, 1997), which covers all types of government from ancient times and in every part of the world.

Websites

http://www.nationmaster.com	Extensive statistical information about many economic, social, political and demographical developments for virtually all states of the world. Probably the best website with which to start any search for information about states.
http://www.un.org	Official website of the UN. Provides information on the UN as well as links to specific organisations.
http://www.cia.gov/cia/ publications/factbook/	Statistical information about many economic, social, political and demographical developments in many states.

Projects

1. Would you call the country you live in a 'nation' (or a 'nation-state')? What makes it a state, and when did it achieve statehood?
2. Draw up lists of:
   (1) the ten largest and smallest states in the world
   (2) the ten oldest and youngest states in the world
   (3) the ten richest and poorest states in the world.
3. Why is the number of states in the world still increasing?

2   The democratic state

Democratic states appear in many different forms. Some are as old as France or as young as Lithuania; some are large like Canada and India or small like Estonia and Namibia; some are as rich as Sweden or as poor as Mali. States can be characterised and classified in endless ways, but for political analysis the *use of power* is a crucial aspect. Once a country is sovereign, it can use its power as it wishes. Here, too, the diversity is astonishing.

Many states gradually accepted the idea that citizens should have the opportunity to be involved in political decision making processes. Even in small communities such as the classical city-state of Athens or a contemporary Swiss town, it is very difficult to base decisions on the participation of many people. For that reason, political decision making is usually left to *officials* who have been elected by citizens. A **democracy** is a system of government in which leaders are chosen in competitive elections, where many parties and candidates participate and where opposition parties can attain power if they gain popular support. Terms such as 'political democracy' and 'liberal democracy' are often used as synonyms for democracy. Together with elections, democracies are characterised by their protection of the human and civil rights of their citizens.

Democracy
'A political system whose leaders are elected in competitive multi-party and multi-candidate processes' (Freedom House).

We deal with democratic states or democracies in this book. These states typically also accept responsibility for the young and old, the sick and disabled and the unemployed and poor among their citizens. That is, democracies usually adopt welfare provisions, although these are sometimes extensive and well developed and sometimes minimal and basic. Democracies that have adopted these kinds of tasks are called 'welfare states'. Since support for the less advantaged social groups is based on *redistribution of resources* among various groups, political decision making in welfare states can be very complicated and controversial.

In this chapter, the main characteristics of democracies and welfare states are presented. We discuss the problems in drawing clear lines between democratic and non-democratic states. We have to also face the question of why we continue to regard states as the most important building blocks of comparative analysis, when some writers claim that they are being replaced in importance in an increasingly global society by agencies of international government and by transnational organisations of various kinds.

In this chapter, we shall deal with the main characteristics of democracies and their welfare provisions, and the reasons for the persistence of the concept of the state in comparative political analysis. The five major topics in this chapter are:

- The modern state and democracy
- Democracy and the rise of democratic states
- Redistribution and welfare states
- Why study states?
- Theories of state and society.

■ The modern state and democracy

As we saw in chapter 1, mass political involvement transformed states into 'mass democracies' when the rights of opposition were recognised and general suffrage granted. Stein Rokkan emphasised the fact that the internal restructuring of the state converts subjects of the state into citizens – 'the people' (see chapter 1). But how do we distinguish between democratic and non-democratic states in the first place? Usually, this question is answered by referring to citizens' *political rights, elections* and *parliamentary accountability*.

■ *Citizens' rights*

Discussions about political power and the rights of citizens have always been at the centre of debates about democracy. As the members of the French National Assembly confirmed in August 1789, the struggle for political power is not an aim in itself. It is what can be done with power that matters. After all, the 'Declaration of the Rights of Man and of the Citizen' published in Paris (briefing 1.1) talks about the end of all political institutions being 'the natural and inalienable rights of man' in its Article 2. In a similar way, the Virginia 'Bill of Rights' – published in the USA thirteen years earlier than the French document, in 1776 – stressed the universal nature of these rights. A first characteristic of democracies, then, is the acknowledgment that it is not power but the protection of rights ('**human rights**') that is of prime concern.

Human rights
The innate, inalienable and inviolable right of humans to free movement and self-determination. Such rights cannot be bestowed, granted, limited, bartered, or sold away. Inalienable rights can be only secured or violated.

Following this line of reasoning the constitutions of many states start with an enumeration of human rights before political institutions and powers are defined (see chapter 3). Some constitutions even borrow heavily from the documents published in Paris and Virginia in the late eighteenth century.

The most common rights include:

- Freedom of speech and the press
- Freedom of religion and conscience
- Freedom of assembly and association
- Right to equal protection of the law
- Right to due process of law and to fair trail
- Property rights to land, goods, and money.

Protecting these rights is the first aim of democratic political systems. Apart from anything else, they have a special political importance for both ordinary citizens and political leaders. If human rights are protected, citizens and leaders can engage in peaceful political conflict and competition without fear of reprisals. After all, free competition for political power should result, in the end, in those attracting most support winning the day. Competition alone is not sufficient to guarantee this, however. Challengers should not only be allowed to join the struggle, but if they win, the losers should not be victimised in any way simply because they were on the losing side. Only in that way can democracy be 'government of the people, by the people, for the people' as the American president Abraham Lincoln stated in his famous Gettysburg

Abraham Lincoln (1809–65)

Address.

Gettysburg Address (1863)

■ *Elections and parliamentary accountability*

The development of mass democracies began in a few countries in the nineteenth century. The basic idea at the time was not that citizens should be directly involved in politics, but that they should rely on being represented by others. The main political task of citizens was to elect *representatives* (see chapter 3 and chapter 6) who would govern on their behalf (**representative democracy**). This was an important step towards democracy, but it was not 'democracy' as we would define it today. Only after long struggles between factions and competing elites was it recognised that democracies could function only with the consent of their citizens, and later still with their active participation (**participatory democracy**). This meant that the principle of *parliamentary accountability* to citizens came to be incorporated into the democratic ideal. It was accepted in France in 1870, in Germany in 1918, but not until 1976 in Spain (see table 2.1). In several countries it took a long time before the new constitutional rules were realised in practice, often because hereditary

Representative democracy
That form of democracy in which citizens elect leaders who govern in their name.

Participatory democracy
Democracy in which citizens actively participate in government.

Table 2.1 *Parliamentary accountability and universal suffrage, selected countries*

	Parliamentary accountability		Suffrage	
	Accepted	Constitutionalised	Male	Female
Austria[a]	1920	1929	1907	1918
Belgium[b]	1831	1831	1893	1948
Denmark[c]	1901	1953	1901	1918
Finland[d]	1919	1919	1906	1906
France[e]	1958 (1870)	1958	1848	1946
Germany	1918	1919	1869	1919
Greece	1974	1975	1877	1952
Iceland[f]	1904	1944	1915	1915
Ireland[g]	1922	1937	1918	1918
Italy	1948	1948	1912	1945
Luxembourg	1868	1868	1919	1919
Netherlands	1848 (1866)	1983	1917	1919
Norway[h]	1905 (1814)	1905	1897	1913
Portugal[i]	1910	1976	1911	1931
Spain	1976	1976	1869	1931
Sweden[j]	1809	1975 (1809)	1909	1921
Switzerland	1848	1848	1919	1971
UK	1215 (Magna Carta)		1918	1918

Notes:

[a] Austria: The constitution of 1920 was supplemented in 1929. As a consequence, the political system had a more parliamentary character.

[b] Belgium: Constitutional monarchy in 1831 with a potential for further parliamentarisation.

[c] Denmark: Parliamentary accountability from 1901 onwards, constitutionalisation in 1953.

[d] Finland: An autonomous Russian district until 1919.

[e] France: Only for Fifth Republic. Parliamentary accountability for the Third Republic from 1870–5 to 1940 and for the Fourth Republic from 1946–58. In the Third and Fourth Republic, the parliament had more control than during the other periods.

[f] Iceland: Independent of Denmark since 1944.

[g] Ireland: Independent of Great Britain since 1937.

[h] Norway: Enforced political union with Sweden, 1814–1905.

[i] Portugal: An unstable, semi-presidential, parliamentary republic, 1910–17.

[j] Sweden: The 1809 constitution was formally effective until 1975.

Sources: Parliamentary accountability: Jan-Erik Lane and Svante Ersson, *Politics and Society in Western Europe* (London: Sage, 1998); Suffrage: Jan-Erik Lane, David McKay and Kenneth Newton, *Political Data Handbook* (Oxford: Oxford University Press, 1997: 118).

monarchs and emperors had to give up their privileges first. For instance, the Dutch constitution of 1848 formulates the principle of accountability, but it was not actually put into practice until 1866.

Similarly, *voting rights* were extended only slowly and in stages. Several democracies completed universal male suffrage in the nineteenth century and many followed directly after the First World War in 1918. But only in a few countries were men and women given voting rights in the same year. In France, for instance, women had to wait almost a hundred years (until 1946) before they had the same voting rights as men.

■ Democracy and the rise of democratic states

The crucial importance of free political competition and a real chance of taking over the powers of government, either alone or in coalition with others, is found in the definition of democracy applied by Freedom House. This independent institute, which monitors political developments in the world (see fact file 2.1), defines democracies as:

> political systems whose leaders are elected in competitive multi-party and multi-candidate processes in which opposition parties have a legitimate chance of attaining power or participating in power. *(http://www.freedomhouse.org/reports/century/html)*

Fact file 2.1

The Freedom House rating of states

Freedom in the World is an institutional effort by Freedom House to monitor the progress and decline of political rights and civil liberties in 192 nations and in major related and disputed territories . . . The Survey assesses a country's freedom by examining its record in two areas: political rights and civil liberties. A country grants its citizens political rights when it permits them to form political parties that represent a significant range of voter choice and whose leaders can openly compete for and be elected to positions of power in government. A country upholds its citizens' civil liberties when it respects and protects their religious, ethnic, economic, linguistic and other rights, including gender and family rights, personal freedoms and freedoms of the press, belief and association. The Survey rates each country on a seven-point scale for both political rights and civil liberties (1 representing the most free and 7 the least free) and then divides the world into three broad categories: 'Free' (countries whose ratings average 1–3); 'Partly Free' (countries whose ratings average 3–5.5); and 'Not Free' (countries whose ratings average 5.5–7).

The ratings are not only assessments of the conduct of governments. They also reflect the reality of daily life. Thus a country with a benign government facing violent forces (for example terrorist movements or insurgencies) hostile to an open society will be graded on the basis of the on-the-ground conditions that determine whether the population is able to exercise its freedoms. (*Freedom in the World 2002: The Democracy Gap*, The Freedom House Survey Team; http://www.freedomhouse.org/research/freeworld/2002/about.htm)

There is certainly no inevitability about a state becoming democratic, and many reasons why ruling elites resist giving up or sharing power, but nevertheless the number of democratic states is rising. If we use the definition presented by Freedom House we find that:

- In 1900, not one of the fifty-five states in existence could be called 'democratic' according to current Freedom House standards. Even the most democratic, such as the USA or Britain, restricted the voting rights of women or black Americans. Monarchies and empires were the dominant state forms.
- The picture changed dramatically in the second half of the twentieth century. By 1950, the total number of states had risen to eighty, and twenty-two of them could be characterised as 'democracies', which meant that about 31 per cent of the world population was living under democratic rule.
- After the decline of colonial rule in Africa and Asia, changes in Latin America, and the collapse of communist rule in East and Central Europe, the number of democracies rose to 119 states by 2000. As a result of this **'third wave'** of democracy, some 60 per cent of the 190 or so states in the world, covering 58 per cent of the world's population, could be called democracies.

The twentieth century, then, was not only an age of devastating wars, genocide, bloodshed and totalitarian ideologies; it was also the 'Democratic Century'. Table 2.2 shows all states of the world that reach the highest democracy scores on the Freedom House scale and have more than 1 million inhabitants. The score combines the two major characteristics of democracies mentioned earlier: protection of basic human rights and of basic political rights. Low-scoring countries are the most democratic.

Although the Freedom House scores are based on two crucial features of democracy, other definitions and measures have been developed that include these two and other criteria. Most of them refer to democracy as a system of government and use labels such as 'political democracy' or 'liberal democracy' as synonyms for what are here called 'democracies' or 'democratic states'. The political scientist Seymour Martin Lipset provided one of the clearest definitions, explicitly spelling out the main features of a democracy as a system of government:

> First, competition exists for government positions, and fair elections for public office occur at regular intervals without the use of force and without excluding any social group. Second, citizens participate in selecting their leaders and forming policies. And, third, civil and political liberties exist to ensure the integrity of political competition and participation.
>
> (Seymour M. Lipset, *The Encyclopedia of Democracy*, London: Routledge, 1995: iv)

Democracy is a variable not a fixed phenomenon; it changes and develops over time, so that what was regarded as good democratic practice a hundred years ago may not be now. There are disputes about whether states differ in their degree of democracy – as the Freedom House index suggests – or

Third wave
Democratisation across the world is often divided into 'three waves'. The first, from the mid-nineteenth to the mid-twentieth century, saw between twenty-five and thirty states achieve a degree of democratic stability, depending on how 'democracy' is defined. The second, from about 1950 to 1975, was mainly the result of decolonisation. The third, from about 1975 to 2000, was mainly the result of the disintegration of the Soviet Union and the spread of democracy in Latin America and Asia.

Table 2.2 *Free and independent countries, 2001–2002 (only states with more than 1 million inhabitants are listed)*

State	Freedom House Index (2001–2)	Population (million, 1999)	Size (000 km²)	GDP *per capita* (PPP,[a] US$, 1999)
Argentina	1.5	36.580	2,780	11,940
Australia	1.0	18.976	7,692	23,850
Austria	1.0	8.092	84	24,600
Belgium	1.5	10.226	30	25,710
Benin	2.5	6.114	113	920
Bolivia	2.0	8.138	1,099	2,300
Botswana	2.0	1.588	582	6,540
Bulgaria	2.5	8.208	111	5,070
Canada	1.0	30.491	9,958	25,440
Chile	2.0	15.018	756	8,410
Costa Rica	1.5	3.589	51	7,880
Croatia	2.0	4.464	56	7,260
Czech Rep.	1.5	10.278	79	12,840
Denmark	1.0	5.326	43	26,600
Dominican Rep.	2.0	8.404	48	5,210
El Salvador	2.5	6.154	21	4,260
Estonia	1.5	1.442	45	8,190
Finland	1.0	5.166	338	22,600
France	1.5	58.620	544	23,020
Germany	1.5	82.100	357	23,510
Ghana	2.5	18.785	239	1,850
Greece	2.0	10.538	132	15,800
Hungary	1.5	10.068	93	11,050
India	2.5	997.515	3,287	2,230
Ireland	1.0	3.752	70	22,460
Israel	2.0	6.105	21	18,070
Italy	1.5	57.646	301	22,000
Jamaica	2.5	2.598	11	3,390
Japan	1.5	126.570	378	25,170
Korea, South	2.0	46.858	99	15,530
Latvia	1.5	2.431	64	6,220
Lithuania	1.5	3.699	65	6,490
Mali	2.5	10.584	1,240	740
Mauritius	1.5	1.174	2	8,950
Mexico	2.5	96.586	1,953	8,070
Namibia	2.5	1.701	824	5,580
Netherlands	1.0	15.805	42	24,410
New Zealand	1.0	3.811	271	17,630
Norway	1.0	4.460	323	28,140
Papua New Guinea	2.5	4.705	463	2,260

Table 2.2 (*cont.*)

State	Freedom House Index (2001–2)	Population (million 1999)	Size (000 km²)	GDP *per capita* (PPP,[a] US$, 1999)
Peru	2.0	25.230	1,285	4,480
Philippines	2.5	74.259	300	3,990
Poland	1.5	38.654	313	8,390
Portugal	1.0	9.989	92	15,860
Romania	2.0	22.458	238	5,970
Slovakia	1.5	5.391	49	10,430
South Africa	1.5	42.106	1,219	8,710
Spain	1.5	39.410	505	17,850
Sweden	1.0	8.857	450	22,150
Switzerland	1.0	7.136	41	38,760
Taiwan	1.5	22.091	36	–
Thailand	2.5	60.246	513	5,950
UK	1.5	59.501	243	22,200
USA	1.0	278.230	9,809	31,910
Uruguay	1.0	3.313	175	2,230

Note: [a] PPP = Purchasing power parity.
Sources: Freedom House Index: *Freedom in the World 2002: The Democracy Gap*, The Freedom House Survey Team; http://www.freedomhouse.org-; All other figures: *Der Fischer Weltalmanach* (Frankfurt/ M.: Fischer, 2002).

whether democratic states can be clearly distinguished from other forms of government. The political scientists Samuel Huntington and Adam Przeworski strongly argued for a clear line of demarcation. Others claim that violations of citizens' rights and other democratic imperfections are a matter of degree and, in their view, states can be placed on a continuous scale ranging from the most democratic to the most undemocratic. The Freedom House index tries to offer a middle-of-the-road position by distinguishing between democratic and non-democratic states, on the one hand, and by grading democracies as being more or less democratic, on the other.

Debates like these remind us of the difficult problems of applying the concept of 'democracy' to real political systems. Different measures and definitions give us different results when we try to classify states as 'democratic' or not, or if we try to grade them on a continuum. Nevertheless the Freedom House and other approaches all agree: the number of democratic states in the world has expanded continuously since the mid-1970s.

■ Redistribution and the welfare state

As states move gradually towards political freedom and democracy, so they will be confronted, as Rokkan points out, with growing citizen demands and a need to strengthen national identification by redistributive policies (see chapter 1). This helps to turn mass democracies into welfare states and gives every citizen a stake in their public services and hence a sense of common national purpose and identity.

As can be seen in the right-hand column of table 2.2, democratic states vary enormously in their level of economic development. A widely used indicator for economic development – the **gross domestic product** (GDP) per citizen – ranged in 1999 from as low as US$ 740 in Mali to a record high of US$ 38,760 in Switzerland. Most democratic states are wealthy, though not all of them are, but what most of them have in common is a rapid expansion of state activities since the Second World War. Even a cursory look at economic trends in democracies over past decades shows a remarkable growth of state spending and employment. Many of them abandoned traditional laissez-faire policies and free-market economics after the traumatic experiences of the Great Depression of the 1930s and the post-war economic problems of the late 1940s. As they increasingly accepted responsibility for the young and old, the sick and disabled, the unemployed and poor, and for education, housing and pensions, so they developed into welfare states (chapter 1).

GDP
The value of all final goods and services produced within a state in a given year. In order to compare the wealth of states the measure used is normally GDP *per capita*.

The expansion of state activities can be illustrated with a few basic figures. For example, average state revenues and expenditures among the industrialised countries rose from 26–27 per cent of GDP in 1960 to 45–47 per cent in 1997. Total spending of the member-states of the European Union had reached about 50 per cent of their GDP by the end of the 1990s! Even more striking, the growth of public expenditure and public services are directly linked to the consolidation of democracy in many states. As figure 2.1 shows, state spending varies very considerably from one country to another, but the longer a state is a democracy, the higher its public spending is likely to be. Although the upward climb levelled off in many countries after the early 1990s, state spending and state services of one kind or another continue to play a major role in the life of the average citizen. In this sense there is no escaping the state, its taxes and its services in modern society.

■ Why study states?

Now that the European concept of a 'state' has captured almost every corner of the world, and at a time when the number of states is at its highest and continues to increase, it is a paradox that the idea of the state seems to be rapidly approaching the end of its natural life. This is because new technologies have made it possible to locate the production of goods and services almost anywhere on the globe. Transport and communications, and especially information technology (IT) have changed the world into a 'global village'. Even wars are no longer restricted to conflicts between neighbouring states, but involve terrorist groups all over the world. As a result, the powers of states

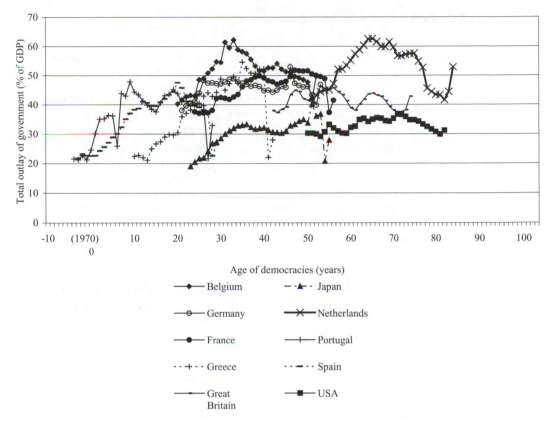

Figure 2.1: The consolidation of democracy and state spending

are increasingly limited by growing *international interdependencies and interconnections*, and by the hundreds of agreements states enter into with other states as a consequence. The world, it is argued, is increasingly forming a single system, and the term **globalisation** is used to describe this trend. Could it be that at the turn of the twenty-first century, the European state, given its seal of approval in the Treaty of Westphalia (see fact file 1.1), is now as outdated as the horse and carriage?

What can we conclude about the future of the state, given what we now know about the emergence of the European Union in place of the old system of sovereign states? The European Union is not alone, for there are other transnational organisations such as the North American Free Trade Association (NAFTA) and the Association of South East Asian Nations (ASEAN), as well as bodies such as the World Bank (IBRD), the International Monetary Fund (IMF), and the UN itself. In recent decades a wave of new organisations (Greenpeace, Transparency International, Médecins Sans Frontières) have joined the long list of older organisations (the Catholic Church, the Red Cross, and the

Globalisation
The growing interdependencies and interconnectedness of the world that are said to reduce the autonomy of individual states and the importance of boundaries between them.

Controversy 2.1

Focusing on the state is . . . . .

Area of debate	Right, because:	Wrong, because:
Euro-centrism	Although the idea of the modern state originated in Europe, every corner of the world is now claimed by states.	The idea of the modern state is Euro-centred and ideologically loaded, and should be replaced by concepts taking account of political arrangements in other cultures.
Integration	States still claim sovereignty and only a very small part of the world (covered by the EU in Europe) has succeeded in establishing a transnational form of government that may render the state obsolete.	The rise of regional and transnational forms of government (EU, NAFTA and ASEAN/UN), of international government agencies (IMF, World Bank), of international NGOs (Greenpeace, ILO) and MNCs (Microsoft, Ford) shows that national sovereignty is losing its relevance.
Legacy and impact	States developed over several centuries and they continue to exercise a powerful influence on social, political and economic life.	States are based on old ideas and practices and should be replaced by more appropriate concepts for the present world, and especially to understand future developments.
Number	The number of states increases continuously.	The number of powerful states does not change; the newest states are unimportant.
Power	States are the most important actors in politics and they are in charge of military and economic power.	Only a few large states are important. Organisations such as the EU, Microsoft and the World Bank have more power than many states.
Separation	Many serious conflicts in the world – the Middle East, Northern Ireland, Chechnya, etc. – are a direct consequence of the struggle for independence and recognition as a state.	Restricting political independence to the founding of states is the cause of these conflicts and hampers more innovative approaches.

Area of debate	Right, because:	Wrong, because:
Terrorism and crime	States are the most important objects of international terrorism.	International terrorism and crime cannot be attributed to states.
Waning importance	Growing interdependencies and contacts between states confirm the crucial role of states. Interdependencies can best be understood in terms of changing relations between states, rather than their decline.	Growing interdependencies and contacts between states show that states are losing their central position. It would be more appropriate to focus on interdependencies and contacts and accept the decline of the state.
War	Wars are waged between states.	With the rise of international terrorism the most important acts of violence are not restricted to states.

International Labour Organisation, ILO), besides the growth of purely private multi-national business corporations (MNCs). Microsoft is wealthier and more powerful than quite a few member states of the UN. Does all this spell the end of the old Westphalian system? If multi-national companies are now beyond the control or regulation of states, then perhaps we should pay less attention to states and more to the really important and powerful actors on the world stage (see controversy 2.1)?

Though this idea may seem attractive and up-to-date, it fails to take account of the fact that states are still the most important single groups of actors, and that states continue to be sovereign within their own territory, even if this sovereignty (chapter 1) is more limited and circumscribed by international forces than it once was. Even international terrorism is mainly directed towards states and their representatives. It is also noticeable that transnational government organisations, such as the European Union, are strongest in the very areas where states are best established, borders clearly defined and recognised and the institutions of national government most widely accepted. States have governments with supreme power within their borders and international relations continue to be conducted on this basis. In short, states remain important, and they are, therefore, the main focus and point of departure for the chapters that follow.

As mentioned already, we shall limit ourselves to studying democracies – that is, to states according to the Freedom House definition, 'whose leaders are elected in competitive multi-party and multi-candidate processes in which opposition parties have a legitimate chance of attaining power or participating in power'. Concentrating in this way on democracies enables us to compare and contrast a group of similar states: we are able to compare apples with apples, and not apples with oranges. But it also has the disadvantage that European,

Anglo-Saxon and North American countries will be heavily over-represented in our analyses. We will return to this difficulty in our concluding chapter (chapter 17).

■ Theories of state and society

As we saw in chapter 1, modern political theories about the state fall into two very broad categories: normative theories about what the state ought to do and empirical theories about how the state actually operates and why it operates that way. We shall discuss empirical theories now. An important feature of empirical theories is the way they *conceptualise the relationship between state and society*. Broadly speaking, there are four major approaches to the relationship between 'state' and 'society':

- State supremacy
- State dependency
- Interdependency
- Separation and autonomy

■ *State supremacy*

Some theories presume the *supremacy or dominance of the state over society*. According to these theories, the state does not so much reflect the characteristics of broader society but is independent of them and above them. This idea is found in legal theories that stress the formal sovereignty of the state. Aristotle, for example, saw the state as a political community 'which is the highest of all, and which embraces all the rest'. According to this view the state is a self-regulating and supreme power. It is not the product of society or the social and economic groups within it; on the contrary, they are part of the state from which they arise. Theories of the state that emphasise its supremacy often see it as a threat to individual rights and liberty. Such theories are summarised

Etatism
A very strong emphasis on state power and an accompanying reduction of social and individual rights.

under the label '**Etatism**'. However, the recognition of the dominant position of the state can also be used to reach very different conclusions. In conventional liberal theories, the main function of the state is to provide *law and order* (a 'night watchman') and to defend society's *independence*.

The view that the state is an independent and dominant power has become more and more problematic as we have gained a better understanding of government. At first sight, the huge increase in the activity and powers of the modern state may, indeed, suggest that it invades society as a conqueror that gains greater and greater control over the lives of citizens. But a closer look reveals a more complicated development in which the relationship between state and society is *mutually interdependent*: the state influences society and helps to mould it, but society also creates the state and both gives it powers and duties and sets limits on them. Besides, states are not simple or monolithic entities that simply control societies as a field marshall might control his troops on a battlefield. They are highly complex 'communities' made up of different institutions and organisations with their own histories and interests, and expressing the outcomes of all sorts of past and present political battles between competing social and economic groups. Most political scientists today therefore do not see the state as something 'above' or controlling society.

State dependency

Some theories see the state not as a supreme agency that dominates society, but, quite the opposite, as *dependent on society*, especially in its economic relations. Disputes about this view of the state and its relationship with social and economic forces have a long and complicated tradition in political analysis. The work of the German theorist Karl Marx inspired the idea that the state is only and always the expression of the struggle between classes in society – or, more specifically, that the power of the state is always an *instrument of the dominant class*. According to Marx, the state is nothing more nor less than 'a committee for managing the common affairs' of the dominant class. In modern society, this is the capitalist class, that owns and controls the means of production. The state is certainly not a neutral referee that adjudicates between the competing interests of different classes or social groups, nor is it an agency that is above and independent of society. It is, and can only be, an instrument to strengthen the *dominant position of specific groups* in society – in a capitalist society, this means protecting the interests of the capitalist class.

Karl Marx (1818–83)

Marxists argue about whether the state can be, to some degree, independent of economic forces and the interests of the capitalist class. The earlier writings of Marx argued that the state is merely a 'superstructure' whose shape and power is the inevitable product of the economic sub-structure. Later, Marx seems to have allowed for a degree of independence of the state, and twentieth-century Marxists have picked up the idea. Usually they emphasise particular 'structural tensions' in capitalist societies, which underline the fact that modern states have *conflicting tasks*. They are expected to protect the free market necessary for making profits but, at the same time, they are also expected to maintain social order and ensure that the population is educated and healthy enough to provide an efficient workforce. This means taxing business, which reduces profits. Another tension results from the great increase in state activities, which over-stretches and overloads the state apparatus, and leads it into all sorts of activities that it cannot really perform well. As a result, the state becomes increasingly intertwined with social and economic forces and becomes increasingly dependent upon them. This leads us away from the notion of an independent state towards an *interdependent* one.

■ *Interdependency*

A third set of theories stresses the interdependence of state and as society, or the relationships of exchange between them. In these approaches the modern state has become ever more and ever deeper involved in social and economic regulation. At the same time, as society has become increasingly complex and differentiated it requires more state coordination, regulation and arbitration. These developments are different sides of the same coin, so and it is not possible to say that one causes the other or that one dominates the other. They are mutually interdependent.

Neo-corporatist theories stress the close mutual dependency of state agencies, on the one hand, and major economic interest groups on the other. In traditional variants of this approach, trade unions and employer associations negotiate directly with state agencies about the formulation and execution of economic policies. More recent variants stress the participation of a wide range and variety of organised social groups in making and implementing public policy of all kinds. We shall have more to say about the interdependency of state and society in our later discussions of neo-corporatism (especially chapter 9).

■ *Separation and autonomy*

Finally, some theories depict state and society as distinct and autonomous areas, each with its own rules and development, and each with its own imperatives and 'logic'. Deep social forces produce social groups, interests and organisations that neither can nor should be controlled or regulated by the state. Equally, the state cannot and should not be captured by any particular interests or class (as the Marxists claim) because the state is a battlefield occupied by many conflicting groups and interests. State activities have their limits, just as social interests and organisations do, and to try to exceed these limits is to underestimate the power of their driving forces. *Pluralist and civil society theories* stress the need for an area of social life and organisation *outside the power of the state* (see chapter 6).

The four approaches are only a brief beginning to our analysis of state and society. We will have much more to say about each as we progress through the chapters that follow and add greater breadth and depth to our understanding. Meanwhile, we can certainly conclude that modern states are characterised by complex connections with their society, and that it is difficult to say which of the four approaches is the best. Each seems to explain some aspect of the affairs of states better than the others. For instance, neo-corporatist and pluralist approaches explain the rise of welfare states in the 1960s in those states where welfare programmes and economic policies and practices were the result of close collaboration between the state and powerful economic interest groups. However, the spread of political dissatisfaction and frustration among large sections of society in some countries after the 1960s seems to be better explained in terms of 'structural tensions' between an increasingly active state that is also increasingly weaker in some respects. Only after looking more closely at the multifarious institutions, structures and activities of the modern state can we come to a more sensible judgement about the strengths and weakness of the various theories.

■ Summary

This chapter has dealt with the difficulties of characterising and defining states, and with the historical development of modern states, especially democratic ones. It argues that:

- The number of democratic states is still rising.
- Accepted ideas about what democracy is, and how it operates, are changing.
- A useful definition of a democracy is provided by Freedom House: a political system 'whose leaders are elected in competitive multi-party and multi-candidate processes in which opposition parties have a legitimate chance of attaining power or participating in power'. Other definitions usually stress the opportunity for oppositions to conquer political power.
- Growing political demands among citizens lead to redistribution and to welfare states that accept responsibility for the young and old, the sick and disabled and the unemployed and poor. Not all democracies have developed their welfare provisions to the same extent, however.
- Although states are increasingly confronted with other powerful organisations, especially international business and **non-governmental organisations (NGOs)**, they are still the most important political actors in the world. However, globalisation implies important changes in the powers and capacities of states.
- Empirical theories of the state and society fall into four general categories: state supremacy over society; state dependency on society; the interdependency of state and society; and the autonomy of state and society.

NGOs
Private organisations (e.g. Amnesty, Greenpeace, Oxfam) that are independent of government and have a humanitarian or service-providing role.

Further reading

A concise overview of the development of modern states and democracy is Roger King and Gavin Kendall, *The State, Democracy and Globalisation* (Basingstoke: Palgrave, 2003). Contemporary debates of the notion of the state in political science are critically evaluated by Gabriel Almond, 'The return to the state', *American Political Science Review*, 82(3), 1988: 855–74 and by Margaret Levi, 'The state of the study of the state', in Ira Katznelson and Helen Milner (eds.), *Political Science: The State of the Discipline* (New York: Norton, 2002: 33–55). Martin L. van Creveld, *The Rise and Decline of the State* (Cambridge: Cambridge University Press, 1999) examines how the state came to replace rival forms of political organisation, and is now in decline. The changing power of states is discussed by Francis Fukuyama, *State Building: Governance and World Order in the Twenty-First Century* (London: Profile Books, 2004).

A short and clear account of democracy is Robert Dahl, *On Democracy* (New Haven: Yale University Press, 1998).

Websites

http://www.freedomhouse.org	Provides information about democracy and human rights for each state of the world.
http://www.oecd.org	Official website of the Organisation for Economic Cooperation and Development (OECD). Provides information on the OECD and about the economic development of its member-states.
http://www.developmentgateway.org	Provides information about sustainable development and poverty reduction in many developing countries.
http://www.worldbank.com/data/	Statistical information about many economic, social, political and demographical developments in many states. Provides information about reduction in poverty, etc. and the World Development Indicators (WDIs).

Projects

1. Explain why all welfare states are democracies, but not all democracies are welfare states.
2. Collect information about Costa Rica, Denmark, Microsoft and the World Bank in order to describe their role and power in the world today. Use your data for a systematic comparison of the political impact that Microsoft and the World Bank may have, and why they are different from states.

PART II

The polity: structures and institutions

Part I of this book considered the nature and development of the modern democratic state in general terms. Part II looks more closely at *internal structures and institutions* – sometimes referred to as the 'machinery of state' or the 'nuts-and-bolts of government', because they are the permanent structures of the political system. They are important because they set the framework within which individuals and organisations behave in everyday political life. In this sense we can distinguish between *government*, with its formal structures and institutions, on the one hand, and *politics*, with its political behaviour and processes, on the other. Following this distinction, Part II concentrates on structures and institutions of government, while Part III focuses on the political behaviour of individuals, groups and organisations. Although this is a convenient and useful way of dividing up the book, we should not forget that structures influence and mould behaviour, just as much as behaviour helps to create structures. Although it is useful to distinguish between the institutions of government and the processes of politics, the two are simply different sides of the same coin.

Chapter 3 deals with the constitutional framework of modern democracies. Constitutions are sometimes overlooked in modern comparative politics, but the fact is that they are enormously important. They try to grapple with the basic problem of all democracies – how to balance the necessary powers of the state against the individual rights of citizens, and how to ensure that government does not become too powerful and remains responsible and accountable to its citizens. Constitutions are the blueprints of power in democracies.

Chapter 4 turns to the three main branches of most democratic governments – the executive, legislative and judicial branches. It shows how, in spite of the bewildering variety of constitutional arrangements, most states fall into one of two general types, either *presidential* or *parliamentary* systems, and how these work in practice.

Chapter 5, on multi-level government, looks at how government is divided in a different way. Few states are so small that they can be ruled by a single centre of national government. Most democracies are divided geographically with national government sitting on top of layers of regional, local and community government.

Similarly, no democratic state can run its own affairs as if it were an island on its own. All have arrangements, agreements and treaties with other sovereign states. Chapter 5, therefore, examines multi-level government from the global and the international down to the local community.

Chapter 6 considers the two most important functions of government – the executive and the legislative. These two overlap to a considerable extent, but the executive is primarily responsible for executing (that is, carrying out) the affairs of state and the policies of the government, while the legislative is mainly concerned with representing the views of citizens, turning them into laws and keeping a watching brief on the executive.

Finally, Chapter 7 examines the administrative backbone of the state – the public bureaucracy. Bureaucrats are important, and potentially enormously powerful, because politicians rely heavily on the people who staff the government ministries to run the daily business of government.

The five chapters of Part II of the book, therefore, examine the main structures and institutions of government:

- Constitutions
- Presidential and parliamentary government
- Multi-level government
- Policy making and legislating
- Implementation.

3   Constitutions

Although the citizens of a given state may feel that theirs is the only or the best way of doing things, there is nothing natural or God-given about having a president rather than a prime minister, a unitary rather than a federal system, or two legislative assemblies rather than one. In fact, it is probably true to say that every modern democracy (chapter 2) has a unique set of government institutions, and combines them in unique ways. It is certainly true that there is no agreed formula or set of rules that will produce a democracy; each country follows its own special path and makes its own special arrangements.

The particular configuration of institutions in any given state (chapter 1) is defined by its **constitution**. This is the most basic set of laws that establishes the *shape and form of the political structure*. We start this chapter, therefore, by considering the nature and purpose of constitutions – what they are and why we have them. Constitutions try to create a complex set of **checks and balances** between the different branches of government, so that no one institution or person has too much power. We then introduce the three main branches of government – the *executive*, *legislative* and the *judiciary* – and outline their basic purpose and design. Constitutions, however, are only the beginning, not the end of the story of comparative politics, so we also discuss the limits of constitutionalism and why it is necessary to go beyond formal laws to understand how democracies work in practice.

Finally, we consider various theories of political institutions and how they help us to understand the structure and operations of the modern state.

> **Constitution**
> A set of fundamental laws that determines the central institutions and offices, and powers and duties of the state.

The four major topics in this chapter are:

- What a constitution is, and why we have them
- The division of powers
- The limits of constitutionalism
- Constitutional and institutional theories.

■ What a constitution is, and why we have them

In *some* respects government is like a game; before the players can even take the field to compete, they need to agree on a set of rules that decide how the game is to be played. Constitutions are the *rules of the political game* – who can vote, who can stand for office, what powers they are to have, the rights and duties of citizens and so on. Without these basic rules politics would degenerate into arbitrariness, brute force, or anarchy. If the rules work well, we tend to take them for granted and concentrate on the day-to-day game of politics, just as we take the rules of our favourite sport for granted and concentrate on today's match. Nonetheless, constitutions are important because they have a profound influence over how the game of politics is played, and therefore over the outcome of the game – who gets what, and when? For this reason,

Briefing 3.1

Constitutions

Constitutions vary so much that no two are likely to be the same in any particular respect. Some are long and detailed (India's has 387 articles and nine schedules), some short (the USA's has seven articles and twenty-seven amendments). Many are general, but others try to specify the kind of society and political system they aspire to – Sweden's sets out specific regulations for social security and labour laws. Some are contained in a single document, some refer to other documents or to international agreements such as the UN Declaration of Human Rights (1948). Some have been changed comparatively frequently, others rarely. Some are old, some new. In a few cases, the constitution is said to be unwritten (Britain and Israel) but, in fact, it is better to refer to them as 'uncodified', because while much is written down, it is not consolidated in one main document.

It is easy to obtain the constitution of every nation in the world from web sites (see p. 59) so no examples are provided here. In spite of their huge variety, most constitutions fall into four main parts:

- *Preamble*   The preamble tends to be a declaration about nationhood and history, with references to important national events, symbols and aspirations. The preamble tends to be inspirational rather than legal or rational.
- *Fundamental rights (Bill of Rights)*   A list of civil and political rights and statements about the limits of government powers. Some constitutions refer also to economic, social and cultural rights. Many of the newer constitutions simply adopt the 1948 UN Universal Declaration of Human Rights.
- *Institutions and offices of government*   The main structures or institutions of government are described, together with their powers and duties. Usually this means the executive, legislative and judicial branches of national government, and sometimes lower levels of government as well.
- *Amendment*   The procedures to be followed in amending the constitution.

some theories of politics place great importance on constitutions, and on the political institutions that they create and shape.

Constitutions are sets of laws, but they are very special ones that lay out the most important institutions and offices of the state and define their formal powers (see briefing 3.1 and fact file 3.1). Consequently, they have four main features:

1. *Fundamental laws*   Constitutions are laws about the *political procedures* to be followed in making laws. They are supreme laws, taking precedence over all others, and defining how all the others should be made. Some analysts call them 'meta-rules' (rules about how to make rules), but the German constitution calls them 'the Basic Law'.

2. *Entrenched status*   Constitutions have a *special legal status*. Unlike other laws, constitutions usually state the conditions under which the constitution can itself be changed. These conditions are often very demanding in ways that are intended to make sure that the change is not hasty or undemocratic, and that it has widespread support.

3. *Codified document*   Constitutions are written down, often in a *single document* that presents the constitution in a systematic manner.

4. *Allocation of powers*   Constitutions outline the proper relations between institutions and offices of the state, and between government and citizens. This is probably the most crucial part because it allocates *powers and functions* to government and specifies the *rights and duties* of governments and citizens – who can do what, to whom, and under what circumstances.

Fact file 3.1

Constitutions

- The first codified constitution was San Marino's (1600), followed by Canada's (1774) and the USA's (1787).
- Since then, there have been three waves of constitution making, linked to the 'waves' of state building discussed in chapter 2: after 1945, when many African and Asian states gained independence from their colonial powers; in the 1970s and 1980s, in Latin America, Africa and Asia when authoritarian forms of government collapsed; and after 1990, in central and eastern Europe when the post-communist nations engaged in a new burst of constitution making.
- Between 1990 and 1995 ninety-six countries – more than a third of the world's total – adopted new constitutions. Twenty were in central and eastern Europe, but thirty-one were in central and southern Africa.
- Most countries have modified their constitutions at some point in their history, but Belgium, Canada, France (twice), The Netherlands, New Zealand, Sweden and Turkey have done so in major ways in recent decades. The Indian constitution has been amended more than seventy times since 1950, but the American has been amended only twenty-seven times since 1787, and ten of these were contained in the Bill of Rights of 1791. France has had seventeen constitutions since 1789.
- About 70 per cent of constitutions date back no further than 1945.

Because constitutions are so important, they are often the focus of fierce political battles between different groups who want to frame the rules in their own interest. Democratic constitutions therefore try to impose rules that are fair and impartial to all groups and interests in society, so that all can compete on a 'level playing field'. They try to do this by incorporating a set of seven basic principles:

Albert V. Dicey (1835–1922)

1. *Rule of law* According to Albert V. Dicey, the nineteenth-century British constitutional theorist, the rule of law underlies the idea of *constitutionalism*. The rule of law, not the arbitrary rule of powerful individuals, is the hallmark of democracy.

2. *Transfer of power* Democracies are marked by a *peaceful transfer of power* from one set of leaders or parties to another. Democratic constitutions typically state the conditions for this – how and when government is to be elected, by whom and for how long. The peaceful transfer of power is so important that some political scientists define a 'democracy' in these terms – e.g. there have been three successive free and peaceful elections.

Separation of powers
The doctrine that political power should be divided among several bodies or officers of the state as a precaution against too much concentration of power.

3. *Separation of powers* and *checks and balances* According to classical political theory, democracy is best protected by creating separate branches of government with different functions and powers, each checking and balancing the power of the others in a system of checks and balances.

4. *Relations between government and citizens* At the heart of any democracy is the relationship between citizens and their government, so constitutions often include (or refer to) a Bill of Rights that enumerates the *rights and responsibilities* of citizens, and the *limits of government power* over them. Those who are suspicious of government in any shape or form see constitutions as setting clear limits on the power of government in order to guarantee the rights of the citizens.

5. *Locus of sovereignty* Since there must be a governing body or office capable of making authoritative decisions, constitutions usually specify who or what is to be the *ultimate authority to make and enforce law*.

6. *Government accountability* Democratic governments are accountable to their citizens, and constitutions normally try to pin down the *mechanisms of this accountability* – who is answerable to whom, and under what circumstances.

7. *Final arbiter* Constitutions are sometimes disputed because none is fully clear, consistent, unambiguous, or comprehensive. The last job of a constitution is to say who is to be the *final arbiter of their meaning* and how they may be *changed*.

■ The division of powers

Democratic constitutions attempt to create limited (not autocratic or totalitarian) government that is accountable to, and responsive to the will of, its citizens. According to classical political theory (John Locke, Montesquieu and the *Federalist Papers* in the USA), this is best achieved by dividing power between the executive, legislative and judicial branches of government, and by creating checks and balances between them so that no one branch can become too powerful.

John Locke (1632–1704)

Montesquieu (1689–1755)

Federalist Papers (1777–8)

■ Executives

Most large organisations have a person, or small group, to take final decisions, decide policies and take ultimate responsibility. Businesses have company chairmen and chief executive officers (CEOs). Governments have political executives (from the Latin term 'to carry out') who do the same job, and who are usually known as presidents or prime ministers – President Bush of the USA, Prime Minister Koijumi of Japan, Chancellor Schröder of Germany, Prime Minister Vazpayee of India, President Escobar of Chile, President Mogae of Botswana and so on. The **executive** branch of government, being at the top of the political pyramid, performs three main functions:

1. *Decision-making* – initiating government action and formulating public policy
2. *Implementation* – executives implement (apply) their policies, which means they must also run the main departments and bureaucracies of state
3. *Coordination* – coordination and integration of the complex affairs of state.

Executive
The branch of government mainly responsible for initiating government action, making and implementing public policy, and coordinating the activities of the state.

In most modern democracies the executive officer is called a president or prime minister. But, to complicate matters, presidents are not always political executives. For example, both the USA and Germany have presidents, but they do entirely different jobs. In America, the elected president is both the head of government and the head of state, which is an enormously powerful and important position, but the German president is only the head of state and a largely ceremonial figure who is, in some respects, rather like a constitutional monarch (see fact file 3.2). In what follows we are concerned mainly with the politically powerful presidents who, as both heads of state and government, are significant political figures, not ceremonial ones.

■ Legislatures

Executives are the decision making branch of government, and **legislatures** are the law-making branch. The term derives from the Latin words 'legis' (law) and 'latio' (bringing). Legislatures evolved from the assemblies that medieval monarchs called to agree to some royal action – to levy taxes or wage war. These assemblies started meeting regularly, and eventually came to be elected by all citizens of the state and so they acquired legitimacy as representative

Legislature
The branch of government mainly responsible for discussing and passing legislation, and keeping watch on the executive.

45

Fact file 3.2

Heads of state and heads of government

■ Heads of state

- In presidential systems, the directly elected president is both head of state and head of government.
- In parliamentary systems, the head of state is a largely ceremonial function carried out either by a monarch or a president, while the head of government, a position of real power, is normally filled by a prime minister or chancellor.
- Presidential heads of state may be elected or appointed, but presidential heads of government in democracies are always directly elected.
- Surprisingly, quite a few heads of state in established democracies are monarchs – Belgium, Denmark, Japan, The Netherlands, Norway, Spain, Sweden and the UK. This is because these countries have often avoided revolution and adapted slowly to democratic pressures, leaving their kings and queens in place while adapting institutions around them.
- Presidential heads of state, performing a largely ceremonial role, are found in Austria, Germany, Greece, Ireland, India, Israel and Italy.

■ Presidential heads of government

- Usually the president is a single person, but a few countries (Bosnia-Herzegovina, Cyprus and Uruguay) have experimented with joint presidencies, usually unsuccessfully.
- There are seventy-eight presidential systems in the world, making them the most common form of democratic government in the world. Fitfy-five of these are new democracies formed since 1990, and it remains to be seen how many of these will remain presidential if these systems change.
- Presidential systems are found mainly in Latin America, which has been influenced by the USA, and in the new democracies of central and eastern Europe.

---

parliaments or assemblies (see fact file 3.3). Technically, a legislature is any law making body, however constituted, but in a democracy the legislature gets its legitimacy from the fact that it is *directly and popularly elected* by citizens.

Legislatures are known by a variety of names – assemblies, parliaments, houses and chambers – but all amount to much the same thing: assemblies are meetings of elected representatives who meet to discuss public affairs; parliaments are 'talking shops'; houses and chambers are the places where assemblies and parliaments meet – the House of Commons, the House of Representatives, the Chamber of Deputies.

Legislatures may be formed by one (*unicameral*) or two (*bicameral*) houses. If we remember that democratic government is already divided between three main branches, one might well ask why the legislative body should

---

Fact file 3.3

Legislatures

- The precursor of modern parliamentary legislatures is probably the *Althingi*, the assembly established by Viking settlers in Iceland about a thousand years ago.
- Legislatures can consist of any number of assemblies, but about three-quarters of contemporary legislatures have one chamber (unicameral) and the rest have two (bicameral).
- Unicameral legislatures include Denmark (*Folketing*), Finland (*Eduskunta* in Finnish, *Riksdagen* in Swedish), Greece (*Vouli*), Israel (*Knesset*), New Zealand (House of Representatives), Portugal (The Assembly of the Republic) and Sweden (*Riksdag*).
- New Zealand became unicameral in 1950, when it abolished its upper house. Costa Rica, Denmark and Sweden later followed suit.
- Bicameral legislatures include Canada (Senate and House of Commons are collectively known as Parliament), France (Senate and the National Assembly), Italy (Senate and the Chamber of Deputies), Japan (the House of Councillors and the House of Representatives, collectively called the Diet), The Netherlands (First and Second Chambers, collectively the States General), the UK (The House of Lords and the House of Commons make up Parliament), the USA (the Senate and the House of Representatives make up Congress).
- The larger the population of a country, the larger its legislative body is likely to be. India, with a population of more than 100 million, has a lower house (the *Lok Sabha*) with 530 members. Brazil, with a population of 160 million, has a Chamber of Deputies with 517 members. At the other extreme, Trinidad and Tobago, with a population of 1.3 million, has a House of Representatives of 36 members, and Iceland, with a population of 300,000, has an Althingi with sixty-three members.
- The larger the country the more likely it is to be bicameral. On average, unicameral democracies have populations less than half that of bicameral countries.
- Four out of five federal states are bicameral, compared with one-quarter of unitary states. The representation basis of many second chambers in federal systems is often regional or local, as it is in Australia, Canada, Germany, India, Switzerland and the USA.

---

be further divided into two chambers. Indeed, two chambers may only complicate matters:

- Which of the two is to be the stronger and have the last word if they disagree?
- If the first is elected in a democratic fashion, how is the second to be constituted, and if it is also elected won't it inevitably clash with the first?

For these reasons, there is a great debate about whether unicameralism is better than bicameralism (see controversy 3.1), but it turns out that most democracies are bicameral. This is because it is usually not too difficult to sort out a system that enables two houses to work together effectively. Whatever the abstract and theoretical problems may be, it is generally possible to solve them in a practical way.

Controversy 3.1

One chamber or two?

Pro-unicameralism	Pro-bicameralism
• Power is mainly located in one assembly. No confusion of roles, responsibilities, or accountability.	• Two chambers provide another set of checks and balances, with powers to delay, criticise, amend, or veto – a constitutional backstop.
• No overlap or duplication between assemblies. Two assemblies can result in rivalry and even deadlock between the two.	• Two forms of representation, usually direct election to the lower chamber, and another form of election (indirect) or appointment to the higher.
• There is room for only one elected, representative body. 'If the second chamber agrees with the first, it is useless; if it disagrees it is dangerous' (Abbé Sieyès).	• A second chamber can reduce the workload of the first by considering legislation in detail, leaving the first chamber to deal with broad issues.
• Most legislatures are unicameral, and the number is increasing. Many new states have adopted unicameralism with apparent success, especially in Africa and the Middle East.	• A majority of democracies have bicameral legislatures – Australia, Britain, Canada, France, India, Italy, Japan, Mexico, the USA.
• Unicameralism is particularly suitable for unitary states (three-quarters are unicameral).	• Bicameralism is suited to federal systems, where territorial units of government within the state can be represented at the national level: 80 per cent of bicameral systems are in federal states.
• Costa Rica, Denmark, New Zealand and Sweden have abolished their second chambers, without apparent adverse effects.	• Some claim the main defence of bicameralism is political – upper chambers are conservative bodies with the job of tempering the actions of the lower house.
• Unicameralism seems to work best in small countries.	• Bicameralism seems to work best in countries that are large or socially and ethnically diverse – it helps to resolve regional conflict.
• Second chambers with appointed members are often criticised as being places where 'has-been politicians' go to die.	

Strong and weak bicameralism

Bicameral legislatures come in two forms: *weak* and *strong*. In the strong systems, both assemblies are of equal strength, but since this is a recipe for conflict – even deadlock – there are rather few cases of successful strong bicameralism. Many of them are found in federal systems (see chapter 5), including Australia, Belgium, Germany, Switzerland and the USA. Most bicameral systems are 'weak', which means that one assembly is more powerful than the other. To complicate matters the stronger (first chamber) is usually known as the 'lower house', while the weaker (second chamber) is the 'upper house', usually called the Senate (after the American Senate). Weak bicameralism is also known as 'asymmetric bicameralism' – i.e. the two houses are of unequal power. Typically in weak bicameral systems, the lower house initiates legislation and controls financial matters and the upper house has limited powers to delay and recommend amendments.

Membership of the second house

Since democratic lower chambers are directly elected by the population, many second chambers are constituted on a different basis. Most are not directly elected by the population as a whole, but are either indirectly elected or appointed, or some combination of both. Some second chambers, however, are directly elected, usually in federal systems (see chapter 5) but on a different basis than the lower house. If they are directly elected at all, upper houses are often based on different geographical constituencies.

Tenure and size

The terms of tenure of upper houses are usually different. They are often elected for a longer term of office (five–nine years, rather than the three–five years of lower chambers). Upper chambers sometimes have an older qualifying age, and they are usually much smaller than lower ones.

■ *Judiciaries*

Should politicians be the final judge of how the constitution should be interpreted? The danger is that the government of the day will try to manipulate matters in its own interests. Therefore, constitutions are, in the words of David Hume a set of 'institutions designed for knaves'. This does not presume that politicians actually are knaves, but takes full account of the possibility that they might be, and that a constitution needs a safeguard against this danger. Since a constitution is primarily a legal document, it is argued that lawyers should be the final arbiter of it. Besides, judges (the **judiciary**) are often thought to be the best independent and incorruptible source of experience and wisdom on constitutional matters. This, in turn, requires judicial independence to protect judges from political interference and from the temptations of corruption. For this reason, judges are often appointed for life and paid well. Some countries have created special constitutional courts, but most use their regular courts (see fact file 3.4).

Not all democratic countries accept the principle of **judicial review** of the constitution. Some reject it, for two main reasons:

Judiciary
The branch of government mainly responsible for the authoritative interpretation and application of law.

David Hume (1711–76)

Judicial review
The binding power of the courts to provide an authoritative interpretation of laws, including constitutional law, and to overturn executive or legislative actions they hold to be illegal or unconstitutional.

Fact file 3.4

Judiciaries

- The principle of judicial review was originally limited to the USA in the nineteenth century. It became more widely accepted in the twentieth century, especially in federal systems where the courts were used to settle disputes not only between branches of government but between federal and other levels of government as well.
- A few democracies, such as Belgium, Finland, The Netherlands and Switzerland, do not have judicial review.
- Some states (Israel, New Zealand, the UK) have judicial review in practice, but not in theory. In the UK, the binding nature of EU law has given the courts the role of judicial review.
- Special constitutional courts have been created in Austria, France, the EU, Germany, Greece, Italy, Portugal and Spain, and many of the new democracies of central and eastern Europe.
- Judicial review is carried out by regular courts in most countries including Australia, Canada, Denmark, India, Italy, Japan, Sweden, and the USA.
- The Federal Constitutional Court of Germany has become one of the most active in the West, rejecting some 5 per cent of all legislation on constitutional grounds, and becoming involved in issues ranging from freedom of speech and abortion to federal–state relations and public finance. The European Court of Justice (ECJ) is also active and powerful in EU matters.

---

1. It is *difficult to guarantee the political independence of the judges*. In many countries, senior judges are appointed by politicians and conservative politicians tend to appoint conservative judges while liberal politicians are more likely to appoint liberal ones. Nor are judges entirely immune from the social pressures of public opinion and the mass media. Most important, judges usually come from conservative social groups and deliver conservative political judgements. In short, it is claimed that judges are not, or cannot be neutral.

2. In a democracy, so it is argued, the *democratically elected legislature* should have responsibility for interpreting the constitution, not an appointed and unrepresentative judiciary.

Judges are involved in more than constitutional law. The meaning of other laws may also be ambiguous and disputed, and sometimes this has political implications – electoral law for example, or tax law with implications that affect government's capacity to raise money for public services. In fact, some legislation is deliberately vague, because it was the only way out of political deadlock between competing groups. In such circumstances, it is the job of the courts to interpret the law and to decide how it should be applied to particular cases. In doing so, the courts may go beyond merely interpreting the law and actually modify or change it in subtle ways. In this respect, judges can play an important political role as the *third branch of government*.

■ Judicial activism

The role of the courts in government is tending to widen. The Supreme Court of the USA was not given power of constitutional review in the 1787 constitution, but had successfully claimed it by 1803. The USA then went through two notable periods of **judicial activism** in the 1930s (when it tried to stop Roosevelt's New Deal legislation) and again in the 1950s (when it promoted racial integration). There is a general tendency now for the courts to take a more active role in government across the democratic world where the judiciary has the right of judicial review. The five main reasons for the expanding role of the courts are:

- An increasing volume of legislation and government actions
- The increasing complexity of government machinery, which means that there is greater chance of conflict between branches and levels of government, especially in federal systems or when new supra-national governments (e.g. the EU) are being developed
- An increasing emphasis on the rule of law and the rights of citizens, and the need to write these down in the legal form, such as in a Charter or Bill of Rights
- A willingness to use the courts (the 'culture of litigation') as a means of resolving conflict
- Possibly, an unwillingness or inability of politicians to deal with difficult political issues; they may be happy to pass on some political 'hot potatoes', especially moral issues, to the courts.

There are problems with judicial activism as there are with judicial review of the constitution. Striking down legislation and choosing between different interpretations of the law can amount to policy making, and sometimes even small differences of legal interpretation of the law can have large policy ramifications. Should judges have this power? And when there is a conflict between elected government and the courts, who should win?

Another quasi-legal development in modern democratic politics is the appointment of ombudsmen. An **ombudsman** is a 'grievance officer', or a state official to whom citizens can appeal if they feel wrongly treated by public bodies. Sweden, which invented the concept, has four ombudsmen covering different areas of public services. They are found in many western Europe states (Austria, Denmark, Finland, The Netherlands, Norway, Portugal, Sweden and the UK) and some other countries, although most modern democracies (about 75 per cent) do not have them, preferring to use normal court procedures. For the most part, ombudsmen are not lavishly funded and their powers are usually limited, so they rarely have a big impact.

■ Unitary and federal states

We shall discuss **federal states** and unitary government at greater length in chapter 5, but it is appropriate to make an important constitutional point

Judicial activism
Involves the courts taking a broad and active view of their role as interpreters of the constitution and reviewers of executive and legislative action.

Ombudsman
A state official appointed to receive complaints and investigate claims about maladministration.

Federal states
Federal states combine a

central authority with a degree of constitutionally defined autonomy for sub-central, territorial units of government.

here. In federal systems, power is divided not only between the executive, legislative and judicial branches of government, but also between *territorial units* of government. These territorial units – states, or regions, or provinces – often have substantial powers and rights that are guaranteed by the constitution. In some ways, therefore, federalism is another form of the division of powers within the state – a horizontal division between geographical areas, to complement the vertical division between the executive, legislative and judicial branches. Moreover, the territorial units of federal systems often repeat the division of powers found at the federal level because each unit has its own executive, legislative and judicial branches of government.

Unitary states

In unitary states the central government is the only sovereign body. It does not share *constitutional* authority with any sub-central units of government.

This distinguishes federal from **unitary states**. In a unitary system, national government ultimately controls all layers of government below it, and can reform, reorganise, or abolish units of local or regional government without any special constitutional restraint. In federal systems, the rights and powers and existence of the federal units are protected by the constitution.

■ The limits of constitutionalism

Constitutions are not like cooking recipes that produce exactly the right result if they are followed to the last detail. They are, after all, only legal words on pieces of paper. How they work in practice is a rather different matter. Constitutions are important documents, perhaps supremely important, but there are seven key reasons why they should not necessarily be taken at their face value:

- They may be completely unimportant simply because they are *not observed*. Most dictatorships have democratic constitutions, and politicians in established democracies have been known to try to flout, break, or go around them.
- They may be *incomplete*. They are general documents that may not even mention some of the more important aspects of the constitution – electoral systems, political parties, or even the office of prime minister.
- A full understanding of a constitution sometimes requires reference to *other documents* – supreme court judgments, historical documents, or the UN Declaration of Human Rights.

Conventions

Unwritten rules that impose obligations on constitutional actors that are held to be binding, but not incorporated into law or reinforced by legal sanctions.

- Written constitutions are often supported by **conventions**.
- Constitutions can *develop and change*, even if the documents do not. The American constitution of 1787 did not give the Supreme Court of the USA the right of constitutional review. The Supreme Court took this power for itself in 1803 when it ruled on the case of *Marbury* v. *Madison*.
- Constitutions can be *vague* or *fail to cover particular or exceptional circumstances*.
- Constitutions can *fail*. History is full of failed democratic constitutions that have been supplanted by revolutions, autocrats and military dictatorships. The lesson is that successful democracy cannot be imposed by constitutional law, no matter how well thought-out this may be; democratic politics must

also be accepted and practised by political elites and citizens alike. Constitutions are like fortresses – they must be well built and well protected by soldiers.

This leads us to the conclusion that constitutions are rather like *maps* or *blueprints* of the main institutions of government (for three examples see briefing 3.2), but actual operations may differ – even differ radically – from the legal documents. This leads to the debate about how important institutions are, and to what extent they actually determine the operations of a political system and the behaviour of political actors within it.

■ Constitutional and institutional theories

■ The 'old constitutionalism'

The interest of political theorists in constitutions dates back at least to Aristotle's famous commentary on the constitution of Athens. In the late nineteenth and first half of the twentieth century, however, the lead was taken not by political theorists but by lawyers and comparative political scientists. Their work was largely legal, descriptive and historical, and confined to a few western states, especially to the UK, the USA and France. After the Second World War this style of political science was fiercely criticised for being too descriptive and legalistic rather than analytical, for its failure to theorise and generalise, for being culture-bound by its narrow western origins and, above all, for its interest in formal and legal documents rather than 'going behind the scenes' to get at the real stuff of everyday politics.

Moreover, as we have already seen, constitutions do not always work as they are supposed to. As a result, many of the constitutions so carefully designed (mainly by constitutional lawyers for the newly decolonised and independent countries of Africa and Asia) collapsed and gave way to dictatorship and military government because they were not adapted to social, political and economic circumstances. The failure of these constitutions made it clear that democracy rests on more – far more – than constitutional design, no matter how good this may be on paper. Consequently, when an interest in constitutions was revived in the last quarter of the twentieth century, it went beyond the 'old' institutionalism of legalistic and descriptive studies of constitutions.

■ The 'new constitutionalism'

The 'new constitutionalism' tried to balance out three main concerns:

1. The *protection of citizen rights* and the *limitation of government powers* – in other words, the classical concerns of constitutional theory.
2. A concern with balancing the limited powers and maximum accountability of government, with the need for *effective government action* in a complex

Briefing 3.2
The Constitutions of Argentina, France and Japan

Argentina

Type of government	Presidential republic: federal state.
Date of constitution	1853, revised 1994
Head of state	President Kirchner
Executive	President Kirchner, cabinet appointed by President
Legislature	Bicameral National Congress
	Senate: 72 directly elected, six-year term, half every three years
	Chamber of Deputies: 275 directly elected, four-year term, half every two years
Judiciary	Judicial review by Supreme Court
Sub-national government	23 provinces and one autonomous city (the Federal Capital of Buenos Aires)

France

Type of government	Republic: unitary state
Date of constitution	1958, amended in 1962, and in 1992, 1996 and 2000 to comply with EU requirements, and in 2000 to reduce presidential term of office from seven to five years
Executive	Head of State, President Chirac, directly elected
	Head of Government, Prime Minister Raffarin, nominated by National Assembly majority and appointed by President, cabinet appointed by President at suggestion of Prime Minister
Legislature	Bicameral
	Senate: 321 seats, indirectly elected for nine years, one-third every three years
	National Assembly: 577 seats, directly elected for five years
Judiciary	Supreme Court of Appeal plus Constitutional Council for constitutional matters
Sub-national government	22 regions, 96 departments

Japan

Type of government	Unitary state with constitutional monarch and parliamentary government
Date of constitution	1947
Head of state	Emperor Akihito
Executive	Prime Minister Koizumi; cabinet appointed by Prime Minister
Legislature	Bicameral
	House of Councillors: 247 seats, six-year term, half every three years
	House of Representatives: 480 seats, elected for four years
Judiciary	Judicial review of legislation by Supreme Court
Sub-national government	47 prefectures

and fast-changing world. It is argued that constitutions are not abstract designs, but practical machines that need careful construction and engineering, and then judged by how effectively they work in practice.

3. An attempt to adapt the constitutional design of a country to its *social and economic circumstances*. It was realised that there is no single constitutional design that is best, but a variety of models to suit different conditions. Constitutional theory tried to solve the problem of how stable democracies could be established in previously undemocratic countries, especially in countries divided by ethnic, religious, linguistic and cultural cleavages. In central and eastern Europe, civil society theorists argued that it was vital that constitutions guaranteed the rights of citizen organisations, and their independence from government. Ethnically mixed societies, it was argued, needed a form of 'consensus' democracy that protected the rights of minorities and gave them effective power to participate in government. We will return to civil society theory in chapter 9 and to consensus democracies in chapter 6.

■ The 'new institutionalism'

Both the 'old' and the 'new' constitutionalism assumes that constitutions matter, and that they are not only a vital part of any democratic system but also an influence – perhaps even a decisive influence – on how political actors behave and how political systems works. This basic idea is expounded in what is known as the 'new institutionalism'. 'The new institutionalism' is not so much a theory as a general approach that focuses on the organisations, structures and institutions of government and politics. There are variations on the general theme, but there is a common argument underlying them:

- Institutions are the *framework within which individuals behave*. Political institutions not only constrain what individuals do, but also what they think is possible to do. As we have seen, actors in a system tend to take its basic structure and rules for granted – as given – and organise their behaviour accordingly.
- Institutions are the products of *past political battles* in which winners create particular forms of organisation that work in their own interests, although they may be quite unconscious of this. Constitutions embody the outcomes of past political struggles over how the game of politics is to be played, and by whom.
- Institutions have a *degree of inertia* built into them. Once established, they will tend to persist, unless circumstances encourage attempts to change them, and sometimes they may be so firmly rooted that this is difficult.

In short, *institutions matter*. They are political actors in their own right. They are partly the products of the society in which they are embedded, but they also help to shape society and its politics. It has been therefore argued that political science should 'bring the state back in' by combining a concern with the major institutions of a political system (not just constitutions) with an understanding of their historical development. The idea of 'constitutional engineering' is based on the premise that instituions are important and that whether it concerns reforming an existing constitution or designing a new one from scratch, getting the right mix of institutions for a society is important for its democratic stability and quality.

However, this is all very general, and what we need now is some examples of how institutions work in order to put some flesh on the bones of the general theory.

The mobilisation of bias

The idea that institutions matter was caught (some time before the 'new institutionalism') by the American political scientist E. E. Schattschneider in the phrase 'organisation is the mobilisation of bias'. This means that all organisations (institutions are one kind) have a built-in capacity to do some things better than others, which may well serve some interests better than others. Politics, therefore, is the organisation of bias in the sense that some issues are *organised into* politics, while others are *organised out.*

E. E. Schatt-schneider (1892–1971)

In some countries, second chambers are used to give membership of the upper house to geographical areas or to occupational groups. This means that some interests will find it easier to gain access to the highest levels of government than in a unicameral system. And since upper chambers tend to be conservative bodies (this is one justification for their existence), there is a tendency for bicameral systems, especially strong bicameral ones, to have a conservative veto-power built into them.

Institutional influence, rules and inertia

In an important article published in 1984 in the *American Political Science Review*, James G. March and Johan P. Olsen argued that institutions were basically a collection of inter-related rules and routines that defined how the members of an institution saw it and their own role within it. These routines included stock responses to problems that were automatically used before trying anything else. How people behaved within the institution, therefore, was determined by *institutional rules and routines* that defined what was appropriate action in the circumstances. Legislative assemblies, especially old ones steeped in tradition, for example, have their own rules and ways of doing things. New members must learn and accept their customs to have a successful political career.

The economist Douglass North has spent much of his life exploring the ways in which economic institutions, once created, can have long-term effects on the content and impact of economic policy. The political scientist Peter Hall also shows that institutions come to absorb and embody a set of policy ideas, such as Keynesian economic theories, that have a long life because they become *institutionalised* in particular structures which gives them a life of their own. To understand the policy choices made now, we have to understand institutional histories and the ideas they stand for. The political scientist Arend Lijphart has investigated the relationship between different types of government institutions and political policies, something we will come back to later in this book (see chapter 6).

Marxist structural theory

An early form of institutional and structural analysis was Marx's account of the capitalist state which, he said, was simply a device that enabled capitalists to stay in power and exploit the workers. As he put it in the *Communist Manifesto* (1848), 'the executive of the modern state' is 'but a committee for managing the common affairs of the whole bourgeoisie'. According to Marx, capitalists create and use the institutions of the state for their own purposes: the police and the courts to protect capitalist property; schools, universities and established religion to indoctrinate people into a state of 'false consciousness' in which they cannot even recognise their own best interests; parliament to give an illusion of democracy; and the military to protect the empire as a source of profit. Marx thus employs a *structural–historical* approach that focuses not on the behaviour of individuals who happen to be capitalists or workers, but on the workings of the whole system and its historical development. He implies that capitalists are not to be blamed for their exploitation of the workers; they are simply following the logic of the situation they find themselves in.

Karl Marx,
Communist
Manifesto
(1848)

Governance

The most recent form of institutional theory revolves around the concept of governance. Although the term '**governance**' can mean rather different things to different people, its core idea is that government no longer revolves around a few institutions of the central state, but consists of a much wider and looser network of organisations and institutions. If government is about 'top-down', hierarchical power relations organised by public institutions, and if politics is about 'bottom-up' participation of individuals and groups, then governance is about bringing these two together by coordinating the activity of the large number of institutions, groups, individuals and organisations in the public and private sector. Government is no longer about a narrow range of organisations and institutions but about trying to give shape and direction to the complex *multi-level activities* of multifarious public and private political actors. In short, governance focuses not on a few institutions of the central state but on a wide

Governance
The act of governing; that is, the total set of government's activities in each phase of the policy making process.

variety of institutions, organisations and associations that blur the dividing between government and the wider society.

■ Summary

This chapter has dealt with how the institutions in a state are configured in its constitution. It argues that:

- Constitutions are a set of entrenched and fundamental laws (laws that determine the procedures to be followed in making other laws) that allocate powers between the main offices and institutions of the state.
- Democratic constitutions establish the rule of law and create limited government that is accountable to and responsive to the will of its citizens.
- The best way of doing this is by dividing power between different offices and bodies, so that each acts as a check on the other and has its power balanced against that of the others.
- In most democracies, power is divided between three branches of government – the executive, legislative and judiciary.
- Democratic constitutions come in a great many shapes and forms with many different institutions and many variations on their themes. All these forms can be democratic, showing that there is no single route to democracy but many different pathways.
- Political systems rarely operate in the precise manner outlined by their formal constitutions, but most democracies operate roughly as the formal constitution requires.
- Institutions have a life of their own, and they have an independent effect on society from that of politics. Among other things, they influence and shape the behaviour of individuals within them, a fact recognised by 'institutional' theories of politics.

Further reading

Robert L. Maddex, *Constitutions of the World* (London: Routledge, 1997), presents a summary of the constitutions and constitutional history of eighty nations. Vernon Bogdanor (ed.), *Constitutions in Democratic Politics* (Aldershot: Gower, 1988: 1–13) presents a useful general discussion. A good collection of classic work on legislatures is in Phillip Norton (ed.), *Legislatures* (Oxford: Oxford University Press, 1990).

Good discussions of the institutional approach, and of new institutionalism can be found in Rod Rhodes, 'The institutional approach', in David Marsh and Gerry Stoker (eds.), *Theories and Methods in Political Science* (Basingstoke: Macmillan, 1995: 42–57) and in Frank L. Wilson, 'The study of political institutions', in Howard J. Wiarda (ed.), *New Directions in Comparative Politics* (Oxford: Westview Press, 3rd edn., 2002: 189–210). For a book-length treatment of different forms of new institutional theory, see B. Guy Peters, *Institutional Theory in Political Science: The 'New Institutionalism'* (London: Continuum, 1999).

Websites

http://confinder.richmond.edu/	Offers constitutions, charters, amendments, etc. Nations of the world are listed alphabetically, each is linked to its constitutional text.
http://www.constitution.org/cons/natlcons.htm	Contains the constitutions of the world.
http://kclibrary.nhmccd.edu/constitutions-subject.html	Contains the constitutions of the world.
http://www.rulers.org	Contains lists of heads of state and heads of government of all countries and territories, going back to about 1700 in most cases. Also sub-divisions of various countries, as well as a selection of international organisations. Recent foreign ministers of all countries are listed separately.

Projects

1. Assume you are consultant brought in to advise a newly independent state that wishes to set up a democratic constitution. Would you recommend:
   a   A unicameral or bicameral legislature?
   b   A special constitutional court?
   c   An ombudsman/ombudsmen?
   Explain the reasons for your decisions.
2. How can institutions be political actors in their own right that constrain what people do? How can they shape what people think they can do?
3. If the French President visits The Netherlands the Dutch Queen would normally welcome him, but the French Prime Minister will normally be welcomed by the Dutch Prime Minister. How do you explain this? Who would you invite to a meeting of 'heads of government' of EU member-states if the meeting was held in your country?

4   Presidential and parliamentary government

We have seen in chapter 3 that each democratic constitution has its own particular and special features, and that each combines them in a different way.
This might produce a severe problem for comparative politics, for if every
system was unique then all we could do would be to describe them in bewildering and endless detail. Fortunately for students of comparative politics,
this is not the case. The great majority of democracies combine their three
branches of government in one of only three general ways – most of them fall
fairly neatly into presidential, parliamentary and semi-presidential systems. Of
course, each particular democracy retains its own special features, but most
nonetheless conform to one of the three general types, and can be classified
accordingly.

The first task of this chapter is to map out the three systems and the main
differences between them. Since each has its own strengths and weaknesses,
the second task is to consider their respective merits and deficiencies. Third,
since constitutions do not exist in a societal vacuum, the next job is to try
to sort out the form of government best suited to each kind of social and
historical circumstances. Some forms of government are more likely to work
better in certain conditions than others, and it is also possible that countries might do well to shift from one form to another as they develop over
time.

The five major topics in this chapter are:

- Presidential systems
- Parliamentary systems
- Semi-presidential systems
- Presidential, parliamentary and **semi-presidential systems** compared
- Theories of parliamentary, presidential and semi-presidential government.

■ Presidential systems

A great many **presidential systems** are modelled on the USA, and they repro-duce many features of the American system, though not in every detail (see fact file 4.1). The main point about a presidential system is that its president is **directly elected** and his or her executive power is balanced by a legislature that is independent of the president because it, too, is popularly elected. The president, alone among all the officials of state, has general responsibility for public affairs. He or she may appoint ministers or cabinet members, but they are responsible only for their own department business, and they are account-able to the president, not the legislature. To ensure a real separation of powers (see chapter 3) neither the president nor members of the cabinet can be mem-bers of the legislature.

Presidential government is marked by four main features:

1. *Head of state and government* Presidents perform the ceremonial duties of head of state and are also in charge of the executive branch of government: they are usually chief of the armed forces and head of the national civil service, and responsible for both foreign policy and for initiating domestic legislation.
2. *The execution of policy* Presidents appoint cabinets to advise them and run the main state bureaucracies.
3. *Dependence on the legislative branch* Presidents initiate legislation but depend on the legislature to pass it into law.
4. *Fixed tenure* Presidents are directly elected for a fixed term and are normally secure in office unless, in exceptional circumstances, they are removed from it by the legislature.

The separation of executive and legislative, each with its independent author-ity derived from popular election, is a deliberate part of the system of checks and balances (see chapter 3). In theory both have powers and are independent of each other, but in practice presidents and assemblies usually have to share power. They must cooperate to get things done, and the result is not so much a separation of powers as a complex mix of them – a separation of institutions (Presidency and Congress in the USA, for example), but a mix of powers in the daily give-and-take of their political relations. The following five examples, drawn from the USA, illustrate the point:

Semi-presidential systems
A directly elected president accountable to the electorate and a prime minister appointed by the president from the elected legislative and accountable to it.

Presidential systems
A directly elected executive, with a limited term of office and a general responsibility for the affairs of state.

Directly elected
Election by the electorate at large (popular election) rather than an electoral college, the legislature, or another body.

Fact file 4.1

Presidential and parliamentary systems

■ Presidential systems

- Influenced by the USA, many Central and South American democracies have presidential government – Argentina, Bolivia, Chile, Costa Rica, the Dominican Republic, El Salvador, Mexico, Peru and Uruguay.
- Most democracies in Africa are presidential including Benin, Botswana, Ghana, Namibia and South Africa.
- Presidential government is often found in the newly established democracies of the 'third wave' (see chapter 2), including Argentina, Croatia, the Philippines, South Korea and Taiwan.
- Switzerland is unique. It has a collective presidency formed by the seven members of the Federal Council (*Bundesrat*), one being selected to be the formal president each year.
- Most democratic presidents are restricted to one or two terms of office, a few to three and most set a minimum age for candidates that is higher than for other offices in order to get more experienced candidates.

■ Parliamentary systems

- There are currently fifty-six parliamentary systems in the world, including thirty-one constitutional monarchies and twenty-five established democracies.
- Parliamentary systems are most common in the older democracies of western Europe, (including Austria, Belgium, Denmark, Ireland, The Netherlands, Norway, Sweden, the UK) and half of them are in British Commonwealth countries, including Australia, Botswana, Canada, India and New Zealand.
- Israel is unusual in having a directly elected prime minister who, unlike a president, can be removed from office by the parliament, thus precipitating an election for both the prime minister and parliament.
- In contrast to presidential systems, the prime ministers or chancellors of parliamentary systems do not have limited terms of office, and in recent decades some of them have had successive election victories and have held on to power for a long time – Gonzales (Spain), Kohl (Germany), Menzies, Fraser and Hawke (Australia), Mitterrand (France), Thatcher (UK) and Trudeau and Mulroney (Canada).
- A large proportion of parliamentary democracies are smaller states (India is an exception) and many are small island democracies.
- Of the newly democratised countries of central and east Europe, only Bulgaria, Hungary, Latvia and Slovakia are fully parliamentary.

- The president can veto legislation, but the legislature (Congress) can override this veto if it has a majority of two-thirds in both houses.
- The president is head of the armed forces, but only Congress can declare war.
- The president makes political appointments, but they can be rejected by the Senate.
- In normal circumstances, Congress cannot remove the president, and the president cannot dissolve Congress, but in exceptional circumstances

Congress can impeach and remove a president from office. No American president has been removed this way.
- Laws are debated and enacted by Congress but presidents are responsible for their implementation. They appoint cabinet secretaries to run the main departments of the federal government.

This has an important effect on the way that presidents work, because ultimately they are *dependent on their legislatures*. It is said, for example, that the American president has little power over Congress other than the power of persuasion. Many in the White House have found this inadequate for the purposes of government, if Congress and the president are of a different political mind they may fight each other and get little done. One image likens the president, the House, and the Senate to participants in a three-legged race – difficult to move along unless they move together, and easy to fall over. The problem is heightened if, as sometimes happens, the presidency is controlled by one political party, and one or both houses by another. If, on top of this, party discipline is weak, the majority party may be unable to pass its legislation. The result is that apparently powerful presidents are sometimes immobilised by elected assemblies.

For this reason, many presidential systems have failed the test of democratic stability and some experts believe that they do not make for effective government. The USA may be the only successful example, although Costa Rica has maintained its presidential system since 1949.

■ Parliamentary systems

In **parliamentary systems** the executive is not directly elected but usually emerges or is drawn from the elected legislature (the parliament or assembly) and, unlike a directly elected president, is often an integral part of it (see fact file 4.1). This form of parliamentary executive usually consists of a prime minister (sometimes called chancellor or premier) and a cabinet or a council of ministers. The cabinet or council is the *collective executive body*. Usually the leaders of the largest party in the assembly, or the governing coalition within it, take the executive offices. Unlike presidents, who are the only officials with general responsibilities for government affairs, parliamentary executives share responsibilities among their members. The theory is that the prime minister is no more than *primus inter pares* (first among equals), and the executive has responsibility for government.

Whereas the executive and legislative branches in presidential systems are separated, this is not so clearly the case in parliamentary systems where:

1. The leader of the party or coalition of parties with *most support in parliament* becomes the prime minister or chancellor.
2. The prime minister or chancellor forms a cabinet usually chosen from members of parliament, and the cabinet then forms the *core of government*.

Parliamentary systems
These are (1) a directly elected legislative body, (2) the fusion of executive and legislative institutions, (3) a collective executive that emerges from the legislature and is responsible to it and (4) a separation of head of state and head of government.

3. The government is dependent upon the *support of parliament*, which may remove the executive from power with a vote of no confidence. The executive (government) is also dependent upon the *legislature* (parliament), because the latter can reject, accept, or amend legislation initiated by the government. Equally, the executive can dissolve the legislature and call an election.

This means that the executive in a parliamentary system is directly dependent, on and accountable to, the legislature (i.e. the parliament), which can veto legislation with a majority vote, and bring down the executive with a vote of no confidence. Since the executive has **collective responsibility** for government (unlike a president), it must stick together, since public disagreement within the cabinet or council on a major political matter will almost certainly result in its being seriously weakened and attacked. The prime minister and the cabinet must be closely bound together by mutual dependence and 'collegiality' if they are to have a chance of remaining in office. The prime minister appoints cabinet members and can sack them, but to remain in power the prime minister must also retain the confidence of the cabinet.

Collective responsibility
The principle that decisions and policies of the cabinet or council are binding on all members who must support them in public.

Presidential systems are usually modelled on the USA and often found in Latin America, while parliamentary systems are often modelled on the British system, and are widely found in the British Commonwealth, but also in western Europe (see fact file 4.1). While, in theory, presidential and parliamentary systems operate in very different ways, in practice they tend to converge. Both types of government depend on a close working relationship between executive and legislature and while the power of a president is formally greater than that of a prime minister, in practice prime ministers in the modern world are said to be accumulating power so that they become more and more 'presidential'. For example, British experts argue heatedly about whether the country has cabinet government characteristic of parliamentary systems, or whether it is moving towards prime ministerial government, akin to a presidential system. In Germany, too, the office of Chancellor, seems to have become progressively more powerful under Adenauer, Brandt, Kohl and Schröder.

One of the advantages of parliamentary over presidential systems is said to be that the former produce strong and stable government by virtue of the *fusion of executive and legislature*. This has generally been the case in Australia, Britain, Canada, Denmark and Japan. But just as presidential systems are sometimes weak, divided, or deadlocked, so also are some parliamentary systems – in Italy and in the French Fourth Republic. The difference between stable and unstable parliamentary systems seems to lie less in their constitutional arrangements than in their *party systems*. Where there is a strong, stable and disciplined party majority (either a single party or a coalition) the result is often strong and stable government, because the executive can usually depend on majority support in the legislature through thick and thin. Where parties are fragmented, factious and volatile, or where majorities are small and uncertain, the parliamentary system is likely to be weak and unstable. This directs

French Fourth Republic (1946–58)

attention from constitutional arrangements to the role of political parties, a theme we will revisit again and again, especially in chapter 12.

■ Semi-presidential systems

The French Fourth Republic suffered from chronic instability caused by party fragmentation and deadlock in the assembly, running through twenty-seven governments in thirteen years. To overcome this problem the French Fifth Republic created a strong, directly elected president with substantial powers to act as a stable centre for government in a **semi-presidential** system:

French Fifth Republic (1958–)

- The French president appoints the prime minister from the elected assembly, and can dismiss him.
- The president can dissolve parliament and call a referendum.
- The president has strong emergency powers.
- The prime minister, in turn, appoints a cabinet from the assembly (the president may do this if he is from the same party as the prime minister) which is then accountable to the assembly. In this way, the French system of semi-presidential government combines the strong president of a presidential system, with a prime minister and the fused executive and legislative of parliamentary systems (see fact file 4.2).

Semi-presidential Government consists of a directly elected president, who is accountable to the electorate, and a prime minister, who is appointed by the president from the elected legislature and accountable to it. The president and prime minister share executive power.

This system worked smoothly in the early years of the Fifth Republic when the president (de Gaulle) and the prime minister (Debré) were from the same political party. During this time the president was the dominant force. To the surprise of many, the system continued to work well later when the president (Mitterrand) and the prime minister (Chirac) came from different parties – what the French call 'cohabitation'. In this period, the balance of power tended to swing in favour of the prime minister.

Semi-presidentialism is found in relatively few democracies (Finland, France and Portugal) but it has been adopted by some of the new democracies of

---

Fact file 4.2

Semi-presidentialism

- Relatively few countries have a semi-presidential form of government, and only Finland, France and Portugal have been so for more than a quarter of a century. Finland's semi-presidentialism has moved towards a parliamentary system.
- Among the new democracies the Czech Republic, Estonia, Lithuania and Slovenia have chosen the system, but there has been a tendency in the Czech Republic, Poland and Romania for the presidential office to be converted into a more prime ministerial one.
- Israel has a hybrid presidential–parliamentary system of government, including the semi-presidential characteristic of a directly elected prime minister.

central Europe (the Czech Republic, Estonia, Lithuania, Poland and Slovenia), which have tried to blend parliamentary systems with a comparatively strong, directly elected president. The attraction of an elected president in the ex-communist democracies is to have a single strong public figure who can act as (1) a *focus of national feeling*, important in a newly independent state that needs a strong central figure and (2) as the centre of executive power to help overcome extreme *party fragmentation* in the new legislatures.

There are indications of a tendency to move away from semi-presidentialism in some countries as political conditions change. In Finland, there have been attempts to reduce the power of the president. The central European states are still feeling their way, and if they develop strong party systems and consolidate their national identity, they may well move from a semi-presidential to more purely parliamentary forms of government.

■ Presidential, parliamentary and semi-presidential systems compared

We are now in a position to compare all three types of government. The main points of comparison are laid out in briefing 4.1. It is clear that there are things to be said both for and against all three as forms of democratic government, but it is also clear that all three can work as effective democratic structures. However, whether all three work equally well in different kinds of countries with different social conditions and political histories is a different matter. One view is that presidential systems can be weak and ineffective, and run into problems of executive–legislative deadlock, leading to attempts to break through the problem by a 'strong man' who promises decisive and effective government. Not many countries have managed the presidential system as well as the USA.

At the same time, semi-presidential systems also have their problems. They can lead to deadlock between presidents and prime ministers, leading to weak and ineffective government. Not many countries seem to be able to handle the problems of 'cohabitation' as well as France. Nor have parliamentary systems always resulted in stable and effective democracy. Some have produced weak, divided and unstable government, while others have tended towards an over-concentration of power (see controversy 4.1). It is clear that we should look more closely at the arguments about parliamentary, presidential and semi-presidential government.

■ Theories of parliamentary, presidential and semi-presidential government

At the heart of debates about the three types of government lies one of the fundamental problems of any democracy, namely how can a political system balance the need for *accountability to citizens* and *protection of their basic rights* against the need for government that is *strong enough to be effective*? Too much

Briefing 4.1
The three major forms of democratic government: main features

Presidential	Parliamentary	Semi-presidential
• Citizens directly elect the executive for a fixed term	• The executive emerges from a directly elected legislature and is an integral part of it	• Executive power is shared between a president (directly elected) and a prime minister who is appointed or directly elected
• Except for a few joint presidencies, the president alone has executive power	• The cabinet shares executive power and must reach compromises to maintain unity	• The prime minister appoints a cabinet, usually from the ruling party or coalition in the assembly
• The presidency is the only office of state with a general responsibility for the affairs of state	• The executive is a collegial body (cabinet or council of ministers) that shares responsibility, though the prime minister, premier or chancellor may be much more than *primus inter pares*	• The president often appoints the prime minister and has general responsibility for state affairs, especially foreign affairs
• The president shares power with a separate and independently elected legislature	• The office of the prime minister/premier/chancellor is usually separate from the head of state (whether monarch or president)	• The president often has emergency powers, including the dissolution of parliament
• Neither can remove the other (except in special circumstances such as impeachment)	• The prime minister and cabinet can dissolve parliament and call an election, but the prime minister and cabinet can be removed from office by a parliamentary vote of no confidence'	• The prime minister and cabinet often have special responsibility for domestic and day-to-day affairs of state
• The president is directly elected and therefore directly accountable to the people	• The prime minister and cabinet are responsible to parliament	• The president is directly elected and directly accountable to the people; the prime minister is responsible either to the president or to parliament
• Examples: USA, many states in Central and South America (Colombia, Costa Rica, Dominican Republic, Ecuador, Venezuela), Cyprus, the Philippines, and South Korea	• Most stable democracies are parliamentary systems – Australia, Austria, Belgium, Canada, Denmark, Germany, Greece, Iceland, India, Ireland, Israel, Italy, Japan, The Netherlands, Norway, Spain, Sweden, Switzerland, UK	• Examples: Finland (until 1991), France and many post-communist states, including Belarus, Poland, Russia and Ukraine

Controversy 4.1

Presidential, parliamentary, or semi-presidential government?

Presidential	Parliamentary	Semi-presidential
Pro		
• The USA is a model	• Most of the world's stable democracies are parliamentary systems	• In theory combines the best of presidential and parliamentary government
• Separation of the executive and legislative institutions of government according to classical democratic theory	• Fusion of executive and legislative can create strong and effective government	• The president can be a symbol of the nation, and a focus of national unity, while the prime minister can run the day-to-day business of the government
• Direct election of the president means direct accountability of the president to the people	• Direct chain of accountability from voters to parliament to cabinet to prime minister	
Contra		
• Conflict between executive and legislation may be chronic, leading to deadlock and immobilism	• The fusion of the executive and legislative, and a large legislative majority, combined with tight party discipline, can produce leaders with too much power	• Conflict and power struggles between prime minister and cabinet, and between prime minister and president are not unusual
• Weak and ineffective presidents have sometimes tried to make their office much stronger	• Parliamentary systems without a legislative majority can be weak and unstable	• Confusion of accountability between president and prime minister
• Few presidential systems have survived long		

government power means too little democracy, but too little government power means too little government. How do our three systems measure up to this dilemma?

At the outset, we have the problem of evaluating semi-presidential systems. There are relatively few, too few of them, in the world and only two examples of established democracies (Finland and France). It is true that many of the new democracies of central and eastern Europe are semi-presidential, but these are rather special cases and it is not clear how they will develop. Only time will tell, and we have to set these aside for the time being at least.

Briefing 4.2

The perils of presidential government

The outgoing president in 1952, Harry S. Truman, is said to have commented about his successor in the White House, the Second World War General, Dwight ('Ike') D. Eisenhower:

> He'll sit here, and he'll say, 'Do this! Do that!' And nothing will happen. Poor Ike – it won't be a bit like the Army. He'll find it very frustrating.
>
> (Richard E. Neustadt, *Presidential Power and the Modern Presidents: The Politics of Leadership*, New York: Free Press, 1960: 9)

A leading writer on the relative merits of presidential and parliamentary systems is Juan Linz. He claims that presidentialism entails a paradox. On the one hand presidents are strong because they are directly elected and have popular support. They can rise above the petty in-fighting of parties and factions and speak for their country and its people. The president is also a single person who takes all the power of the presidential office. On the other hand, presidents are normally bound by all sorts of constitutional provisions that limit their power: they must have legislative support for actions, decisions and appointments; they have to deal with the independence of the courts; and they sometimes face a highly fragmented, undisciplined and effective party system that makes it difficult to shape and implement a coherent policy. Because presidents do not always have the support of the majority in the assembly, they may be unable to implement their policies. In a word, presidentialism is prone to **immobilism** (see briefing 4.2). In addition, unlike parliamentary leaders, presidents have a fixed term of office, which means it can be difficult to remove an unpopular president, but also means a sharp break when a new one is elected. For all these reasons, presidential systems can be *rigid and inflexible*.

Immobilism
The state of being unable to move (immobilised) or unable to take decisions or implement policies.

According to Linz, parliamentary systems are more conducive to stable democracies. They are more flexible and adaptable because they do not impose the discontinuities of fixed terms of presidential office. Since the political executive is rooted in the majority party of the assembly, or in a coalition of parties, it is based on compromise and bargaining within or between parties. And since parliamentary executives are not limited to one or two terms in office, they can maintain a degree of *continuity* – the party leader may be replaced but the party or coalition may continue in power.

How does the theoretical argument about the superiority of parliamentary over presidential government measure up to the empirical evidence? At first sight, the evidence is compelling. The USA is the only example of long-lived democratic presidentialism, and there are a few notable failures – Argentina, Brazil and Chile. At the same time, a high proportion of western European democracies are parliamentary, as are many of the stable democracies of the British Commonwealth. It is estimated that of the forty-three stable democracies in the world that existed between 1979 and 1989, thirty-six were parliamentary, five presidential and two semi-presidential.

A second look at the evidence, however, suggests a more favourable evalua-tion of presidential government. First, while it is true that many presidential systems have failed to sustain democracy, it is not clear why. Many of the fail-ures are in Latin America, which raises the question of whether the explana-tion lies in inherent institutional design faults, or in the economic problems, lack of democratic traditions and fragmented parties of the countries which adopted the system in the first place. Would parliamentary government have worked any better in these countries? It is impossible to know, but it is impor-tant to note that parliamentary systems failed in Greece and Turkey, and did not perform at all well in France and Italy.

There are also different sub-types of presidential government, some giving the office great powers and others limiting them. Similarly some presidents operate within a cohesive and well-organised party system. It may be that com-paratively weak presidents with strong party support in the main legislative body have a better chance of producing stable democracy than either a very strong president or a weak one without party support.

What conclusions can we draw from this?

1. It seems that there is no single recipe for a smoothly working democracy. There are, instead, different routes to the same end result.
2. Different forms of government seem better suited to some conditions than others.
3. As countries develop their political system it may make sense for them to shift from one form of government to another.

▓ Summary

This chapter has dealt with the branches of democratic government and what system is used to combine them. It argues that:

- In spite of great constitutional variety, democratic states fall into one of three categories – presidential, parliamentary systems and semi-presidential systems.
- Presidents are directly elected for a fixed term of office. The main example of presidential government is the USA, but many Latin American and African states have adopted this system of government.
- In parliamentary systems the political executive (chancellor, premier, or prime minister and their cabinet or council of ministers) is not directly elected but emerges from the majority party or ruling coalition in the assembly. The executive continues in office as long as it has the support of the assembly, so there is no fixed term of office. Parliamentary systems are found mainly in western Europe and the stable democracies of the British Commonwealth.
- The semi-presidential system is a hybrid of the other two types, consisting of a directly elected president and a prime minister who appoints a cabinet from the assembly. There are not many semi-presidential systems in the world, and the best known is in France.

- There is no single best formula for a stable democracy. Each system has its advantages and disadvantages. Different systems may be suited to different countries and the same country may change its system as it develops.
- The semi-presidential system seems to be well suited to the circumstances of the new democracies of central Europe, but this may change as they develop.
- Although most stable democracies in the world are parliamentary, and relatively few are presidential or semi-presidential, it may be that weaker presidents with strong and organised party support in the main legislative body can sustain stable democracy.

Further reading

The best collection of work on parliaments and presidents is Arend Lijphart (ed.), *Parliamentary versus Presidential Government* (Oxford: Oxford University Press, 1992). A sustained critique of presidential government can be found in Juan Linz and Arturo Valenzuela (eds.), *The Failure of Presidential Democracy* (Baltimore, MD: Johns Hopkins University Press, 1994), but Scott Mainwaring and Matthew S. Shugart (eds.), *Presidentialism and Democracy in Latin America* (Cambridge: Cambridge University Press, 1997) provide a defence of some forms of presidentialism. Robert Elgie (ed.), *Semi-Presidentialism in Europe* (Oxford: Oxford University Press, 1999) and Alan Siaroff, 'Comparative presidencies: the inadequacy of the presidential, semi-presidential and parliamentary distinction', *European Journal of Political Research*, 42(3), 2003: 287–312, are up-to-date accounts of the subject.

Websites

http://encyclopedia.thefreedictionary.com/presidential%20system	Basic introduction to the presidential system with links to related topics.
http://en.wikipedia.org/wiki/Presidential_system	Basic introduction to the presidential system with links to related topics.
http://encyclopedia.thefreedictionary.com/Parliamentarism	Basic introduction to parliamentarism with links to related topics.
http://en.wikipedia.org/wiki/Parliamentarism	Basic introduction to parliamentarism with links to related topics.
http://www.oup.co.uk/pdf/0-19-829386-0.pdf and http://webpages.dcu.ie/~elgier/SPPoliticalStudiesReview	Introduction to semi-presidentialism
http://www.polisci.com/almanac/world.htm	A website with comprehensive information about the world's governments and links to each one.
http://www.ipu.org	The Inter-Parliamentary Union's website with information on parliaments in the world.

Projects

1. Assume you are a consultant brought in to advise a newly independent state that wishes to set up a democratic constitution. Would you recommend (a) a presidential, (b) a semi-presidential or (c) a parliamentary system? Explain the reasons for your decisions.
2. Why is there no single institutional design for democracy?

5   Multi-level government: international, national and sub-national

Government in all but the smallest countries is organised like a set of 'Chinese boxes', or 'Russian dolls', one unit of government tucked inside another. The smallest units of community or neighbourhood government fit into local government:

- which (in federal systems) is contained by state/regional/provincial government
- which is part of the national system of government
- which is a member of various organisations of international government.

For example, a resident of Wilmersdorf-Charlottenburg lives in one of the twelve *Bezirke* (boroughs) that form the City of Berlin:

- which is one of the sixteen *Länder* (states) that make up the Federal Republic of Germany
- which is one of the member states of the EU in Europe, of NATO in Europe and North America and of the UN across the entire globe.

Government is organised on different geographical levels in this way because no single centre could possibly do everything itself. It must be divided, not only into different branches at the national level (executive, legislative, judiciary) but also into smaller territorial units of local administration and policy making at the sub-national level. Nor can countries manage their affairs entirely on their own; even the largest and most powerful must deal with other countries to solve international problems of security, diplomacy, the environment and trade.

Dividing government into *geographical layers* in this way makes sense, but it also creates problems of its own:

- What should be centralised and what decentralised?
- Which layer of government should be responsible for which tasks?
- How do we ensure that the resulting system is as efficient and as democratic as possible?

We touched briefly on this topic in chapter 3 when we discussed unitary and federal states, but the topic of multi-level government is so important that we will return to it now in greater depth.[1]

There are usually three main layers of government within a country:

1. National, central, or federal government
2. A middle or meso-level that is variously called state, provincial, regional, or county government
3. Local or municipal government, which may cover anything from quite small areas to large metropolitan cities or regions.

Often there is a fourth and lowest tier of government for local communities and neighbourhoods, but it is rarely of great significance as a level of government and will not be discussed here. Layers of government below the national level are collectively referred to as 'sub-national' or 'non-central' government. In addition, there are many kinds of international and supranational organisations that have an important impact on the way that national and sub-national governments conduct their business, all the more so in an increasingly globalised world.

In this chapter, therefore, we discuss the multiple layering of government. It starts at the international level and works down to the most local level of sub-national government, as follows:

- Supra-national and international government
- The national level: federal and unitary states
- The inter-play of multi-level government
- The arguments for and against centralisation and decentralisation
- Theories of multi-level government.

---

[1] The term 'state' is defined in chapter 1. In dealing with multi-level government it has different additional meanings: (1) the whole government apparatus of countries at all levels, (2) national or central government (to distinguish it from local government) and (3) in federal systems, it refers to the middle level of government between central and local levels. To avoid confusion in this chapter we reserve the term 'state' for the middle of level of government in federal systems.

■ Supra-national and international government

Government above the national level is, for the most part, a matter of cooperation between countries that keep their national sovereignty, but nevertheless set up organisations to deal with problems that spread across national boundaries. International government of this kind is replete with an 'alphabet soup' of organisations: including the UN, NATO, IMF, ILO, OECD, OPEC, Interpol, GATT, IBRD, NAFTA, OAU, WTO. They are essential not only to international relations but also to the running of the internal affairs of countries. Among other things they help national governments run their economies, defend themselves, conduct diplomatic affairs, establish trade relations and catch criminals. Most of these are *confederations*, so our first job is to distinguish confederations from their close cousins, the federations.

■ *Confederations*

Confederations
Organisations whose members give some powers to a higher body, while retaining their own independence.

American Continental Congress (1716–88)

The term 'confederation' is often confused with 'federation', because the terms sound similar and have much in common. **Confederations** are looser-knit than federations, and are formed by private or public bodies that want to cooperate with each other but also want to preserve their independent identity and not merge into a single, larger body. Confederations do not encroach upon sovereign autonomy of their members, whereas federations are created by a *pooling of sovereignty* that binds their constituent units together. Because of this, confederations are usually weaker, less centralised and less stable than either federal or unitary states (see fact file 5.1). The American Continental Congress that prefigured the USA's federal system formed in 1789 was a confederation of American states, and it highlights the main problem of such groupings – they are often too loose and powerless to achieve much, and sometimes they fall apart.

Confederations are formed by all sorts of organisations for all sorts of purposes, and they operate at all levels of the political system, from the most local to the most global. Trade unions, for example, often form confederations around their common interests to work at all levels from the most local to the global. Business associations, professional organisations, churches and sports clubs do the same. However, international confederations are particularly well suited to the needs of countries that want to retain their independent identity and autonomy while cooperating with other countries on specific matters such as economic development, defence, environmental policy, or cultural affairs. The World Trade Organisation (WTO), the World Bank (IBRD) and the European Space Agency (ESA) are examples of international government confederations. Briefing 5.1 lists just a few of the international confederal organisations to which the government of The Netherlands belongs.

Fact file 5.1

Confederations

- Confederations include international organisations such as NATO, the UN and the United Arab Emirates.
- One of the earliest confederations was the Swiss Confederacy, dating back to 1315 (some say even to 1291).
- When the USSR (a federation) collapsed in 1989–90, the Commonwealth of Independent States (CIS, a confederation) was created in 1991 as an emergency measure to tie twelve of the former Soviet Republics together.
- Many transnational federations do not last long – the Czechoslovakian Confederation of the early 1990s, the League of Nations, various Middle East confederations of Arab states but some have been successful – NATO, the UN and United Arab Emirates.
- The weakness of the confederal system of the USA (1776–88) lead to the creation of the Federal constitution of 1789.

Supra-national government goes one important step further than international government. It involves the cooperation of countries that are willing to pool sovereignty, at least on certain matters, along federal lines. Since the international system has long been based upon sovereign nations (the Westphalian system outlined in chapter 1), the creation of supra-national government is a rare thing. In fact, the European Union is the first and, by far and away the most advanced, experiment with supra-national government in the world today.

Supra-national government
Organisations in which countries pool their sovereignty on certain matters to allow joint decision making.

Briefing 5.1

The Netherlands: membership of international organisations

The Dutch state is a member of some sixty-eight major international organisations. The following lists illustrates their range and type:

- African Development Bank (AfDB)
- Benelux Economic Union (Benelux)
- Euro-Atlantic Partnership Council (EAPC)
- European Space Agency (ESA)
- International Development Association (IDA)
- International Organisation for Migration (IOM)
- International Monetary Fund (IMF)
- Organisation for Security and Cooperation in Europe (OSCE)
- UN Institute for Training and Research (UNITAR)
- Western European Union (WEU)
- World Trade Organisation (WTO).

(http://www.nationmaster.com/graph-T/gov_int_int_org_par&id=EUR)

■ *The European Union: federation or confederation?*

The European Union is a hybrid of confederal and federal features. Its federal features are a Commission (a quasi-executive), a powerful European Court (ECJ) whose verdicts take precedence over national law and some pooling of sovereignty on particular matters. Its confederal characteristics are an unwillingness of member states to surrender sovereignty on some matters of economic and social policy, a weak parliament and weak coordination of foreign policy. Members can leave a confederation at any time, but the deep integration of the EU along quasi-federal lines makes it difficult for members to leave. France withdrew its troops from NATO military command (a confederal organisation) in 1966, but it would find it a great deal more difficult to pull out of the EU or its currency, even if it wanted to do so.

It remains to be seen whether the EU strengthens its federal or its confederal nature. As things stand at the moment, however, its nearest equivalent is the North American Free Trade Association (NAFTA), but its limited concern with trade relations between the sovereign states of North America means that it is not contemplating the deep integration of the member states of the EU. NAFTA is unlikely to turn itself from an international body into a supra-national one.

■ **The national level: federal and unitary states**

At the national level, government is organised on either a federal or a unitary basis. As we saw in chapter 3, federal systems contain middle-level territorial units of government (states, provinces, regions) which have a guaranteed status in the constitution that gives them a degree of independence and autonomy from the central government. In contrast, **sub-central** units of government in unitary states (chapter 3) are the creatures of central government, which creates them and which can reform, restructure, or abolish them without constitutional limitation. How central government changes local government in a unitary state is a sensitive political issue, of course, and there may be severe limitations to what it can do, but this is a political, not a constitutional, matter.

Sub-central government
All levels of government below central/national government.

Though they vary considerably in the degree to which power is concentrated, unitary governments are still more centralised than most federal systems. The advantage of federalism is that it combines a degree of national government unity with a constitutionally entrenched degree of independence for lower levels of government, variously named states, regions, or provinces. We can see this in figures 5.1 and 5.2 and table 5.1, which show that sub-central units of government in federal states usually account for a greater proportion of public sector taxes, spending and employment, suggesting greater decentralisation of service responsibilities to lower levels of government.

Federal decentralisation is specially important in two situations – where there are *geographically large states* and states with *markedly different geographical regions*.

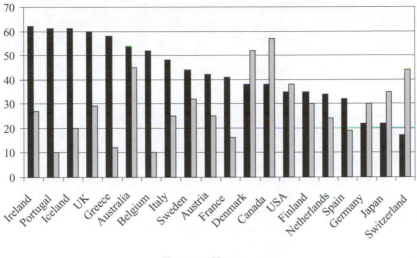

Figure 5.1: Share of total government expenditure: central and non-central
government, 1994, per cent
Note: Central plus non-central plus social security spending = 100 per cent.
Source: OECD, *Managing across Levels of Government* (Paris: OECD, 1997: 35).

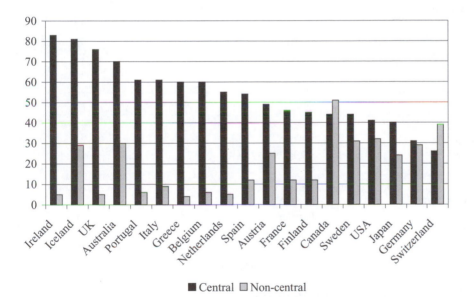

Figure 5.2: Share of total government receipts, 1994 per cent
Note: Central plus non-central plus social security spending = 100 per cent.
Source: OECD, *Managing across Levels of Government* (Paris: OECD, 1997: 35).

Table 5.1 *Share of public employment, late 1990s, per cent*

New Zealand	Central	90
	Local	10
Ireland	Central	87
	Local	13
Portugal	Central	86
	Local	14
France	Central	49
	Sub-national	31
	Health	21
UK	Central	48
	Local	52
Spain	Central	47
	Autonomous communities	31
	Local	22
Austria	Federal	45
	Länder	28
	Local	27
Denmark	Central	27
	Local	73
Finland	Central	25
	Local	75
Sweden	Central	17
	Regional	25
	Local	58
Canada	Federal	17
	Provincial	44
	Local	39
USA	Federal	15
	State	23
	Local	61
Australia	Commonwealth	15
	State	73
	Local	12
Germany	Federal	12
	Länder	51
	Local	37

Source: OECD, *Managing across Levels of Government* (Paris: OECD, 1997: 36).

■ Geographically large states

Large territories may better organised as federations in order to give far-flung territories a degree of autonomy that reduces their dependence upon a distant centre of government. One of the founding fathers of the American constitution, Thomas Jefferson, said: 'Our country is too large to have all

Table 5.2 *Federal states: names and numbers of regional units of government, 2000*

Australia	6 states, 2 territories
Austria	9 *Länder*
Belgium	3 regions
Canada	10 provinces, 2 territories
Germany	16 *Länder*
India	25 states, 7 union territories
Mexico	31 states, 1 federal district
South Africa	9 provinces
Switzerland	20 cantons, 6 half-cantons
USA	50 states, 1 federal district

its affairs directed by a single government.' Many of the largest countries in the world, in terms of area or population, or both, are federal (see fact file 5.2).

Thomas Jefferson (1743–1826)

■ *States with markedly different geographical regions*

Many federal states have multi-ethnic or multi-national populations that are concentrated in different geographical areas (Belgium, Canada, India, Switzerland and the USA). A country with deep **political cleavages** of any kind, whether based on language, ethnicity, religion, culture, or history, may have severe problems with its unity, and these problems will be compounded if the cleavages coincide with geographical divisions. For example, in Canada the French-speaking part of the population is concentrated in Quebec. Federalism makes it easier to hold diverse areas together within a single country by giving regions a degree of control over their own affairs. Belgium turned itself into a federal system in 1993 to prevent its three major regions (French-speaking Brussels, Dutch-speaking Wallonia and French-speaking Flanders) from falling apart.

Federal systems all have a *constitutionally recognised territorial division of political powers*, but there are different forms of federalism: some have many units of sub-central government, others only a few (some names and numbers are given in table 5.2); some reserve the most powerful functions for the centre (Canada, India), others give them to the states (Australia, Switzerland, the USA); some specify carefully the functions and powers of each level of government, others assume that powers and functions not specifically assigned to one level will be the responsibility of the other. In some federal systems, the upper legislative house is reserved for representatives of the states, regions, or provinces (the *Bundesrat* for the German *Länder* and the Senate for American states),

Political cleavage
A political division created when political organisations use social cleavages (p. 13) for their own purposes to mobilise support. Political cleavages are often more important if they coincide with territorially based social cleavages.

Fact file 5.2

Federal states

- Of the 178 states in the world in 1997, twenty-one were fully federal.
- Federal states include Brazil, Canada (sometimes described as quasi-federal), India, Malaysia, Mexico, Nigeria, Switzerland and the USA.
- The first example of federalism in the western world was the Achaean League in ancient Greece. The first federal state in modern history was the Dutch Republic of the United Provinces.
- Modern federal states include some of the largest in the world – Brazil, Canada, India, Mexico and the USA – and cover 40 per cent of the globe's population and nearly half its land. But Switzerland is also a federal state.
- The number of states within federal systems varies. There are three regions in Belgium, six states in Australia, twenty-six cantons in Switzerland and fifty states in the USA.
- Belgium is the newest federal state, being created in 1993 out of the three linguistic areas of Brussels, Flanders and Wallonia.
- No truly federal system has ever evolved into a unitary system, but there are many examples of failed international federations (the West Indian Federation, 1962, the Central African Federation, 1963, the Malaysian Federation (Singapore left in 1965), the East African Federation, 1977 and Yugoslavia and Czechoslovakia, 1992).

Achaean League (251–146 BC)

Dutch Republic of the United Provinces (1579–1795)

which gives them a powerful stake in national as well as regional and local politics.

In theory, there is a distinction between 'cooperative federalism' and 'dual federalism'. In the cooperative type, federal and state government share powers and, consequently, are required to cooperate closely with one another (Germany, Switzerland). In a dual system, there is supposed to be a clearer separation of functions and powers (Australia, the USA), with each level of government having its own sphere of competence. In practice, however, federalism of both kinds requires close and constant cooperation, negotiation and bargaining between federal and state government. In theory, the USA draws a line between the responsibilities of the federal government and the states, but in practice they cooperate closely in many areas of domestic policy. The metaphor of 'the marble cake' is often applied to the USA: a cake where the layers are not divided by clear, straight lines, but mixed and melded in a complex partnership of shared responsibilities. The key fact about any federal system, whether of the Swiss/German or Australian/US type, is not the separation of powers, but cooperation, inter-governmental relations and interdependence. The study of 'inter-governmental relations' and 'fiscal federalism' (the politics of shared taxing and spending powers) is important in federal systems because government is not so much layered as intertwined in a way that makes it difficult to understand how it works in practice.

Federal systems usually have three main levels of government – national government, local government and a middle level between them. To make life complicated the main middle-level units are often called 'states'. To distinguish 'states' in a federal system from central government the latter are often called 'federal' or 'national' governments. Local government is normally under the general oversight of the states, not the federal government. This means that each state or province can determine its own system of local government, with the result that they can vary in a bewildering variety of ways. The picture is often complicated further where large cities are given special powers of their own. Some cities in the USA have 'home rule charters', which give them a special degree of autonomy. In many countries the capital city is also treated as a special case.

Although federalism allows the degree of decentralisation and flexibility that is necessary for large and mixed populations, there is often a price to be paid for it. *Inter-governmental relations* between federal and state government can be complicated and sensitive, and special arrangements and understandings have to be created to allow them to operate effectively. These can be slow, complex and costly as different levels of government, each with its own powers and duties, work out a common programme of action between them. In particular, the growth of federal funding and regulation has often created a tangled mass of complicated inter-governmental relations.

◼ *Unitary and federal systems in practice*

We have drawn a clear distinction between unitary and federal systems so far, but in practice there is less difference between them.

Quasi-federal features

In the first place, some unitary states have *quasi-federal features* such as a degree of 'home rule' for special areas. These include the island of Äland (Finland), Corsica (France), the Channel Irelands and the Isle of Man (the UK) and the Faroe Islands and Greenland (Denmark). Special status is not reserved only for islands. Scotland, Northern Ireland and Wales have long had their own standing within the UK, as do the regions of Alto Adige and Val d'Aosta (as well as the island of Sicily) in Italy. Spain is a unitary state but it gives some regions (notably Catalonia and the Basque Country) so much autonomy that it might be called a semi-federal or regional system. In other words, unitary states can be rather variable and flexible, and not as highly centralised as they first seem (see fact file 5.3). In a word, they also **devolve** power to lower levels of government.

Second, central and local government *depend upon each other*, even in the most centralised of states, such as the UK and France. Just as central government in Paris relies upon the cooperation of local officials in the *communes* and

Devolution
Where higher levels of government grant decision making powers to lower levels while maintaining their constitutionally subordinate status.

Fact file 5.3

Unitary states

- Unitary states include the northern countries of Finland, Denmark, Ireland, Norway, The Netherlands, Sweden and the UK, the southern European countries of France, Italy, Greece, Portugal and Turkey, as well as Japan (the largest unitary state in the world) and New Zealand.
- Among the democracies of the world there are many more unitary than federal systems, but the unitary ones tend to be the smaller in terms of both population and territory.
- Fused local government systems (sometimes called 'Napoleonic systems') were found in their clearest form in France, Italy, Greece, Portugal and Turkey, though late twentieth-century reforms have tended to reduce central government's direct control of local government.
- Dual systems (sometimes referred to as the 'Westminster model') of local government are found in New Zealand, Ireland and the UK.
- The local self-government model is found in Denmark, Finland, Norway and Sweden.
- Since the 1970s, Finland, France, Greece, Ireland, Italy, Spain, Sweden and the UK have all created or strengthened their middle or meso-layer of regional government. This has reduced the difference between fused, dual and local self-government arrangements.

---

départements, so local officials depend upon Paris for resources and support. Each has to negotiate and cooperate with the other to some extent, as in federal systems.

Third, federal systems are tending towards greater *centralisation*. As countries become internally more integrated, and as they face the pressures of globalisation, so federal governments have assumed greater control over some national affairs. Some federal systems have become more centralised in an attempt to reduce economic inequalities between regions, and in order to implement national minimum standards of service provision. Because federal government has greater financial resources it is increasingly funding local services through grants and transfers of various kinds. In doing so, it is exercising greater control over local policies and services.

Although there is a tendency for federal and unitary states to converge, they still remain distinct. Figures 5.1, 5.2 and table 5.1 show that central government in unitary states usually accounts for a higher proportion of public expenditure and employment than central government in federal states: compare France, Ireland, New Zealand, Portugal and the UK at the top of table 5.1 with Australia, Canada, Germany and the USA at the bottom.

Unitary, federal and confederal government compared

Having described the operations of federal, confederal, and unitary government in theory and practice, we can now compare their advantages and disadvantages. This is done in controversy 5.1. We can draw three general

conclusions from a summary of the arguments for and against the three types
of government:

Controversy 5.1

Unitary, federal, or confederal?

Unitary	Federal	Confederal
Pro		
• Central government is clearly accountable	• Another form of the separation of powers	• Permits states (or other autonomous political units) to cooperate while maintaining their sovereignty
• A single centre of power that permits coordinated and decisive state action	• Encourages consensus and compromise between federal and state authorities	
• Best suited to small states, or homogeneous states with similar regions	• Best suited to large states (either population or geographical area), and/or those with markedly different regions	• Best suited to cooperation in one sector or field of government activity – economic (IMF), diplomatic (UN), defence (NATO)
• Can help national integration by focusing on national politics	• Can protect the rights of territorially concentrated minorities	• May be the only form of cooperation possible
• Facilitates the equalisation of regional resources (through national tax system, for example)	• Can maintain the unity of the country by containing regional divisions, so deflecting and defusing potentially dangerous national conflicts	
• It is still possible to grant some areas special powers (e.g. Basque Country in Spain)	• Encourages small-scale experiment, innovation and competition between states: the efficiency argument	
• Helps the creation of a system of equal rights and duties for all citizens	• Creates opportunities to respond to the different needs and demands of groups in different regions	

Unitary	Federal	Confederal
Contra		
• Can result in an over-powerful central state	• Can result in duplication, overlap and confusion of responsibilities and accountability	• Unstable – members can withdraw easily
• Can result in national majorities exploiting or repressing regional minorities	• May lead to conflict, inefficiency, or stalemate between levels of government	• Can be ineffective – when members cannot agree
• Can result in a rigid and hierarchical form of government	• Can result in complex, slow and expensive forms of government	
	• Can be inherently conservative	
	• Can strengthen tendencies towards national disunity and disintegration by encouraging breakaway of territorial units	
	• Can deflect political attention from national groups and interests to geographical interests	

1. Choosing between them is not a matter of deciding between good or bad, or even between better and worse, but trying to decide which is better for what purposes and under what circumstances.
2. Federal systems are better suited to large countries, especially where minorities are concentrated in geographical areas that can be given a degree of independence from central government. Unitary states are better suited to small, homogeneous countries.
3. Confederations are good at dealing with specific policy areas where those who participate in the confederation want to retain their own formal independence.

Decentralisation
Where some functions of the state are carried out by sub-central agencies that have a degree of discretion or autonomy from the central government.

■ *Local government*

Why do we have local government? Why not allow central government to run everything, or perhaps restrict the system to two levels alone – national and regional? The answer is simple: most countries are far too large and complex to be run by a single centre, or even by a few regional units of government. Government must have some **decentralisation** of its operations in the interests of both democracy and efficiency. Most countries rely heavily upon sub-central government to deliver services to citizens. It makes no sense, for example, to have bureaucrats in the capital city deciding when to close park gates in some distant town, or what books to buy for the local library. These are *local services*, and it makes sense to put them in the hands of local people who are affected by them.

The difficulty lies not in justifying decentralisation in theory, but in deciding exactly what and how much to centralise and decentralise in practice. As a general rule, the 'high politics' of state (international diplomacy, defence, monetary policy) are handled by central government, while local government has its own core services (its **general competence**, local planning and transport, refuse collection, sewage). Increasingly, however, there is a larger 'grey area' of services that are shared and mixed between levels of government to various degrees.

Local government in unitary states tends to fall into three broad categories – **fused systems**, **dual systems** and local self-government – ranging from the most to the least centralised.

Fused systems

The clearest example of the fused model is the centralised and uniform system set up by Napoleon in France. He placed agents of central government (*préfets*) in each local government unit (*département*)[2] to supervise their work and ensure that central government policies were carried out. Fused systems have elected local councils and officials, but the most efficient way for them to operate is through the national government in Paris, and the best way to do this used to be for the local mayor to get elected to national office, while remaining the local mayor.

Dual systems

The classic example of the dual system is Britain, where central government retains a good deal of power, though it does not directly control local government through an army of *préfets*. Rather it 'manages' it at arm's length, thereby giving it rather more autonomy. As a result, local government creates a separate political domain of its own – what is called the 'national world of local government' – with a distinct ethos, professional career structure and set of national organisations to represent local government and give it some collective power in its dealings with national government.

Local self-government

The principle of local self-government with more freedom of local action characterises the Nordic countries. Local government is entrusted with the tasks

General Competence The power of local government units to manage their own affairs, provided they observe the laws of the land and relatively few legally defined exceptions.

Fused systems The system of local government in unitary states in which central officials directly supervise the work of local government.

Dual systems The system of local government in unitary states in which local authorities have more independence than in fused systems but within the authority of central government.

[2] 'Prefects' and 'department' in English.

allotted to it by central government, and has freedom of taxation within limits. As figures 5.1, 5.2, and table 5.1 show, local government in Denmark, Finland and Sweden accounts for a relatively high proportion of public expenditure and employment among the unitary states.

Whatever the local government system, it involves a degree of decentralisation of government and a degree of autonomy and legitimacy for local government. While decentralisation of this kind makes a lot of sense in many ways, it also creates two special problems of its own namely:

- Central–local political conflict
- The dilemma of reconciling the needs of democracy and efficiency.

Central–local political conflict

Political conflict between central and local government is endemic in many states. If local government is to play its democratic role, it must be elected by, and accountable to, local citizens; but central government is also elected and accountable. Which level of government is to have the final word in decision making? The problem is likely to be aggravated if central and sub-central government are controlled by different political parties. This is often the case because local elections are usually held between national elections (mid-term elections) when there tends to be a reaction against the central government of the day. The result is that 'opposition parties' are often elected locally. Party political conflict is sometimes thus built into central–local relations. Usually this is resolved by negotiating, bargaining and compromising. In turn, this calls for a set of institutions which enable central and local governments to talk to each other and resolve their problems.

The problem of how best to fund local government is a permanent source of disagreement and conflict in most democracies. On the one hand, central government is ultimately responsible for national fiscal policy and the level of public spending – both local and national. It also controls most of the taxes that raise money (income tax, business and sales taxes) and it is the rare local authority that can fund its own services from its own revenues. In addition, the demands of equality between areas mean that central government redistributes money from rich to poor areas, otherwise the latter would have unacceptably poor public services. Transfers of money from central government are often the largest source of funds for local authorities. On the other hand, democratically elected local councils naturally wish to control their own affairs, which means minimising financial dependence upon central government.

The resulting financial tensions between financial centralisation and decentralisation were heightened in the second half of the twentieth century by the sustained growth of the welfare state and by the increasing amount of public money being spent by sub-national government – money that was often provided by central government grants and transfers. The situation was then compounded by financial problems and cuts in services in the last part of the century, and even more by the tendency for central government to delegate new service responsibilities to the localities without funding them adequately.

■ Democracy, size and efficiency

The second dilemma for local government is how to reconcile the often competing claims of *democracy* and *efficiency*. There are seven main aspects to this problem:

- Democracy in local government requires that it should be based, so far as possible, around small communities of people where participation is easiest and there is a *common identity and set of interests* among citizens. The **subsidiarity** principle requires that decisions are taken at the lowest possible level in the system.

- Some services are most efficiently provided on a small scale, some on a larger one. Parks, refuse collection, local libraries and local transport are small scale, but refuse disposal, central reference libraries, higher education, inter-city transport, water and police services are larger scale. There is *no single optimum size* for multi-purpose authorities.

- *Services are not isolated from each other.* They need integrating so that, for example, residential areas, schools and shopping areas are provided with public transport, and transport integrated with economic development and environmental policies. There is a need for a body that can plan and coordinate a wide range of services, some small scale, some large.

- Local government units should be large enough to have a *tax base* adequate for their purposes, and they should probably be large enough to have a mix of rich and poor citizens so that the financial load can be equitably distributed.

- Some of the largest cities (Calcutta, London, New York, Tokyo) are bigger than some countries, and require large units of local government to run them, even if they have smaller sub-divisions nested within them. On top of this, there is a problem of where to draw the *boundary* around any large city. Should they be defined fairly narrowly to include only densely populated urban areas, or should they include the surrounding commuter suburbs and villages which depend upon the big city for work and recreation? Since suburban commuters use central city services for both work and pleasure, it seems sensible to draw wide boundaries around cities.

- Some features of local geography and history, such as rivers, mountains and historic divisions, suggest boundaries between local government units that may not fit neatly with the most efficient or the most democratic scale of *service provision*. Sparsely populated areas and islands are often

Subsidiarity
The principle of democracy that decisions should be taken at the lowest possible level of government – that is, at the level closest to the people affected by the decisions. Usually the term subsidiarity is used in connection with the territorial decentralisation of government, but it is not limited to this form.

combined into geographically large units of local government with small populations.

- Optimum sizes change according to technical developments and ideas about how public services should be organised. Sometimes this reduces scale, but in other cases it increases it. Computer networks, for example, make it possible to decentralise some town hall functions and create many little local offices that are more accessible to the public. At the same time, the capital and environmental costs of refuse disposal have made it necessary to operate on a much larger scale than before. As city populations grow or shrink, so the *optimum size of service-providing units* also changes – local schools are closed and their pupils sent to larger schools that are supposed to be more effective and efficient.

This means that there is no optimum size for units of local government, nor is there a 'natural' range of service functions for it: it is a matter of trying to balance economies and diseconomies of scale, and weighing up the often competing demands of efficiency and democracy. There are many different ways of organising local government, and the endless search for the best balance explains why local government across the western world has been subject to constant reform.

For the most part, reform has involved the creation of (a) different-sized units of local government with (b) a different range of functions and (c) a set of institutional mechanisms to liaise between them and integrate them. Most countries have experimented with three forms of local organisation:

- General-purpose authorities
- Joint bodies
- Single-purpose authorities.

General-purpose authorities

These deliver a wide range of services and go under many different names – districts and counties in the UK, *communes* and *départements* in France, *Gemeinden* and *Kreise* in Germany, communes and provinces in Italy. They are invariably directly elected, but their function and population size varies enormously from one country to another. Some countries have a single tier of general-purpose authorities that divides the entire territory of the country into local government units with much the same powers and functions. Others divide local government into two or more tiers each with different powers and functions. For example, large cities may have a single overall authority to deal with area-wide services (transport, economic development, planning) and smaller units within them for local ones (libraries, parks, refuse collection). Sometimes large rural areas are run by top-tier authorities, but the towns within them by second-tier ones.

Joint bodies

Small units of local government sometimes form larger joint bodies to provide a range of mutual services (economic development, water supply). Many of the 36,000 French *communes* have grouped themselves into consortia to provide services best provided on a larger scale.

Special-purpose authorities

In some countries, particular services are provided by special single-purpose authorities. These include school boards, river authorities, water boards and police authorities. Special-purpose authorities are most frequently found in the Third World, central and eastern Europe and in the USA.

The result of trying to match services and functions with different types and levels of local government units is often a complex and confusing structure of authorities. Such a structure may have a logic of its own, but one that is difficult to understand. The USA is an extreme case because it is fragmented into more than 85,000 units of local government in the shape of general-purpose authorities, special-purpose authorities, home-rule cities and cities without home rule and a bewildering range and variety of other agencies. The government of New York City, with its tangle of 1,500 local government and service units, has been called 'one of the great unnatural wonders of the world'. The metropolitan region of Philadelphia has more units of local government than there are countries in the entire globe.

■ *Changing local government*

For much of the twentieth century local government has struggled to keep pace with four key powerful social, economic, and political changes:

1. *Social and economic changes* National and local political institutions have had to adapt to huge population movements, large shifts in working patterns, increasing interdependence of urban and rural areas, the growth of huge metropolitan areas and increasing national and global integration. To take one example, road transport has been totally transformed by the speed and volume of traffic, and whereas roads used to be mainly the responsibility of local government national highway systems now require national planning and funding. International cooperation is necessary for rail and air transport, and even for roads.
2. *Financial pressures on central and local government* As the political demands and financial pressures on both central and local government grow, so both have to develop new modes of operating and relating to each other.
3. *Ideological pressure for decentralisation* Politics in the late twentieth century began to favour decentralisation and grass-roots participation.
4. *Technology* Transport, communications and computer technology have affected patterns of work and residence, and they have also made decentralisation and devolution of local government easier, just as they have helped

Fact file 5.4

Sub-central government: patterns of change

▪ Consolidation

• The consolidation of smaller units of local government into bigger ones in Denmark, Finland, Germany, Japan, Sweden and the UK. Sweden has subsequently sub-divided some local authorities in favour of 'small democracy'.
• Consolidation of this kind was resisted in France and southern Europe. Voluntary cooperation between local authorities and the emergence of regional authorities occurred instead.

▪ The growth of meso-government

• Belgium turned itself into a federal state, with three regions, in 1993.
• France, Ireland, Italy and Spain have introduced important regional layers of government.
• Greece has created new regional government, with elected prefects.
• Finland has created new regional joint authorities for regional planning, development and environmental control.
• The UK has created the Scottish Parliament, the Welsh Assembly and a directly elected mayor for the London region.
• Austria, Canada, Denmark and Sweden have shifted functions downwards from the central to the middle layer of government, and strengthened this layer.
• Canada and Denmark have shifted some services upwards from local to meso-government.

▪ Decentralisation in unitary states

• Austria, Canada, Finland, France, Italy and Spain have devolved some services from the central to the middle layer of government.
• Denmark, France, Iceland, Ireland, Japan, Mexico, Sweden, Turkey and the UK have moved some service responsibilities from central to local government.
• Sweden has shifted some functions from local to central government, while transferring other responsibilities in the reverse direction.
• Central government in the UK has begun to exercise greater control over local authorities, and privatised some important local services.
• The number of special-purpose authorities has increased in Canada, the UK and the USA.
• Austria, Canada, Switzerland and the USA (all federal systems) have strengthened their middle level of government by removing some restrictions from them, or giving services to them.

▪ Centralisation in federal states

• In Australia, the states were originally given complete control over education, but gradually both federal and state government have come to share these powers.
• Canadian provinces, originally responsible for health services, now share the responsibility with federal government.

- The federal government of the USA acquired more duties and responsibilities in the 'New Deal' era of the 1930s to try to overcome economic problems, and in the 1940s it centralised around the war effort, while in the 1960s and 1970s it further consolidated power to manage racial integration and social change. Whereas the US states used to decide speed limits on the roads and the minimum drinking age, the federal government has now established a high degree of national unity on these matters.

to centralise other public functions (central police records, national standards for schools and hospitals).

The result is that local government has been the object of constant restructuring in many countries. In fact, few democracies have not reformed and restructured their local government system since 1945, and some have had several goes at it. Amid the huge variety of reforms six general trends stand out (see fact file 5.4), which we shall consider in two main groups (points 1–4 and points 5–6).

1. *Consolidation* In many countries small units of local government have been amalgamated and consolidated into larger units. Sometimes central government has initiated reforms, but in others cases local units have voluntarily merged.

2. *Meso-government* Many unitary states have strengthened or created a middle level of regional government – **meso-government** – that fits between central and local government. In some cases this meso-level has been given substantial powers and service responsibilities so that it is the functional equivalent of state government in federal systems.

   Meso-government A middle level or tier of government between central and local authorities, and often known as state, regional, provincial, or county government.

3. *Decentralisation in unitary states* Local government in unitary states has often been given a broader range of responsibilities and powers. Since this happened at the same time as central governments were coming under intense economic pressure, some observers felt that this was, in effect, 'exporting' the economic problems of central government.

4. *Centralisation in federal systems* As we have already seen, some federal states have become more centralised.

   Most of these reforms have been justified by the government of the day on the grounds that they improved rationality, efficiency and democracy, but there sometimes seem to be political interests at stake as well. For example, in some countries left-wing governments have implemented reforms favouring left-leaning big cities over more conservative and rural areas, while in others right-wing central governments have diluted the powers of 'leftish' urban areas or tried to outflank them by creating higher levels of government that are likely to be more conservative. Politics are important in central–local relations and they account for the last two sets of changes in local government.

5. *Politicisation* Local government became increasingly political in the late twentieth century. As local authorities enlarged their size and

responsibilities, parties and ideological groups penetrated the corridors of power and contested the elections. Few believe any longer that 'there is no room for party politics in local government', or that there is 'only one way to lay a sidewalk'.

6. *Central–local conflict* Politicisation of localities has sometimes brought them into direct conflict with central government, especially where different parties are in power. This occurred in Britain when the Thatcher government in the 1980s was cutting back the powers and budgets of local government, especially Labour-controlled ones. It also occurred in France, when Paris was controlled by the right-wing Gaullist Party and central government by the socialists. In Italy, socialist and communist run cities have often conflicted with centre and right-wing national governments. In Germany and Spain, central–local conflict has often forced moderation and compromise on both sides.

◼ The interplay of multi-level government: the case of the European Union

We have seen how the changing world has brought about greater interdependence between levels of government, and nowhere is this clearer than in the case of the European Union. The mere existence of the Union as a developed form of supra-national government means, of course, a degree of centralisation in Brussels. At the same time, the EU pays careful attention to its regions (as federal systems do), putting regional policy high on its agenda and spending a large proportion of its budget on regional aid. It has created the Committee of the Regions (CoR), which, though only an advisory body, gives regions a direct input into EU deliberations. The result is that the EU often manages to by-pass national governments – which can be a nuisance when they present obstacles to its policies – and deals directly with the meso-level of regional government. This enhances the power, importance and financial resources of the regions, and therefore represents a decentralising tendency. Consequently, the EU is both a *centralising* force, insofar as some national powers have moved upwards, and a *decentralising* one, insofar as it strengthens regional government, while encouraging regional dependence on Brussels for financial and political support.

◼ The arguments for and against centralisation and decentralisation

Having considered the four main levels of government – international, national, regional and local – we are now in a position to form a judgement about the various merits and difficulties of centralised and decentralised forms of government. The basics of the argument are presented in controversy 5.2. This makes it clear that the debate has many sides. It is not a question of whether to have either centralised or decentralised government, but rather

Controversy 5.2

To centralise or decentralise?

▪ Arguments for decentralisation

- *Democracy* Local government adds an important dimension to democracy by allowing people in small communities to participate in, and have some control over, their own local affairs. Because it is also closer to citizens, local government may also be more accessible and democratic.
- *Efficiency* Centralisation may be inefficient, as many large corporations and the highly centralised states of the communist era found, because it means that decisions are taken by people who are far removed from the implementation of the decisions and from first-hand knowledge of their effects. Centralisation may be too rigid and unresponsive to local needs and demands.
- *Adaptation to local circumstances* Should central government officials in the capital city decide what time to lock local park gates, or how to run the local library? Such things ought to be decided by local people according to their wishes and knowledge of local circumstances.
- *Local minorities* Decentralisation allows geographically concentrated minority groups to control their own local affairs.
- *Training ground for democracy* Local government is a citizen training ground for democracy.
- *Recruiting ground for national politics* Local politics help to develop a pool of political interested and talent people who can be recruited into national politics. Many national politicians start off in local government.
- *Experimentation and development* State and local government can experiment on a small scale with new services and new methods of delivering services. Successes can spread quickly; failures are not large-scale disasters.

▪ Arguments for centralisation

- *Democracy* Central government can claim to have stronger legitimacy and support (higher election turnouts), more media attention and a broader and deeper mandate (the whole country).
- *Efficiency* The small-scale provision of some public services can be inefficient if it results in duplication, wasteful competition and high capital costs, as many small units of production have found. Some services can be provided only nationally (defence, national economic planning), some are more efficiently provided this way (population censuses, motor registration) and some are so expensive that they must be provided nationally or internationally (building planes, space research).
- *Equality* Inequalities between areas can be reduced by the redistribution of resources (money, space, human capital) by national government. Central governments usually control the most productive taxes (income tax, business taxes) and they have the money and power to redistribute.

- *Protection of minorities*   Decentralisation may allow local majorities to oppress their minorities. The defence of 'states' rights' in the USA has sometimes been a thinly disguised attempt to maintain racial segregation.
- *Local elites*   Decentralisation can protect entrenched local elites.
- *Disintegration of the state*   It is sometimes feared that decentralisation may lead to the break-up of the country (Basque Separatism, Quebec, Scottish Nationalism).
- *National identity*   Focus on a national government can promote national integration. Some political identities are not local or regional but based upon national factors – class, culture, gender, language and national history.

a matter of what to centralise, and how much, and what to decentralise, and how much. There are no clear answers to these questions and the debate is likely to continue.

■ Theories of multi-level government

Theories of multi-level government tend to fall into three basic types: first, there are philosophical and political defences of decentralised government, including pluralist theory; second, there are rational-choice theories of federalism and local government; and, third, there are the historical accounts of centre–periphery relations.

■ *Philosophical and political theories: Mill and Tocqueville*

Alexis de Tocqueville (1805–59)

John Stuart Mill (1806–73)

The basic philosophical and political arguments for decentralised government were laid out by the French writer on American democracy, Alexis de Tocqueville and the British philosopher, John Stuart Mill. Developing basic liberal values, Mill argued that local self-government was important because, so far as possible, political decisions should not be imposed from above, but developed and accepted from below. Compared with central government, local government gives more people a first-hand experience of public affairs and, according to Mill, it is the chief instrument for *educating people into their citizen duties*. Tocqueville argues a similar case, but his writing concentrates on the benefits of local voluntary associations rather than local government, ideas we shall consider in chapter 9.

■ *Pluralist theory*

Modern pluralist theory builds on Mill and Tocqueville. It argues that democracies cannot have a single, monolithic centre of power but require *many centres of power* so that many people and groups can exercise influence on different issues, in different ways and in different political arenas. Democracies divide power vertically (into executive, legislative and judiciary) and horizontally (into different layers of territorial government) in order to create a variety of *political arenas.* Groups that lose a political battle in one arena can turn to another, and so live to fight another day. If they fail to get satisfaction in, say, central government they can take their causes to the courts, or local government, or perhaps international arenas.

Breaking the political system into geographical units with their own powers and responsibilities also has the advantage of decentralising political problems, and hence of not overburdened the centre with an accumulation of divisive issues. This is especially important where minorities (ethnic, linguistic, religious, or cultural) are geographically concentrated and where they have their own sub-central units of government to tackle their own problems in their own way. What makes local politics important is its very 'localness' – meaning that it is accessible to local people and that they are best placed to understand and deal with local issues (see controversy 5.2).

■ *Economic theories*

Rational choice

Rational-choice theories borrow heavily from economics and assume that politics is based upon the *rational calculations of actors* (individuals, organisations, governments), who are *self-interested* and try to *maximise their own preferences*. Many rational-choice theories start from the position that the political world consists of individuals, as against institutions with a culture and a history, who make rational choices that maximise their own utility – that is, their political behaviour is driven by calculations of what is in their own interest. Rational choice is a high-level general theory and it has been applied to many aspects of government and politics. Here we are concerned with its use to explain (1) the origins of federalism, and (2) its defence of highly fragmented systems of local government made up of very small, competing, jurisdictions.

According to William Riker, the origins of federalism lie in a 'bargain' **William Riker** between national and local leaders, to the benefit of both, which enables them **(1920–93)** to expand the territory under their control, and to defend it against external enemies. Federalism is a rational solution to the problem of how to maintain a balance between the interests of a central power and of geographical regions so that each maintains control of their own affairs but can cooperate to deal with a common, external threat, and thereby increase their own power. Riker **William Riker,** (1964) claims that evidence about the origins of federal systems supports his *Federalism:* hypothesis that *military security* and *territorial expansion* are the driving forces *Origins,* behind the formation of federations. *Operation,*

Significance It can easily be argued that much the same explanation accounts for the **(1964)** historical origins of unitary states as well. Many were forged historically from smaller political units, city-states and princedoms when these were threatened by larger, more efficient and more powerful enemies. A single authority brought together by centralising leaders had a much better chance of developing the economic capacities and military power to compete effectively with external enemies. In other words, the formation of both federal and unitary states is a response to external economic and military threats, and the need to create a larger and stronger political unit to deal with them. What distinguishes them is the historical circumstances of their development along either federal or unitary lines, something best explained by centre–periphery theory.

Rational-choice theory of local government

Rational-choice theory also has its theory of local government, especially the highly fragmented and divided local government in the metropolitan areas of the USA. Splitting the government of a large urban area into many local jurisdictions, and giving each its own taxing and spending powers, means that citizens (the theory calls them 'consumer-voters') are provided with a choice of *different 'packages' of public goods at different prices*. Consumer-voters can move from one locality to another in search of their preferred 'package' of public goods, in much the same way that shoppers choose their supermarket for the goods it sells and the prices it charges. One municipality may have low taxes and few public services, another may tax in order to provide good education for young families, while a third may specialise in services for the retired.

This theory substitutes an economic logic for a political one: consumer-voters can move from one municipality to another to maximise their preferences, instead of using their vote to maintain their influence over civic leaders and local public services. The economic argument is that a highly fragmented system of government is not inefficient, as many argue, but, on the contrary, produces a quasi-market that allows consumer-voters to vote with their feet.

Some political economists find this approach helpful and insightful, but others doubt it doubt its value, for a string of reasons. First, consumer-voters are not free to move at will from one municipality to another. They are severely constrained by the needs of work, family, schools and house prices. Second, survey data shows that few people see local public services as very important when they are deciding where to live. Being near work, family and shops is much more important. Third, there is only a tenuous link between local taxes and services because financial transfers from higher levels of government foot a large proportion of the bill for local services. And last, in most countries other than the USA, local government is not fragmented into hundreds of competing jurisdictions. It is consolidated and coordinated by higher levels of government.

■ *Centre–periphery relations*

Unitary states have typically emerged from *old, centralised monarchies* that kept their local government under the authority of central government as they gradually developed their modern democratic structures. Denmark, Finland, Japan, The Netherlands, Norway, Sweden and the UK are examples. In contrast, federal states are often formed by the merger of *established and autonomous political areas* that come together to form a political union, while retaining a degree of their original independence. In the case of Switzerland, federalism is designed to accommodate a history of autonomous localities created by mountainous geography and reinforced by language and cultural differences. In the case of Australia, Canada, India and the USA federal governments cover large geographical areas that were not previously united under a single (monarchical) centre, but brought together by a colonial power.

According to the widely quoted theory of Rokkan and Lipset (see chapter 1) the historical process of state and nation building involved, among other things, the centralisation of regions and territories under a common central rule. In many cases, a powerful and modernising elite first conquered outlying areas and their local elites and then, by the processes of state and nation building, created a single political system with common political institutions and a common sense of national identity. The processes started many centuries ago in the case of some European countries, and took a long time to complete. Even so, one can often still see the historical imprint of centuries past in modern times, even in the most centralised and uniform unitary state, where the parties, voting and political/social patterns of peripheral regions are often rather different from the metropolitan centres.

However, the centre's attempts to incorporate the periphery has not always been altogether successful, as we can see from the nationalist movements in Italy (the Northern League), Spain (the Basque country and Catalonia) and the UK (Scotland, Wales, and Northern Ireland), and to a limited extent in France (Sardinia). In such cases, the unitary state may best be preserved by devolving powers to the peripheries. In the extreme case of Belgium in 1993, a unitary state turned itself into a federal one in order to maintain the integrity of the country.

Relations between the centre and the periphery are often relations between dominant and subordinate political groups. One variant of centre–periphery theory argues that the institutions of the central state were originally created by powerful interests (a class or ethnic group) that exploited the periphery for its resources, in much the same way that colonial powers exploit the natural resources of the Third World. According to some writers 'internal colonialism' of this kind exists in a subtle form in the UK (where England exploits Scotland, Wales and Northern Ireland) and the USA (where the north exploits the south), and in countries where the capital city region dominates and exploits the surrounding rural and agricultural areas.

■ Summary

This chapter has dealt with the organisation of multi-level government. It argues that:

- The government and politics of the modern world consists of four main levels, with the lower levels nested in higher ones – local government nested inside middle or meso-government, nested in unitary and federal systems, and a layer of international and supranational government above them all.

- Federal systems are more decentralised than unitary states, although to a degree federal systems have decentralised and unitary states have decentralised since 1945.

- Federal systems are better suited to some circumstances (large countries with territorially concentrated minorities) and unitary states are better suited to others (small, homogeneous countries).

- Local government in all countries, federal or unitary, faces two insoluble dilemmas:
  a the conflict that often arises between different levels of democratically elected government
  b the problem of how to reconcile the conflicting claims of democracy and effectiveness.

- Attempts to solve these two dilemmas have often produced a restructuring of sub-central government involving the consolidation of units of local government into a smaller number of larger units, a shifting of service functions both up and down the political system, the creation or strengthening of meso-government, a degree of decentralisation in federal states and centralisation in unitary ones.

- The centralist/decentralist debate revolves around the problem of what to centralise, and how much, and what to decentralise, and how much. In most countries, there is a large 'grey area' of cooperation between central and sub-central government.

- Most organisations at the international level are confederations that are looser than federations and do not encroach on the sovereignty of their members. The European Union is part-federation, part-confederation.

Further reading

Short but comprehensive articles on federalism, unitary states, and local government can be found in Rod A. W. Rhodes, 'Intergovernmental relations: unitary systems', and Grant Harman, 'Intergovernmental relations: federal systems', both in Mary Hawksworth and Maurice Kogan (eds.), *Encyclopedia of Government and Politics*, 1 (London: Routledge, 1992: 316–35 and 336–51). A useful collection of essays on federalism is contained in Michael Burgess and Alain G. Gagnon (eds.), *Comparative Federalism and Federation: Competing Traditions and Future Directions* (New York: Harvester Wheatsheaf, 1993). On meso-government, see Laurence J. Sharpe (ed.), *The Rise of Meso Government in Europe* (London: Sage, 1993). For a comparative study of local government in nine countries, see Alan Norton, *International Handbook of Local and Regional Government* (Aldershot: Edward Elgar, 1994). A more recent study of multi-level government in twenty-six states is the OECD report, *Managing across Levels of Government* (Paris: OECD, 1997). A good account of local government in west Europe is Peter John, *Local Governance in Western Europe* (London: Sage, 2001).

Websites

http://www.forumfed.org	The Forum of Federations is an international network on federalism and related issues. General information about federalism, useful links and a list of countries with federal systems of government.
http://www.iula.org	The website of the International Union of Local Authorities which is a 'new world organisation dedicated to promoting the values, objectives and interests of cities and local governments across the globe'.
http://www.oultwood.com/localgov/index.htm	Many links and information about local government in twenty-one countries, the councillors, members of parliament etc.
http://www.unescap.org/huset/lgstudy/comparison2.htm	On local government in Asia and the Pacific. A comparative analysis of fifteen countries.
www.lgib.gov.uk/ukint/ukint_e2.htm	The website of the Local Government International Bureau from the Congress of Local and Regional Authorities of Europe.
http://www.library.ubc.ca/poli/local.html	A portal to a range of local government websites and related issues.
http://en.wikipedia.org/wiki/Federalism	Basic introduction to federalism with links to related topics.
http://encyclopedia.thefreedictionary.com/Federalism	Basic introduction to federalism with links to related topics.
http://en.wikipedia.org/wiki/Local_Government	Basic introduction to local government with links to related topics.
http://encyclopedia.thefreedictionary.com/Local%20Government	Basic introduction to local government with links to related topics.
www.wordiq.com/definition/Unitary_state	Definition of unitary state and related issues. List of unitary states with links to general information about the state.
http://encyclopedia.thefreedictionary.com/Unitary%20state	Basic introduction to unitary states with links to related topics. List of unitary states with links to general information about the state.

Projects

1. Draw up a table that assigns government functions (international relations, education, pollution control, libraries, parks, economic development, housing, transportation, police) to different levels of the political system (international, national, regional, local, community). What general lessons can you draw from this exercise?

2. Figures 5.1 and 5.2 and table 5.1 tell us nothing about where sub-central government gets its money, or about how tightly central government regulates its use of money and employees. Would you conclude from figures 5.1 and 5.2 and table 5.1 that countries where sub-central government spends proportionately more money and employs proportionately more people are also more decentralised?

6   Policy making and legislating: executives and legislatures

Governments are there to get things done. At the highest level, the most important things they do is formulate public policies and frame the laws of the land in accordance with these general policies, and at the heart of the policy and law making process lie the two main branches of government – the executive and the legislative assembly. This means that the study of the relations between executive and legislative branches is a topic that lies at the very core of comparative government.

Sometimes the executive and the legislative branches cooperate and act together, sometimes they fight and struggle for power. Since democratic constitutions deliberately divide the powers of government between different branches, so that they check and balance each other, there is little wrong with the fact that they sometimes fight. However, some analysts argue that all is not well with the classical system of checks and balances because the golden age of legislatures, some time in the nineteenth century, has given way to the twentieth-century supremacy of executives. What were once powerful elected assemblies with a great deal of control over the affairs of state are now reduced to little more than rubber stamps for decisions made by their executives – their presidents and prime ministers. If true, this has obvious implications for the state of democracy in modern executive-dominated government.

Others claim that presidents and prime ministers have not acquired such great power. They argue that legislative assemblies were never that powerful to start with, and that the balance of power between executives and legislatures has not really changed: ultimately, executives are still dependent upon the support of their elected assemblies.

Another part of the discussion is concerned with correcting a common misperception about what the role of legislative bodies actually is, rather than how much power they have, or how much they have lost to executives. To 'legislate' means to make laws, and who should do this other than those who are elected to sit in the legislative chamber? Do not our national assemblies sit in endless discussion – sometimes solemn debate, sometimes angry and heated argument – about the policies and laws of the government of the day? Yet law making is not actually the main function of the legislature, and may not even be one of their most important functions. The curious fact is that legislatures, in spite of their name, are not mainly there to legislate. To understand why this is the case, we must examine the main functions of legislative bodies.

And last, since things rarely ever remain the same, we will examine the recent efforts of legislative assemblies to modernise. Many of them are in the process of reforming and streamlining themselves for modern government **administration**, so that they can do their work more efficiently and acquire the 'political muscle', necessary to exercise more control over their executives.

In this chapter, we analyse the relationship between executives and legislatures in the policy and law making processes of modern democratic government. The three major topics in this chapter are:

- Making laws: executives and legislatures
- The functions of legislatures
- Theories of democratic institutions: consensus and majoritarian systems.

■ Making laws: executives and legislatures

Classical democratic theory divides government into three main branches, the executive, legislative and judiciary, and gives them different powers and functions so that none can become too powerful. Each should have powers of its own, and each should operate a system of checks and balances to ensure that they are dependent on each other. In this way neither can do its job without the agreement of the other because they are bound together in a relationship of perpetual, mutual dependency (see chapter 3). In virtually all democratic systems **legislation** can be passed only when both the executive and legislative branches agree. Indeed, this condition is formally spelled out in some constitutions. For example, Article 61 of the Dutch constitution states: 'Laws are decided on by government and States-General together.' It is this sort of formal requirement for agreement that tries to ensure that power is shared.

In real life, however, some democratic systems deviate to a greater or lesser extent from the classic formula. Because the two branches should work closely together there is inevitably some overlap and fusion of executive and legislative functions and powers, and it is more accurate to say that their powers are mixed rather than separated. This is most evident in parliamentary systems,

Administration
A term with two meanings. Either (1) a term synonymous with government – e.g. the Bush administration, the Schröder administration or (2) a term synonymous with the management processes of bureaucracies – e.g. the administration of the state through bureaucratic agencies. The term is used in the second sense in this chapter.

Legislation
Legislation is the body of laws that have been passed by the legislature. Legislating is thus the act of initiating, debating and passing such laws.

Controversy 6.1

Parliaments and legislatures

■ What happened to parliaments?

Something has happened to parliaments. Parliaments were the key institutions of representative democracy. They translated the voice of the people into reasoned debate and ultimately into law. They also held governments to account, of all the checks and balances of power they were the most effective. They symbolised the constitution of liberty. For my father – and later for me – becoming a member of parliament was an affirmation of our deep belief in democracy.

Much of this however has to be said in the past tense today. A number of developments have conspired to weaken parliaments:

- Governments have increasingly used orders, regulations and other secondary legislation which is not subject to parliamentary scrutiny.
- There is also a tendency for governments to turn directly to the people – by referenda, but more ominously by relying on polls and the views of 'focus groups'.
- This process goes hand in hand with phenomena like celebrity politics (candidates have to be telegenic), and snapshot or throwaway politics (what counts is the moment, not extended debate).
- Self-elected crowds and groups, demonstrations in the streets, non-governmental organisations, increasingly claim to be the people, to speak for the people.
- All this happens at a time at which important decisions have emigrated to political spaces for which there are no parliaments anyway. This is as true for internal decision making as it is for the role of economic markets.

(Adapted from Lord Ralf Dahrendorf, speech at the Institute for Human Sciences, Vienna, *Newsletter*, 72, Spring 2001)

■ A decline of legislatures?

In what was the first truly empirical study of western governments, James Bryce, devoted a chapter to the subject of the 'decline of legislatures'. He argued that legislatures were weak and legislators incompetent or even corrupt. The idea of the decline of legislatures seemed confirmed in the twentieth century by the weaknesses of western European parliaments, not to mention those of most Third World countries.

While contemporary legislatures are often weak, there is some doubt as to whether they *declined* in quality and power during the period which preceded Bryce's investigation, let alone in the decades which followed. The view that there was a 'golden age' of legislatures seems at best exaggerated . . .

Legislatures are generally weak. Their weakness is due to general causes, many of which are structural and are connected with the complexity of matters and the need for urgent decisions. Only on a very few occasions did they realise the standards which Bryce, and indeed earlier Locke and Montesquieu, would have wanted them to display. (Adapted from Jean Blondel, *Comparative Government*, London: Prentice Hall, 1995: 250) but it also applies to presidential ones where, although there is supposed to be a clearer separation of powers, there is, as we saw in chapter 3, in reality a complex and subtle mix of executive and legislative powers.

James Bryce, *Modern Democracies* (1921)

Some have, however, argued that the classical system of executive and legislative checks and balances does not operate in modern government. They claim that modern executives have acquired so much power that they now dominate the processes of government, reducing legislative assemblies to the role of junior partners, even to little more than rubber stamps for executive decisions (see controversy 6.1). If this is true, then the lack of checks and balances may even pose a threat to democratic government itself.

■ *The rise of executives*

There are good reasons for believing that the balance of power between executives and legislatures may have shifted decisively in favour of executives. Five stand out as particularly important.

Government complexity

The growing complexity and interdependence of the social, economic and political world gives a new importance and role to executives. As technical problems grow ever more complex (nuclear power, the environment, the economy), as society becomes ever more differentiated and difficult to manage, as demands on government grow and as international and global pressures increase, so complex government increasingly requires a single *centre* of *coordination and control*. In addition, one of the major problems in modern government is to keep the multifarious agencies, departments and units of government moving in the same direction, and this increasingly difficult job of coordination is an executive rather than a legislative function.

Delegated legislation

The nature of legislation also changes. It is no longer possible to frame laws for specific and known circumstances – these change too quickly, in accordance with technological innovation, international forces and social pressures. It is necessary instead to devise more general laws, which inevitably leave much of the detail to be decided by executives. This is known as **delegated legislation**, and it gives executives more power.

Delegated legislation
Law or decrees made by ministers, not by legislatures, though in accordance with powers granted to them by the legislative body.

The organisational advantages of executives

Executives have significant advantages when it comes to organising for power. They are usually small in number – presidents and small cabinets – which makes it easier for them to unite around a common interest, and to react quickly and decisively to events. They are often supported by large and well-funded staffs in presidential and prime ministerial offices, and they are headed by highly visible political leaders who are able to appeal directly to the population, over the heads of the members of the elected assembly.

The mass media

Modern executives have equipped themselves with effective press offices to help them exploit every ounce of favourable publicity they can get from the mass media. To some degree, the debating functions of legislatures have also been transferred to the mass media because more public debate about politics now takes place in TV studios rather than parliamentary debating chambers. In contrast, legislatures are rather large and cumbersome bodies consisting of hundreds of elected representatives, divided along party lines, and often unable to act quickly or with a single voice. In such circumstances executives take the lead and acquire power.

Party organisation

Modern political parties are often tightly organised and highly disciplined. This helps executives to maintain control of their parties and ensure that their policies and **bills** are accepted by legislatures. By and large, the stronger the party system, the stronger the executive, and the weaker the legislature. The major exceptions to strong executive power are usually found in countries with comparatively weak parties. Switzerland is probably the best example, but in Israel, the USA and the new democracies of central and eastern Europe, weak and fragmented parties help to undermine the executive and strengthen the legislature.

Bill
A formal proposal for a law put before a legislature but not yet accepted by it.

These are general arguments about the rise of executives, but there is evidence to support them. First, some executives have been given greater law making powers in recent years (Australia and France). Second, the executives in many countries have made increasing use of the power of delegated legislation, which gives them more decision making autonomy. Third, some analysts argue that prime ministers in parliamentary systems have become so powerful as heads of state that they have, in effect, assumed the powers and status of elected presidents. This is said to be occurring in Australia and the UK, where a series of powerful prime ministers have accumulated decision making authority that has transformed their office. Fourth, as we saw in chapter 5, power in federal systems, the most decentralised form of government, has become increasingly concentrated in the twentieth century, and in doing so have given the executive officers of their federal governments greater power than before.

Arguments about the rise of executives are strongly disputed by other political scientists, who claim that the trend is more apparent than real. They point to events that seem to show that even the strongest executives can be reined in by their legislatures. Nixon had to resign to avoid **impeachment**. Clinton was impeached, Thatcher was eventually toppled by her parliamentary party. There are examples of coalition governments losing power because they no longer

Impeachment
To charge a public official, usually an elected politician, with improper

Table 6.1 *The source of legislation: governments and legislatures*

	Government bills as % of all bills	% of government bills passed
Netherlands	98	85
Luxembourg	94	100
UK	92	92
Norway	90	99
Ireland	90	10
Greece	87	77
West Germany	74	100
Portugal	70	14
Austria	65	96
Denmark	59	84
Finland	48	100
Italy	29	51
Belgium	23	100
France	22	82
Spain	5	88

Note: The figures refer to various years in the late 1980s.
Source: Inter-Parliamentary Union, *Parliaments of the World* (New York: Facts on File, 1992).

had the confidence of their elected assemblies (see chapter 12). Consequently, it is said, the old executive systems of prime minister and cabinet continue to function more or less as they did in the nineteenth century, in the sense that power is shared and mixed between the two branches of government.

■ *Increasing power of executives?*

Is it possible to resolve the dispute about the increasing power of executives by reference to some systematic evidence? The figures in table 6.1 show what proportion of bills in fifteen west European countries were introduced by executives, and what proportion of these were duly accepted by legislatures and passed into law. The figures show two things quite clearly. First, most bills are introduced by executives, not legislatures. Second, the overwhelming majority of bills introduced by executives are duly accepted by the legislatures and become law.

What can we conclude about the rise of executive power? Not much, some would say. The fact that legislatures invariably accept executive proposals for legislation simply shows how carefully executives sound out opinion in the legislative body before they present proposals. This argument is based on what Karl Friedrich has called 'The Law of Anticipated Reactions'. This states that wherever there are *mutually dependent power relations*, those involved will try to

conduct in office before a duly constituted tribunal, usually the main elected legislative body, prior to removing the official from office if they are found guilty. Not known much outside the USA, and not often used there.

Karl Friedrich (1901–84)

anticipate the reaction of others and modify their own behaviour accordingly. In terms of the executive–legislative relations, neither is likely to make a move or a proposal that is likely to be rejected by the other, so they sound each other out carefully before taking action. In fact, in most systems of government the two branches maintain an elaborate set of institutions and officials in order to maintain a constant dialogue to find out what each is prepared to accept. Unfortunately for the political scientist, much of this goes on behind the closed doors of party committee rooms, and we do not hear a great deal about the endless process of mutual bargaining and adjustment – what is sometimes termed 'wheeler-dealing' or 'horse-trading'.

Others, however, argue a different story. They agree that a good deal of legislation is based on shared powers and mutual accommodation between executives and legislatures. Nevertheless, the fact that most legislation is introduced by the executive, and that a very large majority of it is accepted by legislative assemblies suggests, to them, that executives are very powerful, even that legislatures have been reduced to little more than 'rubber stamps' and 'talking shops' (see controversy 6.1). A key factor here, it is said, is the presence of increasingly centralised and disciplined political parties. Because party unity is so crucial to modern politics, and because a divided party is unlikely to do well in elections, party members in assemblies are under great pressure to comply with the wishes of their leaders. Strong parties make for strong executives; weak parties make for strong legislatures.

It may well be that the controversy about executive dominance will not be resolved, but one thing is clear. Political systems vary in the relative balance of power between executives and legislative assemblies. The executive seems to have gained the upper hand in some (Britain under Thatcher and Blair seems to be a good example), but mutual dependence seems to characterise others, especially where party systems are weak and legislative committee are strong (Denmark, Switzerland, the USA).

Whatever the strengths of executives, or some of them, we should not slip into the assumption that legislative bodies are powerless in the face of almighty executives. It is one thing to claim that executives are increasing in power, quite another to say that legislatures are powerless. Indeed, elected assemblies still have an important role to play in government, and they are organising themselves to increase their influence and efficiency, as we will see now.

■ The functions of legislatures

Elected assemblies play many roles and have many functions, but these may be conveniently grouped under four general headings:

- The representation of public opinion
- The legitimation of government and the political system
- Law making
- The scrutiny of the executive and the administration of the state.

■ Representation of public opinion

Legislatures are the main representative body in democracies, and therefore the main assembly must be directly elected in order to reflect public opinion. In most cases, this means reflecting party political opinion, because most first chambers are elected along party lines. Some assemblies, however, represent the political interests of specific groups in society (farmers, workers, businessmen, churches, minority groups), or specific areas (cities, regions, or constituencies). No matter how they are elected or how they reflect public opinion, however, legislatures perform the common function of *representing the electorate*. In turn this means that legislative bodies must sort out and represent the main clusters of public opinion – a function known as **interest aggregation** – and then voice them in policy debates – a function known as **interest articulation**.

Elected assemblies are often criticised for not being representative of society, and it is true that many are not a social microcosm of the population they represent. Most are dominated by what might be called the four 'Ms' – that is, middle-class, middle-aged, majority group, males. In fact many elected legislatures are drawn heavily from a rather restricted set of occupations and social groups, most notably the professions (especially lawyers) and the better educated sections of society. Politics is becoming more 'professionalised' in the sense that elected representatives spend less time in ordinary jobs, but go into politics as young adults and stay there as they climb the 'greasy pole' of a political career. In sum: elected politicians in national government are not a good cross-section of society.

Against this, it might be said that it does not particularly matter whether the elected assembly is a microcosm of society or not. In the first place, it is argued that politicians can represent the views of social groups other than their own. For example, middle-class individuals can reflect and defend the interests of the working-class people – and, indeed, many of the early socialist movements of Europe were led by people with a middle- or upper-class background. In the second place, it might be argued that what counts most is to represent the views of political parties, which is how the electorate most usually divides itself when it votes. Most popularly elected legislatures do this fairly well, although exactly how well depends in large part of the voting system, as we shall see in chapter 11.

■ Legitimation

Whatever its composition and method of election, the fact that parliament is directly elected by the population and that it meets regularly in public to debate political issues, is important for the **legitimation** of the political system. Elected legislatures give governments their democratic legitimacy, and they help to give stability to the political system. This means that they not only legitimate the government of the day, but also the whole political system

Interest aggregation
Sorting the great variety of political attitudes and opinions on a political issue, so that it is reduced to a more simple and clear-cut 'package' of opinion.

Interest articulation
The process of expressing political needs and demands in order to influence public policy.

Legitimation
The process of making something

morally
acceptable,
proper, or right in
the eyes of the
general public.

and the rules by which it works. This is important because it means that those who oppose the government will accept it because it is elected. Oppositions can wait patiently for the next election when they have a chance of taking over government themselves and being recognised as legitimate by those who have just been turned out of office.

■ *Law making*

We have already seen that most legislatures do not initiate bills, but they do consider them at some length. In many cases they change and modify details – sometimes important details – and in some cases are able to throw out bills or alter their fundamental intent. The intense pressures on parliamentary time means that some bills, or parts of them, are not scrutinised in any great detail. All, however, are processed according to a complex set of rules governing the passage of bills through parliament before they become law. This usually involves a sequence of debates or readings in one or both chambers, and a series of hearings in the committees, also in one or both chambers. Bills normally shuttle backwards and forwards between these debates and hearings and are subject to modification along the way before they are finally accepted (see briefing 6.1 for a Swedish example). To this extent, the mutual dependency of executive and legislative branches of government is a major feature of parliamentary systems. The legislative body is more important and powerful in the law making process of some countries (Italy, Switzerland and the USA), but in all democracies the legislature does discuss and criticise new legislation, with a view to modifying it, or even rejecting it outright.

■ *Scrutiny of the executive and the administration*

A primary function of elected assemblies is to keep a close watch on the executive and on the administrative machinery of the state. Examining government bills is one method of doing this, but there are many others:

- *Veto powers* Some legislative bodies have powers to veto or modify policy proposals made by the executive.
- *Approving executive appointments* Appointments to high positions of state are involved here.
- *Question time* Most presidents or prime ministers are required to present themselves or explain themselves to their legislative bodies either in person or writing. Normally questions are routine parts of the parliamentary timetable (see briefing 6.1), but they can be special (impeachment proceedings against the American president, for example, see below).
- *Debate* Debates are an occasion to consider government policy and actions in some detail. Some debates are concerned with specific pieces of legislation and may be quite technical, others are on general political issues, and

Briefing 6.1
A legislature at work: the Swedish Riksdag

- The *Riksdag* takes decisions on government bills, and on motions from its members concerning legislation, taxation and the use of central government revenue.
- Meetings of the chamber form an important part of the work of the members, but much also takes place in the party groups and in the sixteen *Riksdag* committees. The committees, whose members are drawn from the various parties, are working groups with responsibility for a particular area of business.
- All proposals for a *Riksdag* decision must first be considered by one of its sixteen committees. The committee publishes its conclusions in a report which may then be debated and decided by a plenary session of the *Riksdag*.
- Decisions in the chamber are often preceded by a debate.
- When the debate is over, the matter is decided, either by acclamation, or (if there are dissenting opinions) by vote.
- Occasionally the chamber will refer a matter back to the committee. When this happens, the committee has to reconsider the matter and draw up a new report.
- Members of the *Riksdag* are allowed to submit an **interpellation** (see below) – a question to a ministers about the performance of his or her duties. Such questions enable the *Riksdag* to scrutinise and control the work of the government, to obtain information or to draw attention to a particular issue.
- Question time is held weekly for about one hour. The prime minister and six or seven other ministers answer questions put directly to them by members of the *Riksdag*.
- If a party group in the *Riksdag* wishes to debate a particular matter, which is unconnected with other business under consideration, it may request a current affairs debate. In 1997–8 five were held.
- Occasionally the government provides the *Riksdag* with oral information on issues of current interest. This is often followed by a debate.
- Much of the work of the *Riksdag* is regulated by the Riksdag Act, which regulates the chamber and its meetings, the election of the Speaker and the way in which business is prepared and decided.
- The *Riksdag* board is responsible for the overall planning of parliamentary business, including the selection of work procedures. The Board comprises the Speaker (chairman) and ten other members who are appointed by the *Riksdag* from among its members.

(Adapted from the *Riksdag's* website http://www.riksdagen.se/english/work/chamber.asp)

some about emergency matters. The advantage of debate is that it subjects governments to the glare of public scrutiny and criticism, and can help to improve the quality of the legislation. The disadvantage is that debates in public assemblies are often reduced to party political 'shadow boxing' – ritual events staged for the public.

- *Vote of no confidence or impeachment*   The ultimate power of legislative assemblies is the ability to remove the executive by a vote of 'no confidence' or impeachment. In parliamentary systems the government of the day can

Interpellation
A parliamentary question addressed to government requiring a formal answer and often followed by discussion, and sometimes by a vote.

remain in office only as long as it has the support of a majority in the assembly. If it loses a vote of confidence in the assembly, it can no longer continue in control and will have to resign so that a new government with majority support can be formed. This is the cornerstone of the relationship of mutual dependence between the executive and the legislature, and we shall discuss it again in chapter 12, which considers the formation of party and coalition governments.

- *Committees* Perhaps the most important single legislative development in recent times is the strengthening of committees. In fact, committee work is now such a significant part of legislative operations, and so crucial to the scrutiny of executives that it needs to be considered in greater depth.

■ *Legislative committees*

Parliaments are adapting to changing circumstances and trying to improve their effectiveness by streamlining their procedures, and by providing members with better facilities and resources (offices, secretaries, researchers, information). Most important they are increasingly concentrating on the scrutiny (sometimes know as '**legislative oversight**') of executive and administrative action. They have tried to do this by creating more effective and more powerful committees.

Legislative oversight
The role of the legislature that involves the scrutiny or supervision of other branches of government, especially the executive and the public bureaucracy.

Close scrutiny of government cannot be done in large meetings. It is better performed by small committees with the time, experience and technical expertise to delve into the great complexities of modern legislation. Committees can also avoid the worst aspects of ritual party conflict that is often found in the main debating chamber. Effective and powerful committees, in turn, require their own expert advice and information, bureaucratic support and time for detailed work. If they are to have a major impact they must also be powerful, which means having a loud bark as well as sharp teeth – in other words they need real powers which enable them to influence government action.

Many legislatures are trying to assert their power, or regain lost powers, by developing an effective committee system for executive and administrative action, and reviewing legislation. This is often an uphill battle because committees depend on executives to grant them new powers and resources, and executives are usually unwilling to do this, because they know that these powers may well be turned against them. The clearest examples of powerful and powerless committees are in the USA and the French Fifth Republic. The former has a remarkably complex and powerful system of small and expert committees that can, and frequently do, exert a profound influence on executive appointments and policy. The French system is restricted to six committees, two of which have 120 members, and are therefore pretty ineffective. The Danish parliament also derives a good deal of its influence over government affairs from its effective committee system.

Effective committees tend to have a membership of fifteen–thirty people, with a good core of members who have served long enough to gain specialist knowledge and experience of a particular policy area. If there are enough of them, committees can cover a wide range of government business, including the close and detailed scrutiny of bills, public spending, foreign affairs, all the main aspects of home affairs and any other public matter they think should be reviewed. Each committee has a convener, or *chair*, who usually has a high standing and long experience in parliamentary affairs. The party composition of committees usually reflects that of the assembly as a whole, with a majority of government members.

If they are to be influential and independent of the government, parliamentary committees will probably be constituted in the following ways:

- Their chairs should not necessarily be members of the governing party or parties
- They should have their own staff and expert advisors
- They should have powers to call witnesses and the right to question them closely, including leading members of the government
- They should have had time to build up their own knowledge and expertise in the business handled by the committee
- They should be able not only to issue public reports, which get publicity in the media, but also have the power to require government action following from their recommendations.

Committees may not have all these powers in full, and hence they may not often operate at maximum strength, but nevertheless they are one of the most effective weapons that legislative bodies have in their battle with powerful executives.

■ Theories of democratic institutions: consensus and majoritarian systems

At one point or another in chapters 2–5 on democratic government, we have pointed out that there is an enormous variety of formal democratic arrangements and institutions, and that each country combines them in its own unique manner. We have also observed that this great diversity of constitutional characteristics usually resolves itself, in practice, into only a few general patterns shared by many countries. For example, in spite of their differences in length, detail and content, constitutional documents normally fall into four distinctive parts. Again, of all the different ways of combining executive–legislative relations, these usually revolve around only three types – presidential, semi-presidential and parliamentary. And although there are a great many different ways of organising territorial government within a country, there are only two main types in practice – federal and unitary – and only a few sub-types in each category. Fortunately for comparative political scientists, what

Table 6.2 *The main institutional features of majoritarian and consensus democracies*

Majoritarian democracy	Consensus democracy
Concentration of executive power	Executive power sharing
Fusion of executive and legislative power and cabinet dominance	Separation of powers
Unitary government and centralisation	Territorial or non-territorial federalism and decentralisation
Asymmetric bicameralism or unicameralism	Balanced bicameralism
Constitutional flexibility	Constitutional inflexibility
Absence of judicial review	Judicial review
Examples: Colombia, Costa Rica, France, Greece, New Zealand (before 1996), UK	*Examples*: Austria, the European Union, Germany, India, Japan, The Netherlands, Switzerland

might easily be a confusing mass of detailed country-specific differences turns out, in the end, to fall into a fairly simple general pattern. This is good news for students of comparative government because it means that they can generalise about a number of similar democratic systems rather than pointing out the detailed differences between each and every one of them, although these undoubtedly exist.

In his ground-breaking comparison of thirty-six democracies, Arendt Lijphart observes that despite their enormous variation, democracies tend to fall into only two general categories. He calls these *majoritarian* and *consensus* democracies. Majoritarian systems, as the name suggests, give political power to the majority of citizens and the political parties that represent them, while consensus democracies try to represent as many people as possible. The basic mechanism of the majoritarian model is both to concentrate power in the hands of the political executive and to leave the exercise of this power relatively unconstrained. The consensus model, in contrast, tries to distribute executive power more broadly among parliamentary parties and it also restrains this power in a variety of ways. In other words, the majoritarian model both concentrates executive power and places comparatively few restraints on its exercise, while the consensus model both disperses power and restrains its use.

The main characteristics of the two types of democracy are listed in table 6.2.

■ *Majoritarian democracy, or the 'Westminster model'*

This model:

- Concentrates executive power by giving it to whichever party (or, more rarely, combination of parties) controls a bare majority in the legislative assembly

- Fuses executive and legislative powers in the classic parliamentary manner
- Concentrates power by being either unicameral or, if, there are two chambers, by giving one assembly a clearly superior status
- Gives the courts no special powers to review legislation or decide constitutional matters, because this would diffuse power to another branch of government
- Has a degree of constitutional flexibility to the extent that the constitution itself can be changed by a simple majority vote of the assembly, just as ordinary law can be changed
- Is often a unitary state and gives central government considerable powers not only over its own business but also that of the territorial units of government below it
- Has majoritarian and disproportional electoral systems, two-party systems, banks that are dependent on the executive and pluralist, free-for-all interest group systems.

We shall discuss interest groups, electoral systems and party systems later (chapters 9, 11 and 12) but here can consider the formal constitutional and institutional features of majoritarian government that we have discussed so far in this book. It is no coincidence that the institutional characteristics of majoritarian government tend to go together, for they 'fit' with one another in a consistent and logical way. The British system is one of the best examples of majoritarian democracy, and it was based on the principle of parliamentary sovereignty, at least until membership of the European Union changed this to some extent. If parliament is sovereign then it follows logically and inevitably that no other body or institution of government should be able to challenge parliament – not the courts, nor a written constitution, nor lower levels of government, nor a second chamber. The idea is to create a stable and effective government with power to get things done, but that is still accountable to the population through the elected legislature.

Consensus democracy

Consensus democracy also relies upon majority government, but rather than concentrating power, it shares it. Consensus democracies:

- Try to construct broad coalition government consisting not of a single majority party or a bare majority of them, but of all or most of the important parties in a broad coalition
- Separate and balance executive and legislative power
- Are often federal – which, of course, means a degree of territorial decentralisation, in some cases (Belgium, for example) they may also be a form of non-territorial federalism in which different language, ethnic, or cultural groups are given a degree of autonomy

- Have two legislative assemblies (bicameralism), often with balanced powers
- Have judicial review of political and constitutional matters, as a way of trying to sort out conflict between the different branches and levels of government
- Have a degree of constitutional inflexibility, because they try to maintain their diffusion of power and to include a wide range of opinion in any attempt to change the system
- Have proportional elections, multi-party systems, corporatist interest-group systems, and independent central banks.

These institutional features of government also 'fit' together logically, given the initial assumption that the job of democracy is to include and represent as many people as possible. Such a government would share and separate power between the main parties and between two representative assemblies. It would also divide government territorially, especially if it were a large country in terms of geography, or population, or both. It would make sure that its arrangements were not easily changed by a few vested interests, and would reinforce the rights of all citizens by giving the courts the right to review constitutional matters and public policy. All this would be a particularly coherent package if the society in question were a culturally and ethnically mixed one, or what Lijphart terms a 'plural' society. These are particularly likely to be federal systems, and to have the other characteristics of consensus democracy.

Lijphart's study of democracy is widely discussed and has inspired much other research, but it is not without its critics. Some claim that the typology is too broad and general to apply to all cases, and that there are many exceptions that do not properly fit. The USA is neither majoritarian nor consensual, but a bit of both. Switzerland is a consensual system but it does not have judicial review. Canada is a consensus federal system in some respects, but at the same time it has dominant one-party cabinets.

In spite of the exceptions, however, we can draw two main conclusions from Lijphart's work:

- Although each democratic system of government has a unique combination of particular features; they often combine their general characteristics in only a few ways, so creating some general patterns and only a few general types.
- There are clear links between the social conditions of a society and its system of government. Consensus democracies are often large and pluralist societies. Many majoritarian systems are members of the British Commonwealth and show their British heritage in their government.

We will return to majoritarian and consensus democracies again later in the book (chapter 12) after we have considered voting systems, pressure group and party government, which are additional features of the two types of democracy not yet discussed here.

■ Summary

This chapter has dealt with policy making and legislative processes, especially the roles of the executive and legislative branches of government, whose relationship is at the very heart of policy and law making, the most important functions of government. It argues that:

- In democratic theory, the executive and legislative branches should be separate, and each should maintain a system of checks and balances on the other. In practice, there is a more of a mix than a separation of powers.
- There is a controversy about whether executives have increased their power in recent decades in response to a variety of social, economic and political pressures.
- Legislatures still have an important role in government. They represent public opinion, help the political system, review bills proposed by the executive and keep watch over the executive and state bureaucracy.
- Legislatures have tried to improve their efficiency and authority in different ways, but especially by developing committee systems that enable them to perform their function of scrutiny and oversight more effectively.
- Powerful legislatures often have comparatively weak party systems (and vice versa) and a comparatively strong committee system.
- Democracies tend to come in two main types, majoritarian and consensual. Large plural societies tend to be consensual. Many majoritarian systems are British Commonwealth countries and influenced by Britain, which is the main example of majoritarianism.

Further reading

On executives and legislatures across the world (democratic and otherwise), see J. Denis and Ian D. Derbyshire, *Encyclopedia of World Political Systems*, 1 (Armonk: M. E. Sharpe, 2000: chapters 4 and 5). For an excellent overview of executive–bureaucracy relations in west Europe, see Paul Heywood and Vincent Wright, 'Executives, bureaucracies and decision-making', in Martin Rhodes, Paul Heywood and Vincent Wright (eds.), *Developments in West European Politics* (Basingstoke: Macmillan, 1997). For a comparative work on legislatures, see David Olson, *Legislative Institutions: A Comparative View* (Armonk: M. E. Sharpe, 1994) and for a set of useful essays on Europe, see Philip Norton (ed.), *Parliaments and Governments in Western Europe* (London: Frank Cass, 1998). A good book on committees is Lawrence Longley and Roger H. Davidson (eds.), *The New Roles of Parliamentary Committees* (London: Frank Cass, 1998). Lijphart's most recent work on majoritarian and consensus democracies is *Patterns of Democracy: Government Forms and Performance in Thirty-Six Countries* (New Haven: Yale University Press, 1999).

Websites

http://www.oecd.org/dataoecd/ 17/55/16212507.pdf	A document about the role of parliamentary committees in education policy.
http://www.polisci.umn.edu/ information/parliaments/	List of national parliaments with links to each one.
http://www.ipu.org	The Inter-Parliamentary Union (IPU), a world organisation of the parliaments of sovereign states, has a website with literature on parliaments, and links to national sites.
http://www.ecprd.org/	The European Centre for Parliamentary Research and Documentation deals with European parliaments.
http://wc.wustl.du/parliaments.html	List of national parliaments with links to each one.

Projects

1. Does the composition of your own national parliament show that it is dominated numerically by the 'four M's' – middle-aged, middle-class, majority group, males?

2. The website for your own national legislature is likely to have information about its committee system. What does this tell you about how the system works and how influential and important it is in the government of the country?

7   Implementation: the public bureaucracy

Governments make policy and pass laws but they are not involved in the routine implementation and daily administration of policy. For this, they rely on government ministries and the army of state bureaucrats who work in them. Like armies, the bureaucracy ranges from a small handful of very top officials down to office workers who carry out the daily work. The jobs of the highest officials (in the civil service, sometimes called 'mandarins', after the top officials of the ancient Chinese bureaucracy) are little different from those of the chief executive officers (CEOs) of multi-national corporations in the private sector, while many of the lower ranks are known as **'street-level bureaucrats'** because they come into everyday contact with the general public.

Whether they are mandarins or filing clerks, state bureaucrats are sometimes seen as lazy and inefficient, but alongside this stereotype there exists a completely different one that views bureaucrats as ambitious empire builders who want to expand their own departments in the interests of their own status and salary, and who conspire to take over the policy making function of politicians to make sure that things are run according to the bureaucrats' wishes.

These contradictory images highlight an ambivalence that permeates the public **bureaucracy**. On the one hand, no democracy could even exist without effective bureaucracies to implement public policies and deliver public services. On the other hand, senior bureaucrats are often more experienced and highly trained than their political masters, and their role at the very heart of

Street-level bureaucrats
The bureaucrats who regularly come into contact and deal with the public.

Bureaucracy
A rational, impersonal, rule-bound and hierarchical form

of organisational structure set up to perform large-scale administrative tasks.

government gives them an enormous potential for power in the affairs of state. Yet they are supposed to be servants, not masters of the state.

In this chapter, we examine controversies about the role and power of public bureaucrats. The chapter outlines, first of all, the organisation of the state bureaucracy before looking more closely at the distinction between policy making and administration. It then considers the theory that it is permanent officials (bureaucrats) who run the state, not elected politicians. Politicians, of course, are fully aware of the potential power of their top civil servants, so the chapter continues by looking at how they have tried to counter this power. Finally, the chapter examines the wave of recent reforms that have tried to make the public bureaucracy more efficient.

The five major topics in this chapter are:

* The organisation of the state bureaucracy
* Policy making and administration
* The dictatorship of the official?
* The New Public Management
* Theories of public bureaucracy.

■ The organisation of the state bureaucracy

The administration (chapter 6) of the state – that is, the day-to-day work of implementing policies – is carried out by the bureaucratic departments or ministries of government. These are usually organised around the major functions of the state: economic affairs, foreign relations, defence, home affairs, transport and communications, education, welfare, the environment and so on. There is no logical or best way of dividing these functions, so the list of ministries varies from one country to another. In some, education is grouped with family matters, in others it is organised with employment and vocational training. Similarly transport, the environment and planning may be combined in the same ministry, or remain separate. As a result, ministry sizes vary enormously from quite compact ones (Ministries of Justice are often separate and small) to huge super-ministries. Sometimes there is a special ministry for women and children. Increasingly ministries combine a range of related functions under one umbrella in an attempt to *integrate different aspects of policy* – economic development, transportation and regional affairs, for example. The advantage is that related policy areas are combined under one organisational roof; the disadvantage that the larger the department, the more cumbersome it may be.

The total size of the public bureaucracy also varies greatly from country to country. It is relatively small in Japan, Greece, and Turkey, and relatively large in the advanced 'Nordic welfare states' of Denmark, Norway and Sweden (see table 7.1). But even when it is relatively small compared with other countries, the **public sector** is often a rather large part of the economy in its own country.

Public sector
That part of social, economic and political life that is not private but controlled or regulated by the state or its agencies.

Table 7.1 *Public employment[a] as a percentage of total employment, OECD countries, 1990s*

Country	'Limited' public sector[b]	'Extended' public sector[c]
Japan	6.5	7.0
Turkey	9.4	12.1
Greece	9.6	12.9
Netherlands	11.8	13.9
UK	11.9	16.9
New Zealand	12.1	14.2
Germany	14.1	15.4
USA	14.2	14.9
Australia	14.6	18.7
Portugal	14.8	17.5
Spain	15.1	18.0
Austria	15.8	22.5
Mexico	15.9	26.1
Ireland	16.8	21.1
Canada	17.4	19.9
Italy	18.2	23.2
Belgium	20.0	23.9
France	20.2	27.0
Iceland	21.1	
Finland	25.1	27.2
Norway	30.6	
Sweden	31.7	38.1
Denmark	35.4	39.3

Notes: [a] The OECD warns that it is very difficult to define and compare public employment across different countries, and that therefore care should be taken in interpreting these figures. They refer to slightly different financial years in each country.
[b] The 'limited' public sector column covers central and federal government, regional and state government, and local government and the municipalities.
[c] The 'extended' public sector covers the limited sector plus public enterprises.
Source: OECD, *Measuring Public Employment in OECD Countries: Methods, Sources and Results* (Paris: OECD, 1997).

Japan, for example, has one of the smallest public sectors in the OECD countries, but it still accounts for an eighth of total employment. The largest public sectors account for a quarter of the workforce. Note, however, that the size of a ministry in terms of employment or its budget may tell us little about its power and importance. Japan's Ministry of International Trade and Industry (MITI) is closely integrated with the country's business and political elites, and has played a very important role in Japan's economic success, but it is not a specially large ministry.

For all their power and importance in the affairs of state, departments and ministries are rarely even mentioned in constitutional documents, but nevertheless in the great majority of democracies they are governed by similar crucial principles. At the very top of each department or ministry – the terms are often used interchangeably – there is usually a politician who is *ultimately accountable for its operations*. These politicians may be directly elected and senior members of the representative assembly, or they may be appointed by, and accountable, to an elected politician. In parliamentary systems ministers in charge of departments are usually elected members of the governing party or coalition, and they constitute the cabinet or council. In most countries, government has now grown so large and complicated that a range of deputy or junior ministers is also appointed, but they do not sit in the cabinet. In presidential systems, the heads of the most important departments of state may also constitute a cabinet, but they are usually appointed by, and accountable to, the president, not drawn from the elected assembly or accountable to it.

In all cases, the theory is that the bureaucratic machinery of state should be under the control of elected politicians who are ultimately accountable to the general public, through the ballot box. Public sector bureaucrats are appointed to be servants of the state. They are not accountable to the general public but to their political masters. The policies of departments are supposed to be directed by elected politicians, and the day-to-day administrative work directed by professional bureaucrats.

The politicians in charge of departments work very closely with a relatively small group of the most senior bureaucrats in them. Although ministers are ultimately responsible for the work of their departments, they have to rely upon the experience and specialist knowledge of their civil servants (bureaucracy), both to make policy and manage the daily affairs of the department. Departments are vast machines, and because bureaucrats often know most about the complexities of both policy and its **implementation** they advise their ministers on both these aspects.

Implementation
The process of applying policies and putting them into practice.

There are three main types of senior bureaucrats with administrative and policy advisor functions:

1. *Permanent administrators*   Some public bureaucracies are built on the idea that permanent officials should faithfully and impartially serve their ministers, whether or not they agree on policy matters. Permanent administrators are politically neutral. The British system is based on this 'faithful servant' notion of an impartial bureaucracy, and for this reason its civil servants are not allowed to take any public part in politics. Some countries go to great lengths to select and train the best and the brightest for careers in the public service. France, for example, has an elite administrative corps trained at the Ecole National d'Administration (see fact file 7.1).

Fact file 7.1

Public bureaucracies

- The term '*bureaucratie*' is said to have been used for the first time in 1764 in France to describe a new form of government by officials, which is completely different from democracy, autocracy, and monarchy. The term soon spread to Italy (*burocrazia*) to Germany (*Bürokratie*) and to Britain.

- 'Bureaucracy' predates the French invention of the word. It was necessary wherever the earliest empires created a need for the administration of large territories. The term 'mandarin' – referring to those at the very highest levels of the modern civil service – comes from the civil service of ancient China.

- The French Council of State is a special administrative court with the double function of protecting civil servants against attempts by politicians to manipulate them, and of ensuring that civil servants behave properly. Many other states have set up administrative systems of tribunals and law to regulate the public bureaucracy.

- Being a top civil servant in many countries is very prestigious, perhaps most of all in France and Japan. The French administrative elite are known as 'Enarques' after the Ecole National d'Administration (ENA), while most of Japan's senior civil servants are the products of the University of Tokyo's Law School. Spain has its prestigious system of *cuerpos*, and the British have traditionally recruited from the universities of Oxford and Cambridge.

- In the eighteenth and nineteenth century entry to the very highest levels of the civil service in many western countries was traditionally restricted to an upper-class elite. This is less true today now that top jobs are increasingly open to merit, and to recruits from working-class and minority backgrounds.

- Some state bureaucracies are run along 'generalist' lines, and recruit people of all-round ability and intelligence to work in a wide variety of top jobs – the UK, Ireland and, to some extent, Italy, Portugal and Spain. The more 'specialist' tradition is more technocratic and trains people for particular departments or jobs – France, Germany, The Netherlands and the Nordic countries.

- The practice of incoming governments appointing top layers of the civil service is an old one in Finland, France, Germany and the USA, but it is now spreading to other countries.

- The most radical new public management (NPM) reforms are found in the Anglo-Saxon countries of Australia, Canada, New Zealand, the UK and the USA, and in Denmark, Finland, Norway and Sweden. They are weakest in Germany and Greece, and have had limited success in France, Italy, Japan, Portugal and Spain.

- Almost all countries have implemented NPM since the 1980s, but these have taken different forms in different countries. In France, Sweden and Spain they were designed to strengthen the civil service; in Denmark, Norway and the UK to weaken and reduce it.

---

2. *Political appointments*   Some countries do not believe in permanent administrators. They clear out the very top layers of departments when a new government is elected, and appoint their own people. A new American president typically appoints 3,000 people to posts in Washington, though occasionally nominees are vetoed by Senate. One can see the sense in having people sympathetic to the government running its departments, but there is also the danger of **clientelism** and of using public office for private gain.

Clientelism
A system of

government and
politics based on
a relationship
between patron
and clients.
Public sector
jobs and
contracts are
distributed on
the basis of
personal and
political contacts
in return for
political support.

3. *Policy advisors* To counter the power of permanent officials, ministers increasingly appoint teams of their own policy advisors. They are distinct from appointed administrators because they are concerned with policy, not day-to-day departmental matters. There are two main reasons for appointing policy advisors. First, civil servants may not always be impartial in their advice because they have their own professional and organisational interests. Second, they may have worked so long and so closely with the private organisations they are supposed to regulate that they become 'captured' and 'domesticated' by these organisations and start representing their interests (see chapter 9). Outside policy advisors can bring a fresh approach to old problems.

■ Policy making and administration

In theory, elected and accountable politicians should make policy; appointed officials should implement it. In practice, however, the line between policy and administration is not that clear. It would be exceedingly foolish to try to implement a policy that could not be sensibly administered; at the same time the best administration in the world cannot save a fundamentally flawed policy. Policy and administration are intimately bound together and cannot be neatly separated, a point made effectively in briefing 7.1. Equally, the way that a policy is administered may subtly alter the original intention of policies. There are studies showing how the grand designs of policy makers in central government have been changed as they are implemented at the local level by street-level officials.

There is therefore no clear distinction between policy making and implementation because they are so closely woven together. How are we to draw a line between the policy making functions of ministers and the administrative functions of bureaucrats, and decide whether one has stepped into the role of

---

Briefing 7.1
Policy making and administration

The relations between senior politicians and their civil servants would not seem to be promising material for a successful TV comedy, but it was the theme of the long-running *Yes Minister*, succeeded by the equally popular *Yes Prime Minister*, on British television. In one episode, the wily mandarin, Sir Humphrey Appleby, gives a lesson on policy making and administration to his new and inexperienced Minister, the hapless Jim Hacker:

> I do feel that there is a real dilemma here, in that while it has been government policy to regard policy as the responsibility of ministers, and administration as the responsibility of officials, questions of administrative policy can cause confusion between the administration of policy, and the policy of administration, especially where the responsibility for the administration of the policy of administration conflicts or overlaps with the responsibility for the policy of the administrative policy. (Jonathan Lynn and Antony Jay, *Yes Minister*, London: BBC, 1982: 176)

the other? This question leads into one of the oldest and most hotly debated controversies in government – the *power of public bureaucrats*.

■ The dictatorship of the official?

■ *The power of the official*

Like many other political institutions the state bureaucracy is (a) essential, and (b) dangerous. On the one hand, public bureaucracies are essential parts of the state apparatus, to both implement policies and deliver public services. Can you imagine any contemporary government without a small army of bureaucrats to organise public elections, collect taxes, administer state pensions, run public education, provide welfare services, draw up contracts for military hardware, inspect the roads, ensure that public health and safety regulations are observed, run police and fire services and answer queries about all these from the general public? Whether these are public or private operations makes no difference to the fact that bureaucrats of some kind are indispensable. Bureaucracies are also supposed to administer these services in a consistent, predictable and universal manner, rather than an arbitrary and idiosyncratic one. In this sense, they are not only essential for the administration of large-scale government, but they promote equality and democracy as well.

At the same time, bureaucracies are also potentially powerful and anti-democratic. They have a reputation for being inefficient, rigid, bound by red-tape, secretive and impersonal. They can also nurture a 'bureaucratic ethos' that is managerial, technocratic and undemocratic. Bureaucrats also have their own interests, which may conflict with those of politicians and the wider society. It is important, therefore, that public bureaucracies are controlled by elected representatives who, in turn, are accountable to the public. But are ministers in control? This is the subject of a long-running controversy in the social sciences.

According to the German social scientist Max Weber (see chapter 1), it is the *dictatorship of the official* that is on the march, not that of the worker. He denies the Marxist theory that the workers can seize power by revolutionary action, and points to the enormous power of the permanent officials who run bureaucratic organisations. Among these, central government bureaucrats are especially important, although precisely the same argument applies to all forms of bureaucracy – parties or large pressure groups (see chapters 9 and 12). Weber had three main reasons for claiming that civil servants are the masters rather than the servants of politicians:

- *Qualifications and expertise* Politicians are not necessarily selected for their educational qualifications or managerial abilities. Senior bureaucrats are often carefully picked for their intelligence and ability and then highly trained.

- *Permanence* Politicians come and go as they move political jobs or lose elections, and their influence on any given ministry tends to be short lived. Career administrators stay in post for a long time and have a potential for exercising a long-term influence.
- *Experience* With permanence comes long-term and specialised experience as well as 'inside knowledge' of how things work.

To these three considerations we can add two other factors that make it difficult for politicians to control their bureaucrats:

- *Secrecy* Civil servants sometimes protect themselves with powerful secrecy rules, which makes it difficult for politicians and the public to find out what is going on.
- *Fragmentation* We often think of the state bureaucracy as a single organisation shaped like a pyramid with power to control the smoothly working machine concentrated at the very top. In reality, it is often a highly decentralised – not to say ramshackle – structure of ministries, departments, agencies, commissions, units and offices, each with its own traditions, modes of operation, interests and powers. The 'ship of state' is not so much a huge oil tanker that takes a long time to change direction, as a whole fleet of ships and boats, all going in their own direction, and all handling the winds and tides in their own way. This makes it difficult for politicians to control and coordinate the public bureaucracies.

◼ *Mechanisms of control*

To say that state bureaucrats may be difficult to control is not to say that they cannot be controlled. There are all sorts of ways of trying to enforce their compliance, if enforcement is necessary:

- *Politically appointed administrators and policy advisors* We have considered these on pp. 121–2.
- *Law* Bureaucrats are not above the law, and there is a rapid growth of administrative law regulating their behaviour, as well as a greater tendency to use the courts to overturn administrative action.
- *Recruitment and training* Training can be used to instil in bureaucrats a professional ethos of public service. However, this can cut both ways: intensive training can also result in a bureaucratic culture of isolation, secrecy and self-interest. Increasingly policies of equal opportunities and **affirmative action** are being used to combat the isolation of the civil service culture and to make bureaucrats more representative of society as a whole.
- *Scrutiny, auditing, and regulation* Financial controls are increasingly used to regulate and limit bureaucratic operations, as are elaborate procedures for scrutinising, auditing and monitoring them. Ironically, modern public bureaucracies have sometimes created small armies of bureaucrats to ensure that the bureaucracy is kept as small as possible. Parliamentary committees

Affirmative action
Policies designed to redress past discrimination. In this case, state bureaucracies may be required to increase recruitment of minority groups.

are also increasingly involved, and as we saw in chapter 6, have increased their efforts to keep a 'watching brief' over state bureaucracies.

- *Open government*   Bureaucratic secrecy can be reduced by 'sunshine laws'[1] to promote transparency and public scrutiny.
- *Ombudsmen*   These have been appointed to protect the public against mal-administration and abuse of power (see chapter 3).

The New Public Management: reinventing government

It is clear by now that there is an inevitable tension between (a) the bureaucratic goal of efficiency and the democratic requirements of participation and debate, and (b) the policy making roles of politicians and the administrative jobs of state bureaucrats. In addition there is sometimes, rightly or wrongly, severe and widespread criticism of public bureaucracy on the grounds that it is either inefficient and lazy, or imperialistic and expansionist – sometimes both at the same time. As a result, a wave of '**New Public Management**' (NPM) reforms has swept across democracies since the 1970s. These reforms have taken two main directions (often at the same time).

Privatisation and market efficiency

Many public services have been privatised, which is assumed to make them more competitive and efficient. Some government departments have been transformed into *private* and *semi-private agencies* that are contracted by the state to deliver certain services at a fixed cost. Their CEOs are often not career civil servants but 'hired guns' on short-term, commercial contracts. Bureaucracies remaining in the public sector have often been decentralised, obliged to con-tract out some of their functions (e.g. computer maintenance and servicing), and adopt competitive internal markets in which divisions within the same bureaucracy 'sell their services' to each other. The purpose of these different reforms is to privatise the routine bureaucratic operations of the state, so that they are driven by the competitive forces of the market (or quasi-markets) to become more efficient. Another purpose is to separate those who *'steer'* (think about policy and plan future developments) from those who *'row'* (carry out the routine tasks), on the grounds that those who steer ought not to have to worry about the business of rowing.

Empowerment

A second set of reforms has been designed to change bureaucracies from what are believed to be inflexible and impersonal government agencies into user-friendly ones. Participation in the running of public services (school

New Public Management (NPM)
This refers to the reforms of the public sector in the 1980s and 1990s, based mainly on what was thought to be private sector practice and consisting mainly of privatisation, deregulation, business management techniques and 'marketisation'. Known also as 'reinventing government', it is said to have had the effect of 'hollowing out' the state.

---

[1] Laws that require light to be shone into dark corners of state activity so that we can see what is going on.

boards, user groups, customer complaints departments, even computer chat-rooms and e-mail complaints) has been encouraged. Computers make it possible to decentralise bureaucracies to local communities and neighbourhoods, making them more accessible to local people. 'Street-level bureaucrats' have been given more discretion over individual cases, so that decision making can become less rigid and impersonal. Some say that the empowerment of consumers and street-level bureaucrats has 'depoliticised' the New Public Management in the sense that it has taken decisions out of the hands of politicians. Others claim that it has simply empowered the most vociferous and demanding sections of the community, which is not in the public interest.

In the end, NPM reforms must be judged by their effectiveness in promoting better or cheaper public services. This, however, is extremely difficult to judge and remains a matter of controversy:

- Many services are taken into the public sector precisely because they have no clear *market measures of efficiency*. Education is one example.
- The assumption that the private sector is *necessarily more efficient* than the public sector has been questioned in some cases.
- Some public services are *fundamentally different from private ones*, and cannot be judged by the same yardstick.
- The notion that public service clients can be treated as *customers* is doubted. Are students in public universities, prison inmates, children in public care, or hospital patients to be treated as clients in the same way as lawyers, beauty parlours, and advertising agencies have clients?
- Some privatised services have had to be *re-regulated* in order to deal with private sector inefficiency or failure.
- Decentralisation, **privatisation**, and deregulation have also added substantially to the already serious problem of *coordinating* government services.
- It is difficult to judge the *effectiveness* of the reforms because there are few before-and-after studies – i.e. research showing the state of affairs before and after reform, by which to measure their success.

Privatisation
The process of converting public services and amenities to private ones.

■ Theories of public bureaucracy

Civil service
The body of civilian officials (not members of the armed forces) employed by the state to work in government departments.

Theories of public bureaucracy (sometimes known as the **civil service**) take different views of the power of administrative agencies of the state. According to Weber, the bureaucracy is powerful, but he has little to say about how the bureaucrats will use their power. According to rational-choice theory, the bureaucracy is capable of controlling public policy, and does so to promote its own interests. According to clientelist theory, however, some bureaucracies are used by politicians for their own political purposes.

■ *The rational-legal ideal-type*

Max Weber argues that society *modernises itself by becoming more bureaucratic*. Bureaucracy itself expresses the ethos of modern society because it is based upon legitimate power, and organised in a rational way according to formal rules. Weber defined bureaucracy as the most efficient method of performing large-scale administrative tasks, and created an **ideal-type** of bureaucracy with rationality, legality, hierarchy and formal rules as its core features. An ideal-type bureaucracy is characterised by its:

1. *Hierarchy* (or pyramid) *of command*, with authority based on official position (as opposed to personal characteristics such as age, gender, race, party membership, or religion).
2. A **civil service** of *salaried professionals* appointed and promoted according to their specialised competence, training and experience.
3. *Formal rules* determining individual decisions and behaviour (rather than personal or arbitrary decisions) so that individual cases are treated in the same, predictable way.
4. *Rationality* – the choice of appropriate means to achieve given ends.
5. *Record keeping*, providing bureaucracies with an 'institutional memory' of what has been done in the past, and the rules and precedents governing this action.

> **Ideal-type**
> An analytical construct that simplifies reality and picks out its most important features, to serve as a model that allows us to understand and compare the complexities of the real world.

It is often pointed out that no real-life bureaucracy can function in this way. In the first place, the mechanical application of rules is bound to create injustice and hostility if people feel themselves to be no more than numbers or cogs in a wheel. Life cannot be reduced to rules, precedents and routines, and a human element almost always intrudes into bureaucratic operations. Bureaucracies invariably develop an 'informal organisation' of short-cuts, personal contacts and unofficial procedures that help ease of operation and efficiency.

In the second place, it is said that bureaucratic means will become ends in themselves if bureaucrats blindly follow rules and refuse to take initiatives or responsibility – something known as 'trained incapacity'. What sets out to be an efficient way of running the modern state may becomes inefficient; it may even be anti-democratic if trained incapacity prevents the efficient and responsive delivery of public services. As a result, real-life bureaucracies may work very differently from the ideal-type, something that has given rise to a huge amount of empirical research.

In the best of all possible worlds, public bureaucracies would come close to Weber's ideal-type but combine it with a degree of informal organisation to improve efficiency and responsiveness to clients. However, the informal element must not lead to corruption, such as bureaucrats taking bribes to 'ease' the way for clients, and it is easy to slip into practices that are not at all compatible with democratic principles. This is the problem in some of the new democracies that suffer from clientelism.

■ Clientelism

In contrast to the Weberian model, clientelism involves the political use of public office for personal gain – power, or money, or both. The clientelist government acts as a patron that distributes benefits in the form of public jobs, money, contracts and pensions in return for political support. Jobs in the state bureaucracy are filled not necessarily according to merit, professional training, or experience, but by those who support the government in power. Contracts are given not according to cost and quality of work, but for material and political gain. Voters are rewarded for their support with jobs, money, or gifts, and those who donate money to the party are rewarded with jobs, contracts and special concessions. In other words, clientelism is an institutionalised form of *patronage* summarised by the old adage: 'To the victor belong the spoils.' It can easily become corruption.

Clientelism in the public service is found to a varying degree in most states, but it predominates in some. In some countries it is more or less formalised and public, to the extent that it is known and accepted that members or supporters of a given party will get certain public jobs if that party is in power. In some countries, even professors in universities owe their job to the party they support. In others, an attempt is made to let the public service be representative of the population as a whole, with quotas for different social groups: Austria, Belgium and the EU are examples. There are 'mass clientelist' parties in France, Italy and Mexico. The 'spoils system' has been a feature of national politics in the USA and was a defining feature of many US cities at the turn of the nineteenth century. Clientelism is found mainly in societies that are rapidly modernising, urbanising and industrialising.

▧ *The new right, rational choice and the New Public Management*

The 'new right' theory of bureaucracy is not so much a theory as a political argument about the need to reform government and 'roll back the frontiers of the state'. The argument was developed in the 1980s and 1990s by politicians (notably Ronald Reagan in the USA and Margaret Thatcher in the UK), who favoured a classical liberal belief in a *minimal state*, and therefore favoured cutting taxes and services and privatising the public sector wherever possible, with the exception of public support for such things as farming, business and the military. The new right's belief that government should be 'reinvented', and that the state should be 'hollowed out', borrowed heavily from rational-choice theories of the state and bureaucracy.

William Niskanen, *Bureaucracy and Representative Government* (1971) and *Bureaucracy and Public Economics* (1994)

Rational choice and bureaucracy

In his two influential and widely quoted books, William Niskanen argues that state bureaucrats are self-interested, like anyone else, and try to maximise their position by expanding their budgets and staff. The bigger their departments, the greater their power and prestige, the larger their salaries and the bigger their pensions. Their special knowledge and experience – Niskanen calls this the 'agency problem' – makes it difficult for politicians to resist these expansionist goals. As a result, public goods and services are over-produced at the public expense and the public sector grows fat.

The theory has been widely criticised for the oversimplified assumptions it makes:

- It assumes that bureaucrats are energetically self-seeking, but might we just as easily assume that they are lazy and want an easy life?
- It assumes that bureaucrats pursue their own self-interest, but might they not also be concerned about the public interest?
- It assumes that bureaucrats will not recognise or care about the problem of over-production, but might they equally be trying to combat this problem?
- It assumes that bureaucrats will not serve their political masters, but might they not have a professional ethic of public service?

Though it is an elegant theory, few attempts have ever been made to test it empirically. However, allied with the new right politicians and a revival of liberal free-market economics, rational-choice theory had a strong influence on the 'New Public Management'.

The New Public Management

Central to NPM theories of the public sector is the belief that bureaucracies are costly because they are not *competitive*, as the economic market is said to be, and because they interfere with the *efficient workings of the private sector*. Public bureaucracies should therefore be cut, privatised and decentralised, and market principles introduced wherever possible in order to reduce public spending and prevent government 'interference' with private enterprise. The incentives for public bureaucrats to maximise their spending should also be limited, to encourage small and efficient operations instead. Some government departments have been replaced by agencies that are supposed to be run along business lines to provide government with services and facilities under 'market-like' contractual arrangements. These are run not by career public servants but by business executives on fixed-term commercial contracts. The routine tasks of government (processing forms, emptying dustbins, maintaining public property, even running hospitals, schools, and prisons) can be privatised and decentralised, leaving a small core of top civil servants to 'steer, not row'.

On the consumer side of public services NPM reforms have tried to reduce what are believed to be the serious problems of bureaucratic inertia, secrecy and unresponsiveness to the public. It re-defines public service clients as 'customers' (like those of shops, car salesmen, and cafés), and tries to make public bureaucracies more responsive to the needs of ordinary citizens.

The NPM wave swept across many democracies in the 1980s and 1990s, but the theory has yet to be put to a real test. It will take many years for the benefits and disadvantages to emerge, and even then they will not be clear because of all the problems of measuring and comparing public and private sectors and services. Besides, there are many side effects and **externalities** of market and

Externality
A cost or benefit

that does not fall on those who are responsible for the decision or action that creates the externality, and which they do not take into account when they take the action.

public services, which are sometimes ignored, and are exceedingly difficult to quantify. After a period of deregulation there is now talk of transforming the New Public Management and some action to re-regulate privatised services.

■ Summary

This chapter has dealt with controversies about the role and power of public bureaucrats. It argues that:

- Policy making is the job of elected politicians who head government departments and ministries, but the day-to-day administration of government business is carried out by appointed officials (otherwise known as bureaucrats, civil servants, public servants, or permanent officials).
- Appointed officials are accountable to, and work under the policy direction of, their political masters, the elected politicians.
- However, the distinction between policy making and administration is not clear or unambiguous, and the considerable overlap between the two makes for a confusion of roles, especially since the senior bureaucrats (mandarins) work closely with politicians and act as their policy advisors.
- Appointed officials are said to be able to exercise power over their nominal political masters by virtue of their superior ability, qualifications and experience. State bureaucracies are also known for their secrecy and fragmentation, which makes it difficult for politicians to control them.
- Aware of this, politicians have devised ways of trying to control their bureaucrats: appointing their own political advisors, training bureaucrats in a public service ethos, introducing scrutiny and auditing and using the machinery of 'open government' and ombudsmen.
- The New Public Management (NPM) practices that swept across many states since the 1980s privatised many public services and introduced many market or 'quasi-market' practices to try to make the public services more competitive and efficient. Attempts have also been made to empower public service 'customers' to make public bureaucracies responsive to public demands.
- The reforms of public bureaucracies are controversial, and their effectiveness is difficult to judge.

Further reading

For a general book on bureaucracy, see David Beetham, *Bureaucracy* (Buckingham: Open University Press, 2nd edn., 1996) and on government and bureaucracy, see B. Guy Peters, *The Politics of Bureaucracy* (London: Routledge, 2000). Edward C. Page, *Political Authority and Bureaucratic Power* (Brighton: Wheatsheaf, 2nd edn., 1992) deals comparatively with the problem of how politicians control state bureaucracies. A selection of good comparative articles on public bureaucracy is in Hans Bekke, James Perry and Theo Toonen (eds.), *Civil Service Systems in Comparative Perspective* (Bloomington: Indiana University Press, 1996). For recent evaluations of New Public Management, see Tom Christensen (ed.), *New Public Management: The*

Transformation of Ideas and Practice (Aldershot: Ashgate, 2002) and Tony Verheijen and David L. Coombs (eds.), *Innovations in Public Management: Perspectives from East and West Europe* (Cheltenham: Edward Elgar, 1998).

Websites

http://www.sosig.ac.uk/roads/subject-listing/World-cat/civilser.html	Links to a great many specialist reports on civil services around the world.
http://en.wikipedia.org/wiki/Bureaucracy	Basic introduction to bureaucracy with links to related topics.
http://encyclopedia.thefreedictionary.com/Bureaucracy	Basic introduction to bureaucracy with links to related topics.
http://encyclopedia.thefreedictionary.com/Civil+service	Basic introduction to civil service with links to related topics.
http://en.wikipedia.org/wiki/Civil_service	Basic introduction to civil service with links to related topics.

Projects

1. 'State bureaucracy is essential and dangerous.' What do you understand by this statement, and how can we reconcile these two characteristics of bureaucracy?
2. Assess the nature and effectiveness of New Public Management (NPM) reforms in your municipality:
    *   Who took the initiative?
    *   What were the main reforms?
    *   What were the main goals?
    *   What were the consequences?

PART III

Citizens, elites and interest mediation

Part II of this book has discussed the formal institutions of government. Part III now looks at the politics of everyday life as practised by people – ordinary citizens and political leaders. The division between parts II and III implies a distinction between the *structures and institutions of government*, on the one hand, and the *political attitudes and behaviour of individuals*, on the other. Sometimes a similar sort of distinction is drawn between government institutions and structures, which are relatively fixed, and political processes, which are dynamic. At other times, a distinction is drawn between macro- and micro-analysis. Macro-analysis is concerned with large-scale phenomena, and often compares countries or broad sweeps of historical change. Micro-analysis deals with parts of the whole, usually the smallest 'unit' of political analysis – the individual. For this reason much micro-analysis often studies individual voting behaviour, or uses survey analysis to study attitudes and behaviour.

The distinctions between institutions and behaviour, between structures and processes and between macro and micro, are useful for studying government and politics, but we must always remember that they are simply different aspects of precisely the same thing. Structures and institutions set a framework for everyday political life; political attitudes and behaviour help to shape structures.

Part III starts with an account of the political attitudes and behaviour of individuals. If we understand what people think and believe about politics we are better able to understand their behaviour. Or perhaps we should put it the other way round: unless we understand political attitudes and values, we will never understand why people behave the way they do. Besides, what people believe and how they behave can have a profound and direct impact on what governments do, and they can also help to shape the structures and institutions of the state itself. So the study of attitudes and behaviour is important in its own right, and because of the impact they have on governments and the state. Chapter 8 is therefore about political attitudes, values and behaviour.

However, few of us have much political significance as individuals on our own. Most of us join with others in voluntary organisations, pressure groups and social movements in order to achieve our political goals. What we cannot do as isolated citizens we can try to achieve through trade unions or professional associations, pressure groups or social movements, which try to exercise organised influence over government. Chapter 9 therefore, looks at the politics of pressure groups.

The mass media are crucial in political life because they are the means by which citizens, groups and leaders acquire political information and try to influence each other. The mass media are also thought to be powerful political actors in their own right. Accordingly, chapter 10 turns to the politics of the mass media and their influence.

Elections determine who is to take control of government. They are vital to the conduct of politics and tell us a lot about how ordinary citizens relate to politics. Electoral behaviour is probably one of the best topics for research on mass politics and an important part of comparative politics. Chapter 11 therefore pays attention to voters and elections.

And, last in part III, chapter 12 deals with a very special and particularly important type of voluntary organisation – political parties. Parties have a chapter of their own because they are so important.

The five chapters in part III examine the key aspects of political attitudes, institutions and behaviour:

- Political attitudes and behaviour
- Pressure groups and social movements
- The mass media
- Voters and elections
- Party government.

8   Political attitudes and behaviour

Everyone has their own view of politics, and their own interests and ideas and ways of behaving. But individuals do not exist in isolation and nor are they unique. If this were the case it would make no sense to talk about 'the working class' or 'youth cultures', or to make generalisations about 'left-wing intellectuals' or 'right-wing business interests'. At a still more general level, citizens of the same country usually share similar assumptions and views about politics, which makes the Swedes different from the Chileans, the Spanish different from the South Africans and the South Koreans different from the Irish. Political scientists find it useful to label these shared patterns of beliefs and attitudes 'the **political culture**'. The first part of the chapter discusses the political values and attitudes of individuals and groups, and examines how modern research has tried to understand and explain political cultures.

Values and attitudes are important in their own right, but they are also significant because they tell us something about how people are likely to behave, and behaviour has a big and direct impact on political life. In order to understand what people do, and why they do it, it is necessary to understand what they *think*. For example, it is not enough to know that someone did not vote in an election: we need to know whether their inaction was caused by apathy, alienation, or contentment. In the right circumstances, the alienated may take to the streets in revolutionary action, leaving the apathetic at home watching television.

Political culture
The pattern of attitudes, values and beliefs about politics, whether they are conscious or unconscious, explicit or implicit.

Values
Basic ethical priorities that constrain and give shape to individual attitudes and beliefs.

There is another good reason for trying to understand political cultures. The structures and institutions of government rest, it is argued, on *cultural foundations*. If most people are satisfied with the way their system of government works, then it is likely to be stable over time, but if a large proportion is dissatisfied and prepared to take political action, then the system may come under pressure to change. Democratic political institutions rest upon democratic cultures, and a combination of democratic cultures and institutions produces stable democracy. In other words, there are two good reasons for studying political culture: it helps to explain individual behaviour and it helps to explain the persistence of democratic institutions and structures of government.

In this chapter, we examine the political attitudes and behaviour of citizens and political leaders. The three major topics in this chapter are:

- Political attitudes
- Political behaviour
- Theories of political attitudes and behaviour.

■ Political attitudes

■ *Political interests and identity*

We know from our own experience that political attitudes and behaviour are not random. People with the same background often have a lot in common politically: manual workers differ from managers and professionals, students from their parents and teachers and men from women. Individuals build their political ideas around their personal circumstances and interests, and when we talk about political interests we mean two sorts of things:

- *Material* interests – money, promotion, taxes, security
- *Ideal* interests – political values and ideals, such as a sense of justice and freedom, religious beliefs, or a left–right political position.

We should not underestimate the importance of ideal interests and values in trying to understand what people think about politics, and why they act the way they do. Many of the most important events in political history have been brought about by people prepared to fight and die for their material *and* ideal interests, and this means political beliefs and values that may have nothing to do with their own material circumstances.

How people define their material and ideal interests, is in turn, closely connected with who and what they think they are. They may define themselves as a member of a social class, or an ethnic or religious group, or perhaps as part of a gender, or age, or regional group. How people see the political world depends on how they believe they fit into it, and how they see their own political identity. According to this approach, politics is a struggle between people and groups whose material and ideal interests vary according to their class, region, ethnicity, age, gender, language, or nationality.

■ *Political culture*

One of the most influential approaches to the study of political attitudes and values in the post-war period has been built around the study of *political culture*. The concept is an elusive and complex one, and it can be loose and vague, but we can best see political culture as a sort of *map of how people think and behave*. A map is not the real thing, it deals only with selected and general features of the world, but it can be a useful guide to the real thing. In the same way, political culture does not reproduce every detail of what citizens know and think and feel about politics, but it can be a useful and simplified guide to the most important features of individual beliefs, values and attitudes. Used well, the concept helps us to focus on what is important and to see patterns in what would otherwise be a confused jumble of individual features (see controversy 8.1).

Controversy 8.1

Political culture as a political science concept: for and against

■ For

- Studies of political culture have produced important empirical findings about *political attitudes and behaviour* – e.g. the role of education and the family, and the importance and origins of competence, social trust and national pride. These were often overlooked or underestimated in previous studies.
- Political culture is claimed to be a 'bedrock' variable – it changes slowly and provides continuity. As a foundation of democracy, political values and assumptions are more important than the more superficial *political attitudes* usually discussed by newspapers and opinion polls.
- Political culture is a *key concept* linking (1) the micro-politics of individuals with the macro-politics of institutions and states, (2) subjective (values and attitudes) with the objective (e.g. voting behaviour) and (3) history and traditions with current circumstances and events.
- Sample surveys reveal differences in attitudes and behaviour that may be better explained by *'soft' cultural variables* (values, religious background, education) than by 'harder' variables (social class, wealth) or by structural variables (the institutional framework).
- Political culture certainly *does not explain everything*, but it helps to explain quite a wide range of phenomena from economic development and political stability, to democratic development and political behaviour.
- The study of political cultures is often based upon 'hard' and extensive *quantitative data* drawn from surveys.

■ Against

- Political culture is said to be a 'soft', 'residual', 'dustbin', or 'fuzzy' concept that can be used to explain everything and therefore nothing, especially where it is used when *other explanations have failed* – since the event is not explained by economic, class, constitutional, or other variables it *must* be explained by culture. Culture is often used as a *post hoc* (after the event) explanation that is not put to an empirical test.
- Political culture explanations risk being *circular*: we infer what people believe from how they behave, and then explain why they behave from what they believe. For example: people behave democratically because they hold democratic values, and we know that they hold democratic values because they behave democratically.
- Political culture is closely associated with attitudes and behaviour because it is close to them in the long causal chain of their determinants. Political scientists should search for causes that are *further away in the causal chain* – e.g. historical, or economic, or psychological.
- Cultures and structures are *mutually interdependent* and tend to go together. It is not surprising, therefore that cultures and structures are associated, but which is cause and effect?
- Some argue for a 'bottom-up' explanation in which the system is shaped and moulded by mass opinions and behaviour, others for a 'top-down' explanation in which structures shape or constrain attitudes and behaviour. If *both processes operate*, as they well may, how can we ever sort them out?
- Research can show the existence of sub-cultures, but not their *relative importance*. For example, is the elite culture more important than the mass culture, and how can we tell? Similarly, how much citizen participation is necessary to describe a national culture as 'participant' – 33 per cent, 40 per cent, 50 per cent, or perhaps 66 per cent?
- Where does the political culture come from? It may be useful to describe a nation's culture as 'participant' or 'alienated', but why is it like this? Why do countries have *different political cultures* and where do they come from?
- One argument against political culture explanations is that they deal only with the *last link in a long chain of causes* of political behaviour. The real and basic causes of behaviour may be historical, or economic (Marxist and class theory), or perhaps lie in individual psychology.

Culture is not innate: we are not born with a genetic imprint of a political culture in our brains. Rather, we absorb the political culture that surrounds us **Political** through the process of **political socialisation**, which passes on culture from **socialisation** one generation to the next. Hence cultures *persist over time*. We also absorb the The process by culture of our own social background and group. Hence political cultures are which individuals *patterned.* acquire their political values, attitudes and **Pattern** habits. Political cultures are patterned because members of the same social groups tend to be socialised into the *same set of attitudes and values*. They are also patterned because beliefs are often connected in a *systematic* way. For example, those in favour of minority group rights are likely to approve of Third World aid, and to have liberal social attitudes as well.

Persistence

Political cultures are passed on from one generation to the next so they persist over time. They do change, of course, but they usually change slowly according to the accumulation of events and experiences, unless there is some traumatic event (war, revolution, economic collapse) to bring about a sea-change.

■ *The civic culture*

The first and most influential study of political culture was the book by Gabriel A. Almond and Sidney Verba (1963). They define political culture as a pattern of **political orientation** to political objects such as parliament, elections, or the nation. They then divide orientations into three dimensions:

* Cognitive
* Affective
* Evaluative.

Gabriel A. Almond and Sidney Verba, *The Civic Culture* (1963)

Political orientation
A predisposition or propensity to view politics in a certain way.

Cognitive

To participate in politics, citizens must be aware of, know about and understand something about their political system – its main institutions, historical events, election system, political figures and national background.

Affective

To participate in politics, citizens must believe that politics is important enough to take up their time. It is significant, for example, that two out of three citizens in Austria, The Netherlands and Norway claim an interest in politics, compared with fewer than one in three in Argentina, Chile and Spain.

Evaluative

To know how they should participate in politics, citizens must also evaluate the system:

* Should it be *supported or reformed* (political support)?
* Do ordinary citizens have enough *influence* (**subjective or internal competence**)?
* Does the system operate as it should (**system or external efficacy**)?

Subjective or internal competence
The extent to which ordinary citizens feel that they can make their views and actions count in the political system.

The fact that almost nine out of ten Norwegians are satisfied with their government, compared with fewer than one in ten in Japan, tells us something about the state of politics in these two countries.

System or external efficacy
The extent to which ordinary citizens feel that political leaders and institutions are responsive to their wishes.

According to Almond and Verba, to measure a political culture requires collecting systematic information from a random sample of the population about the most important aspects of these three dimensions. On the basis of their study of (West) Germany, Italy, Mexico, the UK and the USA, they identified three pure types of political culture, and showed that these were combined in different proportions in the countries they surveyed. They also identified a fourth type that, they said, was the mixture that came closest to a democratic culture:

- *Parochial cultures* have a low level of awareness, knowledge and involvement with government. They are usually Third World and rural societies with poor education, low economic development and poor communications, but there are pockets of parochialism in developed countries as well. In *The Civic Culture*, Mexico came closest to the parochial model.
- In *subject cultures*, people are aware of government and what it does (its outputs) but do not participate much (citizen inputs). Subject cultures are mainly found in non-democracies that emphasise the power of government rather than citizen rights and duties. Subject cultures do not encourage enough democratic participation. *The Civic Culture* found West Germany in the 1950s to have elements of a subject culture.
- In *participant cultures*, citizens are knowledgeable about politics, attach an importance to them and participate because they feel competent and knowledgeable. *The Civic Culture* found the UK and the USA closest to this culture. The danger is democratic overload, in which too much participation produces too many political demands.

Therefore, the best political culture for a democracy is:

Civic culture
The term used by Almond and Verba to signify the balance of subject and participant political cultures that best supports democracy.

- The *civic culture*, in which subject and participant cultures are mixed to produce neither too much nor too little participation. Citizens are active and elites respond to their demands, but citizens also trust their political leaders and give them a degree of independence. Almond and Verba found that the UK in the late 1950s came closest to the civic culture.

The Civic Culture argued that political culture was a crucial theoretical concept that mediated between the micro- and subjective properties of a political system, and its macro-, institutional features. Culture is shared by individuals, so aggregate individual statistics (i.e. national averages) describe the properties of the system as a whole. Cultures and structures are also mutually interdependent, so they must 'fit' each other. As we saw in chapter 3, democratic constitutions are like fortresses – their institutions must be well designed and well built, but they must also be well manned by democrats who believe in them. When the culture matches the structure they are said to be *congruent*,

Political alienation
A feeling of detachment,

but when they do not fit, the culture is said to exhibit **political alienation**. According to Almond and Verba, Italy in the 1950s had an alienated culture because the democratic attitudes and behaviour of citizens were not matched by a sufficiently democratic structure. Alienated cultures were likely to produce a demand for change and a degree of political instability. In extreme cases they could generate mass pressures for political change, perhaps even revolution, as they did in central and eastern Europe in the 1980s.

■ Materialism and post-materialism

Almond and Verba's work had a huge impact in its time and stimulated many similar studies in the 1960s, but the approach lost favour in the 1970s and 1980s. It was revived, in large part, by Ronald Inglehart, who conducted a series of social surveys in many countries over a thirty-year period into what he calls *materialism* and *post-materialism*. Whereas Almond and Verba were mainly concerned with the persistence of political cultures over time and their relationship with stable democracy, Inglehart is interested in cultural and political change. His work starts from two basic propositions:

- Rapid economic development in the last hundred years has taken care of the basic material needs of most people in the west. Consequently, their values are shifting from material concerns (food, health, physical safety, social order) to *post-material* ones (civil liberties, the environment, job satisfaction, political and community participation, self-expression and the quality of life). Rising levels of education and an improved standard of living have caused a fundamental *transformation of political values* from material to post-material cultures.
- The shift from material to post-material values is slow because most people acquire their political culture in early socialisation and change their views only slowly after that. The clearest signs of the shift show up in the *younger, wealthier* and *better-educated generation*.

Inglehart's culture shift from materialism to post-materialism is slow and silent. He argues that it nonetheless has profound and far-reaching effects, because it is part of broader changes involving participation, equality, community and self-expression. Post-materialism also involves greater tolerance of abortion, divorce, euthanasia, sexual minorities, single parents and minority groups, opposition to nuclear energy and weapons and to the exploitation of the environment.

Post-materialism first appeared in young, wealthy and well-educated groups in the most affluent parts of the USA and western Europe in the 1960s. Early signs appeared in the generation that produced the student revolutionaries of 1968 in Berlin, California, London and Paris. The shift towards post-material values therefore helps to explain the remarkable fact that the increasing affluence of the 1960s did not induce a sense of satisfaction with society but, on the contrary, resulted in a wave of political protest that tried to change the political system.

Post-materialism, Inglehart says, has now spread to other parts of the west and to other parts of the developed world, as these grow more affluent. As older, more materialist generations are replaced, so the proportion of

estrangement, or critical distance from politics, often because the alienated feel there is something basically wrong with the political system.

post-materialists in these countries is rising, and it is predicted that they will be in a majority in many western countries by 2010. Among the democracies, the highest proportions of post-materialist believers are found in Australia, Austria, Canada, Italy, The Netherlands and the USA, the lowest in Estonia, Hungary, India, Israel and Latvia. Moreover, as the younger generation rises to positions of political power, so post-materialists will gain control of governments. Nor is post-materialism limited to the western club of affluent nations. It is now found in developing countries such as China, Poland and South Korea as they grow wealthier and better educated. In his 1995 book, Inglehart finds a close association between democracy and an emphasis on trust, tolerance, participation and a sense of personal well-being. In contrast, populations with material and survival values centring on money, safety and job security are likely to have authoritarian governments.

Ronald Inglehart, Moderniza-tion and Postmodern-ization (1995)

Six far-reaching consequences of the shift to post-materialism are said to be:

Cognitive mobilisation

The process by which increasing knowledge and understanding of the world helps to activate people to play a part in it.

1. *Cognitive mobilisation*   Education and wealth bring greater awareness of politics and better skills to participate.
2. *Replacement of class with cultural cleavages*   Materialist versus post-materialist divisions based on political cultures will gradually replace the left–right divisions based on class.
3. *Increased religious conflict*   Because post-materialists tend to oppose traditional religion, there may be a religious backlash against them, especially from religious parties of the right.
4. *More political participation*   The cognitive mobilisation of post-materialists results in greater demands for grass-roots participation.
5. *New forms of participation*   Post-materialists favour 'new forms' of direct participation, community politics and new social movements, which means the decline of 'old' forms of participation organised around bureaucratic and hierarchical parties and pressure groups (see chapters 11 and 9).
6. *New political issues*   Post-materialists are less involved in the left–right politics, and more interested in the environment, community politics, feminism, individual freedom and racial equality.

The post-materialist thesis is supported by a good deal of survey evidence from around the world, but not all the findings are consistent with it. The most extensive study of value change in west Europe in the post-war period, by Jan W. van Deth and Elinor Scarbrough (1995), shows a rather different pattern:

Jan W. van Deth and Elinor Scarbrough, The Impact of Values (1995)

1. *Persistent left–right divisions*   The old left–right divisions have persisted, although they have changed and weakened in some respects.
2. *Fusion not replacement*   Post-materialism has not replaced materialism. Rather elements of the old have been fused with elements of the new.
3. *High tide of post-materialism?*   The evidence suggests that the drift towards post-materialism among the youngest generations in west Europe may

be slowing, as economic conditions get harder, but it is too early to say whether this a temporary or permanent trend.

4. *A missing ingredient?* Most post-materialists are young, well-educated and middle class, but most young, well-educated, middle-class people are not post-materialist. There seems to be something else that helps to produce post-materialism.

▪ Sub-cultures and elite cultures

No country has a perfectly uniform political culture and there are often variations between sub-groups and regions. Indeed, the existence of materialist political cultures side by side with post-materialism in the same country is evidence of the existence of sub-cultures. Members of a sub-culture share in the larger culture, but they also have their own characteristics. For example, the Canadian political culture differs in some important respects from that in Finland and South Africa, but at the same time French- and English-speaking Canadians have their own political sub-cultures. Sub-cultures are typically aligned with important divisions in society such as class, gender, generation, religion, region and race. One of the most important sub-cultures in any society, however, is that of the **political elite**.

Elite cultures are normally different from mass cultures, partly because elites are often drawn from the best educated and more middle- and upper-class sections of the population, and partly because they interact so closely with each other over such long periods of time that they tend to develop their own world view. Compared with mass cultures, elite cultures are:

- *Abstract* They tend to be organised around abstract political ideas and ideals as well as dealing with the concrete policy issues of everyday political life.
- *Complex* They are more elaborate and systematic.
- *Informed* They are based on a good deal of information.
- *Broad* They cover most of the general and particular issues in politics.

Because of this, political elites are said to be 'ideologues' who have a broader, more sophisticated and better-informed view of the political world, compared with most ordinary citizens.

Some political scientists argue that the social background and education of western elites make them more democratic and tolerant, and with more liberal and fewer **authoritarian attitudes** than the general population. According to this view, democracy relies upon the civilised and democratic values of educated elites and their capacity to compromise and accept the rules of the democratic game. Others argue, on the contrary, that elites are more conservative than the masses, and that their liberal, democratic rhetoric simply disguises an interest in keeping power. This view argues that elites prevent the mass from developing political skills and interests because this would

Political elite
The relatively small number of people at the top of a political system who exercise disproportionate influence or power over political decisions. If powerful enough it is a 'ruling elite'.

Ideologues
Those with an informed, broad, sophisticated and more or less consistent (systematic) view of politics.

Authoritarian attitudes
A system or syndrome of attitudes based

143

upon: prejudice, dogmatism, superstition, low tolerance for ambiguity, hostility to out-groups (anti-semitism and racism) and obedience to authority.

bring an end to elite power. We shall return to this theme at the end of the chapter.

■ *Political cleavages*

We have already discussed briefly the concept of 'social cleavages' in chapter 1, but we must return to it here because it is so important for political attitudes and behaviour. There is an important difference between sub-cultural divisions in society, that may well result in political conflict and competition, and the deeper social cleavages that can produce serious political conflict, even violence. Divisions in society, and the sub-cultures associated with them, are accepted as a normal part of everyday life, partly because they often cut across each other in a way that helps to sew society together across its own internal divisions. The same person may be both religious and working class, for example, common membership of these social groups will help to build bridges between religious and working-class sub-cultures. In contrast, cleavages (chapter 1) are produced by divisions that are superimposed one on top of another, so that they *reinforce* each other and widen and deepen social differences (see briefing 8.1). For example, if the working-class movement and some

Briefing 8.1
Reinforcing and cross-cutting cleavages: Belgium and Switzerland

■ Reinforcing cleavages

Belgium is divided between Flemish-speaking (Flemish is a version of Dutch) Flanders in the North (57 per cent), and French-speaking Wallonia (42 per cent) in the South (reinforcing language–regional cleavages), with Brussels, the capital city, a contested area in the middle. Belgium is over 90 per cent Catholic (a cross-cutting cleavage) but the north is wealthier than the south (a reinforcing cleavage) and the socio-linguistic/regional cleavage is so important that parties are split along regional lines (reinforcing cleavages) creating highly fragmented party systems and great difficulty in forming stable governments. The linguistic conflict became so intense in the 1970s and 1980s that constitutional changes produced a decentralised federal system of government in 1993.

■ Cross-cutting cleavages

Switzerland is divided by both language (German 65 per cent, French 20 per cent and Italian 8 per cent) and religion (46 per cent Catholic, 40 per cent Protestant). All but four of the twenty-six cantons are linguistically homogeneous (a reinforcing cleavage) but the same language groups have different regional dialects (a cross-cutting cleavage), and most cantons are of mixed religion (a cross-cutting cleavage). Different language and religious groups often have the same economic interests in tourism or banking (a cross-cutting cleavage). There is no dominant city – Basel, Bern, Geneva, Lausanne and Zürich share capital city functions – and most Swiss identify with their nation (a cross-cutting cleavage). Switzerland (a federal system) is a highly stable and integrated nation.

churches are closely aligned and separate from middle-class political and religious organisations, then a gap will open up between the two. Political cleavages are the result of three conditions:

- *Objective social differences*   These are primarily based on class, ethnicity, language, religion and region.
- *Subjective awareness of differences*   It is not enough for objective differences to exist. Those involved must also be aware of their social identities (subcultures) and express them.
- *Political organisation*   Distinct social groups must form parties and pressure groups to promote their own interests, and perhaps develop their own newspapers and TV stations as well.

The most important political cleavages in the western world since the 1850s have involved class, but religious and urban–rural and regional differences have also played a role.

Geographical separation is particularly important for the production of cleavages. Groups that are mixed together in the same area are less likely to develop self-consciousness and their own political organisations than those that are separated in their own geographical areas. Spatial segregation helped to develop one of the most important political cleavages in western society, that between the centre and periphery. In the early stages of the development of modern states (see chapter 1), a cleavage often developed between the modernisers and centralisers of the state, usually concentrated in the main urban centre, and traditional interests intent on preserving the powers of local elites, usually in the geographical periphery. Although such **centre–periphery cleavages** developed several hundred years ago, they can cast a long shadow over modern politics.

A second important cleavage involving geographical separation evolved in the early stages of the industrial revolution when society tended to divide between modernising, rich, urban, industrial and commercial areas, and poorer, more traditional, rural and agricultural areas. The big cities and new capitalist groups often came into political conflict with the traditional landowners in the rural areas.

A third form of territorial cleavage occurs where distinct ethnic, religious, language, or cultural groups are concentrated in a particular area of the state. In such cases, the political struggle has sometimes taken the form of *separatist movements* that want their own government. The Basques and Catalans in Spain, and the Welsh, Irish and Scottish nationalists in the UK are examples. In some cases, peripheral regions and cultures can be absorbed and incorporated into a larger political system, as the American south was after the Civil War, although there are still marked north–south political differences in the USA. Federal systems are better at doing this than unitary ones (see chapter 5), as the example of Belgium shows. In some cases, ethno-nationalism has been forcefully repressed and contained, as it was in the Soviet Union, only to burst out when central control was removed (Bosnia-Herzegovina, Chechnya); in

Centre–periphery cleavage
The political cleavage between the social and political forces responsible for creating centralised and modern nation-states, and other interests, usually on the periphery of the state, which resisted this process. Centre–periphery cleavages are often, but not always, geographical.

145

Fact file 8.1

Political attitudes and values

- *Trust*   Trust between fellow citizens is said to be a crucial underlying condition for democracy. The *World Values Studies* show that the less democratic a system, the lower its social trust. Among the democracies, countries such as Argentina, Chile, the Dominican Republic and Ghana have comparatively low levels of social trust (10–20 per cent), whereas Canada, Finland, Ireland, The Netherlands, Norway and Sweden have high scores (50–65 per cent).
- *Interest in politics*   Of forty-five countries surveyed in 1999–2002 an average of 45 per cent of citizens described themselves as 'very or somewhat interested in politics'. Of the democracies, the highest placed were Austria, the Czech Republic, Israel, The Netherlands, Norway and the USA (80–66 per cent). The lowest placed were Argentina, Chile, Finland, Portugal and Spain (all below 30 per cent).
- *Satisfaction with democracy*   In forty-nine countries surveyed in 1999–2002, an average of 49 per cent of people expressed a satisfaction with democracy in their country. The figures are, not surprisingly, much higher in democracies, but even so they vary quite a lot. The lowest placed are Croatia, Ireland, Lithuania, Northern Romania and Slovakia (all below 30 per cent), and the highest placed are Austria, Canada, Germany, Luxembourg, The Netherlands and Portugal (all above 66 per cent).
- *Post-materialism*   The highest levels of post-materialist values in the late 1990s were found in the comparatively wealthy democracies of Argentina, Austria, Australia, Canada, Italy and the USA (all above 25 per cent), and the lowest in Estonia, Hungary, India, Israel and Slovakia (all below 5 per cent).
- *National pride*   The Australians, Mexicans, Peruvians, Portuguese, South Africans and Uruguayans are proudest of their nation. The Dutch, Germans, Japanese, Lithuanians and South Koreans are the least proud.
- *Ethnic, religious, and linguistic differences*, with correspondingly strong political culture differences, are found in Belgium, Canada, India, The Netherlands, South Africa, Switzerland and the USA. The most ethnically homogeneous democracies are the Nordic countries.
- *Ethno-nationalism*   European examples of regional nationalism include Bulgaria (the Turkish minority), Bosnia (Serbs, Croats and Muslims), Northern Ireland (Catholic nationalism and Protestant unionism), Russia (Chechen and other Siberian minorities), Serbia (Albanian nationalism), Spain (Catalan, Galician and Basque nationalism) and Turkey (Kurdish nationalism).

---

others, it has resulted in peaceful separation (the Czech Republic and Slovakia), or prolonged civil strife (the Basque country, Northern Ireland) (fact file 8.1).

■ Political behaviour

Political behaviour

All political activities of citizens as well as the attitudes and orientations relevant for these activities.

Political behaviour comes in many more forms than voting or joining a party. It includes reading a paper, talking about politics and joining voluntary organisations that play no political role for much of the time (see briefing 8.2). If we include actions that have an unintended effect on politics, the range broadens further to include such things as not paying taxes and not voting. After all, a large minority of non-voters is a cause for concern in democracies, and tax

Briefing 8.2
Varieties of political behaviour

■ Conventional

- Voting
- Reading newspapers, watching TV news
- Talking about politics
- Joining a political group (voluntary organisation, party, or new social movement)
- Involvement with a client body or advisory body for public service (consumer council, school board)
- Attending meetings, demonstrations, rallies
- Contacting the media, elected representatives, or public officials
- Contributing money
- Volunteering for political activity (organising meetings, election canvassing)
- Standing for political office
- Holding political office

■ Unconventional

- Radical and direct action including:
- Unofficial strikes, sit-ins, protests, demonstrations
- Civil disobedience
- Breaking laws for political reasons
- Political violence

Figure 8.1 is a stylised representation of how political participation research has developed since 1940

evasion has a direct effect on government policies. Even clothes, music and food can have a political connotation, as students know.

■ *Modes of political behaviour*

Research in the 1950s and 1960s suggested that the population of western democracies could be divided roughly into three groups, according to their level of political participation:

- *Gladiators* These are the leaders and activists who run parties, political organisations and campaigns, and who hold political office. About 5–8 per cent of the population falls into this group.
- *Spectators* The great mass of the population is not engaged in politics beyond voting in elections, reading a paper, watching TV news and occasion political discussion.
- *Apathetics* The politically inactive who know and care little about politics, and do not vote.

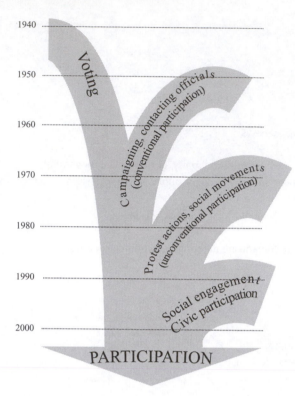

Figure 8.1: Expansion of the political participation research agenda since the 1940s

Sidney Verba, Norman H. Nie and Jae-On Kim, *The Modes of Democratic Participation: A Cross-National Comparison* **(1972),** *Participation and Political Equality: A Seven-Nation Comparison* **(1978)**

Later research on comparative political behaviour by Sidney Verba, Norman H. Nie and Jae-On Kim (1972, 1978), confirmed the existence of a small group of political 'gladiators' (leaders) and a larger group of 'apathetics', but it also found something surprising about the great mass of people in the middle. Their political behaviour could not be placed on a single continuum of political activity ranging from the simple act of voting at one end to the most demanding and time-consuming forms of political activity, at the other. Rather, citizens tended to specialise in different modes of behaviour. Individuals usually concentrated on a group of similar sorts of political activity that clustered together (see briefing 8.3), according to the goals and values of the individuals, and according to the demands that the type of behaviour made on them. Political activity was not cumulative, and knowing what type of behaviour a given individual specialised in could tell us nothing about what other type of activity they might be involved in. For example, community activists were no more or less likely to vote than protest activists, and protest activists were no more or less likely to be party members than those who made contact with specialists.

Briefing 8.3
Modes of political behaviour

Inactives	Rarely vote or engage in any form of political participation
Passive supporters	Vote regularly, pay taxes, support the nation, tacit support for the political system
Contact specialists	Contact political and public office holders about personal matters
Community activists	Cooperate with others in their community, join local organisations, contact local officials about public matters
Party workers	Join parties, volunteer for campaign work, canvass at elections, give money, attend meetings, stand for election
Leaders	Fill major political and public offices – elected representatives in national and sub-national government, party leaders, leaders of pressure groups and social movements, political commentators
Protestors	Specialists in protest and unconventional behaviour

■ *Conventional and unconventional political behaviour*

Democratic political participation has traditionally been confined to voting, attending political meetings, signing petitions, joining a party or political group and so on. These are sometimes known as 'conventional' forms of behaviour, but in the late twentieth century the political repertoire has expanded to include 'unconventional' activities such as protests, demonstrations, boycotts, occupations and unofficial strikes (see briefing 8.2). Surveys show that this type of behaviour is more widely accepted now, though it is still not widely practised. Fewer than 5 per cent of the populations of Austria, Finland, Italy, The Netherlands, Switzerland, the UK, the USA and West Germany have ever participated in an occupation or an unofficial strike, fewer than 17 per cent had participated in a demonstration or consumer boycott.

■ *Patterns of political behaviour*

There are many different types of political behaviour, and these combine in varying proportion in different countries according to their political structures, cultures and histories. However, there are also some striking patterns in participation in the democratic countries of the world which enable us to advance some reliable generalisations.

Most people are not political

Most people do not know or care much about politics. They vote sometimes, and they become active when the need arises. But these people are not necessarily 'apathetic', because there are other reasons for being politically inactive:

Political marginality
The condition of being on the fringes of politics, and therefore of having little influence.

- *Marginals*   People categorised as 'marginals' or who have **political marginality** include lunatics and criminals who are deprived of citizenship rights; illiterates; immigrants and those who do not speak the majority language; the mentally handicapped; the very old and infirm. Students often do not vote in elections simply because they are at university on election day and not in their home town where they are registered to vote.
- *Conflict avoiders*   Some people avoid politics because it can lead to disagreement, conflict and bad feeling.
- *Alienated*   Some people do not get involved because they believe they have no influence in the system (low subjective efficacy), or think the political system is not democratic (system competence). More than two-thirds of the citizens of Croatia, Hungary, Latvia, Lithuania, Northern Ireland, Romania, Slovakia and South Korea are dissatisfied with the way that democracy works in their country, although at the other extreme, more than two-thirds are satisfied in Austria, Canada, Denmark, Germany, The Netherlands, Portugal and Spain.
- *Loss of political salience*   With the huge expansion of income and education since 1945, many people have the personal resources to deal with the problems and opportunities of their daily life. This makes them more independent as individuals. *Politics*, on the other hand, is a collective activity, and become less important and less necessary in a world where individuals have their own money and personal skills to handle their lives. Politics is no longer **salient**: it becomes, as one observer noted, 'background noise' or 'elevator music'. This is not to say that politics is of no importance, but it does mean that, in comparison with other activities – work, family, leisure – it has less significance. This is not to say that people do not participate in political life any more. They participate sporadically when the need arises, but without committing themselves and their time to ideologies or conventional organisations such as parties and trade unions.
- *Apathetic*   Those who are simply not interested in politics. The term 'apathetic' is often used as a critical value judgement, which means it should be avoided, quite apart from the fact that many are politically inactive for reasons other than apathy.

Salient
Something that is important, significant, or prominent in people's minds.

Sporadic political involvement

Though most people are not politically active most of the time, many are involved some of the time: they read a paper, watch TV news and talk about politics. They participate in one way or another when they feel the need, usually because their personal interests are affected. These sporadic acts of participation cover a substantial percentage of the population, and, as table 8.1 shows, more than half and as many as three-quarters of the population of most west European democracies have been politically involved in some way, beyond the simple act of voting.

Table 8.1 *Rates of political participation,[a] western Europe, 1974–1990*

	1974	1981	1990
Britain	31	66	77
Sweden		58	74
Norway		58	68
Denmark		48	59
(West) Germany	34	48	57
France		52	57
Italy	34	50	56
Iceland		40	55
Netherlands	28	37	54
Belgium		27	51
Ireland		32	46
Finland	26	40	38
Spain		32	32

Note: [a] Entries are percentages of the adult population who engage in some form of political participation beyond voting.

Source: Richard Topf, 'Beyond electoral participation', in Hans-Dieter Klingemann and Dieter Fuchs, *Citizens and the State* (Oxford: Oxford University Press, 1995: 69).

Participation rates are rising

As table 8.1 also shows, rates of political activity are tending to rise in the western world, contrary to the common claim that democracies are increasingly apathetic and alienated. Russell J. Dalton's (2002) study of citizen politics in Britain, France, Germany and the USA shows a decline in the 'old' politics of parties and elections, but an increase in the 'new' politics of referendums, community politics, citizen lobbies and single-issue groups. The *World Values Surveys* show a rise in signing petitions in almost every established democracy since the 1980s.

Russell J. Dalton, *Citizen Politics: Public Opinion and Political Parties in Advanced Western Democracies* (2002)

Substantial variations in participation

The percentages involved in political activity often vary greatly from one country to another. This is true of particular modes of participation as well as overall rates of activity, as the figures in table 8.1 demonstrate. Participation in the highest-ranked country is more than twice as high as in the lowest-ranked one.

Voters are not fools

Some political scientists emphasise how little people know about politics, how little they are involved and how poorly prepared they are to perform their citizen duties. Some survey research concludes that voters are often ignorant, irrational and inconsistent and that, as a result, opinion polls and surveys are not to be trusted. Asked about a matter on which they have no opinion or information, many come up with a **'door-step' response**, saying the first thing that comes into their head, or something that they think they should say. Contradicting this dim view of the electorate, the American political scientist, V. O. Key (1966) argued that 'voters [were] not fools'. He produced evidence showing that American voters switched votes between candidates and parties according to their judgement of the political circumstances. They judged candidates and parties according to their past records and future promises. Subsequent research has tended to confirm this, in two ways:

- Electoral behaviour can be explained in terms of *real political trends* and events, especially taxation, inflation, unemployment, economic performance, and social policies, war, and international events. Support for NATO declined after the collapse of the Soviet Union in 1989 because people thought there was no longer a great need for military defence of the NATO type, but when other military conflicts occurred they revised their views again.
- Some research argues that citizens use '**low information rationality**' or 'gut rationality' in deciding how to vote and behave. It is not necessary to have full and detailed information to make sensible judgements; a rough idea is sufficient. If the issue is a complex technical one, people can take their cues from those they trust – party leaders, political commentators, friends, newspapers.

The 'standard model' of political participation

The 'standard model' applies across a wide variety of countries and times. It shows that class and status, plus the closely related factors of education, income and family background, strongly influence rates of political participation. Those with high class and status often have the education to be able to acquire political knowledge and skills, and they are likely to understand the relevance of politics to their own circumstances. They are more likely to have the resources (education, cars, phones, faxes, computers, office support, money) to become *effectively involved in politics* and the social prestige to be influential, and they often have family backgrounds with a political interest. Class and status is often abbreviated to 'SES' or 'social and economic status', where class is closely associated with occupation and income, and status with prestige in society. Some people make a lot of money but have low status (the owner of a string of porn magazines) while others have high status though not much money (aristocrats fallen on hard times). SES is a combination of these two things. In their in-depth study of civic activity in the USA, Sidney Verba, Kay Lehman Schlozman and Henry Brady (1995), find systematic differences along cultural and ethnic lines, as well as between religious groups. *Family activism* is also passed on from one generation to the next. For the most part, different

'Door-step' response
Where those with no opinion or information respond to polls and surveys with the first thing that comes into their head (sometimes known as 'non-opinion').

V. O. Key (1908–63)

V. O. Key, *The Responsible Electorate* (1966)

Low information rationality
Where citizens without great deal of factual political information have a broad enough grasp of the main issues to make up their mind about them, or else they take cues from sources they trust (sometimes known as 'gut rationality').

Sidney Verba, Kay Lehman Schlozman and Henry Brady, *Voice and Equality: Civic Voluntarism in American Politics* (1995)

rates of participation reflect unequal access to resources, with money and education being the most important.

Gender, age and length of residence

The 'standard model' is often modified, though usually only a small degree, by gender, age and length of residence in a community. In many countries, politics is still regarded as something of a 'man's game', and women tend to participate less. Young and old people are less active than the middle-aged, whose involvement with their children's schools, their colleagues at work and their community tends to draw them into politically related activities. The longer people live in their community, and the stronger their social networks, the more they tend to be engaged.

Jean Blondel, World Leaders: Heads of Government in the Postwar Period (1980), Government Ministers in the Contemporary World (1985)

Political elites

Following on from the last point, Jean Blondel's work on political leaders in the world (1980, 1985) shows that such leaders are overwhelmingly of the '3-M' variety – middle-aged, middle and upper class and male. Most have a university education, and many come from three professions – law, teaching and the civil service (fact file 8.2).

Fact file 8.2

Political behaviour

- *Political discussion* On average, 75 per cent of people across forty-three countries claimed to discuss politics 'frequently' or 'occasionally' with their friends. The highest placed were East Germany, Estonia, Latvia, and Lithuania (all new democracies, 90 per cent or more), and lowest Belgium, Italy, Northern Ireland, Portugal, Spain and Turkey (less than 60 per cent).
- *Direct action* Research shows that 'protest behaviour' in the form of strikes, sit-ins, protests, marches and boycotts, is now a widely accepted part of the political repertoire of west European citizens, but that only a very small minority (1–3 per cent) actually engages in such behaviour.
- *Protest behaviour* Among forms of direct action, signing petition is the most frequent (an average of 43 per cent across forty nations in the early 1990s), followed by lawful demonstrations (21 per cent), boycotts (9 per cent), unofficial strikes (6 per cent) and the occupation of buildings (2 per cent).
- *Revolutionary action* Among the democracies, no more than 2 per cent of the Austrians, Danes, Dutch, Japanese, Norwegians and (West) Germans now believe in radical change by revolutionary action, but the figures are much higher in the new democracies of Estonia, Latvia, Lithuania, Poland and South Africa (19–32 per cent).
- *Political inaction* In fourteen West European democracies in 1974–90, between a quarter and a third of the population had no interest and took no part in political life. Another 25–40 per cent were 'active' in the sense that they had an interest and did engage in some way in political life.
- *Political elites* Two-thirds of heads of government in the world between 1945 and 1975 had a university education and more than half (56 per cent) were lawyers, teachers, or civil servants.

■ Theories of political attitudes and behaviour

■ *Marxist and class theory*

False consciousness
The state of mind of the working class induced by the ruling class to conceal the real nature of capitalism and the real self-interests of the workers.

Antonio Gramsci (1891–1937)

Hegemony
Originally a Marxist term, hegemony indicates a class that is so powerful that it does not have to rely upon force or power to maintain its rule because its values and attitudes have been accepted by all other classes.

Marxist theories argue that political attitudes and behaviour are shaped by capitalist institutions that ensure that the system 'reproduces' itself, and that the masses are indoctrinated into a state of **false consciousness**. Education conditions the workers to fulfil their economic function and little else. Religion, 'the opiate of the masses', teaches people their place in life and emphasises spiritual matters rather than the physical conditions of life. The mass media indoctrinate people with a mixture of political propaganda and popular distractions (sport, game shows, films, soap operas, gossip). Political culture is, therefore, largely the creation of the ruling class and designed to protect their economic interests. The Italian philosopher, Antonio Gramsci used the term **hegemony** to refer to the way the ruling class exercised power not by force, but by subtle influence over the hearts and minds of ordinary people. Political culture, viewed this way, is merely a 'superstructure' built on the material substructure of the capitalist mode of production and its class system.

Rigid and 'vulgar Marxist' theories (that is, crude and over-simple Marxism) have nothing to recommend them. They are 'over-determined' in the sense that they do not allow for the many individual and group variations that exist within any political system. The concept of false consciousness also has its difficulties; who can tell others that they do not see the world correctly, or understand their own best interests?

At the same time, there is clearly more than a small grain of truth in the class theory of attitudes and behaviour. Empirically, the 'standard model' that combines class and class-related variables explains a good deal of the variation in political attitudes and behaviour, and it seems to have applied to a broad variety of countries and circumstances for much of the nineteenth and twentieth centuries. However, it certainly does not explain everything, and its explanatory power declined in the late twentieth century. The class model though far from defunct, seems to be on the wane.

■ *Elite theory*

Robert Michels (1876–1936)
Gaetano Mosca (1858–1941)
Vilfredo Pareto (1848–1923)

Elite theory grew up in opposition to Marxist class theory and is associated mainly with the names of the German sociologist Robert Michels and the two Italian political sociologists Gaetano Mosca and Vilfredo Pareto. Both elite and class theory argue that politics are dominated by a small number of people, but whereas Marxists argue that the **ruling elite** or ruling class reproduces itself by passing on its privileges and power to its children, elite theory claims that elites cannot perpetuate themselves in the long run. They *change and circulate* because elites inevitably decay after a time in power, to be replaced by a new, more successful and more vigorous elite. New elite groups rise to the top because of their superior political skills of cunning, force, or popular appeal. There are different versions of elite theory, but all claim that mass democracy is impossible because a small group will *always* dominate politics. This is a rather startling claim, and Michels cast his theory as the 'Iron Law of Oligarchy', which states that minorities *always* rule organisations.

Probably the best known empirical examination of a national elite is C. Wright Mills (1956) a study which argues that the USA is run by a small group of people representing the 'military–industrial complex' and consisting of military leaders (the warlords), top businessmen (the corporate directorate) and political leaders. Mills argues that this group comes from the same middle- and upper-class background of interconnected families, schools and universities, thinks and acts the same way, interacts closely and circulates among the top positions in public and private life. The power elite makes all the 'key decisions' in the USA, although less important decisions may be made by middle levels of power in a more or less democratic manner. Mills' theory is discussed in greater detail in chapter 15 and pluralist theory, the main challenger to elite theory, is discussed in chapter 9.

Ruling elite
A political elite that is so powerful that it can make all the important decisions in government.

C. Wright Mills, *The Power Elite* (1956)

■ *Rational-choice theory*

Some applications of rational choice have already been discussed (chapters 5 and 6), but since the theory is mainly about individuals it should be particularly applicable to the study of individual attitudes and behaviour. One of the earliest and most influential books by Anthony Downs (1956), argues that rational, self-interested voters will support the party most likely to satisfy their preferences. For their part, the political parties will try to maximise power by appealing to the average (median) voter, who holds typical, middle-of-the-road attitudes and preferences.

Anthony Downs, *An Economic Theory of Democracy* (1956)

Early rational-choice theory, following economic models in which consumers were assumed to have perfect knowledge of the market, assumed that individuals were well informed about politics. Since this is obviously implausible, given that many people know rather little about politics, later versions relaxed this assumption and accepted that most people had little political information, but perhaps enough to make political judgements. Indeed, rational-choice theory turned its earlier assumptions about perfect knowledge into a strength, arguing that it is not rational to spend a lot of time gathering political information. The chances of any ordinary citizen having the slightest effect on any given political outcome (e.g. an election result) is close to zero, so the costs of being well informed far outweigh any likely gain. Indeed, from a rational self-interested point of view even voting is a waste of time, and it is much more sensible to **free-ride** on others. The theory thus comes to the conclusion that very few people will bother to vote. Yet people do vote in large numbers, and they do get politically involved, even though they may gain little from it in rational-choice terms. They do so, in part at least, not because of rational

Free-ride
To extract the benefits of other people's work without putting in any effort oneself.

155

self-interest but because performing civic duties is part of a culture that emphasises *civic responsibility* as an end in itself.

The second main problem concerns the discussion of what is 'rational' and
what is self-interest. Was it rational and self-interested for the early Christians
to allow themselves to be thrown to the lions? If you define 'self-interest' in
terms of the soul and salvation, the answer is 'yes', but then everything can
be rational self-interest. Besides, some people seem to vote for the public interest rather than self-interest. They are, in the jargon, not 'pocket-book voters'
who are motivated by their own material self-interest but carry out **sociotropic
voting**, and take the general interest and the public good into account. They
may even vote for increases in their own taxes for the general good – as middle-
class socialists do. However, rational-choice, social choice and public choice
theorists can argue that it is rational and self-interested to vote in the public
interest because this helps to maintain the social and political conditions of
security, safety and economic stability that enable people to achieve their personal interests. Once again, if it is rational self-interest to vote for the public
interest then perhaps everything is rational self-interest.

Sociotropic voting
Deciding which party to vote for on the basis of general social or economic circumstances. The opposite is 'pocket-book voting' that is based on private interests of the voter.

■ *Social capital theory and civic participation*

The most recent theoretical development in the explanation of political attitudes and behaviour concerns the concept of 'social capital', but since this
approach is also tied up closely with voluntary associations, the topic of
chapter 9, we shall leave it until then. Meanwhile, we need note only that
social capital also has a good deal to do with attitudes and behaviour.

■ Summary

This chapter has dealt with the political values and attitudes of individuals
and groups, and examines how modern research has tried to understand and
explain political cultures. It argues that:

- Political attitudes and values are built around the material and ideal interests that individuals derive from their sense of identity. Hence attitudes and
  values are generally strongly linked to class, ethnic, language, religious, and
  territorial identities.
- The concept of 'political culture' is claimed to be important empirically
  (it is associated with many important empirical findings) and theoretically
  (linking subjective and objective, and macro- and micro-features of the political system). Critics claim that it is a vague and unsatisfactory explanatory
  variable.
- Research on materialism/post-materialism argues that younger generations
  in affluent societies are shifting their values from material ones (jobs,
  money...) to post-material ones (self-expression, job satisfaction, the quality of life...). Critics claim that this culture shift has slowed down, and

that post-material values have not replaced material ones but have been combined with them.

- An important distinction should be drawn between **reinforcing** and **cross-cutting political cleavages**, which can result in severe political conflict and violence.
- People tend to specialise in a particular mode of political behaviour (clusters of similar forms of activity).
- Most people are not political: rates of sporadic political activity are relatively high and participation seems to be increasing.
- Voters are not fools.
- Participation is often associated with class and class-related variables, and to a lesser extent with gender, age and length of residence in the community.

Reinforcing cleavages
These are laid one on top of the other, making them more potent.

Cross-cutting cleavages
These are laid across one another, thereby reducing their capacity to divide.

Further reading

The best general introduction to political attitudes and behaviour is Russell J. Dalton, *Citizen Politics: Public Opinion and Political Parties in Advanced Industrial Democracies* (Chatham: Chatham House, 2nd edn., 2002), although it covers only France, Germany, Great Britain and the USA. Gabriel Almond and Sidney Verba (eds.), *The Civic Culture Revisited* (Princeton: Princeton University Press, 1980) is the best appraisal of the concept of political culture and the research done on it since the publication of *The Civic Culture* in 1963. For a revival of interest in political cultures, see also Ronald Inglehart, 'The renaissance of political culture', *American Political Science Review*, 82, 1988: 1203–30, and on political culture and democracy, see Ronald Inglehart and Christian Welzel, 'Political culture and democracy', in Howard J. Wiarda (ed.), *New Directions in Comparative Politics* (Boulder, CO: Westview Press, 3rd edn., 2002: 141–64). The latest book on post-materialism is Ronald Inglehart, *Modernization and Postmodernization: Cultural, Economic, and Political Change in 43 Nations* (Princeton: Princeton University Press, 1995). For two recent collections of essays on changing political attitudes and behaviour in democracies, see Pippa Norris (ed.), *Critical Citizens: Global Support for Democratic Governance* (Oxford: Oxford University Press, 1999) and Susan Pharr and Robert Putnam (eds.), *Disaffected Democracies: What's Troubling the Trilateral Countries?* (Princeton: Princeton University Press, 2001). For data about political values and beliefs across the world, see Ronald Inglehart *et al.*, *Human Values and Beliefs: A Cross-Cultural Source Book on the 1999–2002 Values Surveys* (Mexico City: Siglo Veintiuno Editores, 2004).

Websites

http://www.esds.ac.uk/International/access/eurobarometer.asp	The European Union's bi-annual survey, called the Eurobarometer.
http://wvs.isr.umich.edu/	Website about the *World Values Surveys*.
http://www.europeansocialsurvey.org/	The European Social Survey website. It is particularly easy to use and allows students to generate their own tables.

Projects
1. What are the most important features of the political culture of your country? Why? (The figures in Ronald Inglehart *et al.*, *Human Values and Beliefs*, will be useful for this question.)
2. Read the section in this chapter on materialism and post-materialism, and then assess the extent to which you and your friends are materialists or post-materialists.
3. Critically assess Marxist, elitist and rational-choice approaches to political attitudes and behaviour. Which do you prefer, if any, and why?

9 Pressure groups and social movements

Few of us have much influence in politics as individuals on our own; we have to *combine with others* to have any impact. And that is exactly what people do in democracies. Using their rights of assembly and free association, they organise themselves into a huge number and variety of voluntary organisations – professional and business organisations, trade unions, charities, social clubs, environmental groups, churches, women's groups, community associations, youth clubs, consumer groups, arts, science, leisure clubs and sports clubs. In recent decades, they have also developed a new weapon in the struggle for political power, namely social movements, which are not the same as pressure groups in all respects but have a lot in common with them.

Voluntary organisations and associations, clubs and social movements play an enormously important role in social and political life, and are said to be one of the main foundations of modern democracy. Politically active groups voice the demands of their members and defend their interests in the political arena, as any peaceful group in a democracy is entitled to do. Many groups play a direct role in the consultative machinery of government. Even if they are not politically active, groups help to create a peaceful, integrated and stable social order in which democratic government can operate effectively.

Voluntary associations organise themselves around the interests of social groups and strata, which makes them another example of the way that government and politics are deeply rooted in social life. In fact, they play a special role in politics as *mediating organisations*. They organise individuals into groups, and then link these groups with the political system by expressing and defending their political interests when the need arises. In this sense, they act as 'input' agencies in the political system that express the demands and concerns of individuals, but they also act as 'output' agencies that help to implement public policy. This means that groups are mediating agencies in a *two-way process* that links society and government – a function they share with parties and the media, which have their own chapters in this part of the book (chapters 11 and 10).

Voluntary associations and organisations are thus crucial to an understanding of government and society: they express the social and political interests of their members, they try to influence the public by putting pressure on government, they often play a direct role in the consultative machinery of government and they play a crucial role in democratic politics by organising, integrating and stabilising society.

The seven main topics in this chapter are:

- Political connections
- Pressure groups and social movements in action
- Determinants of power
- Corporatism, para-government and tri-partism/pluralism
- International NGOs
- Groups, pressure groups and democracy
- Theories of voluntary organisations.

■ Political connections

■ *Voluntary organisations and pressure groups*

Modern government is 'big' government and its activities extend into almost every corner of life. Almost every social group and interest in modern democracies is therefore organised to defend itself and influence government policies that affect it. Perhaps the most conspicuous, because they are often large, wealthy, active and powerful, are the organisations and associations that represent people in their *working lives* – that is business associations, professional associations and trade unions. Known as **interest groups**, many are constantly trying to influence government policies not just on economic and occupational matters but on everything that touches their interests, which is practically the whole span of public policy. Churches are also active on moral issues and a broad range of educational and social ones as well. Community associations are interested in local government and its services, environmental groups with pollution, noise, food and health. Arts groups, educational organisations and sports clubs have their special concerns, and so do pensioners' organisations, scientific clubs and charities. The list is almost endless, and it is difficult to exaggerate the number and variety of voluntary organisations and associations in society.

Interest groups
Sometimes know as 'sectional' groups, interest groups are a type of pressure group that represents occupational interests – business and professional associations and trade unions.

The result is that, at any one time, the political arena is packed with voluntary organisations and associations of one kind or another, and any given political issue is likely to attract the attention of at least one of these groups. This does not mean that all voluntary associations are necessarily 'political' in any sense of the term. In fact, so far as government and politics are concerned, there are three main types of groups:

- *'Episodic' groups*   Most voluntary associations are not at all concerned with public issues and avoid politics if possible because they are controversial and cause difficulty between people. A local football club or film club has no need to get involved in politics in normal circumstances, but if their football pitch or cinema is due for demolition to make way for a road, they may campaign to protect their amenities, but only as long as the issue lasts. Such groups are known as **'episodic' groups**. Their importance lies in the fact that, while most groups are not political most of the time, they are already organised and can be mobilised quickly to defend their interests if the need arises.

- *'Fire brigade' groups*   Some groups are set up especially to fight a particular political campaign as **'fire brigade' groups**, and are disbanded when the issue is settled. For example, a local action group might be set up to keep a park as an open space, but fade away when the issue is won (or lost).

- *Political groups*   Some voluntary organisations are created to engage in long-term political action. Trade unions and business associations are usually set up to do battle in the political arena, although they also engage in other, non-political activities.

In other words, we should distinguish carefully between the *group* world of voluntary organisations, which are usually non-political most of the time, and the *pressure group* world, consisting of those voluntary organisations that are politically active at any given time.

At this point, it would be helpful to clear up a purely verbal matter. This chapter refers to voluntary organisations of all kinds that play a political role as **'pressure groups'**. It uses the term 'interest groups' to refer to those kinds of pressure groups that represent people in their *occupational capacities* – that is the business, professional and trade unions that are particularly important in the pressure group world. All groups other than occupational groups are called **'cause groups'**. Interest groups and cause groups together make up the whole of the 'pressure group world'. This is not how the terms are used in some studies, which refer to politically active groups of all kinds as 'interest groups'. This, however, rather confuses matters because it leaves us with no way of distinguishing between occupational and other groups. We shall see later why this distinction is so important.

This still leaves us with other problems of definition. We have already mentioned that pressure groups and social movements are alike in some respects, and in addition that pressure groups are like political parties in some ways.

'Episodic' groups
Groups that are not usually politically active but become so when the need arises.

'Fire brigade' groups
Groups formed to fight a specific issue, and dissolved when it is over.

Pressure groups
Private and voluntary organisations that try to influence or control particular government policies but do not want to become the government or control all government policies.

Cause groups
Sometimes known as 'promotional' or 'attitude' groups, cause groups are a type of pressure group that does not represent organised occupational interests, but promotes causes or ideas.

All three are voluntary organisations and all are political. How, then, are we to distinguish between them?

■ Pressure groups and political parties

The pressure group world overlaps with political parties but it is helpful to draw lines between them because they usually play a different role in politics:

- Pressure groups want to *influence* government, parties want to *become* government. Trade unions and business organisations want to keep a foot in the door of government, but they do not want to take control of government.
- Most pressure groups are interested in *only one policy area*, party programmes *cover all* (or almost all) *of them*. Welfare groups are concerned with welfare, art groups with art. Neither have any particular interest with foreign policy.
- Parties are primarily *political*, most pressure groups *are not*. Parties are set up to win power by nominating candidates for public office and contesting elections. Rose growers' associations are not interested in politics unless they have to be.
- Parties *fight elections*, most pressure groups *do not*.

These are not hard and fast differences. The Labour parties of Australia and the UK were created by socialist, workers' and trade union pressure groups. Some pressure groups contest elections (especially in Japan), though often for the publicity this brings rather than the hope of winning. Some pressure groups operate as parties (Agrarian Parties in Scandinavia, and religious groups in Israel), or turn themselves into parties (the Greens), but most groups stick to being groups. Some are naturally **aligned groups** – business organisations with right-wing parties, trade unions with left parties. In most cases, however, groups try to maintain a *non-aligned status* so that they can work with whatever party or coalition is in power.

Aligned groups
Pressure groups that ally themselves with a political party, the best examples being trade unions and left parties, and business organisations and right parties. Many groups try to maintain a non-aligned status if they can, because they want to work with whichever party is in power.

■ Social movements

Social movements also have much in common with parties and pressure groups, but differ in some respects. Social movements:

- Bring together a range of different organisations and associations to *work loosely together*. They are not organised into a single bureaucratic structure like pressure groups and parties.
- Have a broader range of political interests than most voluntary associations, but a narrower range than most political parties. Social movements are concerned with a *particular area of public life* – the representation of working-class interests, or minority groups, or religious issues.

Probably the best single example of a social movement is the working-class coalition formed in many countries in the nineteenth century to protect and promote working-class interests. Formed by trade unions, cooperatives and collectives, savings clubs, worker educational organisations and socialist organ-isations of all kinds, they initially formed a broad coalition of forces. Later, many of them formed their own political parties, so they made the transition from groups, to movements, to parties. The suffragettes were another early social movement, though they rarely formed their own parties.

In the modern world, we hear much more about 'New Social Movements'. These differ from voluntary organisations and parties in several ways. They have:

1. A different sort of political agenda insofar as they are counter-cultural, anti-politics and anti-state
2. A broader range of interests (human rights, minority groups, the environ-ment, peace) than most groups, but a narrower range than parties
3. A broader range of members than most groups, but a narrower range than the largest parties; some social movements have been called 'rainbow coali-tions' because they try to link rather disparate social groups and organisa-tions under a single political umbrella
4. A looser and more decentralised form of organisation than groups or parties – they have been described as 'networks of networks'. The 'old' organisations are hierarchical, bureaucratic and professionally run, the 'new' ones are based upon the grass-roots participation of volunteers
5. Political methods that are often innovative and unconventional, involv-ing direct political action, community involvement and sometimes protest action or even violence.

New Social Movements
Loosely knit organisations ('networks of networks') that try to influence government policy on broad issues, including the environment, nuclear energy and nuclear weapons, economic development, peace, women and minorities.

Environmental movements illustrate these points well. They often pursue a self-consciously different style of politics than conventional parties and pres-sure groups, and they have a wider agenda than most groups, as well as attract-ing a broader range of social types. Most groups appeal to specific kinds of individuals for specific kinds of activities – they are sports clubs, or choirs, or mountain walkers' clubs. Environmental movements are often networks of interests that come together as loose-knit coalitions, rather than hierarchically organised and bureaucratically centralised organisations. That is why they are called 'movements'. Environmental movements also often use unconventional political methods, including direct action, grass-roots participation and eye-catching protests.

Social movements are not new. The Chartist and the Suffragette movements of the nineteenth century were followed in the late 1950s in Britain by the Campaign for Nuclear Disarmament (CND). However, the 1960s and 1970s saw a wave of 'new' social movements concerned with the environment, peace, women's rights, nuclear power and weapons, minority and animal rights and racism. Examples include Friends of the Earth and Greenpeace, the Black Power movement in the USA, peasant and land reform movements in South America and the loose alignment of right-wing and racist groups in Europe.

Initially it seemed that these New Social Movements threatened the estab-lished order of the state, and its conventional parties and pressure groups. The causes they promoted were not always new, but the political methods they used were often direct and unconventional. But, as it turns out, 'new' social movements have quite a lot in common with 'old' social movements, political parties and groups. Each has tried to steal the other's clothes. The old have adopted some of the policy goals of the new and, in their quest for power, the new have sometimes adapted and compromised with the world by adopting more conventional and pragmatic methods. The Greens formed political parties to fight elections, and while they initially opposed the formal hierarchies of the old parties and tried to work with a rotating leadership, some gradually succumbed to the old ways of doing things and kept their leaders in power. Meanwhile, the old parties, realising which way the wind was blowing, started to adopt modified Green policies in order to head off their electoral threat.

■ Pressure groups and social movements in action

Pressure groups and social movements perform two main political functions:

- *Interest aggregation* The formation of a single policy programme from a set of rather different interests and views. Student organisations have to aggregate the interests of different students – first- and higher-degree, arts and social science and natural science, home and overseas, young and mature, wealthy and poor. Pressure groups have the important role of sorting and sifting opinion and presenting it as a single package.
- *Interest articulation* Expressing and publicising policies in order to influence government action. This is their 'voice' function, in which they try to make their views heard amid the great confusion of noise made by all groups equally concerned to stress their own point.

Groups and movements use many different methods of articulating their interests – from lobbying politicians and bureaucrats, producing pamphlets, doing research and organising petitions, to organising strikes, sit-ins, non-cooperation, rioting, violence and staging publicity events. But there are two general rules in choosing any one or combination of these methods:

- First, try to get into the policy formation process *as early as possible*, because this is when options are open, when parties have not yet taken a public stand and when government is still undecided.
- Second, to operate at the *highest possible level of government* to which you have access, because this is the best way to achieve the greatest amount of influence with the least possible expense and effort.

This, of course, is easier said than done, because groups have to take account of two sets of powerful constraints that determine how they operate in the political system and how much power and influence they have in it. The first set of constraints concerns the nature of the group and its *interests*; the second, the nature of the *political environment* they are working in.

■ Groups and issues

Some groups have a privileged 'insider' status that gives them direct access to high-level government officials. **'Insider' groups** and governments are sometimes heavily dependent upon each other and are in close and constant contact: groups want to influence policies and receive advance warning about them; governments sometimes depend upon groups for their technical information and expertise, and for their cooperation in the smooth implementation of policy (see briefing 9.1). A great deal of the business between groups and government does not involve major policy issues but technical matters and details; some groups are routinely consulted about these, but to preserve their 'insider' status, they must not disturb the relationship by making extreme demands or attacking the government in public. A professional association of doctors may

'Insider' groups
Pressure group with access to senior government officials, often recognised as theg only legitimate representatives of particular interests and

---

Briefing 9.1
International peak organisations
International NGOs such as Amnesty International and environmental groups are often regarded as key organisations in international governance, but they are only a small part of a huge number. They attract a lot of media attention but it does not mean that they are as influential or powerful as some other NGOs that work effectively without much publicity, especially those in the economic, business, health and labour areas. The following gives a flavour of the range of international NGOs, and of the breadth of their organisation in the world:

- The *World Council of Churches* has a membership of about 400 million Christians representing more than 330 churches, denominations and fellowships in 100 countries and territories (http://www.wcc-coe.org).
- The *International Confederation of Free Trade Unions* is the world's largest trade union body, with 221 affiliated organisations and 155 million members in 148 countries on five continents. It maintains close links with other international labour organisations, such as the European Trade Union Confederation (ETUC) and the International Trade Secretariats (http://www.icftu.org).
- The *Olympic movement* consists of the International Olympic Committee (IOC), sixty-five International Sports Federations, 199 National Olympic Committees, the Organising Committees for the Olympic Games, national sports associations and clubs and their athletes and other organisations recognised by the IOC (http://www.olympic.org).
- *Rotary International* is a world-wide organisation with some 1.2 million members in more than 29,000 Clubs in 160 countries (http://www.rotary.org).
- The *World Association of Girl Guides and Girl Scouts* has over 10 million members in 140 countries (http://www.wagggsworld.org). The World Scout Movement has more than 28 million members in 216 countries and territories (http://www.scout.org).
- The *Union of International Associations* is a clearing house for information about more than 44,000 international non-profit organisations (http://www.uia.org). Its list of organisations includes: The Disinfected Mail Study Circle, The International Group of Priests for Circus and Showmen of All Confessions, The European Council of Skeptical Organisations, The International Goat Association, The International Institute for Andragogy, The International Union of Private Wagon Owners' Associations, Proutist Universal, The Society of Indexers, Toy Traders of Europe, The United Elvis Presley Society and The World Association of Flower Arrangers.

often formally
incorporated into
the official
consultative
bodies.
be very concerned about a health issue and have important information that it wants to feed into government policy making circles, for example. Doctors are a prestige professional group that governments will listen to, and often there are special consultative committees to enable them to meet regularly with top health officials so that they can exchange views.

Many 'insider' groups represent business and professional interests – industrialists, farmers, doctors, bankers, food producers – which play a key role in the economy. This gives them political influence. In some countries close relations between government and private interests are promoted by similar elite backgrounds – Oxford and Cambridge University and the London clubs in Britain, the Grandes Ecoles in Paris, the Tokyo Law School and the Law and Business Schools of Harvard and Yale. In Britain and Japan, it is not uncommon for ministers and senior civil servants leaving public service to work for the very businesses and organisations which they were regulating when in office – the so-called 'revolving door' in the UK, or 'the descent from heaven' in Japan.

**'Outsider'
group**
Group with no
access to top
government
officials.
'Outsider' groups do not have this special relationship. They are excluded from close consultation because they lack bargaining power, are too critical of government, are generally unpopular, or because they prefer to be outside and independent of government. While 'insider' groups rely heavily on their close government contacts, outsider groups use other methods of protest, direct action and publicity-attracting demonstrations. One of the ironies of pressure group politics is that powerful 'insider' groups can operate most smoothly and quietly out of the public eye, while the 'outsider' groups, for all the noise of their public campaigns, are less powerful and effective: protest politics is a weapon of the less powerful. Perhaps the best-known 'outsider' protest politicians in the world were Nelson Mandela and Martin Luther King, which makes the point that protest politics can sometimes be both peaceful and successful.

■ *The nature of government*

The way pressure groups operate is strongly influenced by the nature of the political system they are dealing with, and the location of power within it.

Direct routes
So far as they can, groups start with the most powerful actors:

- *Executives* In presidential systems it is best to approach the president or a staff member, and in parliamentary systems the prime minister or cabinet. Since only a few, special groups have such high-level access, the rest must approach the less powerful points that they can reach.
- *Legislatures* Groups without access to their political executives may start with their legislature, which usually attracts a good deal of pressure group activity, especially in the USA where parties are weak, elections frequent and elected representatives are sensitive to special interest campaigns and funds.

Lobby
A popular term
Powerful groups do not need to waste time in the **lobby** of the legislative

---

Fact file 9.1

Pressure groups

- One of the first pressure groups was The Society for Effecting the Abolition of the Slave Trade, founded in 1787 in Britain by William Wilberforce, a highly effective pressure group leader (http://www.britannica.com/ebc/article?eu=407999).
- The number of registered Washington lobbyists is over 23,000 and their estimated expenditure in 1999 was $1.4 billion (http://www.opensecrets.org).
- There are about 3,750 Political Action Committees (PACs) in the USA. Most represent business, labour or ideological interests. In 1999 and 2000 they raised $604.9 million and gave most of this to chosen election candidates. The biggest spenders were The National Association of Realtors ($3.4 million), the Association of Trial Lawyers of America ($2.6 million), the American Federation of State, County, and Municipal Employees ($2.6 million), The Teamsters Union ($2.6 million), and The National Auto Dealers Association ($2.5 million).
- The European Union's Directory of Special Interest Groups lists 915 lobby groups, mainly in the sectors of agriculture (131), industry (301), services (331) and general interest (394). They range from the Association of European Fruit and Vegetable Processing Industries to the Youth Forum of the European Union (http://europa.eu.int/comm/civil_society/coneccs/index.htm).
- One the largest social movements in India is the National Campaign on Dalit Human Rights. The Dalits are the 240 million in India who are not one of the four castes – the untouchables (http://www.dalits.org).
- The Deutscher Gewerkschaftsbund (DGB) represents nearly 11 million trade unionists in Germany (http://www.dgb.de/sprachen/englisch/grundsatz.htm). It operates at the *Länder* and Federal government level in Germany, with the ETUC (http://www.etuc.org) in the European Union and with the International Confederation of Free Trade Unions on the global level (http://www.icftu.org).
- The UN has a Conference of 374 NGOs which it lists as official consultative bodies.
- The Union of International Associations estimates that the number of international NGOs grew from 176 in 1909, to 833 in 1951, 1,718 in 1972 and 42,100 in 1998 (http://www.uia.org/statistics/organizations/stybv296.php).

---

body. They have privileged contacts in committees and consultative bodies of government, and prefer to use them rather than lobbying the legislature, which is crowded with many different groups all trying to win the ear of politicians, who may well already have a clear view about their policies. Some groups choose to employ professional lobbyists (see fact file 9.1), and some 'buy' their influence by contributing to campaign funds.

- *Government departments*   It is often effective to start with the top bureaucrats in government departments, especially if the political system is blocked by weak and fragmented parties, or by conflict between the executive and legislature. It is probably also best to start with bureaucrats on technical matters because they will probably handle them in the end. Having a friend or ally who is a top public servant is exceedingly helpful, just as it is to have the 'revolving door' or the 'descent from heaven' provide a retired official with special knowledge and contacts on your side.

for pressure groups (based on the mistaken belief that pressure group representatives spend a lot of time in the 'lobbies' or ante-rooms of legislative chambers).

Briefing 9.2

A life of pressure: Peter Jenkins, a public affairs officer with the British Consumers' Association

I wish I were taking people out to lunch all the time but it's not really like that. The Consumers' Association is different from most lobbying organisations in that we are here to represent consumers' interests and we don't have large budgets for entertaining in the same way as some of the private lobbying firms.

I campaign on food and communication issues and work as part of a team made up of specialist advisers, lawyers and staff from our policy unit. Between us we form, draft and carry out strategies on a variety of issues. At any one time I might be working on BSE, GM crops, food poisoning or consumers' problems with the utility companies.

An example of the lobbying work we do would be the work we carried out in the run-up to the formation of the Food Standards Agency. The CA had long campaigned for such an agency to be put in place and once it was announced, the focus of our efforts changed. During the drafting of the White Paper we were in contact with civil servants writing the legislation; once it was published we worked in parliament to produce amendments that we felt were in the public's best interest.

Because the present government has such a large majority in the House of Commons we have found it easier to work in the Lords. It's a case of lobbying sympathetic peers, explaining what the impact of the legislation will be if it is unchanged, and persuading them to table amendments.

Sometimes it involves stalking the corridors of parliament late at night; mostly it's about knowing the right person to call, and picking up the phone.

The other side of my job is representing the organisation to the media. Part of the campaigning involves writing press releases and being on call to do radio and TV interviews. On Monday I came into work thinking I had a quiet day only to be told there was a car waiting to take me to ITN.

The thrill of the job is when you are working on a campaign that is getting MPs excited and there is the perceptible feeling that things are really happening. (Adapted from the *Guardian*, 12 May 2001)

- *State and local government* Many pressure groups deal with local matters, so their natural target is state or local government.

Indirect routes

Since many groups do not have good access to either elected or appointed government officials, they try more roundabout routes to gain influence (see briefing 9.2):

- *Political parties* Aligned groups have special, friendly connections with political parties, while others try to 'buy' influence by contributing to campaign funds (see fact file 9.1). At the same time, parties that have already taken a public stand on an issue will be hard to shift, so it is best to get in early before they have thought about the matter.
- *Public campaigns* Modern methods of advertising, desk-top publishing and computer mail shots have made public campaigns more attractive, but they are still relatively expensive, time-consuming and uncertain in their effects. There are so many groups in the political arena that it is difficult for any one of them to have a big effect, but if a group has public opinion on its side then governments are more likely to treat it with respect.

- *The mass media*   Many groups court publicity with press briefings and events (see chapter 10). News reports may be a cheaper and more effective than advertising, but the channels of mass communication are overcrowded and it is often difficult to get media attention. A big demonstration or an eye-catching publicity stunt may do the trick, but nowadays there is no shortage of these.
- *Courts*   Groups can achieve their goals through the courts, especially since they now play an increasingly important political role. The litigious nature of American society means that pressure groups are constantly in court, but in other countries the courts are a last resort, because the legal process is slow, expensive and uncertain.
- *International and multi-national government*   Pressure groups are increasingly operating at the international level lobbying bodies such as the UN and the European Union. The distinction between 'insider' and 'outsider' groups operates here as well.

Groups often use *different combinations of access points* into the political system, and they will often look for allies and build coalitions with like-minded groups. The political arena is usually so crowded that it is helpful to have other groups that help the struggle. 'Rainbow coalitions' are built upon this principle, but many pressure group campaigns are waged by organisations that come together to fight a specific matter. Sometimes this produces strange bed-fellows: militant groups of ecologists living in trees and underground tunnels have formed an alliance with conservative landowners to protect a valley against the road builders. There may be a price to pay for coalition building if partners want help with their own campaign as the cost of support. Some groups refuse to fight with others if they think they are too militant and extremist, especially if they use violence. Cooperation and coalition building helps to moderate group demands.

■ Determinants of power

It is extremely difficult to estimate the power of pressure groups, or to compare one with another, because so many factors are involved. Environmental groups seem to have been successful in recent years but they have been helped by a shift in public opinion, changes in government and media coverage of nuclear accidents, oil spills and the 'greenhouse effect'. Has government policy changed because of environmental campaigns or because of a combination of these other factors? Of course, environmental groups have themselves helped to change opinion, just as they have used their media skills to publicise environmental disasters in order to bring pressure to bear on governments. These different factors are so closely intertwined that it is virtually impossible to sort them out and say how much is due to environmental groups and how much to other factors. Group influence does seem, however, to depend on two groups of considerations – the *internal features* of groups and their issues, and the *political environment* in which they operate.

■ *Group features*

Groups can be distinguished in eight main ways:

- *Income*   Some groups are wealthy and have offices and a large staff, others are poor and rely upon a few voluntary workers. By and large, interest groups are wealthier than cause groups, because they represent the economic interests of their members, who have a strong material incentive to join and pay a subscription.
- *Membership size*   Large groups can collect membership subscriptions from many people, and then use this income to pay staff to raise more money. Nevertheless, size is not always an advantage, for small but cohesive groups can defeat large and divided ones. Some small groups are in fact remarkably wealthy.
- *Organisational advantages*   Some social groups are easier to organise than others – compare adults with children, producers with consumers, doctors with patients, the healthy with the chronically ill, professors with students, the rich with the poor, home-owners with the homeless, the employed with the unemployed.
- *Membership density and recruitment*   A group representing almost all its potential members is likely to have more influence than one representing only a small proportion of them. Professions (doctors, lawyers, dentists, musicians) often make membership of their association compulsory, so they have membership density of 100 per cent. Farmers' associations often have a high density. At the other end of the scale, organisations for the homeless rely on a few dedicated activists, most of them not themselves homeless.
- *Divided groups*   A united group is likely to have more influence than a divided one, and a group that holds the field on its own more influence than one with a rival that competes to represent the same interests. Groups that are united with a common interest are sometimes coordinated by a single '**umbrella' organisations** or 'peak association'.
- *Sanctions*   Some groups have powerful sanctions. Businesses that can move their capital abroad, professional bodies that can withdraw cooperation with the government and groups that have public sympathy and can influence voters. Other groups have weak sanctions, or none – children can't go on strike, hospital patients don't refuse treatment, the homeless can't withhold rent, the poor may not have access to lawyers. Often this boils down to how important the groups are in the economy, and their structural power within it.
- *Leadership*   A charismatic leader (Nelson Mandela, Martin Luther King) is a great asset.

'Umbrella' organisations
Associations that coordinate the activity of their member organisations.

- *The issue*   Governments and parties often have set opinions about big, controversial public issues. Many groups choose to work on policy details and technicalities.

■ *The political environment*

There are five key features of the political environment that can affect pressure group success:

- *'Insider'/'outsider' status*   'Insider' groups are more likely to be powerful than 'outsider' groups. Their access to top decision makers gives them a 'voice' and influence at high levels of the political system.
- *Public opinion*   Governments are more likely to take note of groups with strong public support. To do otherwise is to risk losing electoral support.
- *Legitimacy*   Groups representing legitimate interests in society (doctors, lawyers, teachers, businessmen, church leaders) often have more influence than marginal ones (chapter 8) (drug addicts, prostitutes, ex-criminals, minorities radical groups of many kinds).
- *Political parties*   Groups that are aligned with the party in government can have 'inside' influence – only to lose it, of course, when their party is out of office.
- *Countervailing powers*   Groups with the field to themselves are likely to be more influential than those which face opposition. Sometimes groups cancel each other out by competing on different sides of the issue (they veto each other). One theory argues that the pressure group world is a 'veto-group system', in which few groups can get what they want because other groups have a capacity to stop them encroaching on their own interests.

   It is not difficult to think of an imaginary case to illustrate the influence of group and political factors on the success of a pressure group campaign. Imagine that students are campaigning for higher maintenance grants from the government:

- The student body in most countries is quite large but since most students are not wealthy, their representative associations do not have a great deal of money, although they may have a small, experienced and enthusiastic permanent staff to organise a political campaign.
- Unfortunately, student bodies are often divided internally because they represent groups from diverse social and political backgrounds.
- Worst of all, students have few sanctions: their strikes are symbolic, they cannot threaten to move their capital investments, shut down factories or paralyse the economy. Withdrawing cooperation with the government and its officials would not have much effect.
- On the political side, student representative bodies may not be 'outsider' groups, exactly, but there are many 'insider' groups with more prestige and

power. Their image in most countries is not one that wins them much public sympathy.

- Students themselves come in all sorts of political shapes and sizes, and it is doubtful if their representative body could swing many votes.
- If it came to a battle about how limited funds should be spent on higher education it is probable that the heads of universities and professors would win, and if it came to a battle over limited funds for different public services, it is probable that doctors, businessmen, trade unionists, farmers, road builders, social workers, or pensioners would win.

■ Corporatism, para-government and tri-partism/pluralism

■ *Corporatism*

In some countries, the relationship between government and economic interest groups representing employers and workers was so closely organised within formal government structures that a special term, 'corporatist', has been invented to describe them. **Corporatism** in democratic states (sometimes called neo-, or liberal corporatism) requires:

1. A small number of hierarchically organised **'umbrella'** or **'peak' associations** to speak authoritatively for all their members.
2. That such groups are recognised, licensed or even created by the government to ensure that it deals only with a small number of dependable, official representatives.
3. A wide array of formal decision making and consultative government bodies that covers all groups and issues in the policy area.
4. An ability to produce policies that are binding on all parties, and implemented by them.

Corporatism was strongest in the economic sphere where the main interests could be coordinated:

- Trade unions agreed to limit wage and other demands in return for full employment
- Employers agreed to maintain full employment in return for industrial peace and cooperation
- The government promised low inflation and social benefits in return for economic stability and stability
- All were willing and able to impose these agreements upon their own members. They came together within formal government institutions to hammer out a compromise public policy which all accepted and stood by.

Corporatism developed in the 1970s and 1980s in west Europe as a method of managing economic growth, but tended to break down in the 1990s under the pressures of economic stagnation. Strong corporatism was found in Austria, Denmark, Luxembourg, Norway and Sweden. Weaker forms were found in

Corporatism
A way of organising public policy making involving the close cooperation of major economic interests within a formal government apparatus that is capable of concerting the main economic groups so that they can jointly formulate and implement binding policies.

Belgium, Denmark, Finland, Ireland, The Netherlands, Switzerland and West Germany.

◼ *Para-government*

In some countries, large institutional groups play the role of *para-public agencies* that provide public services with financial and other help from the state:

- The Catholic and Protestant Churches in Germany collect taxes through the state, and provide social services in return.
- Scandinavian housing associations are neither public nor private, but para-public organisations that cooperate closely with public authorities and receive money from them.
- Farmers, business organisations, professional associations, and churches are involved in close cooperation with the state in Germany and Scandinavia, in order to resolve conflict, regulate society and provide services.

The result is an area of government that is neither purely private nor public, but a mixture of both. The problem is that groups not in the system – students, immigrants, peace and anti-nuclear campaigners and (initially) the Greens, as well as extremist right-wing and racist organisations – are excluded from these circles of power, and hence may explode into direct action in order to make their voice heard. Some student and worker protest movements have referred to themselves as 'extra-parliamentary opposition' to stress the point that they are outside the formal circles of power.

◼ *Tri-partism/pluralism*

Other countries in the West, with neither corporatist groups nor structures, use a much less centralised and coordinated system of economic policy making known as **tri-partism**. Here, the three corners of the 'economic triangle' cooperate in a much looser manner through a variety of different formal and semi-formal committees, consultative bodies and meetings. In such systems it makes more sense to talk about **policy communities** or **policy networks** than about corporatism. France, Italy, Japan and the UK are examples. Canada, India, New Zealand and the USA, tend to be even less centralised and coordinated, and more pluralist and open in their approach. Nonetheless, the relationships between government and private interest groups in America is sometimes so close that political scientists talk of the **'iron triangles'** formed by executive agencies, congressional sub-committees and pressure groups. For example, the farming lobby in the USA is wealthy and well organised and has close intimate working relations with government policy makers.

◼ **International NGOs**

Pressure groups have never been confined to domestic politics, but international organisations are now more visible and active than ever before. Barely a week passes without a major news story that involves Amnesty International,

Tri-partism
A looser and less centralised system of decision making than corporatism involving close government consultation – often with business and trade union organisations.

Policy communities
Small, stable and consensual groupings of government officials and pressure group representatives that form around particular issue areas.

Policy networks
Compared with policy communities, policy networks are larger, looser (and sometimes more conflictual) networks that gather around a policy area.

Greenpeace, Médecins Sans Frontières, Transparency International, or the Red Cross. These organisations are known as **non-governmental organisations**, or by the abbreviation 'NGOs' (see chapter 2) and form an increasingly dense network alongside the growing number of agencies of international governance such as the OECD, UN and WTO. As with domestic pressure groups the international NGOs we hear most about are not necessarily the most powerful. Environmental groups and Amnesty International are certainly not weak, but they can rarely match the power of business organisations. We shall return to them in chapter 17 of the book.

Groups, pressure groups and democracy

'Iron triangles'
The close, three-sided working relationship developed between (1) government departments and ministries, (2) pressure groups and (3) politicians, that makes public policy in a given area.

Freedom of assembly and association are essential parts of any democratic system, and all groups have a right to be heard and to try to influence public policy in a peaceful manner. Besides articulating demands (the *input function*) in the open political arena, they also play an indispensable role within government itself on official consultative committees, working parties, advisory groups and commissions. Most political systems have an elaborate array of these, and rely heavily on groups for advice, information, specialist expertise and help with implementing policies. Groups also have an *output function* in producing services for their members and the general public. They deliver meals to the ill and the old, run community centres, raise money for schools, hospitals and overseas aid, provide sports facilities and organise exhibitions. In some countries they run, with government support and money, schools, hospitals and a wide variety of social services.

Pluralist democracy
The theory arguing that political decisions are the outcome of the conflict and competition between many different groups.

For these reasons groups play a central part in **pluralist democracy**, which is based on free competition between a plurality of organised interests and on supportive relations between groups and government. The opposite of pluralist society is **mass society**, which has a weak foundation of organised groups and which, it is said, is particularly susceptible to extremist politics because the population is not well organised into groups that can defend their interests.

Mass society
A society without a plurality of organised social groups and interests, whose mass of isolated and uprooted individuals are not integrated into the community and

At the same time, pressure groups can also present a threat to democracy. They are often not particularly democratic internally, and they represent the narrow sectional interests of their organisation not the public interest. If they become too powerful, and if they get too close to the top levels of government, they may 'capture' and control government policy in their own interests. This is the wrong way round: governments are supposed to control private groups in the public interest (see controversy 9.1). Policy areas said to be under private control include agriculture (e.g. genetically modified (GM) crops), health (e.g. smoking for much of the twentieth century), the defence industry (e.g. arms manufacturers), business (e.g. finance capital, manufacturing and commerce).

It seems, then, that a successful pluralist democracy depends on a balance of power between government and groups. Too much pressure group power results in private interests running government, too little in autocratic government that pays insufficient attention to legitimate citizen demands. It is a matter of opinion where one draws the line between 'too much' and 'too little'.

Controversy 9.1

Do pressure groups sustain or undermine democracy?

■ Sustain

- Groups perform the essential democratic functions of aggregating and articulating public opinion.
- Voluntary organisations are indispensable ways of organising minority interests, and most groups are minority groups.
- Voluntary associations are the 'free schools of democracy', teaching people political and organisational skills.
- Groups are recruiting grounds for local and national political leaders.
- Groups encourage the politics of accommodation, understanding and compromise by bringing together different people with different backgrounds and opinions in the same organisation.
- Overlapping and interlocking networks of organisations tie society together, counteracting internal divisions.
- Groups give people a sense of belonging, community, and purpose.
- Groups act as channels of communication between citizens, and between citizens and government.
- Groups provide a network of organisations outside and independent of government. They are a ready-made organisational basis for mobilising public opinion against unpopular government action.
- Groups provide governments with technical information and specialist knowledge, and can help implement public policy efficiently and effectively.
- Mass societies are prone to extremist politics and totalitarian political movements.

■ Undermine

- As narrow, sectional interests they may conspire against the public interest.
- Groups can be exclusive, keeping out some sections of the population and not representing their views (e.g. women, minorities). Corporatism and policy communities are also exclusive and work with a limited number of groups.
- Private organisations are often oligarchical, representing the interests of only a few leaders, not their members.
- Pressure groups are responsible only to their own members, but governments are responsible to the whole population. If pressure groups have too much power, then representative and responsible government will have too little.
- Close cooperation between groups and government risks two dangers. (1) Groups may become too 'domesticated', losing their critical independence of government. (2) Governments may be 'captured' by private interests, losing their critical independence and accountability to the public interest.
- Too many powerful groups making too many powerful demands on government may result in government overload and hyper-pluralism.
- Groups tend to fragment public policy, preventing governments developing coherent policies.

who are
therefore
vulnerable to the
appeals of
extremist and
anti-democratic
elites.

■ Theories of voluntary organisations

The very large body of literature on groups in politics tends to fall into one of three major theoretical camps – pluralist theory, Marxist/elitist theory and social capital/civil society theory.

■ *Pluralism*

Pluralists argue that:

- Most political issues are fought over by *competing groups*. Rarely is one of them so powerful that it can get its own way. Most have to compromise but they usually get something they want, even if it is only to prevent other groups encroaching on their interests.
- All groups have some *resources* to fight their political battles – money, numbers, popularity, 'insider' status, leadership skills, popular support, votes. Resources are not distributed equally, but nor are they distributed with cumulative inequality: all groups have some resources; none has all of them: no group is powerless; no group is all-powerful.
- Power is fragmented, fluid, or 'mercurial'. There is no fixed power structure or power elite, but *different configurations of shifting coalitions and power* according to the issue and the circumstances. Today's winners will be tomorrow's losers, and vice versa.
- Groups that fail in one political arena (national government) may be *successful in others* (local government, the courts, international arenas).
- Groups often look for *political allies*, which obliges them to compromise and cooperate with others.
- Groups cannot always get what they want, but they can often *veto* other groups' proposals they do not like.
- The main exponent of pluralist theory, Robert Dahl, argues that pluralist democracy does not work in a perfect 'textbook' manner, but it works reasonably well, 'warts and all'.

■ *Marxist/elitist theory*

Pluralist theory is opposed by Marxist and elitist theories, which claim that the pressure group system undermines democracy:

- The 'iron law of oligarchy' (chapter 12) means that groups are controlled by a *few, unrepresentative leaders*, because they are the people with the skill, knowledge and experience to run them, and because leaders make sure they control group resources and the means of communication.
- The group world is dominated by *educated, wealthy, and upper-class 'joiners'*. Survey research shows that people of higher social and economic status are more likely to join voluntary associations, and that the leaders of such associations are generally dominated by the upper strata.

- Some social groups are *weakly organised*, or largely unorganised – the very poor, children, the homeless, the mentally and physically ill, minority groups.
- Group resources are distributed with *cumulative inequality*. The class-based nature of the group world ensures that middle-class groups have most of the resources necessary to fight political battles.
- Groups with *structural power* in the economy (especially business interests) are particularly powerful.
- Groups fight within a political structure that is systematically loaded in favour of *middle- and upper-class interests*. Government is not a neutral 'referee' in the group battle, but part of a system that favours the wealthy and well organised.
- The group world reflects and reinforces the *power structure* in which wealthy interests with structural power in the economy dominate the political system.
- Some elite theorists argue that a **'military–industrial complex'** (see p. 302) controls key decisions, leaving less important issues to pluralist competition.

■ Social capital and civil society theory

Social capital theory has a lot in common with pluralist theory. Drawing on Alexis de Tocqueville's influential study of *Democracy in America* (1831), and on modern social science evidence, the American political scientist Robert Putnam argues that:

- Voluntary associations – particularly 'bridging' associations that bring different social groups together – are crucial for the development of *democratic attitudes*, such as trust, reciprocity and satisfaction with democracy, and for democratic behaviour, such as civic engagement, voting and membership of parties. The social trust and the personal and organisational networks that groups create are vital for the social capital on which democracy rests.
- Voluntary organisations teach the *political skills* of a democracy – how to organise, how to run meetings, how to compromise and how to work and cooperate with others for collective goals.
- Not all social organisations generate *'good' social capital* that is beneficial to society as a whole. The Italian mafia, for example, generates 'bad' social capital that is of benefit only for the mafia.
- Putnam's research on Italy and the USA suggests that *economic success and democratic stability* is rooted in networks of voluntary associations. Democratic malaise (falling election turnout and party membership, declining trust in politicians and government institutions, cheating on taxes, political fear and cynicism) is caused by a decline in the voluntary organisations that generate social capital.

Among the many possible causes of the collapse of civic engagement in the USA, television seems to be important because it pulls people out of their

'Military–industrial complex'
The close and powerful alliance of government, business and military interests that is said to run capitalist societies.

Social capital
The features of society such as trust, social norms and social networks, that improve social and governmental efficiency by encouraging cooperation and collective action.

Alexis de Tocqueville (1805–59)

Alexis de Tocqueville, *Democracy in America* (1831)

community and isolates them in their homes. TV is said to be responsible for many of the signs of civic and political malaise – distrust, fear, cynicism, alienation, apathy, low political interest and understanding.

Social capital theory has aroused a great deal of interest and controversy. Its critics claim that:

- The definition and treatment of the concept of social capital is vague and all-inclusive.
- Some survey evidence shows that voluntary organisations have rather little effect on political attitudes and behaviour. In any case, which is cause and which is effect?
- Some research suggests that television is not particularly responsible for eroding social capital – on the contrary, television news and current affairs programmes can inform and mobilise people.
- Social capital theory sometimes assumes a 'bottom-up' process in which individuals who join organisations help to create a culture of civic engagement and democratic participation. A 'top-down' approach argues that governments help to create the conditions in which both voluntary organisations and a climate of trust can flourish.

Civil society
That arena of social life outside the state and the family (i.e. mainly voluntary organisations and civic associations) that permits individuals to associate freely and independently of state regulation.

Writing on **civil society** has much in common with pluralist and social capital theory. It argues that:

- *Strong and vibrant private organisations* are essential both for a satisfying social life, and as a counter-balance to the power of the state.
- Transition to democracy depends on building *autonomous, private organisations* and creating a culture and tradition to sustain them, especially in societies where such organisations have been controlled or suppressed by the state.
- So far, civil society in central and eastern Europe has tended to develop in a different way from western pluralism, in that organisations have formed most readily around nationalist, ethnic and religious interests that have become a force for *division and conflict*, rather than compromise and integration.

▨ Summary

This chapter has dealt with the key modern pressure groups and social movements. It argues that:

- The importance of the dense network of voluntary organisations as the social basis of pluralist democracy. Politically active groups mediate between citizens and government by aggregating and articulating political interests. Politically inactive groups help to integrate and stabilise society, permitting democratic government to operate effectively.

- Although a vibrant group life is essential for democracy, groups that are too strong are a threat to it. They can 'capture' policy areas and make public decisions that favour their private interests. Strong group pressures from every side may also cause **hyper-pluralism** and overloaded government.
- The ways in which pressure groups work and the influence they exercise are determined by the nature of the groups, their issue(s) and the political and governmental environment in which they operate.
- The difficulties of trying to establish how powerful groups are, because there are usually many factors at work at the same time.
- In most countries, groups have a close relationship with government, ranging from highly formalised and institutionalised corporatist arrangements, to para-government systems, the 'iron triangles' and tight policy communities of tri-partite politics and to the more open policy networks of the most pluralist systems.
- There are arguments both for and against pluralist, Marxist and elitist, social capital and civil society theories of pressure groups politics.

Hyper-pluralism
A state of affairs in which too many powerful groups make too many demands on government, causing overload and ungovernability.

Further reading

Graham K. Wilson, *Interest Groups* (Oxford: Blackwell, 1990), is a good introduction to the comparative approach to the subject, and Todd Landman, *Issues and Methods in Comparative Politics* (London: Routledge, 2000), contains an excellent summary of some two dozen studies of social movements (chapters 5 and 6). Two other useful books on comparative pressure group politics are Jeremy Richardson (ed.), *Pressure Groups* (Oxford: Oxford University Press, 1993) and Clive S. Thomas (ed.), *First World Interest Groups: A Comparative Perspective* (Westport, CT: Greenwood Press, 1993). The classic studies of social capital are two by Robert Putnam, *Making Democracy Work: Civic Traditions in Modern Italy* (Princeton: Princeton University Press, 1993) and *Bowling Alone: The Collapse and Revival of American Community* (New York: Simon & Schuster, 2000).

Websites

http://www.politicalresources.net/	Lists organisations in many countries, and has a long list of international organisations.
http://www.uia.org/index.html	The Union of International Associations lists international organisations.
http://www.library.ubc.ca/poli/cpwebint.html	Website for Canadian groups with many links to pressure/interest groups and lobbying, research institutes and think tanks, populism/social movements and bibliographic databases.
http://www.psr.keele.ac.uk/parties.htm	Website with many links to international and national parties, interest groups and social movements.
http://www.pscw.uva.nl/sociosite/TOPICS/Activism.html	Social science information system based at the University of Amsterdam that provides a list of sites concerned with activism, collective action, social movements and utopianism.

Projects

1. Each student in the group should take a daily paper of their own country and read it for a few days for news items mentioning voluntary organisations and pressure groups. Classify the groups according to whether they
   are interest/cause, 'insider'/'outsider', peak organisations, episodic/fire brigade,
   aligned/non-aligned. What, if anything, does this tell you about the likely power
   of the groups?

2. Voluntary organisations and pressure groups often have good websites. Search
   the websites in your country for examples of, say, a dozen groups (or for some
   of the groups mentioned in this chapter), and see what you can find out about
   the political activity or inactivity of the groups, how they operate and with
   what success.

3. Local politicians are often closely associated with local voluntary associations.
   Choose either a few local politicians in your area, or a few local organisations,
   and try to find out how they are linked. What are the advantages and disadvantages of such links?

10   The mass media

The role of the mass media in modern democracy is one of the most controversial topics in politics. Politicians are usually locked in a 'love–hate' relationship with the political media, and the media seem to play an ever-larger part in political life. Political scientists dispute whether the mass media are powerful or not, and whether their impact on politics is good or bad for democracy:

- On the one hand, the mass media are supposed to play a crucial role in supplying citizens with a full and fair account of the news and a wide range of political opinion about it.
- On the other hand, the media are often criticised for being systematically biased politically, and for their growing but unaccountable power.

In theory, a free press and television should be the watchdogs of democratic politics; in practice, some analysts believe they are as much a threat to democratic government as a protector of it.

The dilemmas posed by the modern media raise all sorts of political problems. What is the proper role of the media in democracy, and do they perform in the appropriate manner? Given their political importance, how should they be organised? They should certainly not come under the control of government because that would be undemocratic, and this leaves two main alternatives:

- They could come under the regulation of public bodies not controlled by the government, to keep them accountable and responsible to the general public
- Or they could be constrained only by the economic forces of the market.

To what extent are the mass media pluralist – in the hands of many owners who communicate a wide range of political opinion – or are they increasingly under the control of a few conservative media moguls and MNCs? Do the mass media wield great influence over public opinion and the fate of political leaders, or are they relatively weak because market forces oblige them to follow public opinion rather than mould it? What impact will the new electronic media play in politics, and will they hasten the trend towards globalisation?

The five major topics in this chapter are:

- The mass media and democracy
- Regulating the media
- Ownership and control
- The impact of the new media technology
- Theories of the mass media.

■ The mass media and democracy

The mass media are supposed to play a vital role in a democracy. The great majority of us rely almost entirely on them for political news and opinion, and the role we are able to play as citizens depends heavily on the fairness, accuracy and balance of the news we get. We cannot make sensible judgements about politics if we are fed a diet of biased, partial and inaccurate news, and if the range of political opinion expressed in the media is narrow and shallow. This means that the news media should provide citizens with a full and fair account of the news and a wide variety of political opinion about it. If democracy is founded on the peaceful struggle between competing interests and ideas, then we all need full information about these interests and ideas in order to make up our mind about the political issues of the day.

In the same way that the political system should be pluralist – permitting the competition of many political interests and groups – so also should the media be pluralist, reporting a full range of political opinion and interpreting the news from a variety of political standpoints. In turn, this means that the political media must not be controlled by governments, nor must they be dominated by a narrow set of commercial or social interests that presents only one political position. The news media should not only be accurate in their reporting of the news, but open and pluralist in their presentation of opinion about it.

The importance of the media is magnified by the fact that they are not just channels of communication that simply convey news, but *major political players*:

- There is so much news in the world that the media must *choose* what to report and what not to report, and what to make the headline article or tuck away on the back page.
- The news media *help to shape the news*. They want to influence the course of public affairs, not merely report them. In some countries, they take up strong political positions on issues, they support this or that party and they attack or defend this or that political leader. In others, their partisanship is more muted, but still present.
- The mass media are important *socialising agents* that have an impact on how people think and behave politically.
- The mass media, some claim, are *replacing parties* as the main means of informing and mobilising citizens (see chapter 12).
- The mass media are even said to be *replacing legislatures* as the main arena of political debate (see chapter 6) so that we are now living in 'teledemocracies'.

None of this is made any easier by the fact that the mass media would face contradictory dilemmas and demands even if they operated in a perfectly pluralist fashion:

- Democracy requires that citizens are provided with a *comprehensive coverage* of the political news, but the evidence suggests that many are bored by this and would rather watch films or game shows, or read gossip and sports columns.
- The news should be *scrupulously accurate*, but it is extremely difficult to achieve high standards, given increasingly rushed news deadlines.
- The news media must *choose* what to report, and what to ignore. What is important and, what is not, is a contested matter.
- The media must offer news and opinion – facts and judgements about the facts. The news should be detached and neutral, but opinion is engaged and subjective. How can the political media be both? The usual answer is that the media should separate *facts* (the news) from *opinion* (editorial and opinion pieces), but this is either difficult or impossible, depending on whether you think there can be objective reporting or not.
- The news media must resist the pressures of **spin-doctors** who work for governments, parties and groups, and try to get the media to report their views. It is quicker, easier and cheaper to rely on their nicely packaged press releases than to delve into issues and probe behind the spin-doctors' version of them.
- The mass media should be critical of politicians, when they feel it necessary, but they are often criticised by politicians for not being 'fair and impartial'. The problem is that journalists may feel that being 'fair and impartial' means *getting to the truth of the matter*, while politicians feel that it means simply reporting accurately and fully what they say.

Spin-doctors
Public relations specialist employed to put the best possible light on news about their clients. Often used in political life to imply attempts to manipulate the news.

In sum, this section shows that the mass media are very important in democratic politics, but that their role is riddled with dilemmas, contradictions and problems. Individuals depend upon the fairness, impartiality and accuracy of the news in order to play their role as informed citizens in a democracy. At the same time, the mass media do not, and cannot, merely report news. They have to decide what it is – and, besides, many newspaper and TV stations want to be a power in the land and *influence* politics, not just report them. They are active players in politics, and major ones at that, not just passive conveyors of political information. Their central part in democratic politics raises the question of how they should be organised to best play their role. Should they be controlled or regulated in the public interest, or should they be left to run themselves as they think best?

Regulating the media

The public service model

Public service model
The system of granting broadcasting licences to public bodies, usually supported by public funds, for use in the public interest rather than for profit.

There are two main answers to the question of how to organise the mass media. One recommends a **public service model** for the electronic media, the other a market model for all mass mediums, whether electronic or not. The merits of the public service and market models are a hotly debated topic in politics (see controversy 10.1).

The media market has long been recognised as divided between the print and the electronic media. The *print media* consist of newspapers, journals, and magazines while the *electronic media* cover radio, television and the Web. In principle, anyone can publish a paper, magazine, or newsletter (many student organisations do), and it is getting easier and easier to do so as desk-top publishing becomes faster and cheaper. Electronic communication is different. Until recently, broadcasting frequencies for radio and television were limited by **spectrum scarcity**. Spectrum scarcity, in turn, meant that radio and TV broadcasting was a natural monopoly or oligopoly, and since broadcasting waves were a scarce public asset of great public importance it was argued that they should be regulated in the public interest. Consequently, in the early days of radio and TV, most democracies controlled and regulated broadcasting according to the public service model. This has six main characteristics:

Spectrum scarcity
The shortage of terrestrial broadcasting frequencies for radio and TV, which meant that there could be only a few channels.

Market regulation
The regulation of the media market by public bodies.

1. *Market regulation*   Spectrum scarcity makes a competitive market in electronic broadcasting impossible, so the state set up **market regulation** for radio and TV, usually by giving broadcasting licenses to organisations that are required to operate under public interest rules.

2. *Content regulation*   When spectrum scarcity meant that there were only a few radio and TV stations, it was thought necessary to regulate not just the market, but also the content of public broadcasting. Since there were only a few radio and TV stations, and since they operated under licences issued by public bodies, broadcasters were required to abide by **content regulation** – public interest rules about what they broadcast. In terms of politics this meant a full, fair and impartial treatment of the news and

Controversy 10.1

Public service versus commercial media?

■ Public service

- The market does not ensure that truth will prevail, or that the best ideas will survive, only that popular demand is satisfied.
- News and political opinion is not a commodity, like soap powder, or something that can be road-tested, like motor cars. It is not subject to the same laws of supply and demand as consumer durables or commercial services.
- Only regulation in the public interest can ensure balanced, accurate, and impartial news reporting. To leave the news media to the market is to hand it over to a few multi-millionaire media moguls, or to MNCs that are often right-wing, resulting in strong and systematic media bias.
- The dangers of state control of the media can be, and have been, avoided by using regulators that are not controlled by government or the state (QUANGOs, see below).
- Bad media drive out the good, or force the good to adopt low standards. Commercial news reporting is often of a low standard (tabloid newspapers and 'tabloid TV'). TV news is often poor in the most commercial countries (e.g. the USA), and best in those that have retained important elements of public service broadcasting (Germany, Scandinavia). The amount of 'hard news' on American TV has fallen, commercial pressures have cut budgets for news programmes, and there is little coverage of international politics.
- The state must step in to exercise market and content regulation where market failure or spectrum scarcity results in oligopoly or monopoly.

■ Market model

- The public service model stifles innovation and is patronising – it gives the public what broadcasters think they need, rather than what they want.
- Whatever their faults, the commercial forces of the market are better than government or independent regulation of the media.
- The end of spectrum scarcity means that the electronic media market is the same as that of the print media, and should be subject to the same regulatory principles – minimal content regulation and market regulation only to avoid market failure.
- Regulation of the political media is not consistent with free speech. Regulation by agencies that are theoretically independent of government merely means 'backdoor regulation' by government, if only because it controls funds for public broadcasting.
- Low standards of journalism and news reporting are better than government control, regulation, or manipulation of the mass media.
- Market competition ensures that all main bodies of opinion will get a hearing, and that there will be free competition of ideas.

Content regulation
Regulation of the content of the media by public bodies in the public interest.

QUANGOs
Organisations that are partially or wholly funded by the government to perform public service functions but not under direct government control.

shared time for the political parties, especially at election time, so that all sides were given an equal hearing.

3. *Self-regulation, or regulation by QUANGOs* If public broadcasting agencies were to avoid the danger of state regulation of the news, they should be self-regulating or regulated by public bodies that are independent of government. Such bodies, known as '**QUANGOs**', operate at 'arm's length' from government.

4. *Public funding* Public service broadcasting is funded, partially or wholly, by public funds, and is not dependent upon profit.

5. *Education, information and entertainment* Public service broadcasting involves a wide range of programmes, including news and current affairs and educational and cultural programmes, as well as entertainment. It serves the public interest, rather than responding to market forces.

6. *National broadcasting* The function of public broadcasting is to serve the nation, including its minorities (linguistic, cultural and regional) and to serve as a focus for national identity. It works best within states rather than over the global broadcasting system.

Broadly speaking, the public service model of radio and TV operated in many western democracies from the start of radio broadcasting in the 1920s up to the 1970s.

■ *The market model*

The print media, in contrast to radio and TV under spectrum scarcity, are usually subject to market regulation only when there was a danger of forming an oligopoly or monopoly. Newspapers in some countries are subsidised or protected by the state (see briefing 10.1) but in the great majority they are wholly commercial enterprises. The reason is that the print media are thought to be no different from any other kind of competitive commercial market, which means that they should operate without public regulation, except in

---

Briefing 10.1

Newspaper subsidies in Norway

Daily newspapers are considered an essential commodity in Norway, in their contribution not only to the workings of democracy but also to cultural life. In relation to its population, Norway probably has Europe's highest number of dailies, with each town, as well as more sparsely settled districts, provided with a local paper.

In order to sustain such a press structure, Norway has developed a resource-consuming system of public support, in the form of subsidies towards paper, government advertising, direct grants, loan arrangements and cheaper distribution. Certain newspapers may receive annual subsidies of up to 20 million Norwegian Kroner. In addition, the Norwegian daily press is exempt from VAT. It has been calculated that subsidies to the press as a whole account for about 20 per cent of all newspaper income. (http://www.reisenett.no/norway/facts/culture_science/culture_under_int_pressure.html)

cases of market failure. In these circumstances, a monopolies board or commission is entitled to intervene in order to establish a competitive market. Similarly, since the print media are thought to be open and competitive, their political content should also be unregulated, partly because there is no obvious need for content regulation, as there is for radio and TV under spectrum scarcity, and partly because of the principle of free speech (freedom of the press). The market model therefore recognises some need for market regulation to guarantee market competition but sees little or no need for political content regulation.

Since the 1980s, however, the distinction between the print and electronic media has broken down. New broadcasting technology has effectively ended spectrum scarcity. There are now many different national and local radio stations, an increasing number of terrestrial TV channels and a rapid growth of cable and satellite channels. If one adds to this the new forms of communication in the shape of videos, DVDs, e-mail, the Net and text messaging, then the electronic media market is increasingly pluralist and competitive. There is, so the argument goes, no longer any need for the market and content regulation of the old spectrum scarcity days. In principle, it is claimed, the market for news and political opinion is no different from that for washing powder or motor cars. News is a commodity like any other and should be produced and consumed, so far as possible, according to unregulated market forces. Indeed, increasingly global broadcasting makes it more and more difficult for states even to attempt such regulation. How can states regulate satellite TV or the Internet?

Technological change has resulted in a rapid shift towards the organisation of the mass media according to market principles. This means that the news media are increasingly driven by the commercial pressures of profit. Many commercial radio and TV stations have been created and some of the old public services stations privatised. The electronic media have joined the print media in being largely unregulated so far as both market and content are concerned.

In many countries, however, this has resulted not in the wholesale adoption of the market model but in a mixed model that combines increasingly commercial principles with some forms of public service funding and regulation (see fact file 10.1). The mixed model applies mainly to electronic media, with the print media left largely to the market. Even in the most commercial systems, however, there is still a fair amount of public regulation, which takes two main forms:

1. *Regulation to ensure market competition* *Cross-media ownership* is often restricted, parts of the mass communications system thought to be essential to national interest are kept in national hands and attempts are made to prevent monopolies and oligopolies. The rules are being progressively relaxed because of economic forces.
2. *Content regulation* Some public service channels are required to observe strict rules to ensure political fairness and balance, and some commercial

---

Fact file 10.1

Public service and market media

■ Public service broadcasting

- Public service broadcasting characterised much of western Europe up till the 1960s, and is still comparatively strong in Austria, Denmark, Finland, Hungary, Norway, Sweden and Switzerland.
- The job of regulating the media is carried out by such bodies as the Federal Cartel Office in Germany, the Monopolies Commission and OFCOM (Office of Communications) in Britain and the Federal Communications Commission in the USA.
- In France and Italy, parties and the government have had considerable direct influence over the public media. In Germany, public broadcasting is in the hands of the *Länder* (to avoid the dangers of a national propaganda machine of a pre-war Nazi kind), in Belgium it is divided between the Flemish and French communities and in The Netherlands it is apportioned between the main social and religious 'pillars' of society.

■ Commercial broadcasting

- Britain introduced commercial TV in 1955, and commercial radio was legalised in 1971. This was soon followed by waves of commercialisation across the rest of west Europe. By 1990, there were more commercial TV channels than public ones.
- TV is largely privatised in Belgium, Greece, Japan, The Netherlands, Portugal, Switzerland, Turkey and the USA.
- The Greek broadcasting system was deregulated and privatised in the late 1980s, when its two TV channels and four radio stations were state-owned. Now it has 158 private TV channels and 1,200 private radio stations.
- In most central and east european countries, the old state media monopolies have been abolished and TV is either privatised (e.g. the Czech Republic) or a public–private model (e.g. Poland), or public (e.g. Hungary). Some companies have been sold to western multi-media conglomerates (Bertelsmann, News Corp, Springer and Time Warner), but some are in the hands of ex-communists, and some are still under heavy government influence.

---

channels follow the same rules. There is still a lot of content regulation over things such as *cigarette advertising*, *pornography* and the amount, content, and distribution of *advertising*.

If the media market was, indeed, competitive, as the market model supposes, we might leave this part of the story happily at this point. Unfortunately, however, there is a very large fly in the ointment. Increasingly, the commercial mass media are moving towards greater *concentration of ownership and control* in a few oligopolistic hands.

■ Ownership and control

Since the 1950s, the mass media market has developed in six related ways, with far-reaching implications for the workings of democratic government:

1. *Fragmentation of specialist media markets* Modern technology has made it possible for *small, niche media* to become increasingly specialised and varied. Local TV and radio, satellite and cable broadcasting, desk-top publishing, and the Web have made it possible to tap into ever-smaller and more specialised markets. A look at the magazines for sale in a high street shop will show how many specialised products there are.

2. *Concentration of ownership and control of the mass market* Modern technology has made it possible for the mass media to reach larger and wider audiences around the globe but this, in turn, has vastly increased the capital costs of production and distribution. In this respect, the mass communications business is like other industries that grow in size and costs. The motor industry, for example, is moving towards a few major global producers of 'world cars', which will force even huge companies (Daimler Benz and Chrysler) to merge to be able to compete. So it is with the mass media. Their history is one of mergers and takeovers, increasing concentration of ownership and control, to the point where pluralist and competitive markets have been replaced by a small number of *giant media empires*.

3. *Multi-media conglomeration* Many media companies collect together many different media businesses that span the range of publishing, music, films, radio, TV and the Net. This is known as **cross-media ownership** or **multi-media conglomeration** (see below).

4. *Horizontal and vertical integration* Conglomeration entails the *vertical integration* of the communications industry, so that the same company controls all aspects of the financing, production, distribution, and marketing of its products. It also means companies *move sideways* into closely related industries. Film, music, video, DVD, radio, newspaper, the Web, and magazine businesses feed off each other economically, so media companies increasingly stretch to cover them all. They also expand to cover spin-off businesses such as theme parks, entertainment and leisure centres, professional sports clubs and chains of shops.

5. *The integration of the media with other business activities* There is nothing new about a few media moguls dominating press or TV, but in the past they have usually confined their interests to the communications business. Multi-media conglomerates are now increasingly incorporated into a wide range of industrial and commercial activities, making it difficult to distinguish between the mass communications business and *'big business' in general*.

6. *Internationalisation* Communications technology has produced a *borderless world*. Media conglomerates are no longer limited to countries or continents, but span the whole globe.

Cross-media ownership
When the same person or company has financial interests in different branches of mass communication – e.g. when they own a newspaper and a TV channel, or a publishing house and TV network.

Briefing 10.2

Mass media ownership: the case of Time Warner

When the publishing and film company Time Warner merged with the internet company America On Line (AOL) in 2000, it marked the fusion of the 'old' media and the 'new' and the creation of the largest communications corporation in the world. With revenues of close to $40 billion, the company has interests in films, music, publishing, television, the internet, sports, leisure and entertainment and other commercial holdings across the globe. Its media interests (some in association with other companies) include:

Magazines

More than sixty-five magazines with almost 300 million readers including *Time, People, MAD, Sports Illustrated, Golf Magazine, Yachting Magazine, Money, Entertainment Weekly, In Style, Fortune, Asiaweek, Popular Science* and The Health Publishing Group and IPC (a large magazine publisher in the UK)

Television

Wholly- or partly-owned channels in the USA, Europe, Asia and Latin America: Warner Bros, HBO, Cinemax, CBS, TNT, Cartoon Network, Turner Classics, CNN

Cable

HBO, CNN, Court TV and Time Warner

Internet

America On Line, CompuServe, Netscape, ICQ, Spinner, Winamp

Films

Warner Bros, Hanna-Barbera Cartoons, The Warner Channel (on five continents), Warner Theaters (in twelve countries), the library of MGM, RKO, and pre-1960 Warner films

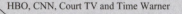

TIME WARNER

Sports

Atlanta Braves, Atlanta Hawks, Goodwill games, Phillips Arena

Music

More than 200 labels in fifty-four countries, including Warner Bros., Reprise, Elektra, Rhino, Atlantic, MCM, Nonesuch and music publishing, packaging and distributing companies

Books

Publishing houses including Warner Books, Time-Life, Book-of-the-Month Club, Little Brown

Theme parks

Warner Bros. Movie World Theme Park, Warner Bros. Recreational Enterprises

Other

Time Warner Telecom, Sportsline Radio, Studio Stores, iAmaze, Streetmail, DC Comics License Rights

Derived from http://www.cjr.org/tools/owners, http://www.fair.org/extra/9711/gmg.html; http://www.thenation.com/special/bigten.html.

These six interwoven trends are illustrated in briefing 10.2, which provides information about Time Warner, the world's largest communications conglomerate. Less detailed information about smaller media companies is in briefing 10.3. A different view of the same concentration of ownership and control is presented in briefing 10.4, which outlines the political and economic activities of Globo, the largest media company in Brazil.

There are two main democratic dangers to increasing global concentration of ownership and control:

Briefing 10.3
Global communications corporations

Much of what we see, hear, or read in the mass communications media is produced and provided by only a few gargantuan multi-media, multi-national media **conglomerates** (see below). Time Warner is the largest in the world (see Briefing 10.2), but others have huge interests in the communications industry, either alone or jointly with other companies. Many of the largest corporations are joint ventures (JVs). The following are among the largest after Time Warner:

- **General Electric** $130 billion revenues. Twenty-eight TV stations and networks in the USA, Europe and Latin America (including NBC and CNBC); TV production and programming; twelve film companies (Universal Pictures); leisure and entertainment in the USA and Europe; sports (New York Knicks, New York Rangers, Madison Square Garden); four large film production and distribution companies with rights to 4,000 films and 40,000 TV episodes; military production (F-16 fighter, Abrams tank, Apache helicopter, U2 bomber); consumer and commercial finance companies in thirty-five countries.
- **AT&T Corporation** $66 billion revenues. Television stations and networks; TV distribution in 175 countries; cable TV; forty-three radio stations; music; cell phones; theme parks.
- **Sony** $54 billion revenues. Financial interests in television networks (in India, Japan, Latin America, Spain and the USA) and eight TV stations; film production and distribution companies (Columbia Pictures); music (including Columbia, Epic and Sony) and recording studios; internet services; electronics equipment, games, tapes, disks; insurance and credit financing; shops.
- **Liberty Media** A spin-off from AT&T in 2001, this company has assets of $42 billion. Interests in TV networks (Discovery, Animal Planet, Fox International Sports, TV Guide Channel and in eight cable and satellite systems); fourteen TV stations; the largest cable operator in Japan and cable interests in Europe; TV production; seventy radio stations in north America; more than 100 magazines; films; sports clubs; internet services; other holdings in car hire, phone services and chains of shops in Europe, Japan and South America.
- **Vivendi** Originally French, now global, $37 billion revenues. Books (Houghton Mifflin) and magazines; TV production and distribution in Australia, Brazil, France, Italy, Japan and the USA (Canal Plus, Cineplex Odeon, United Cinemas); music (Decca, Deutsche, MCA, Polygram, Grammophon, Universal Music, which has the largest catalogue of recorded music in the world); the production and distribution of CDs, DVDs and video games and software; telecommunications and internet access in Britain, France, Germany, Hungary, Italy, Kenya, Morocco, Poland and Spain; websites and music subscription services; theme parks, hotels and entertainment centres; recycling and incineration plant; commercial and industrial cleaning; rail networks; bottled water; transport; heating; advertising agencies.

- First, giant communications corporations are increasingly *beyond public accountability* and wield growing power without responsibility.
- Second, *pluralist competition* is weakened, placing the news media in the hands of a few business corporations with similar social, political and economic interests: in some countries, competition has largely disappeared. It is pluralist competition that is supposed to ensure that the general public gets a diverse diet of news and opinion in the political media. Instead,

Conglomerates
Single business organisations consisting of a number of different companies that operate in different economic fields.

Briefing 10.4
Media ownership: Globo in Brazil

With a population of 150 million, a high illiteracy rate and TV penetration of 99 per cent Brazil has the largest TV audiences in Latin America. This makes Globo, Brazil's largest TV company, the fourth largest in the world behind the three American giant networks – CBS, ABC and NBC. Built on wall-to-wall soap operas and populist news broadcasts from its 115 TV stations, Globo has a national audience share of 54 per cent and takes some $500–$600 million in TV advertising revenues (about 75 per cent of the national total). It is the world's largest exporter of soap operas in the world, selling its products in sixty-eight countries. It publishes one of Brazil's largest-circulation newspapers, controls the largest private radio network, has interests in book and magazine publishing, the internet, cable, films, music, land, agriculture, insurance and banking. With annual revenues of only $2.2 billion, Globo is by no means a major global media player, but nevertheless operates some forty companies world-wide.

The company was created and controlled by its sole owner, the Brazilian media tycoon Roberto Marinho, one of South America's richest men, who died aged 98 in 2003. Radio Globo played an important part, some claim, in supporting the military *coup* of 1964 and the military *junta* that ruled until 1985. It was Marinho's closeness to the dictatorship that enabled him to create his first TV station, with the help of the Time-Life Corporation (see briefing 10.2) in a deal that was later ruled to have contravened constitutional rules about foreign shareholding in the national media. It also helped him to be the first to use government provision of satellite broadcasting in 1968. In 1989, Globo came out strongly against Brazil's left-wing presidential candidate, who lost the election to the conservative Collor de Mello, whose family had business connections with Globo. Globo's TV power is said to be based on the weakness of educational and political institutions, the result of twenty-one years of dictatorship. Since 2002, however, the company has run into severe debt problems.

the multi-media moguls and multi-national corporations that increasingly control the news media are likely to restrict the public agenda to one that favours their interests. In short the problem with the market model is that it assumes market competition, but this is in rapid decline.

Once again, we cannot leave our story here. Media technology is changing incredibly rapidly and it seems likely to revolutionise itself all over again in the next generation when the full potential of interactive multi-media is realised. Some experts argue that this will transform the political media.

■ The impact of the new media technology: globalisation and E-politics

Communications are no longer limited by national boundaries; they are no longer merely international, but *global*. Journalists can dispatch reports and pictures from almost any part of the world which can be broadcast almost instantaneously to other parts of the globe. More than 2.5 billion people watched the football matches played in the 2004 European Cup, and an estimated 63 million people watched the final of the 2002 World Cup. Some soap operas have a world-wide appeal, and some programmes (*Big Brother*) are replicated in many countries. There are only three major news agencies in the world (Agence France Presse, Associated Press and Reuters), which distribute the vast majority of international news material to the national media. In this sense, the 'global broadcasting village' is a fact now, not something waiting just around the corner.

The consequences of this are sometimes said to be nothing short of rev-olutionary. Soon, it is claimed, we will all be watching the same TV news coverage of the same international events, even as we now concentrate on the American election, the Iraq war, the Olympic Games and protests against a G-8 summit. The new technology is also said to be transforming old patterns of *political participation* because new social groups adept with the new technology – especially the computer-literate young – will use it to become informed and involved. The newest technology will make it possible to use the interactive information super-highway to engage in *direct democracy*. It is also claimed in some circles that the new technology will fragment the mass media market as it has the specialist market.

These arguments are appealing, but we must be careful not to exaggerate the impact of global communications technology. Most of the world's population has yet to make its first phone call, much less send a text message, use a computer, or call up a website. TV saturates the wealthy democracies, but not the poorer ones which still lag behind, especially in access to cable and satellite. Computer use is further behind, even in some of the comparatively wealthy OECD countries, and in some of the poorer democracies Internet use is limited to very small minorities (see table 10.1).

In the early years of international cable and satellite TV news (BBC World News, CNBC, CNN) it looked as if the English language would dominate the world. However, the trend since the 1980s has been to broadcast TV news in local languages and to tailor it to the interests of local populations (Ara-bic speakers in the Middle East, Cantonese-speaking Chinese, Hindi-speaking Indians and Portuguese-speaking Brazilians). The days when we all watch the same CNN–CNBC–BBC news in the same language are further away than before. Not only have international TV news channels opted for more regional broad-casting, but national TV is also becoming less international. A majority in most countries still watches national programmes of all kinds, especially national news. The penetration of global TV is still rather limited, and national TV stations are increasingly relying on domestic, not imported TV programmes. Although it has a 'global reach', the new communications technology does not have a 'global grasp', and, if anything, its grip on world markets seems at the moment to be weakening.

The old communications technology, especially the printed word, was associ-ated with the '**knowledge gap**'. This gap increasingly separates those with the education to understand and keep up with political developments, and under-stand them, from those who have neither the education nor the inclination to do so. Some commentators argue that new electronic communications will

Knowledge gap
The gap
between those

Table 10.1 *TV ownership and internet users: selected democratic countries, 2004 (percentage of total population)*

	TV	Internet
High		
Denmark	59.4	69.4
Norway	46.2	69.2
Sweden	51.9	69.0
Australia	55.5	66.0
Netherlands	51.9	64.0
USA	80.6	64.0
Middle		
France	59.5	43.8
Greece	24.0	35.6
Chile	21.5	33.5
Estonia	41.8	30.7
Hungary	43.5	30.3
Bulgaria	39.4	21.8
Low		
Namibia	3.7	2.3
Botswana	2.0	2.1
Ghana	9.3	1.0
Bolivia	11.6	0.9
El Salvador	67.7	0.6
Benin	1.1	0.4

Source: Computer Industry Almanac, *World Factbook*; http://www. odci.gov/cia/publications/factbook/index.html.

with a good education and understanding of the world, which enables them to acquire knowledge and understanding at a faster rate than those with less education and understanding.

break down the 'knowledge gap' because different social groups will use them to inform themselves and become politically active. Some of the young who are not in the habit of newspaper reading will pick up political news and opinion from the Net, and perhaps from text messages and e-mail. Political parties have started text messaging and using websites in their election campaigns. Can the new technology break down the old patterns and bridge the knowledge gap?

So far, there is little evidence that it will. In fact, the new technology has generally reinforced the old patterns because the wealthy and educated have been the first to use it. Political elites in most democracies have so far also made rather little use of interactive, multi-media communications for political purposes. Some governments in the wealthiest democracies have started to explore some of the possibilities, but their efforts are modest and unimaginative so far. However, it is early days, and things may change as the new technology spreads and even newer technologies are introduced. One striking new pattern is that the youngest generations are using multi-media communications most and things may change as they move into positions of political influence. Meanwhile, E-politics has still to be fully exploited in modern democracies.

■ Theories of the mass media

Everyone is an expert mass media theorist because everyone is exposed to the mass media in huge doses. Unfortunately, everyone's theory differs from the others:

- Some claim that the mass media are extraordinarily powerful in political life, others that they are weak.
- Some believe that they are a 'good' thing because they inform and educate politically, others that they are nothing but a corrupting political influence.
- Some argue that most of the news media have a systematically left-wing bias (some right-wingers are inclined to believe this), but others are no less convinced that the bias is right-wing (left-wingers are given to this view).
- Many assume that the mass media affect others but not themselves, since they believe they are too intelligent and well informed to be taken in by bias, propaganda, and superficial sensationalism.

Before we consider sorts of claims, however, we should pause to consider how difficult it is to establish clear-cut media effects on political attitudes, opinions and institutions. Four methodological problems stand in the way:

1. The mass media are *only one of the many influences on our lives*, which include the family, education, work and the community. Media effects are tangled up with these other influences and it is virtually impossible to sort out their independent influence. Educated people are usually better informed about politics and more active, and they also spend more time with their newspaper and TV news. Is their knowledge and activity the result of education or news media exposure, if either? Perhaps their political family background causes all three?

2. It is impossible to generalise about the *impact of the media*. There are many different media and they probably have different effects on different kinds of people. Watching TV news and current affairs programmes has a different political impact than watching entertainment TV. Reading a quality newspaper is different from reading a popular newspaper. Using the Web for political research is different from shopping on it. Most generalisations about 'the effects of the media' are too wide-ranging.

3. The mass media and their audiences are linked by *interdependence*. The media select their audiences and tune their messages to appeal to them. Some papers are designed for intelligent and educated readers, some for a different market. Audiences also select what they want to attend to (self-selection). They read a certain kind of paper, or no paper at all and they watch certain kinds of TV, or no TV at all. This *mutual adjustment* of media

to audiences and audiences to media makes difficult to know what comes first, the chicken or the egg.

4. It is very difficult to measure the *effects of television*, the most important of all the mass media, because we have so few control groups which are not exposed to TV. Just as fish will be the last form of life on earth to discover water, so we find it difficult to know the effects of TV.

Each of these methodological problems is severe, and all of them together make it difficult to say anything with much confidence about media effects. This helps to explain why we can all hold our pet theories of the media: who can challenge them with hard and conclusive evidence? It also helps to explain why political scientists themselves cannot agree: how can they design research projects to answer the key questions when there are so many methodological difficulties? This helps to explain why there are four distinct theories of media effects:

Reinforcement theory
The theory that the mass media can only reflect and reinforce public opinion, not create or mould it.

1. *Reinforcement theory*   **Reinforcement theory** argues that the mass media have *minimal effects*. Bound by the 'golden chains' of the market, they *reflect and reinforce* mass opinion, rather than creating it. The theory is built around four points:

   (a) In the same way that supermarkets sell what their customers want and are willing to pay for, so the mass media give customers *what they want*.

   (b) Audiences select what they want from the media, often to fit their pre-existing attitudes and predispositions (*self-selection*).

   (c) Individuals have a wide range of *psychological mechanisms* for processing media messages, including projecting their own beliefs (projection), forgetting unwanted messages (suppression), misinterpreting (distortion), and refusing to believe what they don't like (rejection).

   (d) Competitive media systems have a wide variety of channels of communication and present a variety of political views, allowing audiences to *pick and choose* what they like best.

Agenda setting
The process by which a multiplicity of political problems and issues are continuously sorted according to the changing priority attached to them.

2. *Agenda setting*   **Agenda setting** theory argues that the media cannot determine what we think, but they can and do influence strongly *what we think about*. The mass media often cover particular issues intensively for a time, and such 'feeding frenzies' help to put the issues on the agenda, or climb up it. Examples include the Monica Lewinsky affair in the USA, the Iraq war, international terrorism, the death of Princess Diana and ecological disasters and famines such as the Bhopal chemical leak in 1984. The persistent interest of the press in crime is said to make people more afraid of it than is justified by the crime figures.

Priming
The theory that the mass media can prime us to

3. *Priming and framing*   Recent theories argue that the mass media have an influence over how the public see and evaluate politics, but in a subtle and indirect way. Imagine an election in which party *A* is thought to be good on domestic matters, while party *B* is better at foreign affairs. If the press emphasises domestic matters then the public is primed to think about an issue that favours Party A. This is **priming**.

Similarly issues can be presented in ways that affect their political impact. This is **framing**. For example, a TV programme on homelessness might be presented in terms of figures and trends that relate homelessness to unemployment, poverty, or housing supply. It might also present it as a human issue, presenting an in-depth life history of a homeless person. The former is more likely incline people to think that homelessness is linked to government policies, while the latter will present it as a personal issue associated with the characteristics of drunkenness, laziness, or individual inadequacy. Human interest stories, it is argued, tend to absolve politicians and governments of responsibility.

focus on certain things and in certain ways by highlighting some issues rather than others.

Framing
The theory that the way news stories are set up (framed) influences how audiences interpret them.

4. *Direct effects*   A small but increasing volume of research on the mass media argues that they have a strong and direct effect on politics, especially on the attitudes and behaviour of citizens and political leaders. Yet even the direct effects school disagrees about what the effects actually are. Some argue that the effects are beneficial, because increasing educational levels are allied with ever increasing amounts of news and political information, at lower and lower prices. This has the effect of cognitively mobilising citizens and increasing political awareness and interest, at least for some sections of the population (see chapter 8). For example, there is evidence showing that, other things being equal, those who watch TV news regularly are better informed about politics than those who do not. Newspaper reading has a bigger impact on political knowledge, but only as far as quality papers with their range of political information.

Others argue, on the contrary, that media effects are pernicious and have coined the term '**mediamalaise**' to describe them. Market competition and the pursuit of profits force the media to adopt the worst standards of sensational, trivial and superficial journalism (sound-bites and photo-opportunities). The obsession with bad news in the form of crime, political corruption, scandal, disaster and political incompetence creates a dismal view of the world (the 'mean world' effect). If journalists cannot find political conflict, they create it. Their highly critical style ('attack journalism') undermines politicians and political institutions. Since news is a highly perishable commodity the media are constantly searching for 'new news', so the public is presented with a bewildering flow of news and information that it cannot understand (the 'fast-forward effect'). Television is said to undermine both 'social capital' and community life (see chapter 9). In short, the modern media are said to create widespread political cynicism, distrust, suspicion, apathy and dissatisfaction with government, and even with democracy itself.

Mediamalaise
The attitudes of political cynicism, despair, apathy, distrust and disillusionment (among others) that some social scientists claim are caused by the mass media, especially TV.

One theory that assumes that the mass media have direct effects on attitudes and opinions concerns what is termed 'cultural imperialism'. In the nineteenth century, imperial nations enforced their rule with gunboats, now they use television, films and Western fashion in clothes, food and music. As a result, it is claimed, Third World cultures are dying out, mainly because of American cultural influences. Critics of the theory argue that it overestimates the penetration of American TV and films into Third World countries, and underestimates the cultural resistance of Third World cultures: drinking Coke and wearing baseball caps doesn't indicate that people think and feel like Americans.

The controversy about the mass media and their impact on government and politics is not going to be resolved in the near future. The four big methodological problems outlined on pp. 195–6, plus the passion with which different views are held, ensure that the debate will continue for a long time.

■ Summary

This chapter has dealt with the media in democracies. It argues that:

- The ability of the news media to deliver a full and accurate account of the news, and a wide range of opinion about it, is crucial for democracy. They should therefore be free from government control and not dominated by any particular set of social and economic interests.
- Radio and TV broadcasting in the era of spectrum scarcity was often run according to the public service model. This involved both market and content regulation. Broadcasting technology has changed this, by making it possible for many radio and TV channels to operate. Consequently, many national radio and TV systems have been deregulated or privatised to a greater or lesser extent. The print media are not normally subject to either content or market regulation because they are presumed to constitute a competitive market.
- Ownership and control of the media has become increasingly concentrated in the hands of a few giant, multi-media, MNCs.
- It is exceedingly hard to pin down the political impact of the mass media, and research is divided between four main schools of thought – minimal effects, agenda setting, priming and framing and direct effects. Researchers are also divided between those who believe that media effects are either benign or malign.
- The new media technology has had a huge impact in some respects (the spread of global news, the diffusion of the Web), but less effect in others (the resilience of national TV programmes – especially news – the slow progress of E-politics and the persistence of the 'knowledge gap' based on the old technology).

Further reading

For an excellent account of the way in which the media operate and impact on democratic politics, see Pippa Norris, *Virtuous Circle: Political Communications in Postindustrial Societies* (Cambridge: Cambridge University Press, 2000). For another general discussion of the mass media and modern democracy, see John Street, *Mass Media, Politics and Democracy* (Basingstoke: Palgrave, 2001). Richard Gunther and Anthony Mughan, *Democracy and the Media: A Comparative Perspective* (Cambridge:

Cambridge University Press, 2000), contains essays on politics and the media in Britain, Germany, Italy, Japan, The Netherlands, Spain and the USA. A useful set of essays on the mass media is in John Downing, Ali Mohammadi and Annabelle Sreberny (eds.), *Questioning the Media: A Critical Introduction* (Thousand Oaks, CA: Sage, 1995).

Websites

http://www.cjr.org/tools/owners	*Columbia Journalism Review* website with detailed information about who owns what in the global media market.
http://www.fair.org/extra/9711/gmg.html	Interesting article about 'The global media giants: the nine firms that dominate the world'.
http://www.thenation.com/special/bigten.html	Website from *The Nation* with some information about 'The big ten' and links to these companies.
http://www.mediamonitor.nl/HTML/ documents/Ward-webversie.pdf	Media concentration and ownership in ten European countries.
http://www.ejc.nl/resources.html	The European Media Landscape provides a comprehensive overview of media situation in selected European states.
http://www.cultsock.ndirect.co.uk/ MUHome/cshtml/index.html	For a basic account of media effects research.

Projects

1. Think of five reasons why the mass media may have rather little impact on politics, and then think of five reasons why they may have a big impact.
2. In a group, compile a list of all the different channels of political communication (newspapers, radio, TV, the Web, etc.) and then of who in the group has used what channel in the previous week. Which are the most frequently used channels, and which do you think are the most influential?
3. Examine the following figures and discuss what conclusions they suggest about the impact of newspaper reading on voting.

	Left-wing voters	Right-wing voters
Left newspaper readers (%)	63	26
Right newspaper readers (%)	37	74
Total (%)	*100*	*100*

11 Voters and elections

Elections have fascinated political scientists for a long time, and with good reason. They determine who is to *take control of government*. They involve a large proportion of citizens and are probably one of the best topics for research on mass political behaviour. They tell us a lot about how ordinary citizens relate to politics, what they think is important and how they make up their mind about governments and issues. On top of this, voting figures in democracies are relatively 'hard' and reliable, so researchers have a great deal of evidence on which to base their generalisations.

Given their importance in any democratic system of government, a great many questions can be asked about voting and elections:

- How should democratic elections be organised?
- What is the best voting system?
- What determines how many people turn out to vote?
- Should we worry about declining election turnout?
- What determines party voting?
- Have voting patterns been transformed by recent social, economic and technological change?

In this chapter, we tackle these questions. The three major topics are:

- Elections
- Party voting
- Theories of voting.

Fact file 11.1

Voters and elections

▦ Referendums and elections

- The minimum voting age in the great majority of countries is eighteen.
- Referendums are still used relatively rarely, and often for constitutional changes, but they have been held in almost every democratic country in the world, exceptions being Argentina, Germany, India, Israel, Japan, The Netherlands and the USA (where some states do hold them).
- Referendums are most common in Australia, Denmark, France, Ireland, Italy and New Zealand, but Switzerland stands out with almost 300 since 1941.
- Voter registration varies from 42 per cent in Switzerland, 58 per cent in India and 66 per cent in the USA, to 91 per cent in Belgium, 92 per cent in Iceland and 96 per cent in Australia. It averages 75 per cent in established democracies.

▦ Voting turnout

- Voting is technically compulsory in a few countries, including Argentina, Australia, Belgium, Costa Rica, Cyprus, Greece, Italy and The Netherlands (before 1970). Turnout is only about 4–5 per cent higher in these countries compared with non-compulsory systems. This is partly because the formalities of compulsory voting are sometimes not followed up in reality. Voting turnout in older, established democracies tends to be about 15 per cent higher than in all other countries (73 per cent and 59 per cent respectively), but the gap between them has been closing slowly since 1945, and is now less than 10 per cent.
- If one excludes the two deviant cases of very low turnout among the most advanced democracies – Switzerland and the USA – average turnout is close to 80 per cent. If one then allows for the fact that a proportion of the non-voters are old, or ill, or temporarily absent from their voting district, then some nine out of ten citizens in democracies normally vote.
- Average voting turnout in PR systems (68 per cent) is higher than in semi-PR systems (59 per cent) and in plurality–majority systems (59 per cent).
- Founding election turnout in central and eastern Europe in the 1990s was on average 12 per cent higher than in later elections, but in Africa, Asia, the Middle East and Oceania turnout was actually lower in founding than in subsequent elections.
- Competitive elections (where the largest party wins less than half the votes) have a turnout 10 per cent higher than less competitive elections (where the largest party wins more than 50 per cent of the poll).
- Turnout is not closely related to national wealth or population size, but it is closely associated with the UN **Human Development Index**. Countries with the highest HDI ratings had an average turnout of 72 per cent, those with the lowest 56 per cent.

Human Development Index
A UN index of national development that combines measures of life expectancy, educational attainment and wealth into one measure.

■ Class voting

Alford index
A measure of class voting that calculates the difference between the proportion of working-class people voting for a left party, and the proportion of middle-class people doing the same. The higher the index, the greater the class voting.

- Britain has one of the purest class voting patterns in the western world but its **Alford index** fell from 41 per cent in the general election of 1951 to 19 per cent in 1997.
- In the same period the Alford index for Germany fell from close to 30 per cent to less than 10 per cent, and for Sweden from 50 per cent to less than 20 per cent.

■ Religious voting

- In most of the predominantly Catholic countries of west Europe (Austria, Belgium, France, Ireland, Italy and Spain and in the south of Germany and The Netherlands), the largest centre-right party is a Christian Democratic one that relies heavily on Catholic votes. Christian Democratic parties are also found in Australia, Chile and South Africa.
- In the Protestant countries of west Europe (Scandinavia, the UK and the north of Germany and The Netherlands) the main centre-right party is a secular one.
- In France (80 per cent Catholic) almost half the Catholics voted for a centre-right party in the 1980s, compared with fewer than one in seven of the Protestants. At the same time about a third of those who attended church of any kind voted for a left party, compared with seven out of ten of those who did not attend church.
- In the 1950s, more than 90 per cent of Dutch Catholics voted for the Catholic People's Party (KVP), the second largest in the country. By 1977, 67 per cent were still doing so.

■ Elections

■ *Democratic elections*

The preconditions for democratic elections are demanding, and we should not take them for granted, even in advanced democracies. They include universal adult **suffrage**, a secret ballot, impartial administration of voting and vote counting, free and equal access to the polls, freedom for candidates and parties to contest elections and an absence of **gerrymandering**. Free elections also require basic democratic rights, including freedom of speech, association and assembly, access to accurate and fair news reporting and parties that are not too unequal in resources. Relatively few countries meet all these requirements. Indeed, the American presidential election in 2000 suggests that registration and vote-counting practices are far from perfect in the USA.

Suffrage
The right to vote.

Gerrymandering
Drawing electoral boundaries to favour a particular party or interest.

Referendum
The submission of a public matter to direct popular vote.

Voting comes in two main forms: a general election for different levels of the political systems, and a **referendum**. Referendums are particularly useful for expressing public opinion on a particular issue, and they often involve either a constitutional change or a major policy issue, often one that is morally and emotionally charged. Democracies have increasingly used referendums since the 1960s, but except for Switzerland they are far less frequent than general elections. Most of this chapter will be about general elections for executives and legislatures (see fact file 11.1).

Briefing 11.1
Main voting systems

No two countries have identical voting systems, but there are three main types: plurality–majority, proportional representation (PR), and semi-proportional, each with its own variations.

■ Plurality–majority

1. *Simple plurality/First-past-the-post*   The winning candidate gets more votes than any other (a *simple plurality*), no matter how many candidates and how small the winning margin. Usually used in conjunction with **single-member districts**, so the combination of single member and simple plurality is often known as the SMSP system. Its advantage is simplicity and direct democratic accountability, because each district is represented by only *one representative*. SMSP is also likely to produce single-party governments with stable majorities, and this favours clear lines of *political accountability*. The disadvantage is **disproportionality** in election results. The SMSP system favours large parties and discriminates against small ones, to the extent that voting for one of them is often seen as a 'wasted' vote.

   A variation on SMSP is the *block vote* which combines first-past-the-post counting with **multi-member districts**.

   Plurality–majority countries include: Argentina, Bolivia, Canada, India, Jamaica, Mauritius, the Philippines, Thailand, the UK and the USA. Italy adopted a mainly plurality–majority system with single-member districts in 1994.

2. *Second ballot*   The second-ballot (SB) system tries to avoid the disproportionality problem of SMSP systems by requiring the winning candidate to get an *absolute majority* of the votes (i.e. 50 per cent + 1) in the first round – or if not, a second run-off ballot is held between the two strongest candidates. The advantage is simplicity, the disadvantage the need for a second ballot shortly after the first. The French use this system in presidential elections.

3. *Alternative vote* (AV)   A variation on simple plurality. Voters mark their first and subsequent preferences among the candidates for their own constituency. If no candidate receives an absolute majority of first-preference votes on the first count, the candidate with the smallest number of first-choice votes is eliminated, but their second-choice votes are redistributed among the remaining candidates. This process continues until one candidate has an absolute majority.

   The system is simple to understand, but its results are no more proportional than the SMSP system, and it can produce unpredictable results. It is used only in Australia.

■ Proportional representation

Proportional representation (PR) allocates seats according to a formula that tries to ensure *proportionality*. The three main forms of PR are:
* The list system

Single-member districts
One elected representative for each constituency.

Proportionality
The ratio of stats to votes. The more proportional the closer the ratio.

Multi-member districts
These have two or more elected representatives for each constituency.

- The single transferable vote
- The mixed-member proportional system.

1. *List PR system*   One of the simplest ways of ensuring proportionality is to distribute the seats on a *national basis* or else on a large regional one. Parties rank their candidates in order of preference, and they are elected in proportion to the number of votes for that party, starting from the top of the list. A party getting 25 per cent of the poll will fill 25 per cent of the seats from the top of its list. The advantage is simplicity and the proportionality of the results. The disadvantage is that voters cast a preference for a party, though they may prefer to vote for an individual candidate. The system also gives power to party leaders, who decide the rank order of candidates on their lists. Because list PR voting requires multi-member districts it also breaks the direct and simple link between representatives and their districts. List PR is highly proportional and it can encourage very small parties and fragmentation of the party system. An **electoral threshold** can overcome this problem, but this increases disproportionality.

   Many democratic countries have adopted the list PR system, including: Argentina (compulsory voting), Belgium, Chile, Costa Rica (compulsory voting), Cyprus (compulsory voting), Czech Republic, Denmark, Dominican Republic (compulsory voting), Estonia, Finland, Greece, Israel, Italy (before 1994), Latvia, The Netherlands (compulsory voting before 1970), Norway, Poland, Portugal, Slovakia, South Africa, Spain, Sweden and Switzerland (compulsory voting).

2. *Single transferable vote* (STV)   Voters rank candidates according to their order of preference, and elected candidates must either get a specified number of first preferences or else the second preferences are taken into account. If no candidate has an absolute majority, the third preferences are counted, and so on until all seats are filled. STV must be used in conjunction with multi-member constituencies. The advantage of the system is its proportionality and the avoidance of 'wasted' votes. The disadvantage is the complexity of the STV formula (although this is now easily and quickly done by computer) and the fact that multi-member constituencies do not create a direct link between constituencies and a single representative. The system is used only in Australia, Estonia (1989–92) and Ireland.

3. *Mixed-member proportional*   The mixed-member proportional system runs two voting systems at the same time. Plurality–majority districts are used to keep the link between representatives and constituencies, but a list PR system is added for a certain number of seats (usually 50 per cent) in order to compensate for any disproportionality that arises from the plurality–majority system. In Germany, half the seats are allotted at district and half at national level, and citizens have two votes, one for their district and one for the national list. The second vote is used to compensate for disproportionality in the district vote. MMP is found in Germany, Hungary, New Zealand (since 1996) and Uruguay.

Electoral thresholds
These discourage small parties by requiring them to get a minimum percentage of the poll to be elected.

Semi-PR

1. *Parallel systems*   These are like the MMP systems in that they use the plurality–majority system together with a PR system, but unlike MMP the PR

system does not compensate for any disproportionality resulting from the plurality-majority system. Used in Japan (from 1994), Lithuania and South Korea.

2. *Single non-transferable vote*   The single non-transferable vote (SNTV) system combines multi-member constituencies with simple majority vote counting, and one vote for each elector. Used in Japan (before 1994) and Taiwan (for 78 per cent of seats).

Table 11.1 *Liberal democracies: voting systems, 1990s*

		%
Non-PR		
	Simple plurality	44
	Second-ballot	5
	AV	1
	Sub-total	50
PR and Semi-PR		
	List PR	36
	Additional member	8
	STV	3
	Limited vote (semi-PR)	2
	Sub-total	49
	Total	99

Source: Derived from J. Denis Derbyshire and Ian Derbyshire, *Political Systems of the World* (Oxford: Helicon, 1996).

■ Voting systems

One of the most basic decisions for any democracy is what **voting system** it should have. Many have been invented (the main types are outlined in briefing 11.1), but it is no simple matter to say what is the best and most democratic. Each has its advantages and disadvantages, and the choice depends on what one wants from a voting system. Those who value **proportionality** more than anything else choose a proportional representation system (PR), but others say that the system should, above all, produce stable and effective government. Some emphasise clear lines of government accountability to the majority of citizens, and others argue for adequate minority representation, on the grounds that democracies are to be judged on how they treat their minorities. Consequently it may be less a matter of choosing the best voting system than of selecting one of them, knowing what its strengths and weakness are in the light of what is most expected of a good system. In the democracies of the world the most favoured systems are the simple *plurality* system, which is believed to produce stable and accountable government, and the *list PR* system, which results in more proportionate election outcomes (see table 11.1).

Voting system The arrangements by which votes are converted into seats on representative bodies.

■ *Voting turnout*

Voting turnout
The number of citizens casting a valid vote expressed either as a percentage of those eligible to vote (adult citizens), or as a percentage of those on the electoral register.

Protest vote
A way of discouraging small parties, by requiring them to get a given minimum percentage of votes or seats to be elected.

Voting is the most basic and simple duty of the citizen, so **voting turnout** is often treated as a good measure of the basic health of a democracy. Unfortunately, there are two problems with this:

- First, does low turnout indicate an alienated and dissatisfied electorate, or, on the contrary, one that is satisfied and happy to let politicians get on with it? History suggests that sudden and large increases in turnout indicate widespread dissatisfaction. The sudden jump in voting turnout in Germany in 1933, when Hitler's Nazi Party won, was the result of alienated people deciding to cast a **protest vote**.
- The second difficulty of using turnout as a indicator of democratic health is that there are *two different measures of turnout*, and a lot turns on which one is used:
  - Voting as a percentage of the voting-age population, usually all adult citizens
  - Voting as a percentage of those on the electoral register.

Some countries make it easy to register, and some even register people automatically when they pay their taxes. Other countries make it more difficult, or even discriminate against certain groups. As a result, the percentage of all adults on the register can vary quite significantly between countries. There can therefore also be a big difference between turnout figures according to which of the two measures is used. It is thus important to make it clear which *baseline* – adult population or registered electorate – is used. It is also important to use one or the other *consistently* when comparing countries. There is the further complication that some countries make voting in national elections compulsory (see fact file 11.1), and although this may be observed in theory more than practice, it does complicate comparisons.

■ *Declining turnout?*

Although it is common to lament a decline in turnout, especially when it is interpreted as a sign of disillusionment with democracy, the facts suggest otherwise. In the established democracies (countries that have been democratic for twenty years or more) turnout as a percentage of the voting-age population rose from around 70 per cent in the 1940s to around 75 per cent in the 1950s. This figure remained fairly constant over the 1960s and 1970s and then declined slightly to around 70 per cent in the 1990s. This does suggest a slight fall, but only to the previous lower level, and it is not clear how much this decline is due to changing socio-demographic patterns, or to growing apathy, alienation, or political satisfaction. It is, however, the case that social groups with a typically low turnout have tended to increase in size – the old, the ill, students, immigrants and ethnic and language minorities. In short, turnout across the democratic nations has not declined very much, and even this may be the result of socio-demographic change as much as disillusionment with democracy, and the much-discussed apathy of voters.

■ *Determinants of election turnout*

There are considerable variations in voting turnout in the democracies (see table 11.2). In Italy, Iceland and South Africa it is above 85 per cent, but in the Dominican Republic, Poland, Switzerland and the USA it is below 50 per cent. Why is this? Many factors seem to affect turnout, and they may be conveniently grouped under two categories: system and individual influences.

System variables
We can distinguish nine of these:

1. *The importance of the election* Citizens are more likely to vote if they think the election is important. They turn out in larger numbers for national than for local government elections, and for the election of executive presidents and lower chambers rather than upper chambers and weak assemblies. The **democratic deficit** of the European Parliament (EP), a weak assembly, is said to be partly responsible for the low turnout in EU elections.
2. *Democracy* According to Arend Lijphart's (1999) research, turnout in established democracies is higher than in non-democracies.
3. *Electoral system* PR voting systems have a higher turnout than other systems (see briefing 11.1)
4. *Close, competitive elections* Close elections, where every vote counts, tend to have a higher turnout. Similarly competitive elections (where the largest party wins less than 50 per cent of the vote) have high turnouts.
5. *Left parties* Elections that manage to mobilise sections of the population with a low voting turnout will usually register a higher turnout – for example, where left-wing parties appeal to working-class voters.
6. *Frequency of election* Citizens who are often called out to vote seem to suffer from 'election fatigue'.
7. *Founding elections* It is often believed that 'founding elections' (the first democratic elections after authoritarian rule) have high turnouts. One thinks of the long queues at polling stations in the first democratic election in South Africa in 1994. An examination of election statistics, however, shows that this turns out to be true of central and eastern Europe, not generally of other parts of the world.
8. *Presidential and parliamentary elections* In parliamentary elections in the second half of the twentieth century turnout was a good 20 per cent higher than presidential turnout, but by 1997, the two were virtually identical. At the same time, presidential elections increased from 30 per cent of all elections to more than 50 per cent in 1999, so it is not clear whether presidential turnout has changed, or whether presidential elections are now held in a different set of countries affected by different turnout factors.

Democratic deficit
A term used to convey the idea that the institutions of the European Union are not fully democratic, or as democratic as they should be.

Arend Lijphart, *Patterns of Democracy* **(1999)**

207

Table 11.2 *Democratic countries: average voting[a] turnout, 1990s*

Italy	90.2
Iceland	88.2
South Africa	85.5
Czech Rep.	84.8
Greece	84.7
Belgium	84.1
Israel	83.2
Sweden	83.2
Australia	82.7
Chile	81.9
Denmark	81.1
Slovenia	80.6
New Zealand	80.4
Austria	79.6
Spain	79.0
Argentina	78.9
Portugal	78.4
Cyprus	77.3
Philippines	76.7
Slovakia	75.9
Netherlands	75.2
Norway	74.5
Germany	72.7
UK	72.4
Finland	71.5
Ireland	70.2
Panama	70.1
Taiwan	70.1
South Korea	70.0
Hungary	66.9
Ecuador	66.2
Latvia	63.1
Thailand	62.5
France	60.6
Canada	60.1
Lithuania	60.1
India	59.2
Japan	57.0
Bolivia	56.2
Estonia	56.0
Poland	48.2
Dominican Rep.	46.2
USA	44.9
Switzerland	37.7

Note: [a] Voting turnout is defined as the percentage of the voting-age population that cast a valid vote.
Source: Institute for Democracy and Electoral Assistance, *Voter Turnout from 1945 to 1997: A Global Report on Political Participation* (Stockholm: IDEA, 1998: 14–15).

9. *Community characteristics* Socially homogeneous communities (predominantly of one class, religion, language, or ethnic group) with a sense of solidarity, often have high levels of social and political participation.

Individual characteristics

We can distinguish four of these:

1. *The standard model* The standard model of political participation, described in chapter 8, applies to voting turnout as well. The higher an individual's position in the **social stratification** system, as measured by caste, class, status, income, or education, the more likely they are to vote.

2. *Age, gender, length of residence and race* The standard model of voter turnout may be modified by other variables. Young and old people are less likely to vote, so also are women and members of minority groups – unless minorities are mobilised by their own political organisations or political issues relevant to them. Long-term residents with roots in the community are more likely to vote than more mobile people.

3. *Party identification* Individuals with a strong **party identification (party ID)** are more likely to vote.

4. *Values* Post-materialist values, it is said, promote participation and civic responsibility.

Social stratification
The hierarchical layering of society into socially unequal groups.

Party identification
The stable and deep-rooted feeling of attachment to and support for a political party.

▧ Party voting

As one would expect, there is a great deal of variation in party voting from one country to another, but at the same time there are stable and well-defined cross-national patterns. There are also fairly clear trends over time that are found in many countries. Since voting patterns are strongly affected by social and economic developments (another example of the close link between society and politics), and since many countries are affected by similar developments of this kind, it is not surprising that democratic nations share similar voting characteristics. By far the most important of these is the connection between *party voting* and *social stratification*, especially *social class*.

▧ *Stratification and class voting*

Social inequalities in societies are encapsulated by the way they are organised into *hierarchical strata* – such as castes, classes, religious elites, or aristocracies. In most countries, social stratification is the main form of social cleavage and affects most other cleavages, and since party voting in most countries runs along lines set by the cleavages between social strata, party voting patterns are usually (but not always) built around the stratification system. In the western world, social class is the main form of stratification and since this is also the best researched, it is the one we will concentrate on here.

In the late nineteenth and early twentieth century, many western societies developed patterns of party voting based on the most important *social cleavages*

Briefing 11.2
The left–right dimension in politics

At the heart of the left–right dimension in politics lies a profound difference between the left, which favours the welfare state and government intervention in society, and the economy in order to achieve a degree of equality of opportunity and those on the right of the spectrum, who favour less government action and intervention and a market economy, although they often favour strong but limited government in the interests of domestic law and order and national security. The left–right dimensions is becoming less important with the decline of class differences in many western democracies, but more important in some industrialising democracies, where a rapidly growing urban working class is combining with poor agricultural workers.

Class
Class is a form of social stratification that is determined by economic factors, notably the occupational hierarchy.

Seymour Martin Lipset and Stein Rokkan, *Party Systems and Voter Alignments* (1967)

Status
A form of social stratification determined by social prestige rather than economic factors or occupation.

(see chapter 1). For the most part, these cleavages were based on the most important historical divisions, going back centuries in some instances, based on social strata, centre–periphery, urban–rural, language, religion and ethnic groups. For the past 150 years **class** has usually been the most important single cleavage.

The industrial system of the nineteenth century produced a large urban working class, which was then given the vote as the franchise was broadened, so making class one of the most important and persistent cleavages in society. It quickly became the main basis of many western party systems. By the 1920s, many middle- and working-class voters had developed clear and rooted party identifications. According to the most influential study of the subject by Lipset and Rokkan (1967) – the party system then became 'frozen' around the most important cleavages in each society. Or, to put it differently, by the time the whole adult population was enfranchised in the early twentieth century, the parties had no need to adapt to further major changes in the electorate, and so they settled into a stable pattern.

In this context, 'class' is defined in terms of the *broad occupational divide* between manual workers, on the one hand, and professionals, business owners and managers and large farmers, on the other. The importance of class is reinforced by a set of closely related variables such as income, education, family background, trade union membership and life experiences. It is true that the simple and crude distinction between middle class and working class ignores many subtleties of class and **status**, but it also happens to capture the basic realities of party voting across much of western Europe for much of the twentieth century. The struggle for power was formed around parties built upon a basic socio-economic, left–right cleavage (see briefing 11.2) with communist, socialist and social democratic parties lined up against conservative and free-market liberal ones.

In the middle of the twentieth century many western countries had strong patterns of class voting. As table 11.3 shows, the countries of northern Europe often had the highest levels – Denmark, Iceland, Norway – while Canada, Japan and the USA had the lowest. By the end of the millennium patterns of class voting in most countries were both weaker and less clear.

Table 11.3 *Class, religious and value voting, 1990s*

Correlation with party preference[a]	Class voting	Religious voting	Materialist–post-materialist voting
0.37		Netherlands	
0.30		Belgium	
0.29		Denmark	
0.27		Finland, Italy, Norway	
0.26		Austria	Netherlands, Finland
0.25		Spain	Denmark
0.22	Norway	France, West Germany	
0.21	Denmark		Britain, (West) Germany
0.20	Austria	Sweden	
0.19	Iceland		France, Iceland
0.18	Britain, Netherlands		Italy, Norway
0.17		Iceland	Spain
0.16	Belgium, Finland, Sweden	Ireland	
0.15	France, Italy, Spain	Japan	Sweden, Austria
0.14	Ireland		East Germany, Japan
0.13	(West) Germany		Belgium, Canada
0.12		Britain, Canada	
0.11	Japan		Ireland
0.10	Canada, USA		
0.09			USA
0.08		USA	

Note: [a] Table 11.3 shows the strength of the statistical association (the correlation) of party preference with social class, religion and post-materialism in the 1990s
Source: Russell J. Dalton, *Citizen Politics* (London: Chatham House, 1996, 2nd edn.: 171, 180, 190).

Class is becoming more important, however, in some industrialising societies. In India, the decline of the agricultural sector and the growth of urban centres is associated with a more mixed stratification system based partly on caste and partly on class. Caste identities continue to be a basis for political mobilisation, but they have been joined by class-based interest groups, political coalitions and ideologies.

■ *Religious voting*

Religion has been a major source of political conflict for most of the world's history, and it remains a major, if not the major, social and political division in some democratic countries. In India, conflict between Muslims and Hindus is an acute political issue and Hindu fundamentalism is the basis of the Bharatiya Janata Party (BJP), which became the governing party in 1998. Religious issues and voting patterns are still strong in the USA. Religion, ethnicity and language are frequently closely associated, but sometimes the same ethnic group and language groups can be divided along religious lines.

While it is not surprising that religion is a basic foundation of political life in religious societies, it also continues to be a major influence on voting behaviour even in the secular parts of west Europe, where churches and the state came to a formal settlement centuries ago (see chapter 1). In fact, as table 11.3 shows, as class voting tends to decline so religious voting, which has maintained its strength, emerges as being more important. Religious voting tends to be more complex than class voting, since there is no simple working-class–middle-class/left–right cleavage, but there is a more complex set of divisions between many different churches and faiths – including, in some countries, the formation of secular parties in opposition to religious ones.

In west Europe, Catholics traditionally support centre and right parties, by and large, while Protestants more often lean to the left or to the Greens. Historical circumstances in different countries have sometimes created different political alliances in which, for example, middle- and upper-class Catholics and some Protestants have united to form a Conservative Party. The German Christian Democratic Party (CDU) is one such case, and so the level of religious voting is not as high there as in Belgium, Denmark, or The Netherlands. Nevertheless table 11.3 shows that religious and class voting have about the same strength in Germany. Christian democratic parties of a similar kind are in Australia, Chile and South Africa, as well as France, Italy, Norway, Sweden and Switzerland.

What makes the existence of persistent religious differences all the more interesting and important is that politicians in secular societies usually try to push religious issues, such as abortion or matters of faith, off the political agenda. They are *moral and emotional issues* of the kind that politicians try to avoid. Nevertheless, religious cleavages that emerged a long time ago, even before the creation of democratic elections and party systems, are still relevant.

■ *Other voting patterns*

Few things rival class and religion as the major influences on party voting across the broad sweep of modern democracies, but other factors can play a significant role:

- Most countries have *urban–rural differences*, for example, and more especially regional variations in party voting. The latter are particularly likely to be associated with ethnic, religious, class, or language differences, as they are in Belgium, Canada, Italy and Spain. India stands out in this respect as well.
- There is a slight *gender gap* in some societies, although it is rarely of great importance compared with religion or stratification.

Briefing 11.3
Cleavages and politics: Chile

Republican political institutions were able to take root in Chile in the nineteenth century before new social groups demanded participation. Contenders from the middle and lower classes gradually were assimilated into an accommodating political system in which most disputes were settled peacefully, although disruptions related to the demands of workers often met a harsh, violent response. The system expanded to incorporate more and more competing regional, anticlerical, and economic elites in the nineteenth century. The middle classes gained political offices and welfare benefits in the opening decades of the twentieth century. From the 1920s to the 1940s, urban laborers obtained unionization rights and participated in reformist governments. In the 1950s, women finally exercised full suffrage and became a decisive electoral force. And by the 1960s, rural workers achieved influence with reformist parties, widespread unionization, and land reform . . .

As Chile's political parties grew, they attracted followers not only on the basis of ideology but also on the basis of patron–client relationships between candidates and voters. These ties were particularly important at the local level, where mediation with government agencies, provision of public employment, and delivery of public services were more crucial than ideological battles waged on the national stage. Over generations, these bonds became tightly woven, producing within the parties fervent and exclusive subcultures nurtured in the family, the community, and the workplace. As a result, by the mid-twentieth century the parties had politicized schools, unions, professional associations, the media, and virtually all other components of national life. The intense politicization of modern Chile has its roots in events of the nineteenth century. (http://workmall.com/wfb2001/chile/chile_history_historical_setting.html)

- *Race and ethnicity*, important in some of the newer democracies, has also gained in importance in the older ones as a result of global migration patterns.

Chile in the nineteenth and twentieth centuries demonstrates many aspects of the relationships between social cleavages and politics, particularly so far as inequality, religion, class and region are concerned. The Spanish conquest of the country created a dominant white, Catholic, ruling class and a coerced labour force consisting of the indigenous population that worked on farms and in the mines. As the economy and society developed in the nineteenth century it created social and economic groups, including a middle class, a set of regional, anti-clerical and economic elites. But Chile has long had a tradition of constitutional and multi-party government, and it succeeded in gradually accommodating these interests into the political system is a largely peaceful manner (see briefing 11.3).

■ New party voting patterns

Social and economic changes (some brought about by government policies) have had a strong influence on voting patterns. In the industrialising democracies, the decline of the agricultural sector and the growth of the cities populated by the working class and the poor have had a profound impact on the strength of parties and the nature of old social cleavages based on urban–rural differences, regions and ethnic concentrations. In the older democracies of west Europe, the old pattern of class politics, and the left–right party system associated with it, shows clear signs of 'unfreezing'. Class is less important than it was and there is evidence that **class (and party) de-alignment** and **partisan de-alignment** has caused voting patterns to show more **volatility**.

The reasons for changing voting patterns, therefore, are many and varied but they include six key considerations:

Class de-alignment
Decline in the class-based strength of attachment to class-based political parties.

Partisan de-alignment
Decline in the strength of belonging to the political parties.

Volatility
The opposite of stability, volatility involves change in voting patterns from one election to another. Some refer to it as 'churning'.

Partisan re-alignment
When social and economic groups change their old party identifications in favour of new ones.

- Industrialising societies have often mixed old stratification criteria based on caste, religion and ethnicity with new class and status distinctions. Post-industrial societies, in contrast, have tended to increase their proportion of middle-class people, while fragmenting both working- and middle-class strata into smaller sub-groups. This has weakened class voting.
- Urban–rural differences have declined with a shrinking agricultural sector, particularly where the urban and rural poor have formed a political alliance in industrialising countries.
- Education has created a more independently minded electorate that is less bound by class identities. Social mobility between classes has strengthened this.
- The mass media, especially television, have become more important.
- New parties have emerged and old parties have shifted their policies in an attempt to broaden their appeal to and to respond to the demands of new social groups. In some cases, the old parties have stolen policies from the new parties and social movements in their attempt to maintain their electoral appeal.
- The basic bread-and-butter issues of poverty, work, health, housing and education have become even sharper in industrialising democracies, whereas the environment, nuclear issues, gender and minority rights, and (in west Europe) the European Union have often cut across the old politics of class in post-industrial societies.

The result of these far-reaching changes in socio-economic patterns is increased *volatility and unpredictability* in voting patterns in both new and old democracies. Nevertheless, talk of revolutionary and radical transformation is often exaggerated. Changes are usually gradual and involve fusions of the old and the new, and shifts of degree rather than kind. In some cases, even **partisan re-alignment** can be observed. Social stratification and religion remain the basic sources for political mobilisation, even if the nature of the stratification is shifting.

■ *Tradition and change in Mexico*

We can see the interplay of tradition and change in the recent electoral politics of Mexico, where economic inequalities of class are superimposed on old ethnic divisions. The Mexican social and political elite is composed of the *criollos*, people of pure Spanish ancestry dating back to the invasion of Mexico in the sixteenth century by the Spanish conquistador, Hernán Cortés. The middle layer of society is made up of people of mixed blood, the *mestizos* with Spanish and indigenous Mayan and Aztec backgrounds. For sixty years, Mexico had stable one-party government built on the ability of the Institutional Revolutionary Party (PRI) to unite the interests of these groups and those of the lowest class, the *indigena*, by bringing them together in a corporatist structure (see chapter 9). The structure however, largely excluded the interests of the very poorest section of society, the rural farmers who were concentrated in the south of Mexico and consisted mainly of people of Mayan background.

On New Year's Day 1994, the revolutionary National Liberation Front (NLF, the Zapatistas) burst into armed guerrilla activity that shook the foundations of the state and the governing PRI. Zapatista demands were economic, regional and ethnic. They wanted a better economic deal for poor farmers, who were mainly of Aztec origin and concentrated in Chiapas in the south of Mexico. Two new parties then emerged to challenge the hegemony of the PRI, both representing class interests. The Democratic Revolutionary Party (PRD) is supported mainly by poor urban and rural people, and the National Action Party (PAN) mainly by upper-income groups. PAN captured the presidency in 2000.

The Mexican case illustrates several points about changing voting patterns:

- First, change is usually mixed with tradition.
- Second, voting is based on a mixture of factors involving social stratification and inequality, ethnicity and regional and urban–rural differences. Religious differences are not important in Mexico because it is 90 per cent Catholic.
- Third, history is important. The Zapatista movement is the result of the subjugation of the Mayan and Aztec populations in the sixteenth century, and the 1990s movement named itself after the revolutionary leader Emiliano Zapata, who fought for the rights of poor farmers.

■ Theories of voting

There are the three main approaches to the explanation of voting behaviour:

- Sociological/political sociology
- Psychological
- Rational-choice/economic.

■ *Sociological approaches: the Columbia school*

Originating in Paul F. Lazarsfeld and his collaborators' first Columbia University study (1944), the theory argues that people vote according to their membership of *social groups*, and that social groups vote for the party that best serves

Paul F. Lazarsfeld et al., The People's Choice (1944)

their interests. This makes class, religion, race, language, urban–rural differences and sometimes gender, generation and occupation the most important determinants of voting behaviour.

The strengths of the sociological school are that it relates politics to broad social and economic patterns and, as we have seen so often in this book, there is often a close connection between *society* and its government and *politics*. Indeed, research shows a close relationship between voting and factors such as class, religion and ethnicity. However, the theory is not good at explaining the causal links between politics and society. To understand why, for example, the working class votes for left-wing parties, we have to introduce *political elements* – such as values, ideology and party policy – into the explanation. Working-class people do not vote for working-class parties automatically, any more than members of a religious group generally vote for a given party because of instinct. They do so because they see a link between the situation and the interests (material or ideal) of their social group and the things that the party stands for.

The sociological approach works very well in some cases – religion and voting in Northern Ireland, for example – but there are always exceptions to the social patterns, and some of them are so large they cannot be overlooked. Working-class people do not always vote for left-wing parties, just as some middle-class people do not vote for right-wing ones. Ethnic groups are rarely 100 per cent solid in their voting patterns. Sometimes they are split between two or more parties, sometimes divided down the middle. And, as we have already seen, the sociological model seems to be losing some of its power, with the emergence of the 'new' politics based not on group membership but on values and issue areas.

The *cleavage model* is a more complex version of the sociological approach. It also argues that voting is organised around social groups, but points out those cleavages are not the automatic outcome of social divisions. Indeed, many social divisions, such as age or gender, do not normally take on the importance of political cleavages. Social divisions become politically potent only when political interests (elites, parties, movements) manage to give them a political and symbolic significance, and build organisations around them. In other words, parties do not merely respond to cleavages; they play upon them and develop them in their attempts to win support. Parties would find it difficult to mobilise voters without cleavage groups to appeal to, but social cleavages would have little political significance without parties to mobilise them and articulate their interests and values.

The problem with cleavage theory is that while it can explain the historical origins of parties and party systems, it is less successful in explaining changing political alignments. The theory tends to take cleavages as given, and works out their political implications from there. They are rather less interested in why different societies have different cleavages or how and why they reconfigure themselves over time. Since the old cleavages appear to be fading a little, and new ones emerging, this is important to contemporary politics.

Psychological approaches: the Michigan school

Starting with Angus Campbell and his collaborators' work (1960), the school emphasises the *psychological orientations* of voters. Whereas the sociological school emphasises social groups, psychological approaches concentrate on individual characteristics, particularly the role of *party identification* (party ID). This is a relatively stable and enduring feature that individuals acquire as a result of childhood and adult socialisation. Party ID is more than identification with a party, because it acts as a prism through which individuals perceive politics and interpret policies, issues, parties and candidates. It affects voting, and it also helps to mould the way in which citizens relate more generally to government and politics.

Angus Campbell et al., The American Voter (1960)

Campbell develops what he calls 'the funnel of causality', in which all the variables affecting voting behaviour are organised according to their influence. At the 'wide end' of the funnel are a set of the most general constraints on voting, such as social background and socialisation. As the funnel narrows so variables constrain the voting decision more tightly. At the narrowest point are factors that are closest to the circumstances of particular elections, including attitudes towards party policies, candidates and election issues. This is a useful way of organising the many different variables that seem to affect voting behaviour, but at the same time it is a complicated model that is difficult to test as a whole.

The psychological school introduces specifically political elements (party ID) into voting studies that are lacking in the sociological approach. It picks out the significance of political issues (unemployment, public services, economic development), party programmes (left–right dimensions, ethnic, religious, language and regional parties) and the images and appeal of political leaders as influences on party ID. There is also a close relationship between party ID and party voting. However, this is scarcely surprising since party ID and party voting are almost the same thing: if people are asked in surveys which party they identify with, they are likely to think of which party they vote for. In the long causal chain of explanatory variables explaining voting patterns, party ID and the vote are practically next door to each other, so of course we find that they are closely correlated. The problem is not to understand the causal links between ID and voting, but to understand who develops what sort of ID, and why. In addition, survey research shows that the strength of party ID (party de-alignment) is fading in many western countries, although it is alive and well in countries such as South Africa where black South African identification with the African National Congress (ANC) is widely and strongly held.

Rational choice

The rational-choice theory of voting originates with Anthony Downs (1957), a work which starts with the assumption that citizens are rational and vote on the basis of a calculation of which party most closely gives them all the political

Anthony Downs, An Economic Theory of Democracy (1957)

information they need; they then act on the basis of their own self-interest. Voting decisions are similar to those of consumers (voters) in the economic market who calculate the costs and benefits of choosing one commercial product (political party) rather than another. Voting for a party is rather like choosing a basket of goods in a supermarket, in that voters select the 'package' of party policies that best fits their preferences. Similarly, parties are like business competing for customers in the market place. They try to locate themselves and their policies as closely as they can to the **median voter**. Rational choice, in short, can explain the behaviour of individual voters and it can explain the strategies and policies of political parties in terms of an economic theory of *consumers* (voters) and the *producers* of public policies (parties).

Median voter
The median is the middle number in any distribution of numbers. The median voter is in the middle of the distribution with equal numbers of voters to the left and right. The support of the median voter is usually necessary to win an election.

Rational-choice theory – sometimes known as formal modelling because it can be expressed in terms of symbols and formulae – is said to have opened up many promising lines of research by virtue of its deductive and logical powers. Most obviously, the theory suggests that people vote for the party that fits their own preferences. Ethnic groups vote for their ethnic party, workers vote for left parties businessmen vote for right parties and so on. One might reply that it would be very strange if people did not vote in this way – if a socialist voted for a right-wing party, for example, or a Catholic voted for the Atheist Party, or a minority group member for the party of their oppressors. In this sense rational choice may be stating the obvious, rather than explaining it.

Rational choice also has problems with explaining why people bother to vote at all. Logically, the most rational course of action for the voter is not to bother because the costs in time and effort of acquiring the necessary information and then doing whatever is needed to cast a vote, are too high. The difference that one individual voter makes to the election outcome is practically zero in the huge majority of elections. The most rational course of action is not to vote, join a party, or participate in collective decisions. Better to free-ride on the efforts of others, and take advantage of their hard work. However, people do vote, and they vote in large numbers even when the election result is a foregone conclusion and the winning candidate, as expected, has a very large majority. The reason is that voting seems to be a symbolic act in part, and people feel obliged to perform their citizen duty. This is not a matter of the rational calculation of self-interest, but a collective sense based on the value of democracy and the importance of exercising the right to vote. This is not so much a rational-choice explanation of the voting act but a cultural one, rooted in *values* and *social expectations*.

The claim that all voters act in their own self-interest can easily be circular, non-falsifiable, or tautological. How can we tell when people are not acting in their own self-interest, and what counts as non-rational behaviour? Are middle-class socialists running against their own preferences and self-interest? Rational-choice theory suggests not, because some people define their preferences in terms of the public or collective interest. In this case, it is difficult to see what 'self-interest' means, other than in terms of what people say is their self-interest, in which case whatever they do, no matter how altruistic or concerned with the public interest, is a rational calculation of self-interest.

Last, rational-choice theory has helped to stimulate an interest in *issue voting*, which occurs when voters choose one issue rather than a total party programme as the basis of their voting decision. Traditional issues are unemployment and the economy ('it's the economy, stupid'), but it has also been suggested that race, human rights, the environment and peace have emerged in many countries as the focus of single-issue voting. However, research shows that the importance of issue voting may not be as great as some have suggested and that, in any case, voters do not always choose the party with the best policies on the issues they think are important. The voting decision is not simply the net balance of issue-based calculations but involves, in addition, a broader set of values and ideological considerations: voters use their hearts as well as their heads. Rational choice tends to avoid issues of the heart, or takes them for granted.

■ Summary

This chapter has dealt with elections, which are vital to the conduct of politics and an important part of the study of comparative politics. It argues that:

- Democratic elections require a large number of preconditions. They should not be taken for granted even in advanced democracies.
- There is no simple answer to the question: what is the best voting system? Each has its advantages and disadvantages. It is necessary to decide what one wants from an electoral system and choose accordingly.
- Election turnout in the post-war period has declined a little in the democracies, probably because of socio-demographic change as much as increasing voter apathy or disillusionment with democracy.
- Patterns of party voting are based mainly on social and economic cleavage divisions in the population – particularly on the inequalities that are part of social stratification – caste, class and status. Stratification is often tangled up with race, religion, language and region, and sometimes with age and gender as well. Voting patterns usually reflect a mixture of these variables.
- Party voting cannot be reduced to social and economic factors or cleavages because these are partly the product of government policies and political pressures.
- Changing voting patterns are usually a mixture of the old and new rather than a transformation. In general, history and tradition casts a long shadow over contemporary events.

Further reading

A recent and comprehensive account of electoral systems is found in David M. Farrell, *Electoral Systems: A Comparative Introduction* (Basingstoke: Palgrave, 2001). The best short discussion of cleavage systems, voting and coalition governments in west Europe is in Michael Gallagher *et al.*, *Representative Government in Modern Europe* (New York: McGraw-Hill, 2nd edn., 1995). Russell J. Dalton, *Citizen Politics* (Chatham: Chatham House, 3rd edn., 2002) compares electoral behaviour in France, Great Britain, the USA and West Germany, and Pippa Norris, *Democratic Phoenix* (Cambridge: Cambridge University Press, 2002) focuses on voting turnout around the world. A good comparative study of voting and elections, covering a wide range of the literature, is Lawrence LeDuc, Richard G. Niemi and Pippa Norris (eds.), *Comparing Democracies: Elections and Voting in Global Perspective* (Thousand Oaks, CA: Sage, 1996) and Russell J. Dalton and Martin P. Wattenberg, *Politics without Partisans: Political Change in Advanced Industrial Democracies* (Oxford: Oxford University Press, 2000) is a good collection of essays examining the changing politics of advanced industrial societies. On referendums, see Matthew Mendelsohn and Andre Parkin (eds.), *Referendum Democracy: Citizens, Elites, and Deliberation in Referendum Campaigns* (Basingstoke: Palgrave, 2001).

Websites

http://electionresources.org	Links to internet sites around the world which provide detailed information about national and local elections, as well as other election resources.
http://www.fairvote.org/turnout/intturnout.htm	For data on electoral turnout.
http://dodgson.ucsd.edu/lij	Web Site of the Lijphart Election Archive, which is a research collection of district-level election results for approximately 350 national legislative elections in twenty-six countries.

Projects

1. How would you account for the persistent strength of religious voting, and of the old political parties?
2. What do you feel is the best voting system? Present a systematic overview of its advantages and disadvantages.
3. What are the strengths and weakness of (a) the rational-choice approach to the explanation of turnout and party voting, (b) the sociological approach (Columbia school) and (c) the psychological approach (Michigan school)?

12   Party government

Democratic government is party government: electoral competition is largely party competition; parliamentary politics are invariably party politics; and government is rarely anything but party government. For better or for worse, **political parties** pervade all aspects of government and politics in democracies. They mediate between citizens, at the bottom of the political system, and parliamentary parties, presidents and prime ministers, at the top, and they span the segments of society (classes, generations, genders, ethnic groups, religions, regions and voluntary organisations). Parties are essential agents that help to structure public opinions, integrate the political system and articulate interests. No wonder that one of the first things new democracies do is form parties, and one of the first things dictators do is ban all parties but their own.

And yet, parties are also widely criticised for being factious and squabbling. The 'anti-party view' is that they are the cause of needless conflict and division: since there is 'only one way to lay a sidewalk', common sense, and not politics, should guide public affairs. Yet it is precisely because there is no one 'best way' of doing things, and because there is almost always disagreement about what to do and how to do it, that we need the *faction and conflict* of rival parties. Parties formulate and express competing interests and ideas in their unending competition with one another for electoral support. Politics is about the struggle for power, and this chapter is about how parties are at the very centre of this struggle in their attempts to win elections and gain government office.

Political parties
Organisations of politically like-minded people who seek political power and public office in order to realise their policies.

The six major topics in this chapter are:

- Party organisation
- New parties and movements
- Party systems and party families
- Coalition government
- Coalitions and government effectiveness
- Theories of parties.

■ Party organisation

Parties in democracies have two central purposes: to gain power by winning elections; and once in power, to implement their (**public**) **policy**. For both these purposes, *organisation* is vital. It is essential for the conduct of effective elections campaigns, and it is the backbone of a united government that can carry out its policy programme.

Public policy
A general set of ideas or plans that has been officially agreed on and which is used as a basis for making decisions.

Parties have passed through three main stages of organisation since their appearance in anything like a modern form:

Caucus
A small but loose-knit group of politicians (notables) who come together from time to time to make decisions about political matters.

- *Caucus parties* (also known as elite parties) In the nineteenth century, when few people had the vote, political parties were little more than loose alliances (a **caucus** or a clique) of like-minded people. They were usually led by a few elite 'notables', aristocrats, or wealthy public figures.
- *Mass parties* In the twentieth century, with the coming of the universal franchise, parties broadened their electoral appeal by turning themselves into mass parties, with a large membership and a bureaucratic, centralised and hierarchical form of organisation.
- *Catch-all parties* Since the 1970s, the 'unfreezing' of old cleavages and the development of 'new politics' have pushed parties towards a '**catch-all**' organisations, or rainbow coalitions that try to appeal to a wider variety of social groups and interests.

Catch-all parties
Parties that try to attract a broad range of supporters by advocating rather general policies.

It is now suggested that parties are moving towards a fourth stage in which they are described either as *media parties*, *cartel parties* or *electoral-professional parties*:

- *Media parties* The spread of the mass media and computer technology means that party leaders can appeal directly to voters. This reduces the need for a mass membership, a cumbersome organisation and mass meetings. State funding also relieves financial pressures. Media parties do not need such deep roots in society, and it may even be that ordinary party members with views of their own about politics make life more difficult for leaders who want to respond rapidly and flexibly to fast-changing political developments in the world.
- *Cartel parties* Political parties in the late twentieth century adapted to declining participation and turned themselves from mass, competitive

parties into cartel parties that collaborated with each other for state resources (money and patronage) as well as career stability and continuity for their leaders. Parties are increasingly a part of the *machinery of state*. Politics used to be a more 'amateur' affair for people who combined it with ordinary jobs in law, teaching and other forms of public service, but now there are more career professionals. They listen mainly to other career professionals, rather than the general public, and try to secure their own political jobs. The large parties collude with each to exclude the smaller and newer ones.

- *Electoral–professional parties* Drawing from Michels' 'iron law of oligarchy' (see pp. 155, 232), it is argued that modern parties have been 'captured' by professional career politicians who run highly centralised and technically skilled party operations and election campaigns.

Party policy and organisation, it is said, are now more of a technical and professional matter than an ideological one. They involve opinion polling, focus groups, spin-doctors, carefully planned public relations and money-raising campaigns, computer technology and mastery of the mass media. Party conferences are no longer policy making events, where the party faithful debate party policy, but stage-managed public relations events organised around photo-opportunities and sound-bites. At the same time, parties still need a core of supporters and workers to get the vote out on election days and to raise money. Party organisations, albeit in new forms, and grass-roots members are still required, even in the media age.

■ New parties and movements

We have already seen how old voting patterns in west Europe, based on class cleavages, have changed to some extent, causing the old party system to 'unfreeze'. The result has been the appearance of new parties and movements that differ from the old parties in three main ways:

- They are based on the 'new' issues of the environment, peace, feminism, nuclear weapons and energy, animal rights, community participation and minority group rights.
- They are supported mainly by the young, well-educated and relatively affluent sections of the population, so are found mainly in the most affluent democracies rather than in industrialising countries.
- They use different political methods, often direct and grass-roots political action, protests and demonstrations and sometimes violence.

Sometimes the new parties are known as 'anti-party parties' or 'anti-politics movements', because they oppose the ideas and methods of the traditional and conventional parties and pressure groups. The first flowering of such parties is often said to have been in 1968 when a new generation of student activists, intellectuals and some workers took to the streets in many western countries to protest against conventional politics. According to some analysts, the new parties are closely associated with the emergence of post-materialism (chapter 8) and they also overlap with the New Social Movements (chapter 9).

Originally there was speculation that the new parties and movements would cause a crisis in democratic politics by replacing the old party and pressure groups, or at least undermining them, so destabilising conventional politics. This has not happened, partly because the new parties have usually remained quite small, and partly because the old parties have adapted to them by stealing some of their new policies. In fact, some of the old parties have long advocated aspects of the 'new' policies, though they have not always put them at the very top of their agendas. They have now polished them up and pushed them closer to the front of their political stall to try to outflank the new organisations.

The result, as we saw in terms of voting in chapter 11, is not the *replacement* of the old politics by the new, but rather a *fusion* of the two. Few of the old parties have disappeared, although they have adapted their policies and organisation to fit new conditions, and they have sometimes declined in power. At the same time, few new parties seriously rival the old, although some have had disproportionate influence in forcing old parties to shift their political agenda. There has been a slight tendency for **party systems** to fragment as new parties have entered the arena, and some increase in electoral volatility as the electorate rearranged its voting habits. But in general the pattern is one of *change and continuity* rather than transformation of the old system.

Party systems
The pattern of significant parties within a political system, especially their number and the party families represented.

◼ Party systems and party families

Most democracies have many parties, and each country has its own unique combination of them. Nonetheless, the parties of democratic countries have two major features in common:

Party families
Groups of parties in different countries that have similar ideologies and party programmes.

- They often group into **party families**
- They form party systems which can be explained with a few simple rules.

◼ *Party families*

Although parties come in all shapes and colours, they often fall neatly into types because parties of the same sort in different countries often bear a striking family resemblance to each other. Because the main parties are built around the main social cleavages in society, and because urban–industrial societies tend to have similar cleavages in each nation one can usually find a few main parties that appeal to similar social groups, have similar core values and policies that express similar goals. There are seven main party families, and to simplify our task of classifying parties even more most can be arranged more or less neatly on a centre–left and a centre–right scale. We shall look much more closely at the beliefs and programmes of party families in chapter 13; here it is enough simply to identify the types and show how they fit into government coalitions. Starting with the left the families are:

1. Socialist parties, including ex-communist and left-socialist, social democratic, Labour and new left parties   Most parties of this family are affiliated to the Socialist International.
2. Christian democratic parties and Christian socialist parties.
3. Agrarian parties, variously called Farmer, Peasant, Agrarian, or Centre parties.
4. Liberal Parties, often known as Radical, Progressive, Liberal, or Freedom parties.
5. Conservative parties   This party family often goes under the name of Conservative or National parties.
6. Nationalist, regional, and minority ethnic parties   These take all sorts of political positions, from radical left to radical right, so they cannot be placed collectively on the left–right scale.
7. New/Green parties   They also come in different left–right colours, although they are often centre-left.

Briefing 12.1 lists these types, and provides examples of the parties in each family and the countries in which they are found.

■ *Party systems*

Party systems are closely linked with party families; we can also see patterns in the way in which parties combine in any given country to form a *party system*. Once again, each country has a unique combination of parties, but we can see clear patterns in the way in which party systems are formed:

1. Since large parties are built upon political cleavages, there is a connection between the *number of cleavages* and the *number of parties*. Nations with one main cleavage – usually class – tend to have two main parties, one on the centre-left and one on the centre-right. Nations with two main cleavages – class and religion, for example – tend to have three main parties, one to represent the middle class and its main religion, and two others to represent the working class and its different religious or secular values. This association between the number of cleavages and parties is sometimes expressed by the formula:

   $$P = C + 1$$

   where P stands for the number of parties and C for the number of cleavages.
2. Because there is usually room only for one party to articulate one side of a cleavage, we rarely find *more than one large party on the same side*. A large social democratic party is not often found alongside a large communist party, and a large Christian democratic party is unlikely to be opposed by a large conservative party, or a major agrarian party found with a major

Briefing 12.1
Party families

Family	Country	Example
Socialist	Canada	New Democratic Party
	Czech Republic, Denmark, Estonia, Finland, Germany, Iceland, Japan, Lithuania, Sweden	Social Democratic Party
	Australia, Ireland, Mauritius, New Zealand, Norway, UK	Labour Party
	Argentina, Austria, Belgium, France, Greece, Japan, Portugal, Spain	Socialist Party
	Costa Rica	National Liberation Party
	Dominican Republic	Dominican Revolutionary Party
	Jamaica	People's National Party
	Peru	Peruvian Aprista Party
	South Africa	African National Congress
Christian Democrat	Australia, Chile, Czech Republic, Germany, Hungary, Latvia, Lithuania, Netherlands, Portugal, Slovenia, Sweden, Switzerland	Christian Democratic Party
	Romania	National, Peasant or Christian Democratic Party
	Denmark, Norway	Christian People's
	Belgium	Flemish Christians, French Christians
Agrarian	Estonia, Finland, Norway, Sweden	Centre Party
	Latvia	Farmers Party
	Australia	Country, National Party
	Poland	Peasants' Party
Liberal	Canada	Liberal, Social Credit Party
	Sweden	People's Party
	Finland, Japan, Taiwan	Progressive Party
	UK	Liberal Democratic Party
	France	Left Radical Party
	Germany	Free Democrats
	USA	Democratic Party
	Philippines	Liberal Party
	South Africa	Democratic Alliance
	EU	European Liberal, Democrat and Reform Party
Conservative	Canada, Denmark, Norway, UK	Conservative Party
	Japan	Democratic Liberal Party
	New Zealand	National Party
	Sweden	Moderate Party
	Finland	National Coalition

Family	Country	Example
	France	Gaullist Party
	Austria	Freedom Party
	USA	Republican Party
Regional, Ethnic parties	Finland	Swedish People's Party
	Belgium	Flemish, Flemish Nationalist Party
	Spain	Basque Nationalist Party, Catalan Nationalist Party
	UK	Irish Nationalist (Unionist, Social Remocratic and Labour Party), Scottish, Welsh
	Italy	Northern League
	Canada	Quebec Nationalist Party
New parties	Australia, Austria, Belgium, Canada, Finland, France, Ireland, Italy, Israel, Japan, Poland, South Africa, Sweden, Switzerland	Green Party
	New Zealand	Values, Greens and Alliance Parties

liberal party. This, of course, is only another way of formulating the $P = C + 1$ rule.

3. Most *social cleavages are old*, so most of the main parties are well established, dating back to the nineteenth century when the modern industrial system was formed, and voting rights extended.

4. Across western nations the *social democrats* are usually the largest single party, though their strength has declined a little, followed by the conservatives, Christian democrats, liberals and agrarian parties, in that order.

Most discussion of party systems distinguishes between dominant one-party, two-party and multi-party systems. **Dominant one-party systems** are relatively rare, **two-party systems** more frequent and **multi-party systems** the most common (see fact file 12.1). The party system has a great significance for the kinds of governments that are formed in most democracies.

■ *One-party and coalition government*

Democratic accountability in democracies is supposed to be maintained by the fact that free elections allow voters to choose their political representatives. They can either reward good governments with another term of office or kick them out. The overwhelming majority of representatives are elected as party candidates, and it is the *party distribution of seats* in a parliamentary system that

Dominant one-party systems
A party system in which one party dominates all the others.

Two-party systems
Party systems in which two large parties dominate all the others.

Multi-party systems
Where several or many main

227

Fact file 12.1

Party systems, government formation, coalitions and electoral systems

■ Party systems

- Dominant one-party systems are found in India (the Congress Party), Japan (the Liberal Democratic Party), South Africa (the African National Congress, ANC) and Sweden (The Social Democratic Workers' Party).
- The main examples of two-party systems are Canada, New Zealand (until constitutional reform in 1966), the UK (Labour and Conservatives) and the USA (Democrats and Republicans).
- Multi-party systems are the norm and are found in most parts of the democratic world.

■ Government formation

- About 10 per cent of all governments formed in western Europe 1945–95 were single-party governments, about a third were MWCs, another third were minority governments and about one in six were surplus majority.
- Japan has had a dominant party system and one-party-government for most of the post-war period. The two-party systems of Canada, New Zealand (until 1996) and the UK are associated with one-party governments, where a single party forms the government.

■ Coalitions

- The multi-party systems of most western European nations since 1945 are associated with coalition government.
- 'Grand' coalitions ruled in Austria, 1947–66, in Germany, 1966–9 and are often found in Switzerland.
- MWCs have survived well in Austria, Germany, Iceland, Luxembourg and Norway, while surplus majority governments have been formed in Germany and Iceland.
- Minority governments have a relatively good record for stability in Ireland and Sweden, and especially Denmark.
- Coalitions of all kinds have fared relatively poorly in Belgium, Finland, France (Fourth Republic, 1945–58) and Portugal Finland.
- The FDP, a small centre-liberal party in (West) Germany, was in the governing coalition for much of the post-war period, because of its pivotal role. The Christian Democrats (CDA) have played a similar part in Dutch coalitions.

■ Voting systems and party systems

- Of a list of seventy-three liberal democracies in the 1990s, thirty-six had PR electoral systems and thirty-seven non-PR systems. Of the thirty-six PR countries, 81 per cent were multi-party and the remaining 19 per cent were two- or dominant one-party systems. Of the thirty-seven non-PR countries, 13 per cent were multi-party and 50 per cent were two- or dominant one-party systems.

determines the composition of the government. As long as the government can muster the support of a majority of elected representatives in the assembly, it can continue in government.

In dominant one-party systems government formation is straightforward – there is no alternative to the dominant party (see briefing 12.2). In two-party systems, it is usually also straightforward because the majority party will form the government if it has an absolute majority of seats, and if it does not it can probably govern with the legislative support of one or more of the other parties, usually minor ones. As a result, two-party systems generally produce one-party government in which the other party forms the opposition. However, one-party government is the exception rather than the rule.

Most government in most countries is by **coalition** simply because they have electoral and multi-party systems that make it unusual to have a single-party majority in the assembly. This makes it important to understand the process of government formation and maintenance in multi-party systems with **coalition** government.

> parties compete, often with the result that no single party has an overall majority.

> **Coalition**
> A set of parties that comes together to form a government.

■ Coalition government

If no single party is large enough to form the government, then a *party coalition* will have to be formed. Most democracies have quite a few parties that are important enough to claim a position in government, either because their size makes it difficult to overlook them, or because their size or place in the party system gives them a pivotal role in government formation. But the creation of such a coalition often involves long, hard and complex negotiations between party leaders. In some cases, alliances are negotiated before elections, but more normally coalitions are constructed after elections, when the parliamentary strength of the parties is known (see briefing 12.2). This process of bargaining between possible coalition partners is sometimes presented as a secretive form of 'horse-trading' taking place in smoke-filled rooms, but there are some rules governing the process:

1. Normally, the leader of the largest party in parliament/assembly has the first chance at trying to form a governing coalition, and as such is known as the *formateur* but if this fails the job passes to the leader of the second largest party.
2. Some constitutions give the head of state the right to nominate the *formateur*, though there is often little choice given the first rule.
3. Where there is no obvious *formateur* an *informateur* may be given the job of finding one, or to set up negotiations.
4. The job of the *formateur* is to find agreement among coalition partners on government policy and the division of cabinet posts between the parties. Policy agreements can be very specific indeed and result in thick and detailed policy documents. This may take months of hard bargaining.

Briefing 12.2
Government formation: parliamentary systems

Party system	Assembly	Government
One-party dominant	One-party majority	Dominant party government – Japan, Sweden, South Africa
Two-party system	One-party majority or near-majority	One-party government with swings between the two main parties – Greece, Norway, Spain, UK
Multi-party systems Electoral alliance No electoral alliance	Multi-party assemblies	Coalition government Coalitions formed before election Coalition government formed after election Minority government – common in Denmark and not uncommon in Finland, Italy and Sweden MWC – quite common in many coalitions Oversized coalition – quite common in Finland, Italy and The Netherlands 'Grand' coalition – Austria, Canada, Switzerland, (West) Germany

5. Cabinet positions in a coalition are usually distributed roughly in proportion to the strength of the coalition partners in the assembly, and the leader of one of the largest parties usually becomes the prime minister. Which politicians end up with which cabinet posts is usually a matter of tough negotiation, and pivotal parties in the coalition can drive a hard bargain.

6. If a governing coalition is formed it is then formally invested in office by the head of state, and sometimes parliament must give its formal assent as well.

Vote of confidence

A vote of confidence (or no confidence), to test whether the government of the day continues to have the majority support of members of the assembly.

7. A coalition government that loses a **vote of confidence** in the parliament/assembly is normally required to resign, but remains in office as a caretaker government until a new government is formed.

Early theory predicted that coalition governments would usually take the form of **minimum winning coalitions** (**MWC**) because these are the smallest that can count on a majority of votes in the assembly. Anything larger than a MWC has more votes than strictly necessary, and the more coalition partners there are the greater the chance of difficulties between them. Anything smaller, and the government will not necessary be able to count on a majority of votes in the assembly.

However, an examination of coalition governments shows that a large proportion are either smaller or larger than a MWC. A **minority government**, often consisting of one party, is quite common. The reason is that opposition parties can sometimes exercise a great deal of influence within parliament through its committees, or outside it through affiliated pressure groups (trade unions, business organisations). In such systems, it is not essential to have a position within government in order to wield political influence. In other cases, minority governments persist simply because the opposition majorities are not sufficiently unified to be able to remove the minority from power.

Quite a few coalitions are larger than necessary. **'Oversized' coalitions** often exist where the 'surplus' parties have policies that are similar to those of the other parties in the coalition. Drawing from the same party family in this way includes all like-minded groups in the government, and reduces the chances of conflict and instability caused by excluding people who might easily be allies if they were included, and enemies if excluded. Surplus majorities may also help to keep the minority parties within them quiet because they know that they can be ejected from the coalition if they make trouble, without risking the government's majority. In some cases, **'grand' coalitions** are formed, consisting of all the most important parties. These are not common and are usually created in the face of a crisis.

It is easier to form and maintain a government if the coalition partners have a similar outlook and policy. Most coalition governments therefore contain parties that are quite 'close' in policy terms. This gives centre and moderate parties an advantage because they can form an alliance with the moderate left or the moderate right. Sometimes, however, the strength of parties in the assembly makes it difficult to achieve a minimum ideological spread, and then politics makes for strange bed-fellows and greater instability.

Minimum winning coalitions
The smallest number of parties necessary for a majority of votes in parliament.

Minority government
A government or coalition that is smaller than a MWC.

'Oversized' coalitions
A coalition that is larger than a MWC one.

'Grand' coalitions
Oversized coalitions that include all parties or all the largest of them.

■ Coalitions and government effectiveness

It used to be thought that two-party systems were the best because they tended to result in stable, moderate and accountable government. They often produced clear and stable working majorities in parliament. If only one party was in power it could be held clearly accountable for government actions. In two-party systems, there was a strong incentive for both parties to try to hold the middle ground, and hence to be moderate in their policies. The inter-war Weimar government in Germany, and the frequent collapse of coalition governments in the Fourth French Republic and in post-war Italy were often wheeled out as examples to make the point about the instability of coalition government.

It is also claimed that the process of forming coalition government gives too much power to politicians and their wheeler-dealing and secret horse-trading. The outcome of their bargaining may not reflect the preferences of voters, it may also give too much power to pivotal parties, whose support is necessary for successful coalition formation, even if they are rather small and unrepresentative. Experience, however, suggests that coalitions can be as stable as one-party government. Germany, The Netherlands, Scandinavia and Switzerland have all had long periods of coalition government that have been effective, stable and moderate.

It is true that unstable coalitions sometimes require the reconstitution of government between elections – that is, the formation of a new coalition: hence some countries have more governments than elections. But the consequences of instability need not be severe or chaotic. The presence of the same party (or parties) in successive coalitions often gives continuity, and the cautious, inclusive and consensual nature of much coalition government discourages rapid swings of policy from one single-party government to the next. It is also easy to exaggerate the instability of coalition government. While single-party governments are generally the most long-lasting, MWCs survive well in some countries, just as surplus majority ones do in others (see fact file 12.1). By and large, coalitions made up of a small number of parties, and of parties that are quite close on the left–right continuum, are most stable. Finally, coalitions are not unrepresentative of electoral opinion. They often have to be moderate to stay in power, and their frequent inclusion of a centre party as a partner means they tend to be representative of the middle ground of politics.

■ Theories of parties

■ The 'iron law of oligarchy'

Robert Michels (1876–1936)

Robert Michels, Political Parties (1911)

Robert Michels, in one of the most influential works on political parties (1911), argued that parties are, and always will be run by minorities. Michels' famous 'iron law' claims that all large-scale organisations – parties, pressure groups, trade unions, churches, universities – are controlled by a few leaders, no matter how democratic they try to be. There are *organisational* and *psychological* reasons for this:

- Organisationally, leaders are best informed about the business of the organisation and control its internal means of communication. They are also likely to have better organisational skills than ordinary members.
- Psychologically, the masses rely upon leaders because they have neither the time nor the ability to master the affairs of the organisation, and because they feel the need for leadership 'direction and guidance'.

Oligarchy Government by a few.

A more recent version of Michels' theory of **oligarchy** is the *electoral–professional* interpretation of modern political parties discussed earlier in this chapter.

Oligarchy in organisations would not matter so much if it were not also believed that leaders inevitably betray their organisation, using their position either for their own interests – usually the pursuit of personal power, glory, or money, or following policies that are not approved by their rank-and-file members. They may do the latter not because they are corrupt or untrustworthy, though this may be true in some cases, but because being leaders of their organisations who come into contact with leaders of other organisations, they take a wider view of matters. They may also follow longer-term and more strategic policies.

Max Weber, a contemporary of Michels in Germany (see chapter 1), argued a similar case when he said that 'for the time being the dictatorship of the official and not that of the worker is on the march' (see chapter 7). Like Michels, Weber argues that full-time, experienced and trained professionals will always dominate part-time, untrained and inexperienced amateurs. Although Weber applies his theory to the power struggle between bureaucrats and politicians, rather than party leaders and followers, the principles are the same.

There are two possible responses to the Michels–Weber thesis. The first argues that the law, though it may be generally true, is not 'iron' because there are examples of private organisations that are not oligarchical. The second claims that it does not particularly matter if organisations are internally oligarchic if competition between them produces democracy. Business associations and trade unions may not be particularly democratic, but competition between them may be.

■ Duverger's law

The 'iron law' deals with the internal organisation of parties, while another classic 'law', of the French political scientist Maurice Duverger, is concerned with the relationship between electoral systems and party systems. In his key (1954) work, Duverger argued that states that have non-proportional elections (specifically SMSP systems) favour two parties, while proportional elections favour multi-party systems. Non-proportional elections usually discriminate against small parties because they fail to turn their votes into a proportional number of seats. The electorate knows this, and is less inclined to vote for small parties because it may be a 'wasted vote'.

Maurice Duverger, *Political Parties: Their Organisation and Activity in the Modern State* (1954)

Fifty years of debate about Duverger's law has tended to concentrate on two issues:

• First, what is cause and what is effect? Belgium, Denmark, Germany and Norway were multi-party systems *before* they opted for PR, and they may have done so because it was in the interest of small parties to have PR, or because it was the only electoral system that was acceptable to most parties, including the small ones. On the other side of the coin, the USA and the UK seem to keep their SMSP systems because it is in the interests of the two main parties that are the only ones with power enough to change them. Since governing parties gain power through SMSP they are unlikely to change it for a different electoral system that might lose them this advantage.

- Second, in spite of exceptions to the 'law', there is in general a good deal of truth in it. The most proportionate voting systems are much more likely to be multi-party than the most disproportionate (see chapter 11).

■ Coalition theory

William Riker (1920–93) The early and influential work on coalition formation by William Riker (1962) predicted that coalitions would be just big enough to ensure a majority in the assembly, but no bigger or smaller. It was assumed that politicians were motivated primarily by a desire for power or prestige, in which case there was no sense in sharing cabinet posts among more parties than was strictly necessary. Consequently, coalitions would be MWCs.

William Riker, The Theory of Political Coalitions (1962)

A different assumption is that politicians seek office not exclusively for power, prestige, or government office, but in order to influence public policy. Such politicians might consider a course of action that gave them influence over public policy, even if it fell short of government office. Minority governments may thus be successful if there are politicians outside government who are prepared to support their policy. Similarly, surplus majority governments may be formed if they help to achieve policy goals. If it is *policy*, rather than *office-seeking* that counts, one might assume that the limits on coalition formation will be set not necessarily by coalition size but by the *ideological 'closeness'* of parties. Consequently, the theory advocated by Robert Axelrod in his (1970) book argues that coalitions will be of a 'minimum connected winning' (MCW) form – that is, the smallest ideological span necessary to drive policy in a particular direction. Coalitions will be formed by the closest set of parties capable of forming an effective alliance.

Robert Axelrod, Conflict of Interest (1970)

Evidence over the post-war years in the democracies provides support for both the Riker and Axelrod theories, but there is not overwhelming support for either:

- The large group of government coalitions has taken a MWC, but it is also true that minimum coalitions are outnumbered by oversized ones and minority governments.
- It is also the case that nearly a half of all coalitions have taken a MCW, but this means, of course, that half have not.

Giovanni Sartori, Parties and Party Systems: A Framework for Analysis (1976)

- In short, most situations that could result in MWCs have not produced them, although, of all kinds of coalition, the MWC are most numerous.

Giovanni Sartori argues that both the number and the ideological distance between parties are important for understanding how multi-party systems work and how governments are formed. In Sartori's (1976) book, he distinguishes between *moderate* and *polarised pluralism*. The moderate type usually has three–five main parties, which tend to compete for the centre ground, and therefore tend to be moderate. Polarised systems normally have six or more main parties, which tend to move to the extremes in order to find votes in an overcrowded political arena. This makes it difficult to form and sustain coalition cabinets.

Perhaps the only safe conclusion to draw from this discussion of coalition theory is that politicians are not exclusively self-interested (office-seeking), and that they may opt for either surplus majority or minority governments, if this helps them, or they may opt to work outside the government if the system allows them to influence policy in this way. This conclusion is consistent with the conclusion that voters are not always self-interested, but pay some regard to the public interest. It does not follow that politicians are not interested in power and office, but it does seem to be the case that they are not all interested in these things all the time.

■ *Majoritarian and consensus government revisited*

At the end of chapter 6, we presented Arend Lijphart's account of majoritarian and consensus government, but did not complete the discussion, having covered only the formal institutions of government at that point. We can now deal with the rest of the majoritarian–consensus typology, having also discussed its other characteristics in chapters 8–11 dealing with electoral systems, party systems, government formation and pressure groups.

Majoritarian governments tend to concentrate power in the hands of the *political executive* and are associated with the fusion of executive and legislative powers, a unicameral legislature, unitary government, government control over central banks and courts with no special powers to review constitutional matters or legislation. In the classic 'Westminster system', built around the principle of parliamentary sovereignty, these features of government fit together in a logical and consistent manner, given the initial purpose of concentrating a good deal of political power in the hands of the party that represents a majority of citizens. The remaining four key features of majoritiarian government also fit the pattern well:

1. *Majoritarian and disproportional electoral systems* Majoritarian democracies tend to favour single-member districts and first-past-the post voting systems. This favours large over small parties and magnifies the size of the winning party's majority of seats compared with its votes.
2. *Two-party systems* The winner-takes-all nature of parliamentary systems, as well as their electoral discrimination against small parties, encourages the formation of two large parties that alternate in government.
3. *Single-party government* The winning party with a majority of seats becomes the government. All other parties form the opposition.

4. *Pluralist pressure group systems* Pressure groups in society are loosely integrated in the decision making structure of government, sometimes forming policy communities but more usually taking the form of competitive policy networks.

Consensus governments try to represent not the electoral majority and its party but as many people as possible, including minorities. They therefore try to distribute executive power more broadly and are associated with the separation and balancing of executive power, bicameralism, federalism, independent central banks and judicial review. The other four key features are consistent with the goal of broad representation and the distribution of power:

1. *Proportional electoral systems* These systems distribute seats in more or less the same ratio of votes.
2. *Multi-party systems* Multi-party government and proportional electoral systems do not discourage small parties.
3. *Coalition governments* The formation of broad coalition governments can involve sometimes oversized or 'grand' coalitions.
4. *Corporatist pressure group systems* Major pressure groups are formally incorporated into the decision making machinery of government, where they cooperate on policy issues.

This twofold typology does not simply describe the political systems of democracy, it also helps to explain their performance in five interesting and important respects:

1. *The distance between governments and voters* Consensus democracies have governments that are closer to the policy preferences of citizens than majoritarian systems.
2. *Citizens' satisfaction* The citizens of consensus democracies are more satisfied with the democratic performance of their countries than those of majoritarian democracies. In part, this is because the losers in consensus systems are more satisfied than the losers in majoritarian systems, in part because they acknowledge that the electoral system is fairer and they have not been discriminated against and because, even as electoral minorities, they still have influence over government policies.
3. *Turnout* Consensus democracies have a higher voting turnout (by about 7.5 per cent) than majoritarian ones.
4. *Women in parliament* Consensus democracies have about 6.5 per cent more women in the main legislative chamber.
5. *Effective number of parties* Consensus democracies not only have a larger number of parties contesting elections but, because of their proportional voting systems, they also have a larger number of effective parties – that is, parties that are large enough to play an significant role in the assembly.

On the basis of this evidence, Lijphart concludes that the majoritarian and consensus systems have extremely important practical implications for the performance of democracies. The performance of consensus democracies is clearly superior.

■ Summary

Politics is about the struggle for power, and this chapter deals with how parties are at the very centre of this struggle in their attempts to win elections and gain government office. It argues that:

- Parties have passed through three main phases of organisation – caucus, mass parties and catch-all parties. Now they are said to be moving into a new phase of media parties, or cartel parties, or electoral–professional parties, which have strong leaders and few members.
- Old parties, formed in the late nineteenth and early twentieth centuries, have been challenged by new parties and movements, but they have adapted. The result is continuity with change, in which the new has combined and fused with the old, rather than a transformation of party systems.
- Most democracies have one-party, two-party, or coalition government, but coalitions are most common.
- Contrary to early theories, most coalition governments do not take the MWC form. Minority governments, surplus majority governments and (occasionally) 'grand' coalitions are more common.
- There is not much evidence to support the claim that coalition government is unstable, unaccountable, or unrepresentative compared with single-party governments.
- Although there are significant exceptions, proportional voting is associated with multi-party systems and coalition government. Non-proportional voting is associated with a dominant party or two main parties.
- The evidence suggests that politicians are not exclusively interested in prestige or the power that goes with government office (office-seeking). They may support surplus majority or minority governments, and they may choose to work outside government if this helps them influence government policy.
- The evidence suggests that the democratic performance of consensus democracies is superior to that of majoritarian systems.

Further reading

A book with a broad surveys of the literature on parties is Alan Ware, *Political Parties and Party Systems* (Oxford: Oxford University Press, 1995). Three up-to-date collections of essays and articles are Paul Webb, David Farrell and Ian Holliday, *Political Parties in Advanced Industrial Democracies* (Oxford: Oxford University Press, 2002), Richard Gunther, Jose R. Montero and Juan J. Linz (eds), *Political Parties: Old Concepts and New Challenges* (Oxford: Oxford University Press, 2002) and Steven B. Wolinetz (ed.), *Political Parties* (Aldershot: Ashgate, 1997).

Websites

http://en.wikipedia.org/wiki/Political_party	A useful site on parties, party systems, elections, campaigns, elections and lists of parties in the world.
http://sosig.esrc.bris.ac.uk/roads/subject-listing/World-cat/polparties.html	An extensive list of web resources on parties and politics in the regions of the world.
http://www.gksoft.com/govt/en/parties.html	Provides links to political parties in the nations of the world.
http://www.benne.luna.nl/pp/eur	Political parties and youth movements in Europe.
http://www.nationmaster.com	Links to the largest parties and pressure groups in countries across the world.
http://www.wordiq.com	Lists political parties by region, country and ideology.

Projects

1. Collect a list of all the main political parties in your country and try to arrange them into the seven main categories discussed in this chapter. What difficulties do you meet in trying to classify your parties, and why do you think your country produces parties that do not fit the scheme?
2. Are you persuaded that the democratic performance of consensus democracies is superior to that of majoritarian systems?

PART IV

Policies and performance

Most ordinary people are not very interested in political institutions and processes. What interests them about politics is what governments do *to* them and *for* them:

- What do they get for their tax bill?
- Do their children get a good education?
- Is inflation and unemployment low?
- Will they get a decent pension when they retire?
- Are the streets safe?
- Is their nation well protected from its enemies?

Part IV of the book, therefore, is about the *policies* and *performance* of governments. A 'policy' is a general set of ideas formulated into a plan that has been officially agreed, and which is used as a basis for making decisions. So when we speak of 'economic policies' we refer to the activities a government has planned to achieve its economic goals. Although ideas and plans are important, what most people care about is performance. By 'performance' we mean the *actual results* that governments get – is inflation low and economic growth good? Is crime under control? Are schools well staffed and equipped? Is hospital care effective? Plans are no good if they do not achieve their goals, and performance is no good if it is based on muddled or dangerous plans in the first place. Citizens want good plans and good performance together, but they care most about performance.

Part IV of the book has chapters on both the policy plans and performance of democratic states. Since plans and policies are what parties and governments start with, chapter 13 examines the 'isms' of politics – competing ideas about what governments should do, and how they should do it. These are known as 'ideologies', and there are four main ones in western politics: socialism, liberalism, Christian democracy and conservatism. Behind them lie basic values and assumptions about important concepts such as individualism and collectivism, liberalism and the role of the state, equality and freedom. Different attitudes towards these basic concepts and values are what define the 'isms' of contemporary politics and the fundamental difference between parties.

Chapter 14 then focuses not on the theory but on the practice of making government decisions and implementing them. This can be seen as an endless cycle, starting with a general plan of action and ending with an evaluation of the results achieved by implementing it. We will see that for all the variation in the details of their policy making processes, states tend to follow one of two general logics. Some incorporate their main social and economic interests into a formal structure of *cooperative* decision making. Others lean towards *conflict and competition* between different groups.

In chapter 15 we examine the defence and security of the state, and the way states defend themselves against domestic crime and foreign aggression. Security of the state and its individual citizens, however, does not end here because modern life is beset by any number of other dangers ranging from atomic radiation to badly designed toasters, and governments are expected to do something about these as well. The chapter looks at how the democratic state handles all these threats to the safety and security of its citizens.

Chapter 16 looks more closely at a different form of citizen protection – namely the social security and welfare system. It deals mainly with welfare and social security, pensions and health, and with the way that the state raises money to pay for these services. Of course, government is involved with a far wider range of public services than defence and national security and social security and welfare. We have chosen these two fields because they cover one of the oldest of all functions of the state (to protect itself from internal and external enemies) and one of the newer (to provide its citizens with a decent standard of living and security against poverty, unemployment, ill health and the difficulties of old age). These areas of policy making highlight the problems that governments face when it comes to making decisions and implementing public policy. Chapter 17 draws some brief conclusions.

The chapters in part IV, therefore, examine the key aspects of government policies and performance:

* Political ideologies
* Decision making
* Defence and security
* Welfare.

13 Political ideologies: conservatism, liberalism, Christian democracy and socialism

Politics are confusing. A casual look at the daily news shows a great profusion of fast-moving events, with many conflicting and incompatible interpretations of them. How can we ever make sense of such a bewildering and incomprehensible business? The answer lies in how we organise our ideas, preconceptions and assumptions about politics. We develop a framework of ideas known as an **ideology**, which helps us to understand and interpret politics. This system of ideas, values and assumptions enables us to fit events into a pattern that we can understand.

Ideologies are about more than understanding, however. If politics are a struggle for power, then ideologies are part of the struggle. Party politicians in democracies know that they must win the tacit support, if not the 'hearts and minds' of most of their citizens if they are to continue in power. Ideologies are the tools – perhaps even some of the most important tools – by which they do this because ideologies are built around the basic interests of the most important groups in society.

Because people have contrasting interests and ideas, and because they see politics in radically different ways, there are naturally different ideological world views, including liberalism, conservatism, anarchism, Marxism, Maoism, socialism, Christian democracy, social democracy, fascism, nazism,

Ideology
A more or less systematic, well-developed and comprehensive set of ideas and beliefs about politics consisting of both (empirical) statements about what is, and (prescriptive) statements about what ought to be.

and libertarianism, among others. Fortunately, there are only four main ide-ologies to be found in democracies, which helps to simplify the life of compar-ative political scientists to a great extent. These are conservatism, liberalism, Christian democracy and socialism/social democracy. There are also two other systems of thought – nationalism and Green theory – but their status as ide-ologies is disputed so we will discuss them after the main four.

In this chapter, we present an account of the four major and two other democratic ideologies. The chapter also analyses the nature of ideology itself and discusses the future for ideological thinking in a world where ideology is said to have come to an end. The three major topics in this chapter are:

- The nature of ideology
- Six democratic ideologies
- Theories of ideology.

■ The nature of ideology

Ideology is a confusing concept that has been given different meanings in its history. Some have used it as a weapon in the struggle for power, and as a term of approval or disapproval, saying that while they have truth, reason, or science on their side, their opponents have only dogma and ideology. But the term is used here in its social science sense, as a *tool of analysis*, not as a weapon in the political struggle. Ideologies may be defined in terms of their four main characteristics:

1. *Complexity and abstraction*   Ideologies are relatively complex, abstract, com-prehensive and integrated systems of beliefs about politics. They are based on fundamental ideas and assumptions about human nature, society and politics and on a set of basic values relating to the central concepts of political life including justice, liberty, equality, freedom and democracy. Ideologies are, therefore, far more than a bundle of beliefs about politics; they offer a *view* of the political world and a sweeping *interpretation* of it. This means that an ideology must be specific enough to fit particular cir-cumstances, but general enough to be able to endure and travel widely across the globe.

2. *Empirical explanation*   Ideologies claim to explain the political world. They pick out what they think is important from the mass of political details and events and offer *coherent explanations* of what is happening and why. This does not mean that they are right or wrong, only that they try to explain the facts of the political world.

3. *Normative prescription*   Ideologies offer a vision of how political life *could be* and *ought to be*. They present a vision of what good government should be. In this sense ideologies are **normative statements** and prescriptive.

Normative statements
Statements based upon faith, values or evaluations.

4. *A plan for action*   Ideologies spell out a set of beliefs about how political goals should be achieved. They claim to answer Lenin's question: 'What is to be done?' Since there is often agreement about political goals – who is

against liberty, justice, democracy and progress for all? – common ideological differences are about *political means*, rather than goals. Is it legitimate to use violent or illegal politics, or should we stick to the ballot and
persuasion? Should we form political alliances with this or that group, or
remain 'pure' and separate? Should we support this policy or oppose it?

Sometimes referred to as prescriptive, or evaluative statements. They are neither scientific nor unscientific, but non-scientific.

Some writers are suspicious of ideologies, claiming that they are closed systems of thought that are not amenable to reason or disproof. They point
to Marxism as an example, although there are many others like it. The
Marxist claim that the capitalist system will collapse under the weight of its
own contradictions has been repeated many times since the publication of *The
Communist Manifesto*, but somehow capitalism has survived. As one cynic puts
it: 'The imminent collapse of capitalism is the longest running show in the
west.' Marxists, or rather crude Marxists, always have a Marxist explanation
for this, and so they always manage to preserve their own belief system in
the face of evidence that seems to disprove it. Whatever argument is used to
criticise a closed ideology of this kind, and whatever evidence is used against
it, is somehow treated as evidence to confirm it.

Karl Marx, *The Communist Manifesto* (1848)

According to Karl Popper, a philosopher of the social sciences, ideologies can
be closed and totalitarian systems of thought that can always justify themselves
in their own terms. In his book of 1945, Popper showed that ideologies are to
be distinguished clearly from scientific theories that can, in principle, be tested
and falsified.

Karl Popper (1902–94)

There is a lot of truth in this point. In some respects, ideologies are rather
like religions that seek to explain everything, and can be manipulated to fit
the facts, whatever these are. On the other hand, it is difficult to see how we
can avoid this. If we are to have a comprehensive view of the political world
then we must also have a broad and general understanding of what is, what
should be and how best to achieve it. Besides, it is not necessarily true that
ideologies turn into closed and totalitarian belief systems. An ideologist such
as John Stuart Mill (see below) proposed an open and self-critical belief system,
and lived up to his ideological standards in his own life.

Karl Popper, *The Open Society and Its Enemies* (1945)

Some analysts want to reserve the term 'ideologies' for a highly abstract,
integrated and comprehensive set of values, beliefs and ideas. In this case, only
a few intelligent and well-educated people, with a strong interest in politics,
have an ideology. Sometimes such people are referred to as 'ideologues' (see
chapter 8). Others want to use the term more generally to cover more loose-
knit, but still relatively coherent systems of ideas and values. Used in this way
many ordinary citizens have an ideology.

Ideology is not the same as *political culture*, however. Ideologies are more
or less explicit, whereas much of political culture is implicit and built on
assumptions and deep-seated values that are taken for granted (see chapter 8).
The language of ideologies consists of abstract concepts – including liberty,
equality, fraternity, rights, justice and liberalism. Political cultures are built
on assumptions about trust, happiness, political salience, national pride and

competence. To oversimplify a little, one is socialised into and assimilates a culture in the family, at school and in the community, but one learns an ideology by thinking, arguing and reading in a more self-conscious way.

Before we start our exploration of the main democratic ideologies, two last general points should be made:

Essentially contestable concept
A concept that is inevitably the subject of endless dispute about its proper use (e.g. art, democracy, politics, Christian life).

1. Ideologies are an **essentially contestable concept**, which is a 'shorthand' way of saying that there is often little agreement about them, or about what they mean and what sort of action they entail. This is why even members of the same political party sharing the same ideology will often argue interminably with each other.

2. Closely related to this point is that fact that each major ideology has many variations that merge and overlap with each other at different points. It is difficult to draw a clear line around any ideology, or the variations on it, and it is difficult to summarise them in a clear and simple way.

■ Six democratic ideologies

In chapter 12, we organised party families along a left–right continuum according to their general views about the central issue of state intervention in society and the economy. We can do the same with ideologies, from conservatism on the right, to liberalism and Christian democracy in the centre and socialism and social democracy on the left. The other and more minor ideologies of nationalism and Green political thought do not fit neatly on the left–right continuum, and so they will be discussed separately.

■ *Conservatism*

Because Conservatism is pragmatic and flexible, some argue that it is not an ideology so much as a loose collection of ideas defending the *status quo*. However, conservative thought can be based on a systematic set of fundamental ideas. Two ideas lie at the heart of much Conservative thinking about politics. The first concerns social and political life, the second economic matters.

Social and political affairs
• *Organic society* Conservatism places great value upon the preservation of the *status quo* and its traditional institutions. It is a pragmatic ideology that argues that old institutions survive and work well because they are built on the *accumulated wisdom and experience* of the past. Society is like a natural organism that has changed slowly but surely over a long period. Moreover, it is composed of a complex set of interdependent parts, and reform that moves too fast will almost certainly destabilise the system and do more harm than good. Reform should be slow and cautious.
• *Pessimistic view of human nature* Conservatives tend to be pessimistic about human nature, arguing that the worst aspects of human nature – greed,

selfishness and irrationality – will inevitably rise to the surface unless there is a clear social hierarchy to locate citizens in a social order, and a strong state to maintain it. Consequently, conservatism generally rejects competing ideologies that assume the natural goodness or 'perfectibility of man'. Instead it argues for a strong *police force* to maintain the social order, and a strong *army* to protect the state from its external enemies.

- *Representative democracy*   Many conservatives believe that liberal democracy is best preserved in the hands of a relatively small, educated elite. The mass of citizens is not naturally democratic and it is dangerous to give them too much power. Hence conservatives often prefer indirect and representative democracy (see chapter 2) to direct, participatory forms.

- *Inequality*   Many conservatives believe that people are inherently unequal in their intelligence and abilities, and that some economic and social inequality is natural and inevitable. Some streams of conservative thought go on to emphasise the social responsibilities of the rich and powerful for the poor and weak. Since this style of conservatism fits well with a religious emphasis on the importance of the family and traditional social values, it is often aligned with traditional Christian beliefs. Other conservatives, however, do not emphasise the importance of social conscience but argue, instead, that wealth produced by a small minority of *energetic and able entrepreneurs* will 'trickle down' to the poor.

Economics

- *The invisible hand of the market*   The second fundamental tenet of conservatism is a belief in the market, and the claim that *economic competition* will result in efficiency and the achievement of the public interest. The 'invisible hand of the market' (see briefing 13.1) means that the best way of optimising the general interest is to allow each individual to act in her own economic interests. In this way, economic actors will compete with others which, in turn, will force them to produce the best goods and services at the lowest price. Individual competition and self-interest will thus paradoxically, result in efficiency, innovation and the public good. Attempts to improve or modify the workings of the market will result only in inefficiency and poor performance. For this reason one of the main planks of conservatism is the belief that the state should intervene as little as possible in the economy, although the left and right wings of conservative thought argue about how much or how little this should be.

Performance Actual activities and results; how well government is doing or how successful it is in offering citizens what they prefer.

■ *Liberalism*

Liberalism is an ambiguous term. In classical political theory its essence is the belief that individual liberty can be preserved only by *limiting the powers of the state*. In modern politics, especially in the USA, a 'liberal' is, on the

Briefing 13.1
Conservative thinkers

■ Edmund Burke (1729–97)

An English writer and MP, he formulated many of the social and political principles of modern conservatism. He argued that society was like a complex organism that was easily ruined by attempts to reform it too quickly, and pointed to the disastrous experience of the French revolution to support his claim. He believed in a 'natural aristocracy' in society, and that the mass of ordinary people could sustain a democracy only with the guidance of a political elite. Above all, he claimed that practical experience and wisdom are always to be preferred to abstract rationalism.

■ Adam Smith (1723–90)

The Scottish philosopher and economist, Adam Smith laid the foundations of classical economics in his book *The Wealth of Nations* (1776). He claimed that individual self-interest on the part of 'the butcher, brewer, and baker' led, by way of the 'invisible hand' of the market, to the satisfaction of the general good. The butcher and the baker do not provide a good service because of their concern for others, but because the workings of the market economy makes it in their own self-interest to do so. The state should leave this invisible hand to play its part by setting up the right conditions for laissez-faire economics and a free market.

■ Joseph Schumpeter (1883–1950)

An Austrian economist and political scientist, Schumpeter is best remembered for his (1942) book, in which he argues for an elitist form of democracy. Contrary to Marxist theory, and other theories that place faith in the 'will of the people', Schumpeter claimed that the masses are capable of little, other than stampeding. Democracy should be limited to elitist, representative forms, in which the masses have the power only to vote at regular intervals for representatives who compete for popular support.

■ Friedrich von Hayek (1899–1992)

Another Austrian economist, von Hayek is best known for his book *The Road to Serfdom* (1944), which argues that state regulation and collective action of all kinds tends to limit the freedom of the individual, even if it is moderate and well-intended.

contrary, someone who believes in more rather than less state intervention. This is because the term 'socialist' is not politically acceptable in the USA, so those who advocate even modest government action refer to themselves as 'liberals' to distinguish themselves from conservatives. In what follows the terms 'liberal' and 'liberalism' are basically used in their classical sense.

Early liberalism emerged in the seventeenth century in opposition to traditional government by kings, aristocracies and elites, and to the social order

Briefing 13.2
Two concepts of liberty

Freedom (or liberty – the two terms are used interchangeably here) may be defined as the *absence of restraint*. According to this simple definition, we are free when we are not prevented from doing what we wish. In political matters, however, this definition does not get us very far. I may be free under the law to set up my own political party or pressure group, or free to start my own newspaper, but these formal freedoms are no good to me if I am living in poverty, hunger, disease and ignorance. Formal freedom under the law, and substantive freedom – freedoms that people can actually use – are quite different things. As the saying goes, both the rich and poor are free to stay at the Ritz Hotel or to sleep at night under the nearest bridge. But formal freedom from restraint is not the same as substantive freedom to do something.

Along these lines, the British political theorist Isaiah Berlin (1909–97) distinguished between two concepts of liberty, 'liberty from' and 'liberty to'. Liberty from, or *negative liberty*, is the absence of restraint. Those who believe in it will argue for a minimal state as a matter of principle. Liberty to, or *positive liberty*, is concerned with the actual capacity to do things. For example, to play their role as citizens people need to be educated and informed enough to make sensible judgements about political issues. Since the economic market typically makes education available to the small number who are able and willing to pay for it, but rarely for those who cannot afford it, the state must provide free public education for all. The implication of the positive notion of freedom – freedom to – is that the state must ensure that citizens are able to make use of their formal freedoms. This may require state action to lift the restraints on liberty imposed by poverty, hunger, disease and ignorance.

The two main schools of liberal political thought take different views of liberty. Classical liberals, neo-liberals and libertarians favour freedom from state regulation to maximise individual freedom. Radical or progressive liberals and liberal democrats argue for enough state regulation to overcome the main social and economic obstacles to substantive freedom. According to them the state can intervene as a *liberator*, not as an *oppressor*.

and hierarchy they imposed. Liberals rejected the constraints of traditional government, emphasising instead the importance of individual freedom (see briefing 13.2). This idea continues to lie at the heart of modern liberalism and distinguishes it fundamentally from conservative ideas. It has five main characteristics.

Limited state power

Classical liberalism was built around the principle that the state should be limited to the 'night watchman' function of protecting individual rights and property, and should not pretend to any other function. The modern version of this belief claims that 'government is best that governs least'.

Parliamentary government and the division of powers

Because of their concern with individual rights and duties liberals have traditionally placed great importance on parliament, and on the *checks and balances* of divided government that protect citizens from arbitrary power. But though early liberals believed in parliamentary government, they did not necessarily believe in democracy, because they feared that giving power to the mass of uneducated and unsophisticated citizens would threaten democratic practice and values. They feared that the 'tyranny of the majority' would replace the tyranny of monarchs and aristocracies. In the twentieth century, however, liberals came to accept mass democracy, hence the term '**liberal democracy**'.

Liberal democracy
The form of democracy that tries to combine the powers of democratic government with liberal values about the freedom of the individual.

Optimistic view of human nature

Unlike conservatism, liberalism takes an optimistic view of human nature, assuming that mankind is rational and reasonable when left to its own devices. Liberals also assume that individuals should be formally equal before the law – not that they are equal in capacities, ability, or intelligence but that they have *equal rights and duties*.

Slow reform by individual action

Because classical liberalism assumes that most citizens are rational and responsible, they also tend to argue for slow reform brought about by the *individual action of free individuals*, rather than radical collective action, or conservative reaction.

Free trade

Like one school of conservative theory, classical liberalism believes strongly in laissez-faire economics and free trade. Its defence of *market economics* is logically consistent with its strong belief in a limited state, and of the rights of individuals to make their own economic decisions.

As liberal thought developed in the eighteenth and nineteenth, centuries it divided into two schools. One continued to hold to the classical position of individual rights and a minimal state, especially in economic matters, but a second emerged taking the view that some freedoms required a degree of state action to eliminate the obstacles to real or substantive freedom (see briefing 13.2). According to this view, the state can intervene as a liberator, not an oppressor, if it creates the conditions necessary for individuals to be able to develop their potential and use their natural rights. For example, early social liberals argued for the state to raise taxes to pay for education, public health and housing for the poor, on the grounds that poverty, disease and ignorance were incompatible with human freedom. Known as radical, progressive, or social liberals, this school sits somewhere between conservative and socialist thought, arguing not for or against state intervention in principle, but for it when it is necessary, and against it when it is not.

The ideas of classical liberalism have been revived in the late twentieth century by *neo-liberals* who believe that the powers of the state should be reduced and the economy deregulated and privatised. Neo-liberalism of this kind exercised a strong influence over some conservative politicians, notably Margaret Thatcher in Britain and Ronald Reagan in the USA. As a result, they are sometimes referred to as 'neo-liberals', although they were leaders of conservative parties. Many other countries, as diverse as Bolivia, Chile, India, Mexico, New Zealand, South Korea and Taiwan have implemented neo-liberal economic policies to a greater or lesser extent. In fact, some ideologists take neo-liberal ideas to their extreme conclusion. Known as *libertarians*, they argue for the abolition of almost all state regulation, even of such things as pornography, drugs, and prostitution, on the grounds that all regulation infringes liberty, and that responsible adult citizens should be free to make up their own minds about such matters (briefing 13.3).

■ *Christian democracy*

Pope Leo XIII laid out the basics of Christian democracy in an important encyclical *Rerum Novarum* (1891). This was partly in reaction to the (classical) liberalism of the times, which tended to be secular or anti-clerical. It was also a reply to anti-religious socialism, which was gaining rapidly in popular support, and to monarchism and extreme conservatism. But it was also an attempt to incorporate Catholic thought into a practical ideology. Christian democracy is neither liberal, nor socialist, nor conservative, but somewhere in between. It has five main characteristics.

Pope Leo XIII (in office 1878–1903)

Natural law
Christian democracy starts from the premise that *natural law* is the basis of society and its rules of conduct. Natural law is not given by the state (that is, by kings, or courts, or parliaments, or electoral majorities), but by God. It is revealed to human beings by their capacity to reason.

Family, church, community
Christian democracy rejects the conservatism of traditional social orders, the atomistic individualism of classical liberalism and the 'tyranny of the masses' advocated by the political left. In place of these, it stresses the importance of *'natural' groups in society*, above all, the family, the church and the community.

Subsidiarity
Natural groups should be allowed to run their own affairs in their own way, which means subsidiarity (chapter 5). Christian democrats assert the importance of the autonomy of the natural groups in society to run their own affairs, without interference or regulation by the state. Private and semi-private agencies are morally superior to public ones, because they give individuals the opportunity to exercise their Christian conscience. They are also more effective in meeting human needs. The state should, therefore, intervene only when

Briefing 13.3
Liberal thinkers

■ John Locke (1632–1704)

The British political theorist John Locke (1689) wrote that Natural Law guarantees to every individual the right to life, liberty, and estate' (private property). Citizens enter into a 'social contract' with their government to protect themselves against those who would try to infringe their rights. The proper role of government is limited to upholding natural rights. It has no other function.

■ John Stuart Mill (1806–73)

The British political theorist John Stuart Mill (1859) drew a distinction between *self-regarding* and *other-regarding* actions. Self-regarding actions have no impact on others, and should not be subject to any restraint by government or any other power. According to Mill 'the only purpose for which power can be rightfully exercised over any member of a civilized community, against his will, is to prevent harm to others. His own good, either physical or moral, is not a sufficient warrant.' *Other-regarding* actions are a different matter and may be constrained by the force of the law. In some, ways Mill's distinction between self-regarding and other-regarding actions opens up the possibility of broad intervention by the state, on the grounds that there are very few purely self-regarding actions and many examples of them are trivial. The state can therefore often claim the right to regulate social life. Since Mill modified classical liberal theories in different ways, his thought can be interpreted as standing between liberalism and socialism.

■ John Rawls (1921–2002)

John Rawls is among the most influential liberal thinkers of the twentieth century. In his book *A Theory of Justice* (1971), he introduced the idea of 'justice as fairness' and strongly defended the idea that equality and liberty should be closely related. In his view all *social primary goods* – liberty and opportunities, income and wealth and the bases of self-respect – should be distributed equally unless an unequal distribution of any or all of these goods is to the advancement of the least favoured. So, for Rawls, the unequal treatment of individuals is acceptable only if it improves the situation of those who are in the worst social position. He is not, however, willing to accept limitations on basic liberties: each person is to have an equal right to the most extensive liberties and this principle precedes any other principle. Just as John Stuart Mill can be considered a socialist or a social democrat through his emphasis on social equality and the relationship between equality and freedom, so also can Rawls. In fact, libertarian philosophers such as Robert Nozick (1938–2002) have criticised Rawls for his willingness to consider restrictions on individual freedom. Nozick strongly defended the idea of a 'minimal state'.

it has to, and only in order to *restore the natural community* to its proper functioning. In this way, it argues, solidarity and harmony in society will be preserved.

Protection of the weak and poor

Christian morality requires that the state protects the weakest and poorest members of society. In turn, this means a *moderate welfare state* with special support for the family (family allowances), education (financial support for schools, many of them church schools) and the community (to alleviate poverty and protect people against illness and unemployment).

Harmony, integration, consultation

Christian democracy emphasises social harmony and integration. This means the reconciliation of class, religious and other differences by means of formal social institutions that enable social groups to consult and discuss with one another, something known as the 'concentration of interests'. This involves an elaborate *consultative machinery* in which government, business, trade unions and other interests participate.

Christian democracy is a middle way between conservatism and unbridled capitalism, secular liberal individualism and atheistic socialism. It is neither for nor against state intervention in principle, but argues for enough of it to protect human dignity in accordance with natural law. Some forms of it are close to socialism, others to conservatism.

■ *Socialism and social democracy*

It is important, first of all, to distinguish between the kind of socialism found in so-called 'communist countries', including China and the former Soviet Union, and the socialism and social democracy found in the democratic world. Communist countries have undemocratic regimes controlled by Communist parties, and their dominant ideologies are better known as 'Marxist' or 'communist'. Socialist and social-democratic ideologies are strong in democracies. To distinguish themselves clearly from Marxism and communism, some socialist parties prefer to call themselves social democratic (see briefing 13.4). Social democracy has five distinguishing features.

Optimistic view of human nature

Human nature is naturally reasonable, rational and sociable. It is *capitalism and its allies* (religion, capitalist education, capitalist media) that makes people greedy and keeps them in ignorance.

Equality of opportunity

Inequalities in the capacities between individuals are as much a product of their *social environment* as they are of inborn talents. The function of the state is therefore to eliminate inequalities of opportunity and release natural abilities.

Briefing 13.4
Socialist thinkers

■ Karl Marx (1818–83)

The German philosopher Karl Marx, with his friend and collaborator, Friedrich Engels, had an immense impact on western politics, and discussions, amendments and attacks on his work form a whole library of books in themselves. Marx argued that capitalism would inevitably produce an extremely polarised society consisting of a few immensely rich and powerful capitalists, on the one hand, and a mass of poor wage-slaves, on the other. The result was that the workers, encouraged by their overwhelming weight of numbers, and with 'nothing to lose but their chains', would organise themselves, rise up in revolution to capture power and overthrow the capitalist state and economic systems. In power they would set up a socialist state in which the means of production were collectively owned, allowing wealth to be equally distributed. The state would then wither away and a *stateless communist society* would replace it. The Russian Revolution of 1917 was initially driven by Marxist principles, but these did not last long, and the communist systems of the Soviet Union and its central and east european dependencies soon ceased to be Marxist. Outside the Soviet Union, Marx's main impact has been through socialist and social democratic movements, and the revisionist thinkers who guided them.

■ Karl Kautsky (1854–1938) and Eduard Bernstein (1850–1930)

Both leading members of the German Social Democratic Party (SDP), Kautsky and Bernstein were influential revisionist thinkers and politicians who argued for *evolutionary* rather than revolutionary socialism, on the grounds that the working-class movement could and should gain power through peaceful, parliamentary means.

■ John Maynard (Lord) Keynes (1883–1946)

The British economist John Maynard Keynes was perhaps the biggest influence on social democratic economic thinking after Marx. He argued against the conventional wisdom of the time, that governments should reduce taxes and public expenditure in times of economic recession in order to balance their budgets. *Keynesian policies* of economic demand management appealed to many governments because they offered a way of controlling the business cycle of 'boom and bust' without centralised socialist planning and without total state control of the economy. Consequently, Keynesianism was the dominant economic orthodoxy in many western states from 1945 until the late 1970s.

Participatory democracy

Democracy is built upon the free and equal participation of all, and on *participatory* rather than representative democracy.

Mixed economy

At the heart of socialist ideologies is the belief that some of the most important parts of the economy should be *owned or regulated by the state* in order to eliminate the worst forms of inequality and social injustice. Capitalism produces unacceptable inequalities of wealth and opportunity, and market failure means that capitalism is unable even to support itself as an efficient form of production. Economic inequality means injustice, poverty and economic inefficiency. Market failure is a capitalist inevitability and it means periods of economic depression, monopolies and oligopolies and underinvestment in collective goods, including health, education, welfare, research and communications. Socialism, however, differs from communism in that it rejects total state control (the 'command economy') in favour of a mixture of public, private, and joint enterprise (**the mixed economy**).

Mixed economy
An economy that is neither wholly privately owned (a capitalist market economy), nor wholly publicly owned (a communist command economy), but a mixture of both.

Peaceful reform

By gaining power through the *ballot box*, socialist and social democratic governments can change the capitalist system to produce a more just mixed economy.

Socialism, like most other 'isms', takes many forms. Most are to be distinguished not by their political gaols, for most socialists agree that the aim is to achieve general values such as justice, liberty for all and equality of opportunity. Socialists argue mainly about how best to achieve these sorts of goals: the far left argues for revolution, the moderate left for evolution. Moderate and evolutionary forms of democratic socialism have had most influence in democratic states, where socialist and social democratic parties have often been elected to power, sometimes with the support of sections of the middle class, and centre and centre-right parties.

▪ *Nationalism*

Nationalism has been an extraordinarily potent force in politics. Its enduring strength can be seen in the fact that the French Revolution of 1789 set off a train of nationalist movements in the name of freedom. The twentieth century was also the age of nationalism because even more states were born then (see chapter 1). Yet it is hard to capture the ideas of nationalist ideologies in a few short paragraphs because they vary greatly from one state to another. In fact, nationalism has been advocated by communists, fascists, democrats, imperialists, anti-imperialists and conservatives alike. Because nations differ tremendously, nationalist ideologies dealing with specific nations tend to differ, too.

For this reason, some analysts reject the idea that nationalism is an ideology, claiming that it is an empty bottle into which one can pour any doctrine. At the same time, nationalist thought has features in common with ideologies based on the three characterising features of modern states: territory, people and sovereignty.

Ethno-nationalism and territory

All nationalist movements believe that a *common national identity* is more important than any differences of class, race, or religious that might exist within the area. Usually, this common identity is formed by the ethnic, linguistic, religious, cultural, or historical characteristics that distinguish the population of a given territory. Nationalism, territory and ethnicity are thus often linked under the concept of *ethno-nationalism* – in Belgium, Canada, Northern Ireland and Spain, among many other countries.

National independence

Nationalists believe that common identity should be turned by separatist movements into *national self-determination*. Sometimes this takes the form of full-blooded independence and sovereignty, sometimes the devolution of power from the centre. In this sense, there is a difference between *political* nationalism demanding independence and sovereignty, and *cultural* nationalism that is satisfied with greater autonomy for a region within a state. Nationalism was given great impetus by the dissolution of empires after 1945, and then by the collapse of the Soviet empire in 1989, sets of events caused, in part, by the strength of nationalist movements in the first place. Having gained independence, the new nations then added to the nationalist culture of the world with their own flags, national hymns, leaders, full UN membership, national airlines and football teams.

Nationalism does not manifest itself only in the new states of the world, however. On the contrary, it so much a part of the fabric and structure of everyday politics in 'old' states that it is often taken for granted. Nonetheless, nationalism is all around us, not just when our country happens to be playing in the World Cup or participating in the Olympics. Most people simply presume that the territory of the globe should be divided between states – and that the borders of our own state are somehow natural and inevitable, just as we rarely question our own national identity. As a result much nationalist ideology is inconspicuous.

Some people claim that the long era of nationalism is coming to an end. Their theory is that modern society will bury the state and nationalism in the 'borderless world' of the 'global village'. The more integrated the global economy, the more powerful transnational corporations (TNCs) become, and the more urgent the need to take global action against natural disasters, terrorism and global warming, the less relevant the nation-state. The argument may be appealing on theoretical grounds but, as we have seen in chapter 1, there was little sign of anything like this actually happening, even at the beginning of the twenty-first century. Nationalism seems to have a lot of life in it yet, a claim we shall return to in chapter 17.

■ *Green political thought*

Green political thought is the most recent ideology of the six discussed here. Also known as the environmental or the ecological movement, it emerged as a political force in the late 1960s as part of what has been termed the 'post-materialist' ethos. As we saw in chapters 8 and 11, this stresses the importance of the quality of life, self-fulfilment and the protection of the environment, over money, obedience and material possessions. Greens often stress their opposition to all the 'isms' of conventional politics, and argue that they are trying to create entirely new kinds of political organisations, with entirely new political aims.

There are many forms of green political thought including green socialism, green Marxism, green anarchism, green feminism, green libertarianism and even green capitalism, which favours the use of state power and financial inducements to push production and consumption in a 'green' direction. The environmental movement includes those who want to use the traditional means of influencing government policy, and radicals who advocate direct and revolutionary action. There is a tendency for Green parties and movements to fragment into smaller splinter groups because of disagreements about means and ends. Like nationalism, some argue that Green thought is so diverse that it cannot count as an ideology, but like nationalism, it has common themes that are of an ideological nature.

Sustainable development

One is the importance of achieving 'sustainable development'. The term reached a wide audience in 1987, when the Bruntland Report of the World Commission on Environment and Development laid out the case for environmental action and the means of achieving it. The affluent parts of the world, it was argued, would have to adapt their way of life to *ecological demands*, by reducing energy consumption, for example. In addition the existing institutions of government and international relations that are based on nation-states would have to give way to a broad, integrated and comprehensive approach involving popular participation and international cooperation.

Bruntland Report, *Our Common Future* (1987)

Decentralisation

Another Green theme is *localism and decentralisation*. This means the local production of goods and services for local consumption, which reduces the power of large MNCs and the need for long lines of transportation and communication, which degrade the environment and the local **ecology**. It is also argued that local production improves the satisfaction of people, who can see the

Ecology The study of the relationships between organisms and their environment.

255

fruits of their labours. Local markets are said to be more responsive to local demands, and deliver fresher produce. Politically, localism means community participation and self-regulation. One green slogan is 'Small is beautiful'.

Direct participation and democracy

Greens oppose the traditional centralised and hierarchical organisation of political parties, and favour *direct participation* and *the rotation of elites*. Some Green parties have tried (often unsuccessfully) to ensure that no one stays in a leadership position for long, and that no one is paid more than the average wage, or more than a given multiple of the average wage. Some critics argue that Green thought is inherently anti-democratic because it puts the utmost importance on taking action to protect the environment now, before it is too late, irrespective of public opinion and the slow processes of democracy. Others claim that the decentralist and participatory thrust of Green thought guarantees its democratic credentials.

The core of Green support lies among younger, better-educated and secular sections of the urban middle class. Green parties also attract those who are alienated from conventional politics, including feminists and gays. In elections, Green parties are usually quite small, rarely getting more than 10 per cent of the vote: if anything, support seems to have waned since the 1980s and early 1990s. At the same time, it seems that more people support Green objectives than join Green movements or vote for their parties. Some with Green sympathies vote for the socialists. Some of the other parties have also taken Green ideas, and built them into their own programme.

◼ Theories of ideology

We have seen that ideologies themselves mix empirical and normative statements. **Empirical statements** are '*is*' statements about the world, and normative statements are *value judgements* about how it *ought to be*. Some writers have treated the concept of an ideology in an ideological way, claiming that ideologies can be 'true' or 'false', 'good' or 'bad'. In analysing ideologies as political scientists, however, we must be careful to avoid ideological statements of the 'ought' kind. We must try to stick to social science and make no value judgement about them, so far as this is possible, but provide, instead, an account of what different theories have to say.

Empirical statements
Factual statements about or explanations of the world. They are not necessarily true or false, but amenable to falsification.

◼ *Marxist and neo-Marxist theories*

Marxist theory

Marxists theorists distinguish between the *sub-structure* and the *super-structure* of society. The sub-structure consists of the material conditions of society (**materialism**), especially its economic conditions, and the super-structure includes ideas and ideology, art, philosophy and culture. Marxists then argue that the

Materialism
The theory that ideas are rooted in the material or

material sub-structure fundamentally determines the super-structural world of ideas. According to Marx himself: 'It is not the consciousness of men that determines their being, but, on the contrary, their social being that determines their consciousness.' This is the essence of the Marxist materialist theory of political ideas and ideology.

According to Marxist theory, ideologies are systems of ideas that *justify the interests of the ruling class*. Under capitalism, the bourgeoisie uses its ideological power to delude and manipulate other classes into believing that capitalism is not only natural but in the best interests of everybody. It is a false set of beliefs, a mystification of the real world, a myth, or a lie. Those who believe it suffer from false consciousness (chapter 8). In contrast, Marxist theory is not ideology but scientific and 'the truth'.

> physical conditions of life, as opposed to spiritual ideals and values which are constructs of the mind which can be independent of material and physical conditions (*see* Idealism).

According to Marxist theory, religion is no more than the 'opiate of the masses', which justifies the social order as God-given and legitimised by the church. Nationalism is a way in which the ruling class prevents the working class from seeing its common interests with workers in other countries and wars are a way of fighting for capitalist advantage, markets and profit. Respect for the aristocracy, deference towards economic elites and love of the monarchy and the national football team are means by which the ruling class divides and rules, and conceals the nature of capitalist exploitation. Belief in parliamentary government obscures the fact that real power lies with the owners of property. In this way, Marxist theory tries to explain and subsume other ideologies and religions within its own system of ideas.

Neo-Marxist theory

Marxist ideas of ideology were especially developed by the Italian Antonio Gramsci, who spend much of his life as a prisoner of Mussolini's fascist government. Gramsci was struck by the fact that the ruling class in western society managed to maintain its economic and political power, without exercising much overt force. He concluded that it managed this by virtue of its ability to infuse its own values throughout society. It maintained its hegemony (see chapter 8) not by naked power but by more subtle and indirect control over what people thought. It won 'the hearts and minds' of people, and gained their willing consent by use of religion, education and the mass media.

Antonio Gramsci (1891–1937)

Gramscian ideas have been developed more recently by the French structuralist theorist Louis Althusser, who argued that the ideological state apparatus was important for maintaining the capitalist system. The main institutions of this ideological apparatus were the churches, schools and universities, families, the legal system, the means of mass communications, culture and parties and trade unions.

Louis Althusser (1918–90)

Marxist and neo-Marxist theories of ideology have been important for introducing *realist and materialist theories* of ideologies into the social sciences, which focus on the relationship between social and economic conditions and what people think about politics. This aspect of their approach is commonly accepted or assumed in contemporary theories. Nonetheless, criticisms of Marxism and neo-Marxism abound. Four important questions need to be asked:

- To say that a person does not know what is in their own best interests opens up the possibility of *forcing them to do things against their own will*, because they do not know what is in their own best interests. Do you suffer from false consciousness? If not, why do you think others do?
- Is it plausible to argue that most of the major institutions of modern society are instruments of a *hegemonic ruling class*? Is this true of schools and universities, parties, trade unions, families, the legal system and TV and newspapers?
- Is Marxism a *science*? Are all ideologies a matter of false consciousness and Marxism alone a scientific theory?
- It is possible to distinguish between the material sub-structure and the ideological superstructure? Do not *ideas* help to shape social and economic conditions?

Beyond these criticisms there also lies a deeper argument about the role of ideas in politics and history that involves a confrontation between materialist and idealist theories, and theories that claim that both material and ideal interests play their own role in history.

■ *Material and non-material interests*

Born in the year that Karl Marx finished the first volume of *Capital*, Max Weber (chapter 1) was a German professor who managed, for most of his life, as he said, to avoid the 'drudgery' of university life. Weber much admired the work of Marx and declared it to be profoundly true, but he also tried to show that Marx's materialist interpretation of history was insufficient. Weber (1905) argues that modern capitalism could not have developed without the ideas of the *Protestant ethic*. Capitalism is the renewed pursuit of profit, and the Protestant ethic entails a commitment to the sort of hard and systematic work that is capable of producing renewed profit. Moreover, capitalism and Protestantism are linked, because some Protestants came to believe that economic success was a sign of God's favour.

Max Weber, *The Protestant Ethic and the Spirit of Capitalism* (1905)

The link between capitalism and Protestantism was entirely unrecognised and unintended by the leaders of the Protestant Reformation, Luther and Calvin. They were interested in religious matters, not economic ones. Nevertheless, their ideas, Weber argues, were necessary to start capitalism on its successful world-wide career. Once in the saddle the capitalist system would ride forever because its own logic and imperative would force others to copy it, or perish economically, but it took the ideas of the Protestant ethic to launch it in the first place.

Idealism
The theory that ideas have a life

Weber did not try to replace Marxist materialism with the opposite theory, known as **idealism**. Rather his work has been described as a 'debate with the ghost of Marx', in which he argues that it is not material conditions but material and ideal interests that drive the behaviour of individuals. Ideal interests – related to ideological beliefs – are no less important than material ones. In this case, if politics are a struggle between competing forces, ideas and ideologies play an important role in the struggle.

■ The end of ideology and the end of history

In the 1960s, the end of ideology was widely proclaimed by social scientists such as Daniel Bell (1960) or Seymour Martin Lipset (1960). They argued that the appeal of ideologies especially communism, fascism and other utopian theories, were exhausted. The main problems of the industrial revolution had been solved and the main issues of the class struggle resolved. As a result, there was a *non-ideological consensus* about the virtues of liberalism, democracy, the welfare state, decentralised power, pluralism and the mixed economy. This amounted to the exhaustion of political ideas during this period.

The 'end of ideology' thesis depended on the idea that only extreme and utopian systems of thought counted as ideologies. In this sense there may well have been some truth in the thesis. But, as we have argued, the term applies also to liberal democratic ideas as well. Defenders of these faiths are as 'ideological' as anyone, perhaps more so if they are unable to see the ideological nature of their own thought. Moreover, the theory has apparently been overtaken by the events of the late twentieth century, which saw the revival of classical liberal ideas about free markets and minimal government, and the emergence of post-materialist and Green thought, to say nothing of the argument about the clash of civilisations – 'the west versus the rest'.

In the late 1980s when the Berlin Wall came down, and when western liberal democracy had triumphed over communism, the 'end of ideology' thesis was presented again by the American Francis Fukuyama in his (1992) book. He did not suggest that from now on nothing would happen or that everything would remain as it is. In his view, most of the globe seemed to have reached the point where liberal democracy was regarded as the only acceptable form of government. With this decided, there was little need for further ideological disagreement. History, seen as the struggle between competing ideologies, had come to an end, as everyone had agreed upon the fundamentals of the political order. This theory, too, seems to have been overtaken by events, most notably by conflicts within and between states, particularly the international flashpoints in eastern Europe and the Middle East, and between poor and wealthy nations. In these conflicts, a revival and strengthening of nationalist ideologies can be observed.

The moral of the story seems to be that while some social scientists will, every now and again, proclaim the 'end of ideology' or 'the end of history', new (and old) ideological differences will continue to play their usual role in the power struggle within and between states.

(margin note) of their own as the products of consciousness or spiritual ideals and values that are independent of material conditions. In international relations, idealism emphasises the role of ideas and morality as a determinant of the relations between states.

Daniel Bell, *The End of Ideology* (1960)

Seymour Martin Lipset, *Political Man* (1960)

Francis Fukuyama, *The End of History and the Last Man* (1992)

▌ Summary

This chapter has dealt with the frameworks of ideas known as ideologies, which help people to understand and interpret politics. It argues that:

- The term 'ideology' is used here to mean a broad and systematic set of ideas that mix empirical and normative statements about politics with a programme for political action.
- There are four main democratic ideologies – conservatism, liberalism, Christian democracy and socialism/social democracy – and two more minor ones – nationalism and Green theory. These have many different variations, and each overlaps at some points with competing ideologies.
- Conservatism is distinguished by its core beliefs that: society is an organic entity that has evolved slowly and should not be reformed rapidly; the natural failings of human beings are best restrained by a strong state that maintains social order and the social hierarchy; some inequality in society is inevitable; there is representative democracy; and the market is the best way to achieve the public economic good.
- Classical liberalism is distinguished by its core belief that individual rights and freedoms can be maximised only by limiting the powers of the state. Neo-liberals hold to the negative definition of freedom and argue for limited state intervention, but social or progressive liberals argue for some state intervention to secure positive freedom.
- Christian democracy incorporates Catholic thought into a practical ideology that emphasises community, family and church; the devolution of power; institutions to bring different interests in society together to achieve social integration and reconciliation; and state services to protect the weak and the poor and to prevent the failure of key private institutions.
- The distinguishing features of socialism and social democracy are: an optimistic view of human nature; a participatory form of democracy; the legal and peaceful attainment of parliamentary power through popular election; a mixed economy, with state power to control or regulate key elements of the economy: a guaranteed minimum standard of living for all; and equality of opportunity.
- Materialist theories, notably Marxism and neo-Marxism, argue that ideologies are the products of social conditions, but other theorists claim that both material and ideal interests are crucial for an understanding of ideologies.
- Despite repeated announcements neither ideology nor history seems to have come to an end. What seems to have ended, however, is the heyday of conventional political 'isms' such as conservatism or Marxism.

Further reading

General works on political ideologies are Andrew Heywood, *Political Ideologies: An Introduction* (Basingstoke: Palgrave, 1997); Robert Eccleshall *et al.*, *Political Ideologies: An Introduction* (London: Routledge, 2nd edn. 1994); and Roger Eatwell and Anthony

Wrights (eds.), *Contemporary Political Ideologies* (London: Pinter, 1993). A shorter account of ideologies is found in Stephen D. Tansey, *Politics: The Basics* (London: Routledge, 2nd edn., 2000: chapter 4).

For works on the ideologies of parties and party families, see Anthony Arblaster, *The Rise and Decline of Western Liberalism* (Oxford: Basil Blackwell, 1984); Andrew Dobson, *Green Political Thought* (London: Routledge, 2nd edn. 1995); David Hanley, *Christian Democracy in Europe: A Comparative Perspective* (London: Pinter, 1994); Elie Kedourie, *Nationalism* (London: Hutchinson, 1966); Noël O'Sullivan, *Conservatism* (London: Dent, 1976); and Anthony Wright, *Socialisms: Theories and Practices* (Harmondsworth: Penguin, 1987).

Websites

Virtually all political philosophers have websites dedicated to their life and work. Simply submit a name (for instance 'Edmund Burke') to any major search engine and you will easily find these sites. Useful websites are:

http://berlin.wolf.ox.ac.uk	A virtual library of the work of Isaiah Berlin and many links to related websites.
http://www.jsmill.com	A website with all information and publications of John Stuart Mill.
http://www.marxists.org/archive	A very extensive website with all information and publications of Karl Marx, Friedrich Engels, Rosa Luxemburg and many other Marxist authors.
http://www.nationalismproject.org	A very extensive website about Nationalism.
http://www.nationmaster.com/encyclopedia/Christian-democracy	General website with a brief overview of Christian democracy and many links to related websites.
http://www.nationmaster.com/encyclopedia/Social-democracy	General website with a brief overview of Social democracy and many links to related websites.
http://www.nationmaster.com/encyclopedia/Green-parties	General website with a brief overview of Green political ideas and many links to related websites.
http://www.nationmaster.com/encyclopedia/Conservatism	General website with a brief overview of Conservatism and many links to related websites.
http://www.nationmaster.com/encyclopedia/Liberalism	General website with a brief overview of Liberalism and many links to related websites.
http://www.nationmaster.com/encyclopedia/Nationalism	General website with a brief overview of Nationalism and many links to related websites.

Projects

1. Collect the programmes of the two main parties in your country. Summarise the ideological points in these programmes in a systematic way (that is, search

for normative and empirical statements about politics and relating proposals for action). Enumerate the distinguishing features of each programme in order to decide to which of the six democratic ideologies discussed in this chapter these parties belong.

2. Similar ideologies are usually used by various organisations (for instance, in many countries we find social-democratic unions, parties and other organisations). Try to find at least two organisations in two or more countries for each of the six democratic ideologies mentioned here.

3. With growing international dependencies, parties in different countries, but with similar ideologies often try to cooperate and establish a common international organisation. Which parties with what ideologies do you think are most likely to cooperate successfully? Can you support your expectations with examples?

14   Decision making

Government exists to solve problems. To do this it must take *decisions*. In one sense, the whole process of government is little else than a ceaseless process of decision making:

- How to respond to the latest international crisis
- Whether to increase taxes or cut services
- How to balance economic development against environmental needs
- Whether to reform a law or leave it as it is
- What to do about the new problems caused by internet communication or genetic engineering
- How to handle a public health emergency
- What to do about traffic congestion.

Politics never sleep, and governments can never pause for a rest. They are assailed from all sides by an endless flow of demands and events, and they must constantly make decisions about options, priorities, policies and courses of action.

This chapter deals with public policies and decision making. A *policy* is some general set of ideas or plans that has been officially agreed on and which is used as a basis for making decisions. *Public policy* is a more specific term. It refers to the long series of activities, decisions and actions carried out by officials of government in their attempts to solve problems that are thought to lie in the public or collective arena. In that sense, we speak of 'environmental policies' if government shifts from coal and nuclear power to oil and wind-powered generators, and of 'educational policies' if the school leaving age is raised or money is redirected from primary to secondary education. How can we analyse such public policies in general, when there are so many decisions made and each one has its own specific circumstances? How do governments make decisions and which political and governmental structures are relevant for public policies? How do governments respond to public demands?

The four major topics in this chapter are:

- Public policies: their nature and importance
- The public policy cycle
- Public policy structures
- Theories of decision making.

■ Public policies: their nature and importance

■ *Goals and results*

Public policy (chapter 6) is designed to achieve *specific goals* and produce *particular results*. Public policies are supposed to solve public problems, or at least improve them. In this sense, public policies are the main **outputs** of the political system – the actions it takes in response to the demands made upon it and the problems it faces. Two points follow from the idea that public policy and decision making aim to improve the world:

Outputs
Policy decisions as they are actually implemented.

- *Public policy is important* Public policies affect our lives in many trivial ways, but also in many crucial ones, and almost everything we do is affected by them. They determine which side of the road we drive on and whether we carry identity cards. They also decide whether we receive a free university education, have to pay for health care, pay a lot or a little tax and, in the extreme, whether we go to the electric chair if we are found guilty of murder.
- *Public policy is conflict-ridden* Because public policies are so important, they are the focus of fierce and constant political battles. Which policy is adopted depends on the competing and conflicting political forces that operate on the state from both within and without – the executive, legislative and judiciary, the state bureaucracy, other states and international organisations, sub-central governments, parties and pressure groups, public opinion and the mass media. A public policy is the 'end product' of the battle between these political forces. Consequently, public policies and political decision making tell us a lot about how political systems actually work, and about who is powerful. If politics is to be about who gets what, when and how, then the study of public policy making can tell us a lot about who gets what, when and how they obtained it.

◼ *The nature of policy making processes*

Discussions about public policies usually start with the cliché that public policy making is extremely complex and difficult to analyse. This is certainly true. Yet, paradoxically, we all know about decision making because we do it all the time. Take a simple decision: at this minute you are reading chapter 14 of this comparative politics textbook, but you might have made the decision to go to the cinema, drink with friends, read a book for another course, or catch up on sleep instead. If you analyse your decision to read the textbook, you know well enough that you are not completely free to do what you want. Perhaps you have an essay deadline tomorrow, or not enough money to go to the cinema. So the first thing to notice is that your decision is subject to *constraints*. Secondly, your decision is also partly in response to the decisions of others. You made your own decision to go to college and study this course, but your teachers put on the course and set essays, and your friends may have decided to work today, and go to the cinema tomorrow. In other words, your decision is closely tied up with the decisions of others. And, third, you know that today's decision has implications for future decisions you might make – what you do tomorrow, and if you write a good essay, what courses you study in the future, even what kind of job you get. In other words, today's decisions are influenced by a long chain of decisions that reaches back into the past, and has implications for decisions in the future.

These three simple aspects of decision making processes can be used to characterise public policy-making:

Constraints

Policy making is beset on every side by constraints. No government can do what it likes. It is always faced with shortages of time and resources, or by pressure from foreign governments and economic forces. It is subject to the conflicting demands of public opinion, the mass media, pressure groups and opposition parties. It must meet the requirements of the law and the courts. The permanent officials of the state bureaucracies may have views and powers of their own, and so may sub-central units of government. Indeed, governments themselves are invariably composed of *factions* that push and pull in different directions. Politics is the art of the possible, and what might appear to be the most obvious or most sensible course of action is often ruled out by circumstances.

Policy processes

The repeated use of the term 'policy processes', in the plural, is deliberate because there is no single 'policy process' – there are many of them. Governments are not integrated, coordinated and centralised machines: they are fragmented and disjointed, with different departments and units that compete, overlap and work unknown to each other. The agricultural ministry may want to preserve farmland, the transportation department may want to cover it with a road and the military may want it as a training ground. One of the big problems for the huge and sprawling apparatus of the modern state is how to produce 'joined-up' government, where public policies are more or less coherent and push in roughly the same direction. This may be an impossible ideal. Even within the same ministry, there are likely to be different views on any given matter, and each matter may well involve parties, pressure groups, international government agencies, the mass media and public opinion – each with its own decision making processes.

Unending policy cycles

Policy processes consist not of discrete decisions, distinct from one another, but of a *continuous and unending cycle* of decisions and policies which merge into one another without a break:

* In the first place, no policy decision is independent of the decisions *that have gone before*. A government that has decided to invest heavily in nuclear power will frame its current power policies with this in mind.
* In the second place, every policy has *knock-on effects* that require a further round of decisions. Bigger and better roads have been built in an attempt to solve traffic problems and reduce accident rates, only to discover that this has increased the demand for cars, which makes the traffic problem worse than before. Successful promotion of economic growth in the post-war years has resulted in much higher standard of living, which has led to all sorts of environmental problems. Higher standards of living and improvements in public health have also produced an aging population, which has generated severe problems for state pensions (see chapter 16).

Almost every public policy has its unintended and unanticipated side effects, which then become a problem for public policy. The result is an endless cycle of policy and decision-making that tries to solve both the new problems of the world and also the side effects of old policies.

■ The public policy cycle

It is helpful to imagine policy processes as consisting of six stages. Analytically, each policy process starts with selecting the most urgent problems to be dealt with (agenda setting). Then decisions have to be taken about the course of action (decision making) and appropriate means to be used (choice of means). The next stage consists of putting the plan into action (implementa-

Outcomes
The impacts, or effects, of outputs.

tion), which results in specific consequences (outputs and **outcomes**). Finally, the effects and costs of the policy are assessed and conclusions are drawn for future actions (evaluation and feedback). This last stage leads directly back into the first stage, so it is helpful to think of the process as a continuous and unending cycle, not as a one-way flow with a clear beginning and end

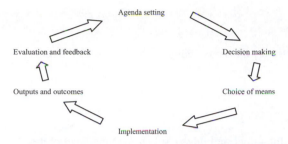

Figure 14.1: The six stages of the policy cycle

(see figure 14.1). In real life the different stages of the cycle are not separate and distinct. On the contrary, they merge and overlap with one another, and sometimes the stages get mixed up, but nevertheless they are helpful analytical categories.

■ *Agenda setting*

The world is full of political problems and it is impossible to give much attention to more than a small number of them at any given time. You can think of the list of problems to be dealt with as a kind of 'agenda' with the more urgent concerns at the top of the list receiving the most attention. An important part of the political struggle is the attempt by different groups and interests to put their issues at the top of the agenda, or at least to push them up the agenda, so they have a better chance of being considered. This struggle is called 'agenda setting' (chapter 10), and being able to *control or influence the agenda* is an important source of political power. The struggle is endless because as the world changes so priorities and agendas also change. For example, according to post-materialist theory (see chapter 8) the public agenda is shifting from safety and security, money and material advantages, to the quality of life, self-fulfilment and environmental protection. Although new political parties, such as the Greens, have rarely played a direct role in government, they have had a political influence to the extent that they have *shifted the political agenda*.

One important aspect of the public agenda is the divide between what is thought to be the proper concern of the state, and what is outside its sphere of action, and therefore off the public agenda. What is thought to be a public matter varies considerably from one country to another, and from one historical period to another (see briefing 14.1). In fact, political conflicts frequently concentrate on the question whether government should deal with specific problems (such as providing day-care for young children or banning genetically manipulated/modified (GM) food), or leave it to private action. The shifting divide between the public and the private reminds us that the nature of politics itself is constantly *contested*.

Briefing 14.1
The public–private divide

The boundaries between the public and the private vary from one country to another, and from one historical period to another.

■ Historical changes

As we saw in chapter 13, the distinction between the public and private sphere is at the heart of the battle of political ideas between liberals, conservatives and socialists. These ideologies have waxed and waned over three historical periods.

The dominant liberal ideology of the nineteenth century argued for a minimal, 'night watchman' state with responsibility for little beyond the defence of the realm, law and order, the protection of private property and the necessary conditions for a market economy.

As the welfare state grew in scope and activities during the late nineteenth and in the twentieth century, so the public sphere expanded. Taxes increased, more public services were delivered and the role and scope of the state grew rapidly, especially in west Europe after 1945 (see chapter 16).

In recent decades the neo-liberals have been successful to some degree in rolling back the frontiers of the state, by privatisation and deregulation and tax/service cuts. In other words, the boundaries of the public sector were first pushed out a great deal in the mid-twentieth century, and then contracted somewhat at the end of the millennium.

■ Country differences

Since we often take the boundary between the public and private for granted in our own country, a few examples will help to illustrate the idea:

- In some Catholic countries in west Europe the names that parents can give their children are restricted to a state-recognised list of Catholic saints' names. There is no such restriction in Protestant or secular countries.
- In north European countries the sale of alcohol is often closely controlled by the government, sometimes through state monopoly shops. In the south, it is not.
- Norwegian municipalities own cinemas and spend the profits on public services. In most countries cinemas are in the private economy.
- In some countries shops can open when they like. In others, their opening hours are restricted.
- In some countries all citizens must carry ID cards. In other, is there is no such requirement.

A good indicator of the breadth of the public sector is what proportion of total national production is spent by all public authorities. Countries vary enormously in this respect, as figure 14.2 shows. At the top of the league (left side), half the nations' wealth is spent by government in Sweden and France. At the bottom (right side), it is less than a third in Australia, Ireland, South Korea and the USA.

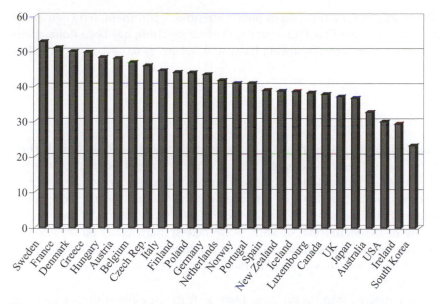

Figure 14.2: Government expenditure as percentage of GDP,[a] OECD member states, 2000
Note: [a] GDP = Gross domestic product, the value of all final goods and services produced within a state in a given year.
Source: http://www.oecd.org.

■ The public–private mix

There is no clear line to be drawn between the public and private. They can overlap a good deal in some policy areas, where private or semi-private groups and organisations cooperate closely with government to provide services, with financial and other help from the state. For example, in Germany the state collects taxes for the Catholic and Protestant churches, which provide social and other services with the money. Scandinavian housing associations are neither public nor private organisations, but **public–private partnerships (PPPs)** (see below) that cooperate closely with public agencies and receive resources from them. Many politicians have turned to PPPs since the 1980s as the best solution to a wide range of problems.

As we have seen in chapter 10, the mass media play an important role in public debates and therefore also in agenda setting. The argument is that although the mass media cannot do much to influence what people think, they can exercise a good deal of influence over what people think about. Television, with its unquenchable thirst for new issues and stories, is constantly engaging in 'feeding frenzies' involving issues such as road rage, football hooligans, new diseases, genetic engineering, crime, drug crazes, political corruption, the sexual abuse of children and terrorism. Known as 'moral panics', these matters

Public–private partnerships
Formal cooperations between government and private groups to obtain specific goals.

hit the headlines for a time, focus public attention upon them, but then disappear in favour of another issue, perhaps before anything has been done about the matter, or perhaps prompting hasty and ill-considered action from policy makers.

■ *Decision making*

Having decided upon the priorities of the political agenda, decisions must then be taken about them. A major decision is usually the end product of a series of decisions leading up to it, each preceding decision being made by different individuals and bodies that feed into the process. In democracies, major policy decisions should be taken by *publicly accountable bodies*, normally the elected executive or the legislature, or both. Nonetheless, many other public and private organisations and officials may have an impact on a particular decision, and they, in their turn, will have to make many decisions in order to exercise influence.

Decision making is by far the most popular research topic of the six stages of the policy cycle and there is a huge literature on the topic. Decisions represent the most important output of the political process, not only for practical politics, but also because they reveal how political forces mix together to produce a policy. Remember, however, that *not* making a decision counts as decision-making as well, because the decision not to make a decision is itself a decision.

Non-decision
The decision not to deal with an issue, perhaps not even to consider it.

A **non-decision** has its consequences and reveals the interplay of political forces just as much as a decision to do something. In fact, refusals to deal with an issue, attempts to sweep them under the carpet (trying to keep them off the political agenda), or decisions to put off decisions, are tactics often favoured by politicians:

- Sometimes the issue is 'too hot to handle' because it is a highly emotional one.
- Sometimes governments may be faced by powerful opponents with the capacity to veto its preferred decision.
- Sometimes it may not be in the interests of the government to make a decision or to leave it until after the next election.

For all their possible importance, non-decisions frequently escape attention for the simple reason that they are notoriously difficult to study. A non-decision is a non-event that involves things that did not happen, and how does one study something that did not happen? Besides, how can we be sure that there was ever a need to consider the issue that produced the non-decision in the first place? 'Conspiracy theorists' are always claiming that governments refuse to investigate their latest pet conspiracy. Is this a case of non-decision-making or a case of governments refusing to take silly theories seriously? The methodological problems of non-decision-making have been heatedly discussed by community politics studies and no firm conclusions have been reached.

▪ *Choice of means*

Choosing the best means available to bring about the goals selected is the next step confronted by policy makers. This may seem a straightforward job after issues have been selected and priorities set, but it is not simple at all. There are usually a wide variety of *possible policy instruments* available to achieve a given end, and deciding which to use is no easy task. The options include:

- *Taxing specific products or services* to change the costs of action – excise duties on cigarettes and alcohol, for example, or lower duties on lead-free petrol to encourage more environmental motoring.
- *Imposing regulations* – shop opening hours can be restricted, dog owners required to have a dog licence, toxic products banned, or industrial plants regulated.
- *Encouraging citizens* to do certain things – some governments carry out intensive and expensive publicity campaigns to persuade people not to smoke, to use condoms, to eat healthily, not to drink and drive and to take exercise.
- *Offering subsidies or grants* – many countries subsidise food production and some offer tax reductions to home-owners, or child benefits to increase the birth rate.
- *Direct provision* of services by the state itself – education, health services, transport, etc., especially if the private provision of these services is problematic.
- *Encouraging private organisations to regulate themselves* – governments are often reluctant to intervene directly in, for example, the conduct of the mass media where the principle of the freedom of the press is involved.
- *Passing new laws* – not only to make things legal or illegal but to introduce one of the measures mentioned in the list above. Changing the law may appear to be the obvious method, but it can be cumbersome and ineffective because it usually takes a long time, and the effects are uncertain.

In most cases, decision makers choose a combination of these, since it is unlikely that any single one will work well.

▪ *Implementation*

As we saw in chapter 6, policy making is supposed to be the responsibility of elected and accountable politicians, whereas implementation (chapter 7) is a matter for state bureaucracies. In practice, the distinction between policy making and implementation is not clear because policy goals cannot be separated from the means of implementing them, and vice versa. Besides, in political life policies often get changed in the *process of implementation*:

- Sometimes, this is for very good practical reasons (economic pressures, bureaucratic procedures, the avoidance of unforeseen side effects) that may not have been recognised when the policy was formulated.

- Sometimes it is because implementing agencies have their own interests, and bend the policy to their own wishes as much as they can.
- And sometimes it is because legislation deliberately gives agencies discretion over how to implement a policy because of difficulties in deciding in advance.

Private organisations and pressure groups may also try to influence implementation in their own interests. One way or the other, therefore, there may well be *slippage* between what policy makers intend and what is actually implemented.

One of the most interesting studies of policy implementation by Jeffrey L. Pressman and Aaron Wildavsky (1973) reveals its main message in its sub-title: 'How Great Expectations in Washington are Dashed in Oakland: Or, Why it is Amazing that Federal Programs Work at All.' They found that federal policies in the USA were distorted as they passed down through a long chain of 'clearance points' between the committee rooms and debating chambers in Washington, and local street-level bureaucrats who made decision on the ground.

Aaron Wildavsky (1930–93)

Jeffrey L. Pressman and Aaron Wildavsky, *Implementation* (1973)

■ *Outputs and outcomes*

After a policy has been applied, its results or consequences become clear. Political scientists find it useful here to distinguish between outputs and outcomes:

- By 'output' we mean the political decisions taken, the laws passed and the money spent. So the decision to build another 10,000 km of roads in order to ease traffic congestion and reduce road accidents is an output.
- The term 'outcome' is used to refer to the results or consequences of the outputs. The new roads are intended to reduce accident rates and traffic congestion, but if their effect is to increase car usage they may well increase congestion and the accident rate as well.

The distinction between outputs and outcomes reflects the often unintended and unrecognised nature of *policy effects*, and the differences between policy decisions and what is actually achieved. Since society is exceedingly complex, and since decision making is no less difficult, governments quite often fail to achieve their intended goals, and sometimes even have an opposite effect.

■ *Evaluation and feedback*

Once the policy has been in operation for some time, its effects can be reviewed. Policy evaluation provides a *feedback loop* enabling decision makers to learn from their experiences. Policies should be evaluated for their *efficiency* (using the least resources to the maximum effect) and *effectiveness* (achieved what was intended). Since all but the most trivial public policy decisions have knock-on effects – intended or unintended – there is almost always something to be learned from evaluation, and it can be a nasty lesson. It is this feedback loop that creates an endless policy cycle. Even if no explicit evaluation takes place, the outcome will be evident and will play a role in future policies. To say that 'the outcome is evident' is not to say that the evidence is perceived correctly. Citizens and governments alike may entirely misconstrue the actual effects of a policy for their own political reasons: they may choose to believe that a policy was not successful simply because they did not like it in the first place. At any rate, one policy decision simply leads to another, or serves as a background context for new decisions. In this sense, there is no such thing as a decision, but only a *ceaseless flow of them*.

In practice, evaluation and feedback are the 'Cinderella elements' of policy processes, for several reasons:

- Policies should be evaluated in terms of their *objectives* but policy makers may deliberately leave their objectives vague in order to avoid political controversy, or in order to avoid responsibility for failing to meet them.
- Policy makers rarely want their *failures* evaluated.
- Policy makers may pay little attention to the evaluation, no matter how well it was carried out, because the *public agenda* has changed already.
- Often little money is set aside for *proper evaluation* of government programmes.
- Governments often *evaluate their own policies*, although they normally insist, for obvious reasons, that other organisations are evaluated by independent agencies.
- Efficiency in the public sector is difficult to *measure*. Some services are taken into the public sector because they are not amenable to the usual market measures of efficiency.

In this brief overview of the policy cycle we have emphasised the complexity of the whole process, and the difficulties of making decisions, implementing them and evaluating them. We have frequently used the phrase 'unrecognised and unintended effects'. However, in spite of all this, public policies are often drawn up and implemented more or less effectively. That is to say, children are educated, health systems operate, transport is available, welfare benefits paid, pensions schemes funded and so on. No doubt no policy works quite as well as it is supposed to, but they work nonetheless and for the most part, they manage to avoid the worst disasters.

■ Public policy structures

Policy and decision making is full of conflict between groups and organisations with different and often incompatible interests. Sometimes this conflict is protracted and bitter, because the stakes are high or the moral issues of great importance. At the same time, the public policy process is rarely a free-for-all battle between warring interests. Few human activities are without *structures and rules* to organise them. Even war is supposed to be conducted according to international agreement and conventions, and even the freest of all free-market competition is tightly regulated and controlled by government regulation and international trade agreement, or by economic interests themselves, which try to limit unrestricted competition in one way or another. Public policy and political decision making are no different. It occurs within 'structures and rules of the game' that try to ensure that it is relatively smooth, ordered, regulated and predictable (see chapter 3).

Pluralism

A situation where power is dispersed among many different groups and organisations that openly compete with one another in different political arenas.

The structures of public policy making can be differentiated according to two main types: corporatism and **pluralism**. Corporatism is the more top-down, state-centred arrangement, whereas pluralism is a more 'bottom-up' and decentralised system.

■ *Corporatism*

In some countries special policy making and implementation structures and institutions have been created in order to minimise conflict, maximise consensus and ensure a smoothly executed policy cycle from agenda setting to implementation and evaluation. The term 'corporatism' (chapter 9) has been invented to describe these sorts of structures. To avoid confusion with the Fascist theory of 'state corporatism', corporatism in democratic states is also referred to as 'neo-corporatism', 'liberal corporatism', or 'social corporatism'. In this chapter, however, we will use the simple term 'corporatism', on the understanding that this is a democratic form of political decision making.

Modern corporatist theory evolved in the late nineteenth century as a reaction to socialism, on the one hand, and laissez-faire capitalism, on the other. It argued that society is an *organic entity* consisting of different functional parts – genders, classes, economic sectors and interests – that should work together in harmony. In this sense, corporatist theory owes a lot to Christian democracy (see chapter 13). To create social harmony and a common purpose it is necessary to create collective institutions in which all major social and economic interests can participate in order to formulate mutually acceptable policies, and implement them effectively.

In modern industrial society, corporatist policy making rests on a set of *specific conditions and formal structures*, without which it cannot work:

- A small number of *hierarchically organised peak associations* or federations that speak authoritatively for all their members. For example, there should be no more than a handful of organisations to speak for the major economic interests – labour, industry, commerce, the financial sector and farming – and ordinary members of these organisations should accept the agreements reached. Usually, a few peak associations are recognised, licensed, or even created by the government as a way of ensuring that the government deals with only a small number of dependable official representatives.
- An elaborate structure of government decision making, consultation and negotiation in the form of consultative committees, advisory bodies and

social and economic councils. The most important groups and interests are formally co-opted into this machinery and have a *recognised place* in it.

- An ability to produce policies that are binding on all parties, and implemented by them. This means that the system is *hierarchical and centralised* – there is only one decision making centre in any policy area. Its decisions are passed down and implemented by centralised and hierarchical groups.
- All participants in corporatist arrangements must be prepared to *compromise*. They cannot get everything they want, but they can get some of it, by 'playing by the rules'. It may be much better to stay within the system, where one can be heard, than be on the outside.

In modern societies, corporatism has generally worked best in economic policy making where business interests, trade unions and government have been brought closely together in specific institutions in order to consult and negotiate with each other. Trade unions, for example, might agree to limit wage and other demands in return for full employment, whereas employers would agree to maintain full employment in return for industrial peace and cooperation. Under these circumstances, the government could work more effectively for low inflation and good social benefits. The system can work – as indicated – only where a small number of interested organisations is committed to the policy and able to implement it.

Countries may be more or less corporatist, for corporatism is a variable, not a clear-cut category (chapter 9). In fact, such countries can vary considerably in their degree of corporatism. There is, however, a good deal of agreement among experts about which are the most corporatist countries, and the least. The north European countries Denmark, The Netherlands, Norway and Sweden are among the most corporatist countries, but Austria also belongs to this category. Corporatism, however, is by no means restricted to west Europe, as the account of Mexican corporatism in briefing 14.2 shows. On the other hand, decision making in the Anglo-Saxon democracies of Australia, Britain, Canada, New Zealand and the USA do not have much in common with the corporatist model (see table 14.1).

Corporatism developed in the 1970s and 1980s, especially in west Europe, as a method of promoting and managing economic growth. Its achievements in this respect were substantial. According to an article by Markus Crepaz (1992), corporatist countries had lower rates of unemployment, lower inflation, less working time lost from strikes, but no better rates of economic growth. Although its main goal – promoting exceptional economic growth – was not reached, the successes of corporatism were evident and are widely recognised.

Markus Crepaz, *Comparative Political Studies*, 25 (1992)

In spite of these successes, however, corporatism began to break down in the 1980s:

- Corporatism is easier to work in periods of *economic growth* (the 1960s and 1970s), when there are additional resources to distribute, than in harder economic times (the 1980s), when some groups lose.

Briefing 14.2

Mexican corporatism: rise and fall

In the 1920s President Calles reorganised Mexican government along corporatist lines. Given the factious, unstable and violent nature of politics his first priority was to produce an inclusive, peaceful and stable system. He created new 'umbrella organisations' that brought together the disparate parts of the broad functional sectors of society and then gave them state subsidies to encourage their dependence upon the state and their links with Calles' ruling party. The trade unions were organised into one organisation run by a friend. The civil service was expanded to handle the corporatist machinery and disperse state funds.

A successor of Calles in the 1940s – Cárdenas – built on these foundations, expanding the social base of the ruling party to include and incorporate the four sectors or 'legs' of Mexican society – the working class, the peasants and rural workers, the military and middle-class civil servants and businessmen. Their organisations were legally recognised and incorporated into the machinery of public policy making. The system, in its general form, remained in place for the next forty years. In the 1980s the corporatist structures created by Calles and Cárdenas began to break down and with it the stable politics of one-party government. Public subsidies to the four organisational sectors were cut back and government programmes reduced, which meant a weakening of the old clientelist arrangements of previous decades. State ownership and regulation of industry gave way to more competitive and privatised forms. Subsidies for consumer goods and services were reduced and the economy opened up more to international trade. Internal schisms developed within the ruling party between a traditional wing favouring the old system and a more technocratic faction that eventually broke away. The old one-party corporatist state gave way to a more open and pluralist one.

- Corporatism works best with issues that are amenable to bargaining, compromise and incremental change, such as those between management and workers over pay, hours and conditions of work. The issues raised by new pressure groups and New Social Movements – peace, rights, environmental protection – in the 1970s and 1980s have often been *moral issues* that are not easily handled by corporatist negotiation and bargaining.

- The shift from heavy industry and manufacturing to service industry has fragmented business organisations and trade unions, making them less amenable to corporatist centralisation and hierarchy. Trade union membership has fallen in many countries making it difficult for *peak organisations to speak authoritatively for their members.*

- *Globalisation* has made it more difficult to control national economies, and to impose regulation upon them.

- Keynesian policies have tended to give way to a belief in *market competition* (see chapter 13).

- Demands for more political *participation* have tended to erode the closed circles of corporatist policy making. Groups that are excluded from the cosy circles of corporatist policy making (students, immigrants, peace and anti-nuclear campaigners and (initially) the Greens, as well as extremist right-wing and racist organisations) may use direct and unconventional forms of political participation to make their voice heard.

Table 14.1 *Corporatism in eighteen democracies, 1950s–1970s*

Country	Corporatism rating
Austria	2.9
Norway	2.8
Sweden	2.7
Netherlands	2.4
Denmark	1.9
Switzerland	1.9
Germany	1.9
Finland	1.8
Belgium	1.6
Japan	1.4
Ireland	0.8
France	0.7
Italy	0.6
Great Britain	0.5
Australia	0.3
New Zealand	0.2
Canada	0.0
USA	0.0

Source: Derived from Arend Lijphart and Markus Crepaz, 'Corporatism and consensus democracy in eighteen countries', *British Journal of Political Science*, 21, 1990: 235–56.

■ *Pluralism*

The Anglo-Saxon democracies in table 14.1, and others like them that rank low on the corporatism scale, make policy in a more fragmented and less centralised/hierarchical manner. In these countries, power is dispersed among many different groups and organisations that openly compete with one another in different political arenas. Because there are supposed to be many competing interests and organisations, and many centres of power, this sort of policy process has been labelled 'pluralism' (see chapter 9). There may be consultation and consensus-seeking in pluralist systems, but the absence of fully-fledged corporatist structures makes it difficult to reach binding agreements. Even if such agreements could be hammered out, the absence of centralised and hierarchical interest groups means that the peak organisations could not ensure the compliance of any or all of their constituent interest organisations and members to implement the agreement.

A lack of corporatist structures does not mean that policy and decision making is an unorganised free-for-all struggle for power. There are two main ways of organising and integrating policy making to make the power struggle more predictable and manageable: tri-partite arrangements and policy communities (chapter 9).

Tri-partite arrangements

Pluralist systems sometimes use what are known as tri-partite arrangements in which the three 'corners' of the economic 'triangle' (business, unions and government) try to cooperate through both formal and informal channels. The formal channels include a variety of official committees and consultative bodies and the informal can include quite close personal relations between the elites of government, business and even unions. Such arrangements existed in France, Italy, Japan and the UK, especially in the 1960 and 1970s, but less so in the 1980s and 1990s. Tri-partism (chapter 9) is most often found in economic policy making, including matters such as employment policy, the control of inflation and unemployment and agricultural policy. The three-cornered relations are known as 'iron triangles' (chapter 9).

Policy communities

Outside the economic sphere pluralist policy making can also be organised and given a degree of integration by what are known as policy communities (chapter 9). These are small and exclusive groupings of government officials (both elected politicians and appointed bureaucrats) and pressure group elites, who agree on many of the broad issues in a particular policy area. They meet often, sometimes in formally constituted public bodies (committees, councils and consultative bodies) and sometimes informally. These groupings are generally influential and sometimes very powerful in their particular policy area, though not necessarily outside it. Policy communities tend to form around food and drink policies, education, health, defence matters and technical issues of government policy making. They often involve the most established of the 'insider' groups drawn from the world of professional and business organisations.

Policy communities have many *advantages*:

- They keep government and those most directly affect by its policies in close contact.
- They exchange information on both policy and technical matters.
- They help to formulate and implement policy in the most effective and efficient manner.

Policy communities also have their *disadvantages*:

- They are exclusive, keeping 'outsider' groups and interests at a distance from policy making.
- Close and constant contact may also result in government officials and group representatives ending up in each other's pockets. Officials may 'go native' and be unable to represent the public interest properly. Group representatives may be 'captured' by government officials, and unable to represent the interests of their organisation properly (see chapter 9).

Nevertheless, by containing group conflict, limiting participation in policy-making and establishing close working relations between public officials and private interests, policy communities can contribute to the stability and continuity of decision making. In pluralist systems, this form of policy making is most usually found in Canada, India, New Zealand and the USA – the more decentralised countries among the Anglo-Saxon democracies.

Policy networks

Policy networks (chapter 9) are looser and less exclusive than policy communities. They consist of all the organisations, groups and actors that cluster around a concern in a given policy area and that participate in public discussion about it. Their advantage is that they are more open and less exclusive than communities, so they are less likely to create resentment on the part of groups and interests that are outside the system. At the same time, because they are more open to all sorts of interests they are also likely to be more conflictual, and therefore decision making involving networks is likely to be less smooth and predictable.

■ Theories of decision making

Decision making theories often mix *analytic* and *prescriptive* elements, in the sense that they try both to help us understand how decision making processes actually work, and to say how decisions should be made. Generally speaking, two broad approaches have been developed, one based on economic theory and rational behaviour, another based on more pragmatic considerations of actual policy making processes.

■ *The rational-comprehensive model*

The rational-comprehensive model draws from economic theory about how rational individuals make decisions in complex situations. Analytically the four main characteristics of decision making according to this model are that:

- First, rational participants collect all the information relevant to a decision, and carefully analyse it. They rank and define their policy objectives, and systematically survey all the means appropriate to achieving these goals, choosing the most efficient and effective.
- They then calculate the consequences of their actions, and compare their costs and benefits with alternative strategies.
- The most cost-effective strategy is implemented.
- Finally, rational individuals evaluate their policies so that they can learn from the experience and improve things in the future.

Applied to public policy making, such a model assumes a single, centralised and coordinated decision making body, and a smooth and efficient government machine that implements decisions in the specified way. It should be kept in mind, however, that the rational-comprehensive model of decision-making is like the Weberian ideal-type of bureaucracy (see chapter 7). It is not an account of how decisions are actually made but an abstract model for judging reality.

The rational-comprehensive model may approximate to the kind of decision making that is possible, even if rarely found, in relatively small and highly effective decision making organisations, especially those concerned with technical problem solving. Something like it was used in the USA by the National Aeronautics and Space Administration (NASA) to land a spacecraft on the moon in 1962. But the model is usually far removed from the reality of decision making by large governments, as the fate of the centralised command economies in former socialist states demonstrates only too clearly. So far as decision making in large-scale government is concerned, the rational-comprehensive model is mainly of use as an abstract ideal by which to measure actual decision making. In real life, decision-makers:

- Rarely have even adequate, much less complete information
- Often handle crises with little time to think or prepare; they have to 'rebuild the ship at sea', sometimes in a Force 10 gale
- Are surrounded by powerful political constraints
- Rarely have adequate resources
- Sometimes are pushed by powerful political forces to make policy decisions that are incompatible or downright contradictory
- May already have invested heavily in other policies that they feel should not be compromised by a later one, even if the latter would be better
- Have limited control of the bureaucracies that implement central policies, especially if state and local government, which has its own democratic legitimacy, is involved
- Have to deal with unknown and unintended consequences that blow their policies off-course
- Have their own blind spots, prejudices and ideological preferences.

Some techniques have been devised to help rational decision making, most notably Cost-Benefit Analysis (CBA). CBA involves the attempt to calculate all the costs of a policy and the benefits it will bring at an early stage of decision making. It assumes that all the important factors to be taken into account can be *quantified* and that the costs (not just financial, but everything including social, environmental and aesthetic) can somehow be weighed against all the benefits. Advocates of the method argue that it forces decision makers:

- To think carefully and systematically
- To take a broad range of factors into account
- To question assumptions
- To make decisions transparent.

Critics have called CBA 'nonsense on stilts': how would you calculate the costs and benefits of, say, building a new motorway through a beautiful and untouched mountain pass? CBA sometimes involves trying to estimate labour costs for a particular project by getting workers on the project to apportion the time they spend on it. This is notoriously difficult and imprecise where, as often happens, office and managerial staff work on different projects at the same time, or where capital costs are shared between different projects.

■ The incremental model

'Muddling through'

If the rational-comprehensive model is an ideal, the **incremental model** is a realistic and pragmatic account of how decisions are actually made. Since political problems are so complex, and since policies have all sorts of unintended and unrecognised effects, it is better to minimise risk by proceeding cautiously, a small step at a time (*incrementally*). The result is piecemeal, gradual, *ad hoc* decision making, not a fundamental reappraisal of all goals and means. Since public policy is a political matter, it is also characterised by political bargaining, negotiating and compromise. This is especially true in fragmented and decentralised political systems where many different actors and organisations can get in on the act – that is, in pluralist systems. These can make centralised, rational decision making very difficult to achieve.

According to the American political scientist Charles Lindblom (1968), in real life decision makers *respond to problems*, rather than anticipating them or creating new goals. Instead of formulating some idealistic model of rational behaviour, Lindblom described the behaviour of decision makers, they:

> **Incremental model**
> The theory that decisions are not usually based upon a comprehensive review of problems, but upon small, marginal changes from existing policies.
>
> **Charles Lindblom, *The Policy-Making Process* (1968)**

- Consider only a *few alternatives* for dealing with a problem
- Pick those that *differ marginally* (incrementally) from existing policies
- Evaluate only a few of the most important *consequences*
- *Continually review* policies, making many small adjustments
- Do not search for the best single solution but recognise that there are many alternatives and pick those that are *politically expedient* and have *political support*.

This, says Lindblom, is the science of 'muddling through'. Though widely accepted as a rough and ready account of how decisions are made, the model has also been criticised for being:

- *Too conservative and too reactive*: It concentrates on existing problems and solutions, instead of widening the search for new solutions.
- Unable to deal with *emergencies and crisis situations*, requiring radical solutions.
- Unable to bring about fundamental re-thinking: the accumulation of incremental decisions over a long period of time can result in a 'policy morass', consisting of all sorts of conflicting and incompatible policies. In such a situation, fundamental re-thinking may be absolutely necessary. Sometimes it actually occurs.

Bounded rationality and advocacy coalitions

Herbert Simon (1916–2001)

Herbert Simon, *Administrative Behaviour* (1957)

Nobel prize laureate Herbert Simon emphasises in his (1957) book the boundaries to rational decision making created by the personal values of decision makers, the culture and the structure of the organisations they work in and the complexity and unpredictability of political events. These constraints mean that decision-makers 'satisfice' – a word Simon coined to describe policies that are not perfect but satisfactory, and suffice (are sufficient) for the time being. Decision makers will not continue to search for the very best policy but accept one that is adequate under the circumstances.

Graham Allison, *Essence of Decision* (1971)

The importance of organisational cultures and structures is emphasised by Graham Allison (1971). He found that American decision making about the Cuban missile crisis was the result of bargaining and negotiating between a small group of key decision makers representing departmental interests. Decisions were made not by a single, rational process, but by departments and departmental coalitions engaging in a political power game of 'pulling and hauling', amid confusion and lack of information.

Paul Sabatier and Hank Jenkins-Smith, *Policy Change and Learning: An Advocacy Coalition Approach* (1993)

This idea is developed further by Paul Sabatier and Hank Jenkins-Smith (1993), who argue that policy areas create 'advocacy coalitions' consisting of interest groups, politicians, professionals, journalists, researchers and others, who compete, bargain and compromise with each other. They also learn as circumstances change, so that policies also change.

■ Summary

This chapter has dealt with public policies and the way governments decide on those policies. It argues that:

- Governments try to deal with many problems, interests, and demands. They develop public policies: long series of activities, decisions and actions carried out by officials of government in their attempts to solve problems that are thought to lie in the public or collective arena.
- Not making decisions also has its consequences, and non-decision making is just one form of decision making (the decision not to make a decision) that is favoured by politicians who do not want to face an issue.
- The development of policies is a continuing and cyclical process that analytically consists of six overlapping phases: 'agenda setting', decision making, choice of means, implementation, outputs and outcomes, and evaluation and feedback.
- The scope of public policy making depends on the demarcation between the private and the public. Where the line is drawn is itself a matter of political controversy.
- Policy making processes are structured in various ways. Corporatist structures are mainly found in north Europe. They are characterised by close cooperation of interest groups within a formal government apparatus capable of concerting the interests of both groups and government so as to

formulate and implement binding policies. Only a limited number of hier-archically organised groups exist.

- Policy making is much less structured in many Anglo-Saxon countries. In these countries, pluralist structures prevail, characterised by cooperation of government and interest groups in networks or communities in restricted areas only. Usually a variety of loosely organised groups exists.
- Approaches to policy making can be broadly divided into models empha-sising rational behaviour (selecting of alternatives and strategies, optimis-ing costs and benefits) and those stressing the limitations of the process ('satisficing' instead of 'optimising') and the relevance of cultural and polit-ical factors.

Further reading

A number of general introductions to policy making and the study of policy making processes are available, among which are: Thomas R. Dye, *Understanding Public Policy* (London: Prentice-Hall, 10th edn., 2001); Charles Lindblom, *The Policy-Making Process* (Englewood, Cliffs, NJ: Prentice-Hall, 1968); William N. Dunn, *Public Policy Analysis: An Introduction* (London: Prentice-Hall, 3rd edn., 2001); and James E. Anderson, *Public Policymaking* (Boston: Houghton Mifflin, 4th edn., 2000). At a more advanced level are the case studies of policy making presented in Stuart S. Nagel (ed.), *Handbook of Public Policy Evaluation* (London: Sage, 2001). A general account of the nature of corporatism, and of its rise and fall in west Europe, can be found in B. Guy Peters, *European Politics Reconsidered* (New York: Holmes & Meier, 1991: 165–92). A fascinating study of policy implementation is Jeffrey L. Pressman and Aaron Wildavsky, *Implementation: How Great Expectations in Washington are Dashed in Oakland* (Berkeley: University of California Press, 1973).

Websites

http://www.uoregon.edu/~vburris/ whorules/policy.htm Extensive website on policy research with a number of links to different organisations and projects.

http://www.aspanet.org Website of the American Society for Public Administration.

Projects

1. Visit your local community council and make a list of the ten issues at the top of the public agenda. Did any issues 'disappear' from the public agenda in your community? Which groups are involved in the present top-three issues, and which groups find it difficult to get their issue high on the agenda?
2. Select a Scandinavian country and an Anglo-Saxon country, and search for information to compare the influences on public policies. Is their influence explained by the corporatist–pluralist nature of the political system?
3. Suppose you decided to spend a term abroad while a student. Present a clear description of your complete policy cycle for this decision.

15   Defence and security

What would happen if everybody did just whatever they liked? Why do we need police, courts, and armies? Can't people take care of their own business without violence and oppression? Do citizens need protection against the consequences of GM food, atomic energy, or toxic paint? Is the exercise of force compatible with democracy's claim to peace and justice?

Living together is based on *mutual understanding* and the acceptance of certain rules, conventions and habits, yet these are not enough on their own. In the end, severe conflicts of interest can be resolved only by force. Therefore, the traditional tasks of government include the enforcement of rules and the regulation of social life. Governments preserve law and order by protecting their citizens from internal disorder (internal security), and their country from foreign aggression (external security). Increasingly they also offer protection against potentially harmful products such as unsafe cars, dangerous food additives and toxic substances. Governments also regulate the construction and operation of many other things – from atomic plants to electric toasters – to protect their citizens against the dangers of modern life.

In this chapter, we examine the efforts of governments to protect citizens from assault, interference and physical danger of many kinds. The provision of social security to protect citizens against the consequences of illness, poverty and unemployment is discussed in chapter 16. Meanwhile, this chapter deals with national defence and domestic law and order – that is, with measures to secure the life and property of citizens against threat, especially crime and foreign aggression. The six main topics in this chapter are:

- The state and security
- Defence and national security
- Internal law and order
- Other forms of protection
- The limitations of state security
- Theories of security and conflict.

◼ The state and security

In 1651, the British philosopher Thomas Hobbes published a classical defence of the need for security in society. Starting from the premise that completely free and independent people are naturally selfish and self-seeking, he concluded that only the provision of collective security could banish the risk of injury or violent death. What was needed was a third party commanding enough power to make sure that each citizen respected the security of everybody else. This is where the state – or the 'King' or 'Leviathan' as Hobbes preferred to call it – comes in. According to this line of reasoning the state's main task is to provide physical security for its citizens. Without this protection, everybody is under threat and life becomes, as Hobbes put it 'solitary, poore, nasty, brutish and short' (briefing 15.1).

Thomas Hobbes (1588–1679)

Hobbes' argument still underpins the case for a state that wields a monopoly of the legitimate use of physical force in order to protect itself and its citizens. Although people were never free and independent in the way the romantic idea of a 'state of nature' suggests, the need for protection and the enforcement of rules is self-evident. Without them, peaceful social life is impossible. Even the mafia and terrorist cells insist on obedience to their own rules and, as we have seen in chapter 1, there is a close connection between the development of

Briefing 15.1
The life of man [is] solitary, poore, nasty, brutish and short

Whatsoever therefore is consequent to a time of Warre, where every man is Enemy to every man; the same is consequent to the time, wherein men live without other security, than what their own strength, and their own invention shall furnish them withall. In such condition, there is no place for Industry; because the fruit thereof is uncertain: and consequently no Culture of the Earth; no Navigation, nor use of the commodities that may be imported by Sea; no commodious Building; no Instruments of moving, and removing such things as require much force; no Knowledge of the face of the Earth; no account of Time; no Arts; no Letters; no Society; and which is worst of all, continuall feare, and danger of violent death; And the life of man, solitary, poore, nasty, brutish and short. (Thomas Hobbes, *Leviathan*, Harmondsworth: Penguin, 1968 [1651]: 186) the modern state and the need of early capitalism for protection of property, including its investments and markets at home and abroad.

Defence and national security

Protecting the state and its citizens from outside aggression is probably the most conventional task of any government. Of course, many contacts between states or their citizens result in cooperation, collaboration, or peaceful exchange between nations, but disputes and conflict cannot be avoided, and so the need for regulating the relations between states is evident. In the final analysis, international conflict of values and interests can be settled only **Karl von** by force – war if necessary – because war, in the words of Karl von Clausewitz **Clausewitz** is nothing more than the continuation of politics by other means. **(1780–1831)**

Conflict resolution

Conflicts involving states can be classified according to the degree of *violence* involved. At one end of the continuum are non-violent conflicts that entail no more than a clear expression of different interests. Such mild conflicts can, however, easily escalate when participants start to press their case by means of diplomatic pressure, economic sanctions, or threats of violence. Usually some arrangement is reached between conflicting parties to settle their disputes, so many conflicts between states and other groups remain at a non-violent level. Arrangements can be formalised in treaties or pacts, with special agencies to enforce them and avoid further conflict.

By reaching agreements with other parties, states try to protect the interests of their citizens as well as their position in the world. Notice that the term 'non-violent conflicts' does not mean that there are no real victims, for the use of economic sanctions and blockades in non-violent conflicts can results in deep misery or death for thousands (see briefing 15.2).

Briefing 15.2
Economic sanctions or genocide?

The death sentence for hundreds of thousands of Iraqis was pronounced on August 6, 1990. With Resolution 661 the UN Security Council imposed a full-scale economic embargo against the country, four days after Saddam Hussein's army had invaded Kuwait. The brutal dictator was not overthrown by the sanctions; the Iraq people, however, has had to endure almost inconceivable suffering in the last twelve years. According to a Unicef study, by 1999 the sanctions caused the death of about half a million people. Due to shortages of food and medicine, or due to polluted drinking water, about 5,000 to 6,000 Iraq children died each month . . . In a report to the UN Commission on Human Rights, the Belgian international lawyer, Marc Bossuyt, wrote: 'The sanctions against Iraq intentionally generates living conditions that aim to destroy a group (of people) physically – this is a literal definition of genocide'. (*Sanctions: who gets punished?*, Amnesty International Switzerland: www.amnesty.ch/d/id/idamd/m0208d/sa.html).

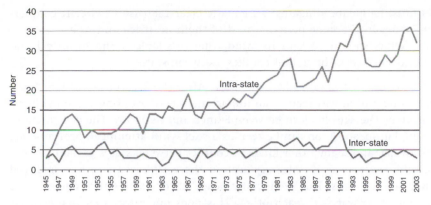

Figure 15.1: Intra- and inter-state conflicts of high intensity, 1945–2003
Source: Konfliktbarometer 2003: 5; www.konfliktbarometer.de.

Severe conflicts cannot be solved easily by exchanging views and trying to reach agreement. In cases where there is little trust, those involved may use third-party **mediation** or **conciliation** to try to find common ground – turning to an 'honest broker' who can break the deadlock. Alternatively, conflicting states may bring their case to the Security Council of the UN or to the International Court of Justice (ICJ), or to some other authoritative international body. The problem here is that states are *sovereign* (see chapter 1): they can accept or reject the legal decision, just as they can accept or reject mediation in the first place. Instead of trying to reach a peaceful settlement, states can, and do, use force to reach their goals.

The **Charter of the United Nations** (UN) starts with the statement that the purpose of the UN is: 'To maintain international peace and security' (Art. 1.1) and it obliges member states 'To settle their disputes by peaceful means' (Art. 2.3). The Charter clearly bans the initial use of force and spells out the peaceful means that are available as an alternative:

> The parties to any dispute, the continuance of which is likely to endanger the maintenance of international peace and security, shall, first of all, seek a solution by negotiation, enquiry, mediation, conciliation, arbitration, judicial settlement, resort to regional agencies or arrangements, or other peaceful means of their own choice. (Art. 33.1)

The use of violence between states is – measured by the number of conflicts – rather limited. As can be seen in figure 15.1, violent conflicts between states since 1945 show a modest increase only in the late 1970s and into the 1980s. Of the total of thirteen wars fought in 2003, only one was *between states* (the war of the USA and its allies against Iraq). What has been growing constantly, however, is the number of violent disputes *within states*. After the Second World War internal violence increased steadily to reach the figure of about 30–35 conflicts each year. In short, the clear decline in wars between states in the

Mediation
Attempt by a third party to reach an agreement between disputing parties on the basis of an investigation of the facts of the dispute.

Charter of the United Nations
Founding treaty of the United Nations (UN) that defines the purposes of the UN and confers certain powers on it (see chapter 1).

1990s must be balanced against an equally clear increase in violent conflicts within states in the same period – most of them in Africa and Asia.

Two factors should be kept in mind when we look at the historical and geographical changes in violent conflicts between states:

- First, many used to take place in *Europe*. After the Second World War European integration was seen as an important way of avoiding these conflicts, especially the age-old clash between France and Germany. The development of the European Union can be seen as a successful attempt to prevent wars in Europe, and many other kinds of conflict between states as well.
- Second, the spread of *democracy* around the world seems to have reduced international wars. The 'democratic peace' theory states that democracies do not go to war with each other. This does not mean that democracies are not warlike – as the examples of the USA and Britain clearly show – for democracies do make war against non-democratic states. Yet, the fact that democracies do not go to war with each other means that the increasing number of democratic states in the world reduces the incidence of war.

■ Just wars

In the international community, violent action is accepted only if (1) force is used in self-defence, or (2) the action is authorised by the UN. Straightforward as these principles may seem, they are highly disputed in any given case. Self-defence against aggression seems relatively unproblematic, but what about pre-emptive strikes against anticipated attack? Apart from the ethical and diplomatic problems that go with attacking first, the danger is that pre-emptive strikes may overestimate the aggressive intentions of the other country and thereby intensify the conflict. On the other hand, it is difficult to see how one can deny the right to pre-emptive strikes, especially when, in retrospect, history shows that it might have been beneficial in reducing conflict in some cases.

One of the problems is that it is very difficult to reach consensus about the meaning of terms such as 'aggression', 'attack' and 'self-defence', so that the use of violence in self-defence remains highly contested. Nonetheless, three points about self-defence are clear:

- The force used must be *proportional* to the force used by the assailant. A minor violation of a frontier is no pretext to start a full-scale war. The problem, of course, lies in stating exactly what is 'proportional'.
- Self-defence does not mean a right to *reprisal*. For instance, an attack on country A by terrorists who happen to operate out of country B does not justify country A attacking country B or its residents. The problem, of course, comes when country A claims that the terrorists were agents of country B, or otherwise aided by that country. Country A might then justify its counter-attack in the name of self-defence.

- Self-defence can usually be invoked by states whose *territory is violated* (see chapter 1). Attacks on its citizens who are living abroad does not entitle a state to use force against another state as an act of self-defence. The problem, of course, lies in defining what is 'home' and what is 'abroad', as the examples of the West Bank, North and South Korea, North and South Vietnam, Taiwan and the Falkland Islands show.

The self-defence problem is even greater in the case of conflict within a state:

- Is a corrupt government entitled to defend itself against attack by rebels who are clearly supported by the population?
- Are violent separatist movements legitimate if the government suppresses the rights of minorities?
- Does international terrorism establish a general right of self-defence, including a declaration of war, or is a large-scale violent response excluded by the principle of proportionality of means?

In a world where violent internal conflict is more common, states are increasingly turning to self-defence arguments to justify their own violence, and so the meaning of the term 'self-defence' is becoming increasingly unclear.

Instead of relying on self-defence, states may try to protect their interests by turning to the UN, for both peaceful intervention and peace-keeping by force. Since the 1990s the UN has increased its armed peace-keeping activities by sending military forces to areas of conflict all over the world. In 2003, thirteen peace-keeping missions were active (see table 15.1) with a total of 43,000 soldiers and police officers from ninety-two countries. The largest contributions came from Pakistan (5,250 men), Bangladesh (4,000 men) and Nigeria (3,300 men). Four missions were in areas with a very high level of violence (Congo, Israel, Kashmir and Liberia). In fact, since its start in 1948 more than 1,800 men have been killed in UN peace-keeping missions all over the world.

◾ Military expenditure

In spite of the determined attempts to regulate conflicts by peaceful means or to rely on UN action, many states maintain large armies or manufacture large amounts of military equipment. The 'top five' states in the world with the largest defence budgets are:

1. USA
2. France
3. Japan
4. Germany
5. Britain.

With total spending of almost $400 billion a year, the USA's budget is by far the largest. Even before the Iraq War of 2003, the USA's defence budget equalled

Table 15.1 *UN missions around the world*

Mission	Name	Start (or period)	State/Region
MINURSO	UN Mission for the Referendum in Western Sahara	1991	West Sahara
MONUC	UN Mission in the Democratic Republic of the Congo	1999	Congo
UNAMSIL	UN Mission in Sierra Leone	1999	Sierra Leone
UNDOF	UN Disengagement Observer Force Golan Heights	1974	Syria–Israel
UNFICYP	UN Force in Cyprus	1964	Cyprus
UNIFIL	UN Interim Force in Lebanon	1978	Lebanon
UNIKOM	UN Iraq–Kuwait Observer Mission	1991–2003	Iraq–Kuwait
UNMEE	UN Mission in Ethiopia and Eritrea	2000	Ethiopia–Eritrea
UNMIBH	UN Mission in Bosnia and Herzegovina	1995–2002	Bosnia-Herzegovina
UNMIK	UN Interim Administration Mission in Kosovo	1999	Yugoslavia (Kosovo)
UNMIL	UN Mission in Liberia	2003	Liberia
UNMISET	UN Mission of Support in East Timor[a]	2002	East Timor
UNMOGIP	UN Military Observer Group India and Pakistan	1949	India–Pakistan
UNMOP	UN Mission of Observers in Prevlaka	1996–2002	Croatia
UNOMIG	UN Observer Mission to Georgia	1993	Georgia
UNTSO	UN Truce Supervisory Organisation Middle East	1948	Middle East

Note: [a] Successor of the UN Transitional Administration in East Timor (UNTAET), start 1999.
Source: Konfliktbarometer 2003: 8; www.konfliktbarometer.de.

the total of Britain, China, France, Germany, Italy, Japan, Russia, Saudi Arabia and Taiwan!

The picture of military spending changes dramatically when we calculate it as a percentage of gross domestic product (or GDP) (chapter 2). Measured this way, spending in the USA is only 3.3 per cent of GDP – and this figure does not even get into the top forty states! The list is headed by North Korea, which spends an estimated 31 per cent on defence, followed by Angola, Eritrea, Saudi Arabia and Ethiopia. West European countries such as France or Britain spend only 2.5 per cent of GDP on defence, while Germany, Spain, The Netherlands and Norway are even lower, with less than 2 per cent. Notice, however, that obtaining reliable figures on military expenditures is a tricky business. Many states manipulate information about military expenditure for obvious reasons, so that estimates by independent institutes are usually (much) higher than the official figures.

Controversy 15.1

Is government the greatest threat to human security?

The production of security must be undertaken by and is the primary function of government. As far as empirical – historical – evidence is concerned, proponents of [this] orthodox view face obvious embarrassment. The recently ended twentieth century was characterised by a level of human rights violations unparalleled in all of human history. In his book *Death by Government*, Rudolf Rummel estimates some 170 million government-caused deaths in the twentieth century. The historical evidence appears to indicate that, rather than protecting life, liberty, and the pursuit of happiness of their citizens, governments must be considered the greatest threat to human security. (Hans-Hermann Hoppe, *The Myth of National Defense: Essays on the Theory and History of Security Production*, Auburn: Mises Institute, 2003: 2)

Selling arms is big business, although it is sometimes difficult to know exactly how big. For leading exporting countries such as Britain, France, Germany and the USA, it is difficult to distinguish between the production of arms for defence purposes and for the economic benefit of the arms industry. Global trading is heavily dominated by US firms. In many countries, military expenditure is mixed up with spending on general research and development (R&D), making it very difficult to disentangle 'pure' military efforts from civilian and applied research. In Britain, France and the USA, substantial proportions of public expenditure on R&D are used for military purposes.

Military budgets have been reduced in most countries since the late 1980s. The main reason is political: when the Cold War between the Soviet Union and the west came to an end, a number of states no longer used conscription but turned to professional soldiers instead. These forces are much smaller and do not concentrate on the defence of national territory, but can be deployed for military tasks all over the world. A second reason is the serious economic problems faced by many countries, resulting in growing financial restrictions on public spending of any kind. Even in prosperous times, military spending is not popular and an easy target for politicians looking for cuts.

States still attach high value to their military capacity for self-defence. Despite their growing military capacities, however, modern states have not been very successful in protecting life (see controversy 15.1). Consequently, some argue that high levels of military spending are part of the problem of security in the world, and not the solution.

■ Internal law and order

For most citizens, the protection of life, liberty and the pursuit of happiness start at home: they expect government to protect their life and property and to punish those who break the law. Punishment for crime is strictly regulated and can be carried out only by order of a proper court.

■ *Law enforcement*

Law enforcement and punishment of offenders are among the traditional tasks of the state but, as we saw in chapter 3, the autonomy of the legal system is based on the idea that judges should be independent of the government and final arbiters of the law. Since punishing citizens generally implies a very significant violation of their rights, law enforcement, tracking down of offenders, convicting suspects and punishment are carried out by two or more different branches of government. Their organisation varies considerably between states:

Police
The branch of government employed to maintain civil order and to investigate breaches of the law.

- Usually, a national **police** force deals with grave offences and threats to the internal security of the state, and usually it has jurisdiction throughout the country and is responsible to the national government. National **police** forces can have a military or semi-military character, such as the *Guardia Civil* in Spain or the *Carabinieri* in Italy. In addition to their national police, many countries also have a local or regional police corps – a *gendarmerie* or civil guard – that is responsible for law enforcement in specific geographical areas. In addition, there are usually national organisations to deal with special criminal activities and intelligence, such as the Federal Bureau of Investigation (FBI) in the USA. Police forces are usually part of the Ministry of the Interior (Home Office).
- Deciding who should be prosecuted, of those charged with an offence by the police, is the main tasks of *public prosecutors*. Here, too, we find substantial differences between countries depending on the judicial system and the division of labour between police and prosecutors. Generally speaking, public prosecutors are part of the Ministry of Justice, and independent of the police.
- Convicting and punishing those found, as well as issuing judgements resolving disputes, are tasks assigned to judges and courts or the judiciary (chapter 3). Their job is to *interpret* the law and *apply* it to particular cases. The judiciary has to be protected from political interference and from the temptations of corruption. The police and the judiciary are usually housed in different ministries.
- Finally, convicted offenders may be *punished*, and it is usually the job of the Ministry of the Interior or the Ministry of Justice to organise this, by running prisons, receiving fines, or organising community work.

The complicated and lengthy procedures that follow, from notification of an offence to conviction of the offender, differ noticeably between countries, and can involve a set of independent public agencies and departments. Consequently, it is difficult even to estimate the overall costs of law enforcement in any given country, much less compare a range of them. Even apparently simple indicators such as the number of police officers per 100,000 citizens

Table 15.2 *Criminal offences, selected countries, 2001, per 100,000 inhabitants*

	Murder	Sex offences	Assault	Theft	Fraud	Other	**Total**
Belgium	5.97	41.99	552.99	4258.40	85.86	366.74	**5311.95**
France	3.91	60.58	199.20	4310.32	621.70	160.66	**5356.37**
Germany	3.21	64.31	146.30	3682.05	1125.95	306.09	**5327.91**
Italy	3.75	4.24	53.17	2257.74	67.44	62.44	**2448.78**
Netherlands[a]	10.87	42.42	242.77	5302.51	112.22	64.18	**5774.97**
Norway[b]	2.14	72.77	70.38	4329.84	265.00	1128.45	**4742.27**
Spain	2.90	16.80	21.23	1940.92	43.45	44.20	**2069.50**
UK	18.51	237.95	242.40	12130.41	1049.43	999.42	**14678.12**
USA	5.61	–	318.55	3804.58	–	–	–

Notes: [a] 1998.
      [b] 2002.
      – Missing data.
Source: Interpol; www.interpol.int/Public/Statistics/ICS/downloadList.asp.

can be misleading if the organisation of regional, national and special police forces is not carefully taken into account.

■ *Crime, punishment and prevention*

Citizens in virtually every western country consider crime – especially violent crime – to be an increasingly serious threat to their well-being, and want the government to do something about it:

- Does this widespread feeling of insecurity indicate real danger?
- Are crime rates rising?
- Or is it mainly a matter of the insecurities of modern life, magnified by the popular and sensational mass media?

These questions are difficult to answer, for six main reasons:

- Estimates of the *number of real crimes* are influenced by how the police register crimes, on the ways different sorts of crimes are recorded and counted and on the willingness of the public to report them. Similar countries can have remarkably different crime statistics (see table 15.2), which is at least partly due to differences in crime reporting and counting.
- Feelings of *insecurity and threat* are difficult to measure, and the figures one gets from surveys depend on the precise question asked.
- Different definitions of *delinquent behaviour* produce different crime rates. For instance, if corruption and bribery is part of the traditional culture, it will not appear to the same extent in the crime statistics.

- Different *ownership rates* cause different crime rates. Bicycle theft is espe-cially high in The Netherlands, Denmark and Japan, where cycling is common.
- Different *demographic factors* can account for differences in crime rates. Since young men are the most crime-prone group, their decline in the population may result in a changing pattern of offences.
- Instead of focusing on feelings of threat and insecurity, information from *victims of various crimes* can be used to analyse crime and crime rates. Research in this area – *The International Crime Victims Survey*, for instance – shows that the pattern of crimes differs across countries, with Spain (Catalonia) and Portugal having a crime problem with cars and Finland an unusually high number of sexual incidents.

The conventional way to deal with crime is to search for offenders, bring them to court and punish them for their behaviour. The most common measure against grave breaches of the law is to send offenders to jail. Prison figures appear to be highly dependent on national and demographic characteristics. Several studies even conclude that there is no relationship between the size of the prison population in a country and its level of recorded crime. The main factors influencing the size of the prison population are the length of sentences imposed and the number of serious offences recorded by the police. Among some democratic states, especially in the USA, imprisonment is very high, with some 700 prisoners per 100,000 of the population (see briefing 15.3). Comparative figures for western European countries are much lower, ranging from 130 in Portugal and Britain to as little as 50–60 in Scandinavia. In fact, the number of prisoners per 100,000 citizens is below 150 in about two-thirds of all states in the world. Nevertheless, growing feelings of insecurity are reflected in steadily increasing numbers of prisoners held in many countries.

Law and order is an expensive business. Even if the police and public pros-ecutors give priority to serious crimes and pay less attention to minor ones – bicycle theft, parking violations and small tax evasions – large bureaucracies are required to trace and prosecute suspects, while securing their individual rights. Prisons are also expensive, but even long sentences do not seem to act as a deterrent so the preferred solution of many politicians to the crime problem does not seem to work. The crime rate seems unaffected by sentencing poli-cies, and many of those who go to prison return for the crimes they commit after their release. As a result, prison space remains scarce because in spite of additional facilities being built, the prison population appears to expand to fill the space available.

As Hobbes forcefully argued, citizens want governments to protect their prop-erty and rights, more than they want punishment for those who have violated

Prevention
Attempt to hinder or deter delinquent behaviour.

their rights. Most people would prefer their car was not stolen in the first place than that the thief was punished for stealing it. Policy makers are there-fore increasingly looking to **prevention** as an alternative to punishment, espe-cially since many politicians realise that imprisonment is an expensive and

Briefing 15.3

The world prison population

- More than 8.75 million people are held in penal institutions throughout the world, mostly as pre-trial detainees (remand prisoners) or having been convicted and sentenced. About half of these are in the USA (1.93 million), Russia (0.96 million), or China (1.43 million plus pre-trial detainees and prisoners in 'administrative detention').

- The USA has the highest prison population rate in the world, some 700 per 100,000 of the national population, followed by Russia (665), the Cayman Islands (600), Belarus (555), the US Virgin Islands (550), Kazakhstan (520), Turkmenistan (490), the Bahamas (480), Belize (460) and Bermuda (445). Almost two-thirds of countries (63 per cent) have rates of 150 per 100,000 or below.

- Prison population rates vary considerably between different regions of the world, and between different parts of the same continent. For example:
  - In Africa, the median rate for western and central African countries is 50–55 whereas for southern African countries it is 260
  - In the Americas, the median rate for south American countries is 115 whereas for Caribbean countries it is 295
  - In Asia, the median rate for south central Asian countries (mainly the Indian sub-continent) is 55 whereas for (ex-Soviet) central Asian countries it is 425
  - In Europe, the median rate for southern European countries is 65 whereas for central and eastern European countries it is 210
  - In Oceania (including Australia and New Zealand), the median rate is 105
  - Prison populations are growing in many parts of the world.

(World Prison Population List, 3rd edn., 2002; www.homeoffice.gov.uk/rds/pdfs/r166.pdf)

ineffective way of reducing crime. Prevention programmes are often based on the fact that adult crime is linked to the social and behavioural problems of criminals when they are young, and so early intervention is preferred.

■ Other forms of protection

Besides trying to protect citizens against *crime* governments are involved in another huge area of public activity concerned with protecting citizens from *harm*. They regulate the production and sale of an extraordinarily wide range of goods and services, from food, cigarettes and alcohol, to dental, legal and insurance services, and from the manufacture of cars, electrical goods and building materials to the construction and operation of tools, factories and engines – from nuclear power stations to electric toasters, in fact. They do so to protect citizens against the dangers and harmful effects of modern life.

Government activity in this area takes four main forms:

- Information
- Certification
- Permission
- Product safety.

■ *Information*

Governments try to protect their citizens by requiring the producers of goods and services to *inform consumers* about what they are buying – food is labelled, the effects and side-effects of medicines are described, operating instructions for machines are provided, the details of contracts are presented in simple language.

■ *Certification*

Governments issue rules not only for the *standardisation* of products (electric plugs should be the same size and shape) but also for safety standards, and they then certify the products as suitable for public use. The European Union is very active in this area of consumer protection.

■ *Permission*

In many countries, potentially harmful products such as medicine, industrial equipment, chemicals, and guns, can be sold only by registered dealers.

■ *Product safety*

Information, certification and permission are ways of increasing *product safety*, based on the idea that individuals can decide for themselves once they are provided with the relevant information and safety guarantees. However, risk and liability looks quite different when we are dealing not with electric shavers or pharmaceutical drugs, but with polluted streams, atomic plants, or GM food. In these cases, government protection is not about individuals who can make informed and responsible judgements about what they consume, but about *public goods* and *collective resources* such as clean air and water, or *public 'bads'* such as noise and exhaust fumes. By definition, public goods and public 'bads' have to be collectively regulated and this is becoming one of the most important and controversial modern functions of government.

Most governments have developed complicated laws and policies to deal with modern technology and its consequences for individuals and the environment. Since all technologies have their dangers, and since these are often hard (or impossible) to estimate given that some may materialise only many years after their introduction, discussions usually focus on the question: 'how safe is "safe enough"?'. The state cannot protect citizens against all risk, any more than it can ban all new technologies. Nor can governments ignore the possibly considerable advantages of atomic energy or GM food: they have to take into account both positive and negative aspects. The result is very difficult and complicated decisions involving the actual and possible risks, both present and future, to individuals and the environment. This inevitably involves unknowns, and a continuous monitoring of the risks. We now know that smoking is a health risk, but what about mobile phones, or GM and irradiated food, or high-tension electricity cables, or hormone replacement therapy (HRT)?

One important principle of democracy is that government intervention can only *follow* and not *anticipate* adverse effects. The government can put you in prison for committing a crime, but it cannot sentence you before you have committed the crime on the grounds that you might commit it at some time in the future. Effective environmental protection, however, is not possible if government has to wait until rivers are polluted or billions of Euros spent on nuclear reactors. At the same time, rapid technological innovation means that governments risk running years behind the latest developments if they are too cautious.

◼ The limitations of state security

Although governments devote an increasing amount of time and money to protecting the state and its citizens, their powers in this respect are strictly limited:

- In the first place, no government can guarantee a 'no-risk society' any more than it can prevent all crime.
- In the second, punishment may satisfy the desire for revenge and retaliation, but it seems to contribute little to the prevention of crime.
- And in the third, the world is changing in ways that make the problem even more difficult. With growing interdependence and interconnectedness in the world, national borders become less effective and states exercise less control over their own territory (see chapter 1).

Globalisation (chapter 2) presents new challenges to security, the most significant of which are:

- Terrorism
- International crime
- Corruption.

◼ *Terrorism*

States, democratic or otherwise, have never been safe from **terrorism** but recent events have concentrated attention on the problem as never before. Palestinian suicide bombers, Basque nationalists, Al Qaida and the Shining Path in Peru are only a few examples. Although most terrorist groups take action against a particular state or government, they also hijack and kill innocent third parties, if they feel it can increase political pressure. Terrorism, however, can also be seen as the only means available to the poor and repressed of the world to defend themselves against the overwhelming strength of their oppressors (see controversy 15.2).

Terrorism
The use of violence for political aims. What some regard as terrorism is seen as 'freedom fighting' by others.

Controversy 15.2

Terrorism: a fundamental mind-trick?

The poor, the weak and the oppressed rarely complain about 'terrorism'. The rich, the strong and the oppressors constantly do. While most of mankind has more reason to fear the high-technology violence of the strong than the low-technology of the weak, the fundamental mind-trick employed by the abusers of the word 'terrorism' is essentially this: The low-technology violence of the weak is such an abomination that there are no limits to the high-technology violence of the strong that can be deployed against it.

Not surprisingly, since Sept. 11, 2001, virtually every recognised state confronting an insurgency or separatist movement has eagerly jumped on the 'war on terrorism' bandwagon, branding its domestic opponents – if it had not already done so – 'terrorists'. (John V. Whitbeck, 'A world ensnared by a word', *International Herald Tribune*, February 18, 2004)

The demolition of the World Trade Center in New York on 11 September 2001 made it clear that terrorism is not at all the same as conventional warfare, and requires entirely different methods to deal with it. At the same time, the end of the Cold War and the decline of wars between states has left quite a few western countries with defence and intelligence capacities that are 'surplus to requirements'. One response has been to re-deploy defence and intelligence staff to fight the 'war on terrorism'. In addition, some countries have created new anti-terrorism units; the USA has created an enormous federal agency to coordinate its anti-terrorist efforts, and justified the war in Afghanistan (2001) and Iraq (2003) in these terms.

■ International crime

Crime does not stop at national borders. On the contrary: the most profitable crimes are organised internationally. Drugs, women and arms are exported to places with the highest profits – often from poor and rural areas to rich ones in west Europe and north America. Organising this business is extremely lucrative, and the chances of arrest are lower because of international legal and policing arrangements. In other words, international crime is running ahead of national and international capacities to deal with it.

■ Corruption

Political power is crucial for the distribution of resources and the protection of interests, so it comes as no surprise that politicians are under constant pressure from many different quarters and many different interests. Lobbying is an integral part of democratic decision making, but as we saw in chapter 9, the line between legitimate pressure and less savoury activities is difficult to

Controversy 15.3

The price of security?

The claim that if you want security you must give up liberty [has] become a mainstay of the revolt against freedom. But nothing is less true. There is, of course, no absolute security in life. But what security can be attained depends on our own watchfulness, enforced by institutions to help us watch – i.e. by *democratic institutions* which are devised (using Platonic language) to enable the herd to watch, and to judge, their watch-dogs. (Karl R. Popper, *The Open Society and Its Enemies, 1: The Spell of Plato*, Princeton: Princeton University Press, 1961 [1943]: 315, emphasis in the original)

draw. Clientelism, patronage and outright bribery and **corruption** are by no means unknown in democracies, although they can be defined and evaluated very differently. In some countries they are seen as inevitable, even good or 'functional', in others they are unambiguously rejected and prosecuted. Since it makes sense to try to corrupt only the strong and influential, and since these are often powerful politicians, it is also difficult to root out such abuse. For this reason, it is seen more and more as a major threat to democratic politics. The NGO, Transparency International (TI), has been set up to investigate and draw attention to the problem.

Corruption
The use of illegitimate means (bribery, blackmail, or threats) to influence or control the making of public decisions, or the secret use of public offices or resources for private purposes.

■ *The limits of state power*

Concerns about international crime, terrorism and corruption draw fresh attention to the old problem of the limits of state power. For modern democracies, however, the question is whether they are particularly *vulnerable* to these threats. Their strict rules about individual rights and freedoms make it easier for criminals and terrorists to work within and cross their borders, and more difficult to take effective measures against them. Hence the claim that 'if you want security, you must give up liberty' (see controversy 15.3). Debate about this claim is likely to persist.

Meanwhile, as a reaction to the risks of modern life, businesses and wealthy citizens are turning to private security arrangements. They live behind walls and gates in protected communities, employ private bodyguards and armed watchmen and install closed circuit TV (CCTV) and expensive alarm systems. This, in turn, means that the state no longer has a monopoly of physical force, a point we will return to in chapter 17.

■ **Theories of security and conflict**

Over the centuries social scientists, philosophers and military experts have tried to understand war and formulate general theories about it. Their attempts have not been very successful, so far. This is partly because it often seems that each war is the product of very specific and particular circumstances, especially if the focus is on the more spectacular phases of violent confrontation rather than the protracted negotiations to avoid war, or the long chain of events that leads up to war. Violent conflict is also a special interest of modern historians who are often interested in the unique aspects of each case. As a consequence, research on conflicts and peace tends to be fragmented and not cumulative.

Theoretical work is perhaps more successful when it focuses on the role of the state in protecting its citizens. In fact, this is one of the most important arguments for the existence of states and their legitimate use of political power (see chapter 1). According to one view, states should be little more than 'night watchmen' with the job of protecting life and property. Notice that such a 'protectionist' approach says little about the social and historical origins of states, or why they function as they do. It is a normative theory (chapter 1) concerned with what states ought to do, and with the limitations that should be placed upon them. Thomas Hobbes' famous account of the Leviathan is widely recognised as a basic attempt to legitimise strong government in order to protect freedom.

■ *The origins of conflict*

More empirical approaches to conflict and security have been formulated in several social science disciplines. Three are particularly well known:

* *Animal behaviour theories* focusing on biological aspects of animal and human behaviour, especially on the aggressive and competitive instincts that are said to be inherent in human nature.
* *Social–psychological theories* examine the inter-relationships between individuals either within small groups or in large ('anonymous') masses. Social psychologists tend to stress the importance of socialisation, especially in childhood, in the development of character, norms and values. They emphasise human 'cultures' rather than 'instinct'.
* *Structural–functional theories* emphasise neither culture nor instinct. They start from the structures and institutions of society and the functions they perform in maintaining social stability and continuity. Societies are seen as an organic 'system' in which each part performs a set of functions, so that to change any one part may have consequences for all the others. If one part of society does not perform its function adequately, the result is likely to be some sort of conflict, until society readjusts itself to establish equilibrium once again. Conflict can, therefore, be 'functional' if it draws attention to a social problem that is then rectified.

Each of these approaches has its problems:

* Can we use animal behaviour to explain human behaviour, and to what extent can we explain human conflict in terms of basic instincts?

- Are human beings 'animals' in this sense, and how can we know what is 'instinctive' or 'hard-wired' into our genetic make-up?
- Equally, how do we know what is learned in society and therefore cultural?
- Can we understand conflict as the product of how people are socialised into their cultures, or perhaps the result of inadequate socialisation? And is it not rather odd to say that conflict is functional?
- If it persists over a long time, as it often does (think of religious and racial conflict), is it functional?
- Is serious conflict more functional than less serious conflict?
- Would it not be much better if there was no conflict to start with?

Realism and idealism

Such theoretical problems have pushed students of international relations to take a different approach towards international conflicts which concentrates neither on individuals and their instincts or socialisation, nor on society and its organic nature, but on *states and their reasons for operating in the international system* as they do. As so often, there are two opposing theories:

- *Idealism*   On the one hand, the idealist approaches that dominated before the Second World War saw politics as the struggle between competing ideas and ideologies (see chapter 13). The behaviour of states in the international system was guided, so far as possible, by *ideals and morality*, and by the possibility of peaceful coexistence.
- *Realism*   **Realism**, which can be seen as a reaction to idealism, sees politics as a struggle between *competing material interests*. The basic assumption is that international politics is shaped by relatively autonomous actors (especially states, but also other organisations such as MNCs) who act more or less rationally to promote their own interest. These actors are confronted with an unpredictable international system, where few common norms or values exist, and where no single body rules, as states rule the countries of the world. The logic of the international system is for each state to further its own interests by means of economic and military power. Unfortunately, this rational behaviour of state actors results in the continuing insecurity and unpredictability of the international system. Rather than the ordered Westphalia system (chapter 1), we have a 'dog-eat-dog' world that could be described as a 'west failure' system.

Realism
In international relations, realism refers to the view of politics that emphasises the role of self-interest as a determinant of state policies and hence the importance of power in these relations.

Policy communities

Defence policy and the arms trade are often used as a prime example of the policy communities that operate in some areas of public policy, and policy community theory has had some success in explaining decision making in government (see also chapter 14). Policy communities:

- Are relatively small and stable groups of people representing the *main interests* involved in a policy area
- Work closely together in both the formal decision making bodies of government (committees, consultative groups and official working parties) and in various informal and private ways
- Usually have common interests, and develop a *consensual approach* to the policy area
- Will do their best to exclude outside groups and interests that try to disturb their close working relations with different ideas and interests. Policy communities are *closed*.

In the case of defence policy and the arms trade, two closely related issues, there is likely to be a single policy community bringing together three sets of people:

- Senior government ministers and their most senior civil service advisors
- Military leaders in the army, navy and air force
- The business interests that finance, manufacture and sell arms at home and abroad.

Although their interests are not identical, they are likely to overlap to a great extent and they will have a common interest in keeping out other groups that want to get involved. While policy communities build up a great deal of expert and inside knowledge, and can work smoothly, efficiently and consistently over time, the danger is that they can become a closed conspiracy against the public interest. In some cases, those who are responsible for the public interest (elected politicians and public servants) may be 'captured' by private interests (the businessmen) in the community.

■ *The military–industrial complex*

C. Wright Mills (1916–62)

C. Wright Mills, *The Power Elite* (1956)

In his (1956) book on the power elite, C. Wright Mills goes a long way further than policy community theory, arguing that the military–industrial complex (chapter 9) controls *all* important decisions in American government. The national and financial issues of foreign and defence policy are so important in terms of national security and profits that a tiny group of politicians, top military officers and businessmen forms a tight political elite that makes all key decisions – social, political, economic, domestic and foreign policy.

This elite is united by a common social background and the same financial interests. Members attend the same schools and universities, join the same exclusive clubs and are related by intermarriage. Most of them are from enormously wealthy families and inherit large fortunes and business interests. This gives them the same vested interests in big business and 'big' government, and in protecting these interests at home and overseas. The elite is not interested in the middle levels of power, which it leaves to pluralist competition between whoever wants to get involved, but it keeps tight control of all 'key' decisions.

Critics of the power elite thesis argue that never once does Mills actually show how the elite makes any given decision, nor does he tell us how many people are in the closed circle – 50, 500, 5,000, 50,000? Another problem concerns how the elite maintains its unity – do the army, navy and air force not have different interests, each fighting for a larger share of the defence budget, and are the financial interests of oil companies always the same as those of, say, finance capitalists or the electronics industry? And even if Wright Mills is right about the USA, does the same model apply to Denmark, Namibia and Peru?

■ Summary

This chapter has dealt with the defence and security of the state. It argues that:

- Traditional tasks of governments include the defence of the state against its external enemies, the maintenance of domestic law and order and the protection of citizens and their property. In fact, many theories of the state and political power are based on the idea that security and protection are the ultimate reasons for the existence of states and governments.
- Wars between states have declined in recent decades, but armed conflict within states has increased since the Second World War.
- States have the right to defend themselves, subject to certain conditions (proportionality of response, taking action against attackers and not reprisals against innocent third parties, the maintenance of territorial integrity), but pre-emptive strikes are a different matter.
- Defence, military power and the arms trade are important economically for many countries, resulting in tightly knit policy making communities consisting of government, the military and arms producers. Some writers have even argued that 'the military–industrial complex' makes all the really important political decisions in some states.
- Crime rates vary highly between similar states. This may be because crime rates really differ, or because of differences in the definition and recording of crime. There are even larger differences in the number of prisoners, ranging from about 700 per 100,000 inhabitants in the USA to 50–60 per 100,000 inhabitants in Scandinavia.
- Since the deterrent effects of punishment and imprisonment appear to be limited and not very cost-effective, states increasingly develop programmes for crime prevention.
- International terrorism, organised crime and corruption are very difficult to handle, partly because police activity has traditionally been organised at the national level, and states are unwilling or unable to operate at the international level.

Further reading
Research on defence, security and conflict is fragmented and spread over many disciplines. A good way to start with the study of international conflicts is offered

by introductions to international law, such as Michael Akehurst, *A Modern Introduction to International Law* (London: Allen & Unwin, 1973) or international relations, such as Robert Jackson and Georg Sørensen, *Introduction to International Relations: Theories and Approaches* (Oxford: Oxford University Press, 2nd edn., 2003); or Scott Burchill, Andrew Linklater *et al.*, *Theories of International Relations* (Basingstoke: Macmillan, 1996). An extensive overview of crime and criminological research is offered by Horst Entorf and Hannes Spengler, *Crime in Europe: Causes and Consequences* (Berlin: Springer Verlag, 2002). Empirical findings about victimisation in several countries are reported by John van Kesteren, Pat Mahay and Paul Nieuwbeerta, *Criminal Victimisation in Seventeen Industrial Countries* (The Hague: NSCR, 2000). See, for a provocative challenge of the traditional claim that the primary function of government is to provide security and protection, Hans-Hermann Hoppe, *The Myth of National Defense: Essays on the Theory and History of Security Production* (Auburn: Mises Institute, 2003).

Websites

www.cdi.org	Website of the Center for Defense Information. Information and alternative views on security and issues of security policy, strategy, operations, weapon systems and defence budgeting.
www.curia.eu.int	Website of the ECJ, with extensive information about its functions and procedures.
www.echr.coe.int	Website of the European Court of Human Rights (ECHR), with extensive information about its functions and procedures.
www.homeoffice.gov.uk	Website of the UK Home Office. Provides information on imprisonment in many countries of the world (World Prison Population List).
www.icj-cij.org	Website of the principal judicial organ of the UN, the ICJ, with extensive information about its functions and procedures.
www.iiss.org	International Institute for Strategic Studies (IISS). This is the primary source of accurate, objective information on international strategic issues, weapons and strategy.
www.interpol.int	Website of the largest international police organisation in the world. Information about cross-border criminal police cooperation among its 181 member countries spread over five continents.
www.konfliktbarometer.de	Website of the Heidelberg Institute of International Conflict Research. Provides extensive information on conflicts, crises and wars in the world since the Second World War.
www.nato.int	Website of NATO, the major alliance of nineteen countries in North America and Europe to safeguard the freedom and security of its member countries by political and military means.
www.transparency.org	Website of TI, the only international NGO devoted to combating corruption, with information about corruption in many countries.

Projects

1. Even in countries with high numbers of prisoners, fewer than 10 per cent of the prison population are female. How many female prisoners are in jail in your country at this moment? Why is the figure so low? Can you imagine reasons for an increase of the number of female prisoners in your country?

2. Make a list of terrorist actions in the world since 2000. What was the main objective of these actions? Which countries – if any – were involved in these actions and what was their main role (victim, supporter, opponent, mediator)?

16 Welfare

Life can be very pleasant in democratic countries. The state provides schools and hospitals, roads and bridges, parks and libraries and sometimes it even subsidises opera and sport. But consider the following:

- What happens if you are ill or disabled? Will the state help you?
- What about those who are too young or too old to work? Should the state support them?
- What of the poor and vulnerable? For that matter, who is poor and vulnerable?

Welfare state policies are based on the *redistribution of resources* between parts of the population: taxes and contributions are collected from citizens who can afford to pay and the money is used to support those in need. A detailed list of welfare state provisions would be long in most countries, and the administration of even the simplest of them is exceedingly complex. The politics of the 'taking and giving' that the welfare state involves is also highly controversial and the source of fierce political debate. We cannot cover all aspects of social security in one chapter, so we focus on the most typical welfare state arrangements and use them to illustrate the ways in which democratic states try to improve the well-being of their citizens and redistribute resources between them. In this chapter, we examine social security programmes because these are basic welfare programmes, pensions and health programmes because they are common to all welfare states and, third, the ways in which security programmes are funded because their high costs affect a great number of people.

The five major topics in this chapter are:

- Welfare states and redistribution
- Social security
- Pensions and health programmes
- Social security and taxation
- Theories of the welfare state.

■ Welfare states and redistribution

Modern states have passed through several phases in their development: after the consolidation of their territory and sovereignty many of them gradually provided citizens with equal civil rights and with services to protect the poorest and most vulnerable parts of their populations (see chapter 1). Initially, the intention was to provide no more than a minimal safety-net for those in the greatest danger, but gradually public services were extended to include larger sections of the population, and then to work towards equality of opportunity for all. The processes of *equalisation* and *redistribution* usually involved conflict between social groups, and the social security programmes we find in many democracies after the Second World War were often the result of political fights. A central issue was:

- Which risks were 'private', and therefore the responsibility of individuals?
- Which risks were 'social', requiring government involvement and public policies (see chapter 14 on the private–public distinction)?

Closely related was the issue of how to define and measure *poverty* and *vulnerability*. The 'poverty line' shifts from one generation to the next: poverty now is not the same as poverty in 1950, even less in 1900. Similarly, poverty in Taiwan or Portugal is different from poverty in Sweden or Canada.

For a long time, most states refrained from 'too much' social and economic intervention. The dominant liberal theory of the state held that its purpose was to provide physical security, not protect the poor and vulnerable. But the traumatic experiences of the Great Depression of the 1930s and the post-war economic chaos of the late 1940s changed the traditional **laissez-faire doctrines** that were associated with emerging capitalism in many countries. Gradually, democratic states accepted the idea that markets did not always function well and that government intervention was necessary to correct market failures. Some states began to accept more responsibility for the very young and very old, the sick and disabled and the unemployed and poor. They developed what are called welfare states, particularly in western Europe after the Second World War, but in other areas of the world as well. We can define five major goals of such states, in general terms:

Laissez-faire doctrines
The literal translation from the French is 'to allow to do': maximum freedom for the economic forces of the market, and minimum intervention from the state.

Controversy 16.1

What is a welfare state?

■ Definition

What is the welfare state? A common textbook definition is that it involves state responsibility for securing some basic modicum of welfare for its citizens. Such a definition skirts the issue of whether social policies are emancipatory or not; whether they help system legitimation or not; whether they contradict or aid the market process; and what, indeed, is meant by 'basic'? Would it not be more appropriate to require of a welfare state that it satisfies more than our basic or minimal welfare needs? (Gøsta Esping-Andersen, *The Three Worlds of Welfare Capitalism*, Princeton: Princeton University Press, 1990: 19)

■ Decline of the welfare state?

The contemporary state is very much the product of the collectivisation of health care, education and income maintenance. A modern life, in its most intimate and pervasive aspects, is shaped by this collectivising process. The recent welfare backlash and budget cuts affect the welfare society only superficially, even if they cause much individual distress and institutional upheaval. Cut-backs, also, are central interventions and in the end may even contribute to centralisation. (Abraham de Swaan, *In Care of the State: Health Care, Education and Welfare in Europe and the USA in the Modern Era*, Cambridge: Polity Press, 1998: 11)

- Reducing poverty
- Promoting equality of opportunity
- Promoting individual autonomy
- Promoting social stability
- Promoting social integration.

Nowadays these general goals are widely shared in many countries; it is mainly when specific policies are under discussion that conflict emerges (see controversy 16.1). This is usually because welfare – desirable and benign from the social, humanitarian and economic point of view – has to be paid for, like any other policy, and this involves the redistribution of resources – taking from some in order to give to others. For this reason, welfare states are also *tax states*.

Although it is invariably a political issue, the considerable burden of taxes and contributions is accepted with surprisingly little complaint and protest in many countries. In fact, the rapid expansion of social security programmes in the 1960s and 1970s was widely accepted and fundamental disagreement did not figure very largely in legislative debate. The reasons for this broad support are easy to understand if we look at the many accomplishments of successful social security programmes:

- *Political*   Social security programmes do a great deal to ease political conflict between groups, not least by including all of them as citizens of the state with their own rights and duties.
- *Economical*   Social security programmes improve the quality of the labour force, and its **productivity** – that is the average production per labourer – by maintaining a healthy and educated population.
- *Social*   Social security programmes stabilise society by protecting the family and communities on which society itself depends. Conservative forces opposed to socialism in most of its forms place great importance on family and community.
- *Cultural*   Social security programmes help to create a fair and just society, which serves to enhance the legitimacy of the state and its social arrangements. Welfare helps to create a culture of support for society and the state.

Productivity
The average production per labourer in a specific period (for instance, the average number of ballpoints produced per labourer in a ballpoint pen factory in one year).

Social security is in the interest of many diverse groups in society, ranging from big business in search of efficient workers or early retirement schemes to local charities for disabled children. Put somewhat strongly, welfare states are widely accepted because they meet the diverse needs of many different social and economic groups in society, while their costs are spread collectively. It does not follow that each and every welfare state provision is universally welcomed, only that the basic principle is widely recognised.

■ Social security

■ *Social security and social expenditure*

Provision for the young and old, the sick and disabled and the unemployed and disadvantaged can be organised in many ways. Individuals can, for instance, buy private nursing care for their elderly parents, send their children to private schools and buy private insurance to cover themselves against unemployment. Welfare states, however, are based on the idea that at least some of these services should be *collectively provided and funded* because some individuals are unable to provide them for themselves, and because the collective costs of not providing them are too high:

- Imagine, for example, how well the economy would work if the state did not provide free, universal education.
- Imagine the public reaction if accident victims were left to die on the roads because there were no public hospitals to take them to.

The total of all payments for public and private welfare expenditures are called **social expenditures**. The Organisation for Economic Cooperation and Development (OECD) (see briefing 16.1) defines these payments as:

Social expenditures
The provision by public (and private)

Briefing 16.1
The OECD classification of social expenditure

Category	Examples
1 Old age cash benefits	Pensions, veterans' pensions, early retirement pensions
2 Disability cash benefits	Disability pensions, disabled child pension
3 Occupational injury and disease	Paid sick leave, occupational injury compensation
4 Sickness benefits	Inability to work due to sickness
5 Services for the elderly and disabled	Residential care, day care and rehabilitation services
6 Widow and widower pensions	Pensions and benefits in kind for dependants of deceased persons.
7 Family benefits	Children's allowances and family benefits
8 Family services	Day care for children, household and personal services for the disabled.
9 Active labour market programmes	Labour market training, youth training, subsidised employment
10 Unemployment	Unemployment benefits, severance pay
11 Health	Hospital care, home health care, ambulance services
12 Housing benefits	Rent subsidies, sheltered accommodation for the old and disabled
13 Other contingencies	Income support for those below the poverty line, indigenous people, refugees and immigrants

(*1980–1998: 20 Years of Social Expenditure*, The OECD database, Paris: OECD, 2003: Annex 2).

the provision by public (and private) institutions of benefits to households and individuals in order to provide support during circumstances which adversely affect their welfare.

The OECD definition of social expenditures contains a number of elements that require a little more discussion:

- 'circumstances which adversely affect their welfare' are mainly related to old age, illness or invalidity, unemployment, family problems, poor housing and some aspects of poverty.

- 'provide support' can be done in several ways. Most important are (1) **cash transfers** where individuals or households obtain direct financial support, and (2) the **provision of goods and services**. Examples of (1) are pensions and family allowances for children and of (2) are housing programmes and labour market initiatives, such as retraining. Reimbursements – such as compensation for the costs of medicine or sick leave pay – are a special variant of cash transfers.

- 'provision by public (and private) institutions of benefits' is probably the most complicated aspect of the OECD definition. Some benefits are universal

institutions of benefits to households and individuals in order to provide support during circumstances which adversely affect their welfare.

Cash transfers
Providing social security by giving citizens money.

Provision of goods and services
A way to provide social security by

and available to all citizens, but in some countries they may paid through **means testing**. Some benefits are provided without any obligation, but others are combined with special requirements, such as participating in a job-training programme. In other words, social expenditures are not necessarily free, or unconditional, or universal. For them to be 'social', however, they must not be a transaction in which money is paid to cover the full market costs of the goods or services. To give a concrete example, buying a pain killer at a drugstore at your own expense is not a social expenditure, but getting it through a public health system doctor is, provided that the cost is covered in whole or in part by some public or quasi-public institution. It immediately becomes clear that exactly what counts as 'social' varies enormously from one country to another, depending on exactly who pays for the benefits. The question is not who provides what but how it is *financed*. If it is financed in whole or in part by a public or private institution, and not by a private individual, it counts as social expenditure.

- 'public (and private) institutions' are responsible for social expenditure programmes. *Public* institutions can be any government agency at any level (national, regional, communal), or a special social security fund. *Private* institutions, on the other hand, are restricted to institutions that operate according to government rules. Private programmes can be compulsory (employed people are often legally required to pay into social security funds) or voluntary (employees may pay for additional benefits such as a higher pension). It is very difficult, therefore, to draw a clear line between different kinds of private institutions involved in social security programmes, because different agencies are 'public' and 'private' to varying degrees. What is clear is that payments within families (from parents to children, for example) and payments from purely private organisations (the Red Cross) are not included.

Social security is organised in very different ways in different countries. Some states – Denmark, The Netherlands, or Sweden – have very extensive programmes covering a wide variety of risk. Others – Japan, the UK, USA – offer more restricted cover. Moreover, in some states, such as The Netherlands, the UK and the USA, private sources play a more important role than others. Comparing social security programmes between states is thus a complicated matter.

■ Comparing social security systems

To compare social security systems we might try to measure the *amount* of service delivered, or its *quality*, or its *effectiveness*, but these are complicated matters to define and quantify. The easiest yardstick for comparison is *cost*. Even measuring costs requires us to be clear about the differences between (1) *levels* of social spending in different countries, (2) the *composition* of these expenditures (how it is divided between health, education, pensions, etc.) and (3) the *trends*

offering specific facilities such as housing or job training.

Means testing
Investigating a person's income and means of support to ensure that they quality for public assistance and services.

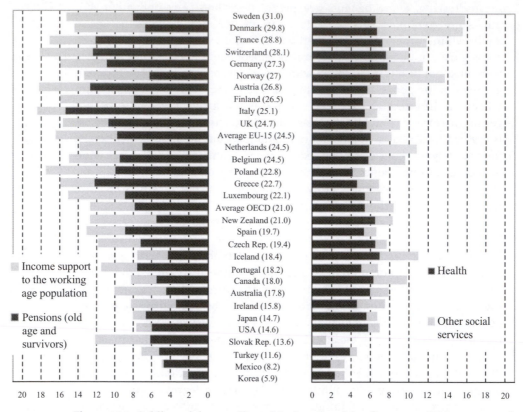

Figure 16.1: Public social expenditure,[a] by broad social policy areas, 1998, per cent of GDP

Note: [a] Countries are ranked by decreasing order of public social expenditure as per cent of GDP.

Source: 1980–1998: 20 Years of Social Expenditure (Paris: OECD Data Base, 2003: 6).

over time of expenditures in one or more countries. All are important, and we will consider them now.

■ *The level of social expenditure*

Since prosperous countries can afford more generous social security programmes, the costs are typically related to economic capacity (measured as gross domestic product, or GDP). Even expressed as a percentage of GDP, the differences between states are significant.

As can be seen in the central column of figure 16.1 about 30 per cent of GDP was spent on public social security in Denmark and Sweden in 1998. At the other end of the scale, we find countries such as Korea (5.9 per cent) and Mexico (8.2 per cent). A large group of European countries – including France, Germany, Norway and Switzerland – devote more than a quarter of their income to social expenditures. The average for member states of the European Union is 24.5 per cent; for the OECD it is 21 per cent.

When we look at the level of social security as a percentage of GDP two important conclusions can be drawn. First, some states spend much more than others – compare France and Mexico – and even similar countries vary a lot – compare Denmark and The Netherlands, or the Czech Republic and Slovakia. Second, although variations within west Europe are considerable (compare Iceland and Sweden), Europe as a whole spends more than other parts of the world. All the places in the top half of figure 16.1 are filled by European countries. The first non-European state on the list is New Zealand, which spends less than the EU average. The bottom half includes some wealthy countries such as Japan (14.7 per cent) and the USA (14.6 per cent), as well as poorer ones such as Korea and Mexico.

■ *The composition of social expenditure*

Figure 16.1 presents information about the composition of social security spending; that is, the way social security is provided (cash benefits versus the provision of goods and services) and about client groups for these services (the working population, pensioners, disabled, poor, etc.). Even though the categories in figure 16.1 are broad, they show how much countries vary. Cash benefits account for a larger proportion of spending than goods and services, but there are exceptions (compare Canada and Iceland). The two types of spending usually balance each other: a state spending relatively large amounts on cash benefits normally spends less on goods and service (compare Italy, Switzerland and Slovakia). The reverse is also true: where cash benefits are comparatively low, goods and services are high (see, for instance, Iceland, The Netherlands and Norway).

Differences between states are even more evident in the services they provide. A glance at figure 16.1 reveals astonishing variation, and not just between rich and poor countries, or First and Third World ones. It is no great surprise that Belgium and Mexico have little in common, but what do we make of a comparison of Germany and Italy or Poland and Slovakia?

A closer look at social expenditures is presented in figure 16.2, which shows how total social security expenditures in six selected countries are divided among different programmes. In all countries but Denmark the largest part is for elderly people, in Greece, about 45 per cent of social security payments are for this group. In European countries, health is usually the second largest, ranging from 21 per cent in Greece to 29 per cent in Germany. The gap between Europe and the USA is evident, since the latter spends no less than 41 per cent of its total social security bill on health. Family-related spending follows a similar pattern of comparisons and contrasts. In Denmark, and Greece this

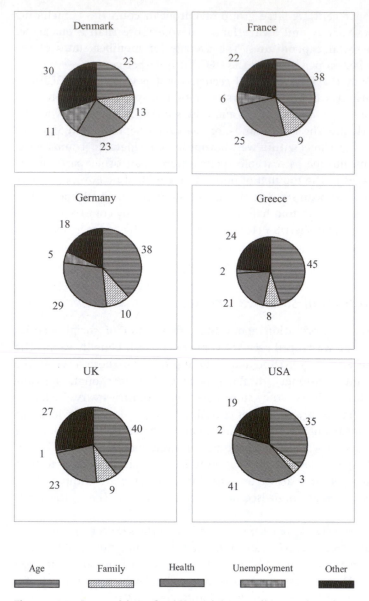

Figure 16.2: Composition of public social expenditure, selected countries, 1998, per cent of total social expenditure
Source: 1980–1998: 20 Years of Social Expenditure (Paris: OECD Data Base, 2003).

accounts for 13 and 18 per cent of total social expenditure, respectively whereas in the USA it is barely 3 per cent.

The conclusion, once again, is that there are huge differences between countries. Even among west European states the variation is usually large, but the west European average is usually well above other regions of the globe.

■ Trends in social expenditure

Social security programmes began in Germany and Austria in the 1880s. A second phase of development followed the First World War when other countries took up the idea, and a third phase followed the Second World War when there was a very rapid expansion of a wide variety of programmes in many western countries. These were generally well established by the mid-1970s, but from then onwards until the 1990s there was a fourth phase of stability or reform. We have already seen how the *levels* and *composition* of spending varies from one country to another, but to talk about 'phases of development' in a collection of countries suggests that their *trends* over time may be rather similar. In fact we have already seen this in chapter 2, which showed how redistribution of resources was a characteristic of developing democracies in the nineteenth century. We can make two points:

- Could it be that since most industrial democracies are confronted with similar problems as they develop, so they also show similar trends in their social security spending?
- Have democratic countries become more alike (converged) in this respect?

Trends in the level of spending as a percentage of GDP in selected countries are presented in figure 16.3. A first glance confirms our conclusion about the huge differences between countries. Furthermore, the *trend lines* show more or less similar developments, so that differences between countries do not narrow:

- Social security *expanded rapidly* in many European countries in the 1960s and 1970s, when the worst damage of the Second World War had been repaired and economic growth provided the necessary finances. In the period between 1960 and 1980 social expenditure rose in Denmark, for instance, from 11 per cent to almost 30 per cent of GDP. On average, the OECD countries doubled their spending from 10 per cent in 1960 to 20 per cent in 1980. This was primarily because social security was extended to larger sections of the population and because higher-quality services were provided at higher cost.
- Expansion *reached a ceiling* in the 1980s, when few new commitments were added, and spending started to flatten off or even declined slightly. The economic recession of the 1970s made it clear that economic growth could not be taken for granted, and several governments started to curtail social expenditures.
- However, severe economic problems and rising unemployment at the end of the 1980s and the early 1990s forced some countries to *spend more on social security*. Increases were evident in Austria, Denmark, Finland, France, Germany, Portugal and Sweden.

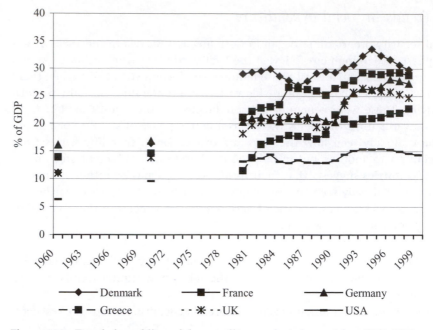

Figure 16.3: Trends in public social expenditure, selected countries, 1960–2000 per cent of GDP
Source: 1980–1998: 20 Years of Social Expenditure (Paris: OECD Data Base, 2003).

- Social spending again *declined* in many countries in the 1990s, once more for economic and financial reasons – benefits were cut, the people eligible for them restricted and private provision, especially private pensions and insurance provision, encouraged.

The expectation that states converge and become more alike in their social expenditures as their economies develop is not supported by the data. Each country has its own combination of social security programmes and its own approach to reform. What we observe, however, are similar *patterns in the time trends*, with rising expenditures and attempts to reform social security in economically difficult periods. European countries show such trends since the 1960s, but there is little evidence of convergence.

◼ Pensions and health programmes

Pensions and health are the two largest spending programmes in virtually every country. Together, they account for more than three-quarters of all social security expenditures in the USA and about two-thirds in many European countries. We now take a closer look at them.

◼ *Pensions*

Provisions for the old were one of the first forms of social security in many countries. These included pensions, war veterans' provisions, early retirement pensions and reduced costs for things such as public transport and medicine. The share of these programmes ranges from no less than 45 per cent of all social expenditure in Greece, to 23 per cent in Denmark.

In principle, there are two ways of providing the elderly with benefits:

- *General population or state pensions* provide everybody of a certain age – usually sixty-five years and older – with a *basic income*. Entitlements are not based on earnings nor on contributions to a pension fund, but simply on age and residence, on the grounds that each person is entitled to financial security in their old age. Because it is *universal*, the high cost of such a pension scheme means that payments to individuals are usually modest. A standard, universal pension, however, does guarantee a minimum income for all.
- *Pension insurance programmes* provide people with a retirement income according to how much they have *contributed to a pension fund*. This can lead to severe problems, especially for those who have not had paid employment or who have had it for less than a normal working life. Pension insurance programmes are increasingly found in almost all countries. They tend to reproduce in the retired population the same income inequalities that are found among those with paid employment.

There are also great differences between countries in how pension funds are collected. In all countries the state supports pension programmes with public funds, although this varies from 10 to 30 per cent of the total costs. Both employees and employers are required to contribute to funds in every country. But while general population pensions rely heavily on general taxation, insurance pensions are mostly paid from funds collected from employee and employer contributions.

Whether they are paid from general taxes or specific pension funds, pensions are based on the idea that the *current working population* pays for the pensions of those who are *currently retired*. The pensions of those who are currently working will, in turn, be paid by the next generation of workers. The problem with this system is obvious: what happens when, as in many countries now, the population ages, and the smaller proportion of working people cannot afford the pensions of the larger proportion of retired (see controversy 16.2)? The solution often advocated is a *capital investment scheme* in which each citizen invests their pensions savings during their working life, and lives off the pension income this generates when they retire. The problem with this system is also obvious. What happens if people do not or cannot afford to invest enough for a decent pension income, and what happens if investments do not generate a

Controversy 16.2

The end of the welfare state?

With few exceptions, systems of social protection are still recognisably the same as they were some forty or fifty years ago. They still revolve around cash support to individuals who are temporarily absent from the labour market, and ensuring that those who are elderly receive an adequate standard of living . . . long-term trends, which are requiring a new approach to social and health policies, are:

- People are living longer. Dependency ratios will rise.
- The increase in elderly people living alone raises the demand for care services.
- The proportion of children in lone-parent families has risen.
- The increase in dual-earner households, caused by increased female labour force participation, makes childcare and parental leave policies more important for the well-being of families.
- Fertility rates have fallen. Labour market developments appear to strongly influence family formation.
- Low-skilled workers have a higher risk of unemployment, other forms of non-employment, or low wages insufficient to support their families.
- People are leading healthier lives because of declining disability. Demographic changes will nevertheless lead to an increase in demand for health services unless remedial action is taken.
- Previously fatal illnesses are being converted into chronic conditions, implying a need for long-term support.

(OECD, *A Caring World: The New Social Policy Agenda*, Paris: OECD, 1999: 15)

good financial return? Stock markets can and do go down as well as up, and people can and do lose some or all of their pension funds.

This brief look at pension programmes underlines the conclusion we reached earlier about country variations. Even for the universal phenomenon of old age, there is a bewildering variety of pension schemes and an even greater variety of different kinds and forms of special provisions and services for the elderly. Nevertheless, an aging population has forced many states to reform their pension system and restrict entitlements. In turn, more private and individual elements are being introduced in many countries and private insurance schemes are becoming increasingly important.

■ Health

Ill health, like age, is universal, and many people attach supreme importance to good health. Health expenditures now account for a third to a quarter of social expenditures in welfare states, and as the population ages, and ever more expensive medical technology and drugs are developed, so health costs inexorably rise.

As with pensions, health services can be organised as a general and universal benefit ('health care for all'), or as a health insurance matter funded by private contributions. But unlike pensions there is an additional aspect to health insurance: covering the costs of medical treatment, on the one hand, and compensating for income loss while ill, on the other. We need to look at:

- Social security programmes to *cover the costs of medical treatment* have common characteristics in many countries. These measures are usually a general population programme which offers health care, but entitlements vary: in Britain and Denmark, for instance, health care is available, in principle, to all citizens, whereas in France and Germany, payment into a health insurance programme is required. All countries demand that patients carry some of the costs of medical treatment themselves (often such things as dental costs), but some hospital or medical costs are also charged to patients in some countries. There are clear differences between countries in the way health care programmes are paid for. While Britain and Denmark rely heavily on general taxation, countries such as France or Germany prefer transfers based on contributions. A mixture of taxation and additional contributions is found in Spain and Sweden.
- *Compensation for income loss*, which is more diverse. The amount paid, and the length of time it is paid for, varies greatly: in Denmark, Germany and Sweden benefits are directly related to income loss; Britain provides a minimum payment and France and Spain occupy a middle position.

Fierce controversies about the rising costs of health schemes have broken out in many countries since the 1980s. Increased spending is mainly due to an aging population and to the costs of high technology medical equipment and drugs, but some critics claim that it is not demographic and technological factors that are responsible so much as the lack of *transparent rules* about the provision of medical care. On the one hand, demand for care is limitless; on the other, it is difficult to ration because lives, health and well-being are at stake. It is also extremely difficult to lay down general rules about who should and should not receive medical care:

- Should overweight smokers be given the same care as those who have taken trouble to look after themselves?
- If there is only enough money for a hundred operations of a given kind, who should be the hundred and first to go without?

In many cases, and in an increasing number of them, the rationing of medical care is not by general rules, but simply by *cost*.

Attempts to control costs take three main forms:

- Limiting the *public costs* of treatment, either by making less available, or by requiring patients to cover more of the costs themselves.

- Limiting *compensation for income losses*, by lowering payments or restricting the time period of payments.
- Introducing *market measures*; that is, abandoning the idea of free, universal medical care paid for from general taxation and leaving more to market mechanisms based on supply and demand. Usually this, too, requires patients to contribute more to their own costs. As with pensions, private medical care and insurance is the result.

■ Social security and taxation

The reasons for the growth of the welfare state and its associated expenditure are well understood in broad outline:

- First, it is generally true that the wealthier the country, the greater the proportion of its income it will spend on welfare and public services. This is partly because services are *labour-intensive* and labour costs tend to rise faster than the other costs of production, especially the costs of the highly trained professionals employed by the state – teachers, social workers, doctors, administrators, lawyers and so on.
- Second, as society becomes more and more complex so the costs of *social coordination* rise – the costs of police, transport and communications, education, public health, R&D.
- Third, as technology develops, so the capital and running costs of public services rise.
- Last, of course, with economic development comes higher standards and expectations of public services.

There are also political reasons for the growth of the welfare state, although these are much disputed. As the scope of the state widens so the number of interests organised around its activities grows. The more a state becomes involved in taxing its citizens to pay for public services – especially those that equalise opportunities and resources – the more it becomes involved in conflicts between 'winners' and 'losers' and the more these groups press for additional services. Consequently, the state becomes even more involved in other public services. As it has been said: 'Big government breeds big pressures.' Once this process is started, the circle is hard to break. Each new task of the state produces a new set of interest groups organised around it to put it under pressure to do more, which then attracts new groups, and so on *ad infinitum*. There is always great demand for free public services provided by the state, and also strong resistance to the idea of paying for them.

The growth of the state can be seen clearly enough in the growth of *taxation*. The average level of total taxation was about 31 per cent in OECD countries in 1970; by 1988, it had grown to 41 per cent. This is not to say, of course, that citizens happily bear their share of the costs of the welfare state. On the contrary, as taxes rise so a larger proportion of the population is drawn into the tax net and taxation becomes more and more controversial. On top of this, the link between the welfare state and the economy as a whole is a highly disputed matter which pervades modern politics across the democratic world.

Taxes increase labour costs, and high labour costs affect the economy in two important ways:

- First, they *increase production costs*, and if these cannot be passed on to the consumer in the form of higher prices they may result in attempts to reduce employment or move production to countries with lower costs. In both cases, the result will be *unemployment*.
- Second, individuals will try to *reduce their own tax costs*. The rich will employ accountants to devise ways of avoiding taxes. Other parts of the population will try to evade taxes by working in the informal '**black economy**'. In these instances, social security programmes have the opposite of their intended effect: instead of raising money to pay for services for the poor and vulnerable they reduce the income of the state, but not demand for its services. Notice that this outcome is not the result of political incompetence, corrupt administrators, or poorly designed welfare services, but of the behaviour of ordinary citizens trying to reduce their taxes.

'Black economy' The 'informal economy' in which goods and services are traded for cash, without bills, receipts, or financial records that would enable the authorities to levy taxes on them.

Another reason for the controversial nature of the welfare state concerns what is called *dependency*, or the 'cycle of deprivation'. This argues that the very success of social security programmes breeds a new generation which is used to living on benefits, and is content to do so. In other words, the children of the poor on social security grow up in a culture of dependency that makes them, in their turn, unable to be self-supporting, and so the process reproduces itself.

A final point about social security and taxation is of a very different nature. Many social security programmes are based on *cash transfers* as a form of income support. Should these be taxed? Different states answer this question in different ways:

- Some withhold tax at source paying, say, a notional €400 a month in benefits, but actually passing over €300, and keeping €100 in taxes.
- A more generous state might pay the full €400 and cash €100 in taxes afterwards.

This difference is important when it comes to comparing the total cost of welfare services in any two countries, and on this basis some have even challenged the conventional wisdom that the welfare state in the USA is much smaller that its European counterparts (see controversy 16.3).

Controversy 16.3

The American welfare state: unusually small?

Comparing social security programmes is a complicated matter requiring us to take into account different tax systems, exchange rates, costs of living and the value of benefits in cash and in kind. Most analysis is based on *gross payments* (total payments to fund welfare service) or an estimation of income deductions made by the state. A careful estimate of these deductions, however, may change our conclusions about the differences between welfare states:

> I challenge the most commonly made claim about the exceptional nature of the American welfare state – that it is unusually small. This judgement, in my view, is misleading. It is based on an over-statement of the social benefits received in other nations and an underestimate of the social benefits distributed by the United States. The latter results from a narrow focus on just two tools of government action, social insurance and grants, and from a misleading measure of welfare state effort . . .
>
> In short, the American welfare state may be unusual less for its small size than for its reliance on a wide variety of policy tools to achieve what many European welfare states do primarily through social insurance. While it is hard to be 100 per cent sure of this conclusion, given the difficulties of comparing direct spending, tax expenditures, regulation, loan guarantees, and the like, the evidence certainly suggests that we should be highly suspicious of anyone who declares that the United States has a small welfare state. (Christopher Howard, 'Is the American welfare state unusually small?', *Political Science & Politics*, 34(3), 2003: 411–16)

■ Theories of the welfare state

The question of how and why democratic states gradually came to accept responsibility for their young and old, sick and disabled, unemployed and poor has fascinated scholars. Their interest is related to the fact that welfare systems vary hugely between states, and that social security expenditures, as a form of *redistribution* between citizens, are most usually the source of serious social, political and economic conflict. The welfare state also involves some fundamental moral issues about social justice, the nature of the modern state and its relationship with its citizens. As a result, theories of the welfare state typically mix normative and ideological approaches (see chapter 13) with empirical research. There are two fundamentally opposed views of the nature of the welfare state, for example:

- *Liberal* approaches regard the welfare state as a left-wing institution that taxes the rich, invades their liberty and encourage laziness and dependency on the part of the workers.
- *Socialist* approaches see the welfare state as a right-wing device that enables the capitalist system to function (that is, to maintain an educated and healthy working population) without having to rely on force or paying too much for it.

We do not wish to cover the ground of chapter 13 again, but shall concentrate instead on empirical theories that explain why very different types of social security programmes arose in various countries and why these expenditures occupy an ever-larger share of GDP. Empirical theories come in four major forms.

■ Conflict-oriented approaches

These explain the very different paths taken by social security programmes in various countries on the basis of *power conflicts* between groups in society. A well-known example of this approach is the work of the Danish political scientist Gøsta Esping-Andersen. In his view, the historical role and position of the labour movement was decisive, especially its resources and its ability to mobilise workers. Opposing social elites – capitalists, some churches, and politicians – were forced to compromise on redistribution policies if they were faced by a strong labour movement. Since the division of power varies in different countries according to their historical circumstances, different social security programmes are likely to arise (see briefing 16.2). Other scholars believe that conflicts between political parties are decisive, particularly given the important role that Christian democratic parties have played.

A special version of these theories tries to explain the absence of political conflict between workers and capitalists in Britain in the late nineteenth century. At the time, Britain was the most advanced capitalist economy in the world and precisely the place where Marxist theory predicted a revolutionary working-class movement. British workers, however, were anything but revolutionary. On the contrary, most were comparatively conservative and strongly supported what the Marxists regarded as the 'capitalist' Empire and the First World War, which was fought mainly for capitalist reasons. According to the Russian revolutionary Marxist, Vladimir Lenin, **Vladimir Lenin** this was because late nineteenth-century and early twentieth-century Britain **(1870–1924)** could afford to pay higher wages and finance some rudimentary welfare services out of the huge profits is made by exploiting its colonies. These kept the British workers not just happy and docile but turned many of them into counter-revolutionary supporters of the Empire and of the First World War.

■ Functionalist explanations

The oldest accounts of diversity in social security systems focus on functionalist explanations. Emerging capitalism requires state intervention to support workers and stabilise families. According to this view, social security differences between countries are mainly the result of different levels of *socio-economic*

Briefing 16.2

A typology of welfare states

One of the most comprehensive treatments of welfare state policies and the various ways of organising them is presented by the Danish political scientist Gøsta Esping-Andersen (1990). He distinguishes between different types of welfare states according to entitlements to benefits, levels of support, degree of redistribution and success in reducing or reinforcing inequalities. The three major types are:

■ Liberal welfare capitalism

A liberal type of welfare capitalism is found in Anglo-Saxon countries, particularly the Australia, Canada and the USA. Benefits are modest and available mainly for low-income groups. Conventional work-ethic norms play an important role and entitlement rules are strict. The state encourages private initiatives to provide social security.

■ Conservative welfare capitalism

A conservative type of welfare capitalism is found in continental Europe, including Austria, France, Germany and Italy. This type is characterised by corporatism – that is, unions, employers' associations and governments collaborate closely to arrange social security programmes (see chapter 14). Because the government relies heavily on the collaboration of trade union and business organisations, the degree of redistribution is usually limited: entitlements are linked to status and class. Because the church plays a major role in corporatist regimes, social security programmes emphasise traditional family values.

■ Social-democratic welfare capitalism

A social-democratic type of welfare capitalism is found in Scandinavian countries. The goal of social security is not 'equality of minimal needs', but equality based on the highest standards. This means, first, that cash benefits are generous and service of a high quality and, second, that every citizen participates equally in the system (the principle of universal entitlement). The ideal is to maximise individual independence, rather than emphasise either the family or the market.

Esping-Andersen's typology was at the core of debates about the welfare state in the 1990s. Although critics point to severe limitations – such as the neglect of gender issues, the special features found in southern Europe and the interdependence of 'welfare capitalism' and negotiations between unions and employers' associations about benefits – his typology is indispensable. As with every good typology, its main advantage is the way it groups a large number of disparate systems into a *few categories* that make sense and are helpful. See Gøsta Esping-Andersen, *The Three Worlds of Welfare Capitalism* (Princeton: Princeton University Press, 1990).

development. A recent revival of functionalism argues that welfare policies enable modern societies to shift from industrial to post-industrial economies – for example, to enable coal mines and textile factories to be closed down by pensioning off miners and textile workers, or retraining them for different jobs.

■ Institutional approaches

These are a rather mixed set of explanations, but they all focus on the importance of institutional structures. Broadly speaking, the idea is that the more institutions are involved in policy making, the more difficult it is to create extensive social security arrangements. States with complex federal structures, and those making most use of referenda, are less developed than unitary states where decision making power is unified and centralised. *Institutional inertia* may also explain the persistence of welfare states once they are established, because they are surrounded by bureaucracies and institutionalised interests that protect them against reform (see chapter 7 and 9).

Two versions, of the institutional approach can be applied to different countries according to their decision making institutions in the welfare field. The first involves the idea of policy networks. We discussed policy communities in chapter 14 and again in chapter 15 in the context of military and defence matters. Policy networks are looser and more open than communities, generally involving a wider range of interests and, therefore, more disagreement and conflict. Welfare policy networks involve government leaders and top administrators in welfare departments, a wide range of welfare professionals and employees and a wide range of pressure groups representing welfare service consumers. These come together in the network of committees, working groups and consultative bodies set up within government institutions and private bodies such as think tanks. Policy networks in the welfare field are found in Britain, France and Italy, and in a weaker form in the USA.

In other countries welfare policy making is more highly formalised within corporatist institutions (see chapter 9). Under these arrangements government and a few private interests work closely together within official structures that formulate and implement public policies. Each set of private interests (welfare professionals, for example) is organised into a single *peak association* that acts authoritatively for all its members and takes decisions on their behalf. This means that all the actors involved at the highest levels of the corporatist structure can bargain and negotiate in the knowledge that the policy outcome will be accepted and implemented by those lower in the system. The advantage is that *binding decisions* can be made, and *stable and predictable policies* can be followed. The disadvantage is that the system is more *closed and exclusive* than policy networks, so that groups outside the corporatist system are excluded from decision making. Corporatism in its most developed form was found in Austria, Luxembourg, The Netherlands, Norway and Sweden between the 1960s and 1980s. Less pure forms were found in Belgium, Denmark, Finland, West Germany, Ireland and Switzerland in the same period.

■ International and transnational dependencies

Finally, there are approaches focusing on international and transnational dependencies. These explain the variety of social security systems in terms of relations between states, as Lenin's theory of colonialism does. A heated debate has more recently broken out about whether *globalisation* forces states to cut their welfare programmes in order to make their economies more competitive in the world market. New Zealand is sometimes presented as the classic case of a country with a protected economy and a strong welfare state that transformed itself into a market economy with a modest welfare state. Small or vulnerable economies are said to be under pressure to reform welfare policies. In order to protect themselves from the consequences of global capitalism they have to decrease costs, which means cutting their welfare costs; to do anything else risks being priced out of the international market. To this set of explanations also belong theories focusing on the impact of the European Union on the social policies of its member states: in an open market countries with expensive welfare systems are under pressure to reform these systems in order to reduce costs.

At first sight these various approaches seem to be rival explanations. Yet none seems to be satisfactory on its own. A much better explanation involves all of them, because each explains only a part of the puzzle. For instance, the rise of the welfare state has invariably involved acute conflict between workers and employers with different resources and different capacities to mobilise support. At the same time, this conflict has been played out in different institutional contexts, in different legal frameworks and according to different rules. The outcomes are certainly influenced by international circumstances, in which developed economies – especially colonial powers – had greater surpluses to devote to welfare. And none of these explanations prevents the welfare system supporting the family, which may, in turn, fulfil an important function in capitalist society.

It is worth pointing out finally that just as there are different and equally effective ways of setting up a democratic political system, so there are also many different ways of setting up a welfare state. Cash transfers may be better suited to some circumstances or some purposes than others, but cash transfers are not necessarily better or worse than the direct delivery of services. If this is correct, then a variety of welfare state provisions is no more strange than a variety of democratic states: they are simply different ways of getting to the same place.

■ Summary

This chapter has dealt with the welfare state and its policies of redistribution of resources. It argues that:

- Democratic states that accept responsibility for the young and old, the sick and disabled and the unemployed and poor among their citizens are called 'welfare states'.

- Many democratic states use between a fifth and a third of their GNP for social security programmes, most being spent on pensions, medical care and income support for the sick and disabled.
- Welfare states organise their social security programmes in a variety of ways: they offer different entitlements, with varying restrictions, to different social groups, and with varying obligations. They raise money to pay for services in different ways, some relying on general taxation, others on contributions to specific funds.
- Most welfare states pass through a similar pattern of growth in which welfare spending increases faster than economic growth in the later stages of industrialisation. This period lasted from about 1950 to 1975 in most of the OECD countries.
- All welfare states have recently confronted the need to limit the growth of social security spending, resulting in a slight decrease in many countries over the past ten–twenty years. The aging of society will make further reforms unavoidable.
- Just as welfare states grew in nation-specific ways, so it seems likely that they will be reformed or cut in nation-specific ways. There is little evidence of 'welfare state convergence' among the democracies.

Further reading

A general overview of the historical development of social security programmes is provided by Abraham de Swaan, *In Care of the State: Health Care, Education and Welfare in Europe and the USA in the Modern Era* (Cambridge: Polity Press, 1998). An important attempt to classify the various national social security systems is Gøsta Esping-Andersen, *The Three Worlds of Welfare Capitalism* (Princeton: Princeton University Press, 1990). Much of the literature on welfare, social security and taxation is rather technical and focused on budgetary and financial aspects. The OECD provides very valuable statistical information on social security and many of its reports are accessible for non-specialists. A general overview of public expenditure is Vito Tanzi and Ludger Schuknecht, *Public Spending in the 20th Century: A Global Perspective* (Cambridge: Cambridge University Press, 2000), and a good study of public policy, including welfare policies, is Francis G. Castles, *Comparative Public Policy: Patterns of Post-War Transformation* (Cheltenham: Edward Elgar, 1998).

Websites

www.oecd.org	Website of the OECD. The OECD groups thirty member states sharing a commitment to democratic government and mixed economies. Statistical information about social expenditures in many countries as well as a number of reports on welfare state policies can be found on this site.
www.who.int	Website of WHO, which offers reports and overviews about health and health-related problems.

Projects

1. What would happen to you if you could not earn an adequate income? Could you apply for public support? What are the requirements and conditions of support in your case, how much would you receive and for how long?

2. Many states have tried to reform their welfare policies. Present a systematic comparison of these attempts in the 1990s in two different democracies. What was the main aim of these reforms? How successful were they?

3. Why do welfare reform policies differ between countries facing very similar budgetary, financial and demographic challenges?

17   The future of the democratic state

At the start of the third millennium, states and democracy seem to be the big winners in the fierce conflicts and wars that scarred the twentieth century. With only a few special exceptions every place on earth falls within the territory of a state. The number of states has increased rapidly from about fifty to not much fewer than 200 since the 1950s. States still claim absolute authority and control over their own territory and its residents, and conflicts between them are still hard to handle. Moreover, modern states are not the puny 'night watchmen' of the liberal era at the start of the twentieth century: they now extract vast amounts in taxes, provide an enormously wide variety of services and pervade almost every aspect of daily life.

Democracy also seems to have triumphed in the twentieth century. Three successive waves of democratisation – driven mainly by post-war de-colonisation after 1945 and the collapse of the Soviet Empire in 1989 – have expanded the number of stable democracies to approximately 120 countries, covering about 60 per cent of the world's population. Democracy has grown in depth and strength to cover far more than the most basic rights and duties and now includes universal adult suffrage, referendums, a wide range of legal, social and economic rights, direct participation, greater control over government and fewer privileges for elites.

If the forces of statehood and democracy seem to be taking over the world, it may be because they are inseparable twins: states are essential for the *democratic organisation* of political life and democracy is essential for the *legitimation* of the state. Only a few utopians and anarchists can imagine democracy without the power of the state to create and enforce democratic rules and structures. In the twentieth century, and especially in the last half of that century, states and democracy developed together so that they seemed to be different sides of the same coin.

It is ironic that the present time – the very heyday of the democratic state – produces widespread predictions of the imminent decline of the state and a crisis of democracy:

- Could it be that widespread and confident announcements about the end of the state and the crisis of democracy show that they are both past their best?
- Should we now start searching for a new understanding of state and democracy in the twenty-first century, with different theories, fresh concepts and original approaches adapted to the 'post-state' and 'post-democratic' twenty-first century?

'The Owl of Minerva spreads its wings only at dusk', wrote the German philosopher Hegel, by which he meant that we understand reality *only after events have taken place*. It may be that the democratic state is so popular today precisely because it is an outdated model!

Georg Wilhelm Friedrich Hegel (1770–1831)

Those who followed Hegel's approach to the state in the nineteenth century focused on the French Revolution, with its emphasis on citizenship and human rights. They substituted the early morning crowing of the French rooster for the hooting of Minerva's owl. But the great revolutions of France and America that have shaped the development of our contemporary democracies are more than two centuries old. Do we need a new approach and new theories for a new world?

In this concluding chapter we return to questions about the contemporary relevance of states and the future of democracy:

- Is the state and its sovereignty 'withering away' and, if so, what will succeed it?
- Can democracy survive?
- What reforms might help to preserve both the state and democracy?

The terms on everybody's lips, of course, are *globalisation*, *internationalisation* and the *crisis of democracy*. The four major topics in this chapter are:

- States and sovereignty
- The retreat of the state?
- Democracy without borders
- The future.

■ States and sovereignty

The usefulness of the term 'state' may be limited by two difficulties. First, the concept has to cover a huge variety of different forms of political organisations, from the comparatively tiny state of Switzerland to the huge land mass of Australia, the old established democracies of Denmark and New Zealand to the new ones of the Czech Republic or autocratic ones such as North Korea, and from ethnically homogeneous Norway to multi-cultural India. Is it helpful to apply the same term to such a wide variety of political systems? Second, the traditional supremacy of the state is now challenged by globalisation (chapter 2) and the 'borderless world' which can no longer be understood in terms of national independence and sovereignty. It was one thing to defend your country against soldiers massing on the border, quite a different thing to defend it against the power of MNCs, satellite TV and international terrorists. We shall argue that in spite of all this states are still the main building blocks of modern government and politics.

■ *Conventional states, proto-states and supra-national states*

States are characterised by their territory, people and sovereignty, and if we are to analyse their development or their decline, it is helpful to do so in terms of these three elements. In fact, we can distinguish three *broad types of state*, according to how they combine their three defining characteristics:

- Conventional states
- Proto-states
- Supra-national states.

Conventional states

Conventional states have a well-defined territory, a developed sense of nationhood (a 'people') and all the institutions of sovereignty. They are found all over the globe and the fact that they are associated with peace and stability seems to have a lot to do with democracy and the balance of power between democratic states. Conventional states remain sovereign within their own borders. In some cases, outside influences are crucial for their creation and persistence (the USA playing a defining role in this respect) but in the majority of cases the territory, people and sovereignty of conventional states are not disputed, and they conduct relations between each other on this basis.

Proto-states

States in some parts of the world do not have secure boundaries, or a body of citizens who form a 'people', or a single sovereign power with a monopoly of the legitimate use of physical force. They are threatened by putsches, insurrections, separatist movements, foreign intervention, ethnic clashes, or civil wars. Sometimes a conventional state divides itself, to be replaced by one or more new ones (the Czech Republic and Slovakia, Croatia and Slovenia), but the successors are not guaranteed to turn themselves into conventional states. They may be torn apart by chaos and anarchy, with competing factions and warlords replacing sovereign power. In some instances, no ultimate authority, no sovereign power, no state exists (Afghanistan and Iraq in 2004). The label 'proto-state' suggests that conventional states may emerge in these places. This often occurs with the help of foreign assistance, as happened in the Balkans in the 1990s when the Republic of Bosnia-Herzegovina was created on the basis of an international agreement in order to end war and genocide. UN peace-keeping forces are still required here because large parts of the population reject the Republic. And although ethnic war has ended, it will take a long time to establish a conventional state with sovereign power, undisputed territory and a united body of citizens.

Supra-national states

Serious conflicts between states do not necessarily result in state disintegration, separation, or chaos. In Europe, the conventional state is in the process of being transformed by cooperation, negotiation and agreement. The member states of the European Union are still characterised by their territories and populations, but national borders are becoming increasingly porous and even irrelevant, and the claim of absolute national sovereignty has been given up. Power has not been shifted to other states, however, but to a new supra-national organisation that coordinates its member states and lays down binding rules for them. The European Union is the only clear example of a supra-national organisation of its kind, and to this extent it remains a risky adventure that is as ambitious as it is experimental. It is a striking fact that the prototype of the post-conventional state is being created in west Europe, the cradle of the conventional state. Nonetheless, we should not forget that many important policy areas – such as foreign politics and defence, taxation and social security – remain firmly in the hands of national governments, despite attempts by the European Union to coordinate and standardise them. Furthermore, recent enlargement of the European Union will make it more difficult to deepen integration. Indeed, attempts to produce a European constitution in 2003 were delayed because of divisions among the member states. For all this, the European Union is a post-conventional state.

Conventional states remain the most common form of organising political power, a situation that will not change overnight. It does not follow that every part of the earth, the sea and the sky is subject to the sovereign power of a given state, any more than it means that all political power is state power, but the modern state remains the anchor point for our understanding of modern comparative government. Apart from anything else, the strongest political power in the world and the only global power of our time is the USA – a conventional state *par excellence*.

■ Challenges to the state

Although conventional states rule the world, their position as sovereign bodies is challenged by five developments:

- Concentration of commercial power
- Rise of international NGOs
- Globalisation
- Changing nature of conflicts
- Importance of international organisations.

Concentration of commercial power

Some commercial organisations are wealthier than states, and are able to challenge their power. The GDP of Ethiopia – one of the poorest countries of the world – was only US$ 6,543 million in 1999. Even in wealthy Europe, Portugal and Slovenia had GDPs of US$ 107,716 million and US$ 20,653 million (in 1999). These figures are far below the US$ 200 billion of the largest business companies in the world. Not even the total wealth of Portugal puts it within reach of the largest companies, and for that matter, some individuals are worth more than whole countries (see table 17.1). If power follows wealth and if wealth generates power, then it is no surprise that the big MNCs can influence economic development and set their own terms when dealing with national governments, not least because the mobility of their capital gives them great locational flexibility.

Rise of international NGOs

International NGOs (see chapter 9) are neither branches or agencies of the state, nor are most of them created by states. They include, for instance, Amnesty International, Greenpeace, Médecins Sans Frontières, the Scottish Catholic International Aid Fund and Volontari nel Mondo and their main characteristics are that they are:

- Founded and run by citizens independently of governments and states
- Non-profit or charitable organisations, which
- Reject the use of violence.

In their modern form, international NGOs were founded in the nineteenth century, but their numbers and importance increased after the Second World War. It is difficult to estimate their numbers, but according to the UN there were 1,083 international NGOs in 1914, which increased to more than 37,000 in 2000. Nearly one-fifth of them were formed in the 1990s. Most developing countries have seen an even sharper increase in the number of domestic NGOs: in 1996, Brazil had 210,000 non-profit making organisations and India had more than 1 million (UN *Human Development Report*, 2002).

Table 17.1 *The largest corporations of the world, 2002*

Corporation	Origin	Main business	Employees	Revenues (US$ million)
Wal-Mart Stores	USA	Retailing	1,383,000	219,812
Exxon Mobil	USA	Oil	97,900	191,581
General Motors	USA	Automobiles	365,000	177,260
BP	Britain	Oil	110,150	174,218
Ford Motor	USA	Automobiles	352,748	162,412
Daimler Chrysler	Germany	Automobiles	372,470	136,897
Royal Dutch/ Shell Group	Britain/ Netherlands	Oil	91,000	135,211
General Electric	USA	Diversified Industrial	310,000	125,913
Toyota Motor	Japan	Automobiles	246,702	120,814
Citigroup	USA	Diversified Financial	268,000	112,022
Mitsubishi	Japan	Automobiles	43,000	105,814
Mitsui	Japan	Industrial Services	36,116	101,206
Chevron Texaco	USA	Oil	67,569	99,699
Total Fina Elf	France	Oil	122,025	94,311
Nippon Telegraph & Telephone	Japan	Communication	213,000	93,425

Source: http://www.fortune.com/fortune/global500.

NGOs are non-state organisations and for the most part they are privately financed, but some of them receive financial and other support from states or international organisations such as the European Union and the UN. When they are heavily dependent on public money, and when NGO and government activities are closely interwoven, the sharp distinction between 'private' and 'public' vanishes. Governments also find it useful to create organisations that are independent of them, but which provide public services with the help of public finances. Such organisations are known as QUANGOs (chapter 10), and are useful in politically sensitive areas which fall within the public sector but which governments do not wish to control directly (see chapter 9). Public broadcasting is the classic case where QUANGOs operate in the public sector at arm's length from government. Like NGOs it is exceedingly difficult to estimate QUANGO numbers, but they are also rising steeply.

NGOs (and QUANGOs to a lesser extent) are widely believed to be increasingly powerful actors in national and international government. This is not so much because they are wealthy, like the MNCs, but because NGOs often have a powerful *emotional* and *moral* appeal. Organisations such as Christian Aid, Greenpeace, Oxfam and the Red Cross use their popular appeal to gain widespread publicity for their activities, and they can use this to 'leverage' political influence. They represent another force that challenges the power of the state.

Globalisation

The 'interdependence' and 'connectedness' of the world today is evident when we look at the environment and the use of natural resources, or at terrorism and the global drug trade. It is most evident in the economic and financial sectors, where capital and production is free to move around the world in pursuit of the highest profits and lowest taxes. Since welfare states are tax states with high labour costs, they are under pressure (they can even be blackmailed) by businesses threatening to relocate investments and jobs. A whole range of *mini-states* – the Bahamas, Liechtenstein, Luxembourg – serve as *international tax shelters* and places where companies can be legally registered. Not only does this have implications for the ability of states to control international business, but it reduces government revenues that are used to pay for public services. Some countries (Brazil, for example) encounter difficult problems if large amounts of money are transferred to foreign bank accounts.

Changing nature of conflicts

As we saw in chapter 15, violent inter-state conflict has not increased in recent decades in spite of an increase in the number of states. Indeed, where national borders are no longer disputed, and even less the borders between post-conventional members of the European Union, there is no longer even a need to guard them. To this extent, the age-old justification for the military power of the state is reduced. Even one of the most important justifications for the existence of the state itself – that it is necessary to defend its territory against foreign threat – may have been removed. At the same time, new threats to the state have appeared:

- First, *violent conflict within states* has increased and the role of armed forces is certainly not reduced in many pre-conventional states (the Balkans and many parts of Africa and Latin America), and in some conventional ones as well (Northern Ireland, Spain). This creates a need for highly trained and specially equipped peace-keeping forces, which are provided mainly by the conventional states.
- Second, the *threat of terrorism* took a dramatic form with the attack on the World Trade Center in September 2001 (see chapter 15). States that are no longer endangered by foreign armies have to deal with a completely different problem that cannot be handled by the conventional armed forces.

Importance of international organisations

States have created a large number of international organisations to deal with relations between them and to try to settle conflicts in an orderly and peaceful manner. These organisations are *institutionalised forms of cooperation and collaboration*, and although they work at the international level they are still the product of state cooperation and states take their own decisions about whether to join or leave, and to comply with their decisions or to reject them. The main example is the UN and its many subsidiary organisations, but the list includes thousands more, such as the OECD and the Organisation of Petroleum Exporting Countries (OPEC). International organisations such as these are clearly different from states in that each has a clear and limited task:

- The OECD is concerned with economic matters and collecting statistical information for a comparatively small number of wealthy nations.
- The WHO deals with medical matters.
- The IMF fosters global monetary cooperation, stability, trade and employ-ment.

A very few international organisations can give orders to states (such as the Security Council of the UN) and military force may be required to have states comply with these decisions (see chapter 15), but most do not have this sort of power.

As the intensity and scope of relations between states has increased so has the number of international organisations. As a result, states are increasingly caught up in a 'web' of directions, advice and instructions. Globalisation and rising numbers of NGOs will further stimulate this process. Even if most of the decisions taken by international organisations are voluntarily accepted by states, their scope for action is still restricted.

■ The retreat of the state?

The combination of MNCs, NGOs, globalisation, the changing nature of con-flict and the importance of international organisations casts doubt on the *continuing relevance of the state*. It seems to be only one actor among many, and one that is rapidly declining in power and importance at that (see contro-versy 2.1). Should we even drop the concept of the state, and concentrate on the 'real' and important actors in the world today? This suggestion, however, fails to notice that states are still the most important actors on the world stage, and that sovereignty and the legitimate use of physical force within their given territories is still the main form of organised political power. States continue:

- To be the main actors in modern warfare (Afghanistan, the Falklands, Iran, Iraq)
- To create international and supra-national agencies of government such as the European Union and the UN, and control them
- To be responsible for the vast majority of public services delivered to citizens
- To raise vast amounts of money in taxes
- To be mainly responsible for the defence of their territory and their citizens and for the maintenance of internal law and order

- To define the rights and duties of citizens in most democracies (with certain EU exceptions)
- To decide who will live and work within their borders (though admittedly with the increasing exception of illegal immigrants)
- To issue passports and travel documents to their citizens
- To control and influence almost every aspect of the daily life of their citizens with their accumulated laws and with literally millions of ordinances, rules, orders, commands, regulations, precepts, decrees, directives, instructions, edicts, dictates, injunctions, promulgations, guidelines, advisory documents, circulars, specifications and requirements
- To be attacked: even international terrorism is mainly directed towards states or their representatives, even when it attacks ordinary citizens.

Arguments about the decline of the state also seriously underestimate the force of another characteristic of our times: the rising strength of *nationalism* (see chapter 13). While it is true that technology promotes global integration and weakens national boundaries in some respects, in others it makes it easier to sustain nationalism. Communications technology helps to preserve minority languages and culture with local radio and TV stations, and desk-top publishing. Moreover, as each ethnic minority creates its own independent state so it is likely to create another minority within its own borders. Nationalism seems to have a lot of life in it yet – and by definition it implies a *strengthening* of the state.

Summarising the confusing and contradictory trends and arguments about the state, the political scientist Susan Strange (1996) presents three hypotheses: **Susan Strange, *The Retreat of the State* (1996).**

1. Political power has shifted *upwards* from weak states to stronger states. Strong states are able to influence, even determine, developments far outside their territory. The best example is, of course, the USA, but one can also think of the influence of France in north and west Africa, and of Russia in central Asia.
2. Political power has shifted *sideways* from states to markets, strengthening the position of giant MNCs and of international organisations such as the G-9, the IMF and OPEC. Some writers prefer to use the term 'governance' rather than government (chapter 3), because the term implies the coordination of many actors in the political system rather than the old 'top-down' system whereby government controlled everything else.
3. Some political power has *'evaporated'*, in the sense that no one is exercising it any longer. Examples include some areas of the former Soviet Union, and some parts of Africa and Asia (Afghanistan, Congo, Ethiopia), where legitimate authorities have been replaced by local potentates, warlords and gang leaders.

Although some organisations have successfully challenged the claims of the state to be the sole source of legitimate political power, and although political power has shifted, or even 'evaporated' in some parts of the world, states remain the point of departure and main focus of organised political power. The state is not 'withering away': on the contrary, it seems to be changing and expanding its power to deal with new circumstances and forms of organised power. So the answer to a key question of this chapter – Are states disappearing? – is an unambiguous 'no'. Circumstances are changing, and states with them, but the result is that states are both stronger and weaker in some respects, just as some states have become stronger and others weaker.

■ Democracy without borders

We know that states can do very well without being democratic, but so far it has taken the organised and limited forms of political power of the conventional state to promote democracy (see chapter 1). To put it in a nutshell: *no state, no democracy*. To this extent, our conclusion that the state is likely to survive, and even grow stronger in some respects, is a comfort for the foreseeable future. But it does not necessarily follow that future developments of the state will continue to promote democracy, even less improve the quality of democratic government. A second key question of the chapter, therefore, is: What is the future for democracy?

■ *The quality of democracy*

Neither states nor democracies are created overnight. The first democracies developed over a period of two hundred years or more, and suffered war, civil disturbance and national trauma in the process (see controversy 17.1). In many cases the most important democratic milestones have been relatively recent ones: the French Revolution secured basic rights for every citizen in the late eighteenth century, but French women had to wait until the 1940s for the right to vote; violations of human rights occur in such countries as The Netherlands and Sweden even now. It no surprise, then, that democracy has a fragile presence in many of the states that have recently joined the list of free nations in the world. Besides, democracy itself is not a fixed or given entity. It is constantly changing and developing as citizens make new and greater demands upon it.

The end of the Cold War resulted in a great deal of optimism about the spread of democracy. The 'triumph of liberalism', 'the end of history' and the 'victory of democracy' were announced (see chapter 13). But in 2002 the UN concluded that although a majority of the people in the world lived in nominal democracies, political freedoms and civil rights were limited in more than a hundred countries. Worse still, the spread of democracy had not done much for many people in the world: civil wars claimed 3.6 million lives in the 1990s, and about 2.8 billion of the world's 6 billion people live on less than 2 US$ a day (UN *Human Development Report 2002*). Democracy, it seems, takes more than organising free, multi-party competitive elections at regular intervals.

Controversy 17.1

Complaints about democracy?

Complaints about states that have emerged from dictatorship but have not effectively democratised lack perspective. It took American democracy 86 years to abolish slavery, 144 years to enfranchise women and 189 to assure black people the vote. After a century and a half, American democracy produced the Great Depression. Democracy is not a rose garden. It is as fallible as human beings. (Joshua Muravchik, 'Democracy is quietly winning', *International Herald Tribune*, August 21, 2002)

After a hopeful start, the third wave of democracy seems to have lost its momentum in some countries, because it turns out that it is fairly easy to mix formal democratic processes with political corruption, civil rights abuses and autocratic rule. While only a few countries have slid backwards into military rule (Pakistan 1999), many more seem to have reached a 'stand-off' or 'cease fire' between democratic and non-democratic forces where elected government has failed to regulate or take control of the most powerful social and economic groups in society. It was easier to introduce free multi-party elections and the semblance of democracy than to guarantee civil and social rights for all. In such cases, it is not too much to claim that elections do less to guarantee political freedom than to legitimise illiberal democracy. In many of the new democracies violations of freedom and human rights are hard to prevent because these countries lack adequate institutional safeguards for minority, or even majority rights. As a result, simple electoral democracy has swept countries such as Russia and Venezuela toward authoritarian rule that has little in common with the broader principles of democracy.

Nonetheless, Freedom House continues to record the spread of democracy around the world (see chapter 2). In its *Annual Report* of 2004, it concludes that since the start of global action against terrorism in 2002, fifty-one countries had showed overall progress, while twenty-seven had slid back, a real gain of almost 2:1. Most improvement has been made in central and eastern Europe and in east Asia, least in the Middle East, north Africa and central Asia. Happily, the survey clearly reveals that freedom and liberty are not restricted to wealthy countries, since many poor and developing states have a record of respecting political rights and civil liberties.

■ *Reform of state and government*

Democracy, it is worth saying again, involves a *continuous search for improvement*. Even the world's most advanced democracies such as Denmark, Finland, The Netherlands, Norway and Sweden, debate reforms. In fact, discussion about how political life should be conducted is in many countries as important as the actual substance of politics in the form of taxation, services and support or opposition for the Iraq war or for the European Union (see controversy 17.1).

Virtually every institution of democracy discussed in this book is currently disputed, but the ten most important items on the agenda for democratic reform are:

- *Constitutional reform* Since constitutions define the major political institutions and their relationships (see chapter 3), proposals for reform are often basic and far-reaching. Some countries have recently added social rights and a ban on discrimination in order to guarantee equal opportunities for all citizens. Because constitutional matters are so basic and controversial it is sometimes difficult to reach agreement about them. The European Union failed to get agreement on its new constitution in 2003.
- *Strengthening parliaments* Monitoring and controlling the executive is one of the main functions of parliaments in representative democracies (see chapter 4 and 6) and many parliaments have attempted to strengthen their powers in this respect. Some are using parliamentary commissions or committees to investigate specific policy matters, and to hold ministers to account.
- *Freedom of information and open government* This concerns public access to documents and the use of electronic media to improve communication between citizens and MPs. Some countries have adopted legislation making government information accessible to the public.
- *Decentralisation of power* Recent decades have seen a wave of attempts across many democracies to decentralise and deconcentrate power to regional, local and community levels of government (see chapter 5). An example is the creation of regional units of government for Scotland and Wales in the UK. In other countries the positions of city and urban authorities have been strengthened and budgetary powers have been decentralised. Within cities, neighbourhood and community councils have been created or strengthened in order to reduce the 'distance' between citizens and government. Some believe that central governments are trying to decentralise power in the interests of democracy, others that this is simply a way of 'exporting financial problems' to lower levels of government.
- *Making bureaucracies more responsive and efficient* Bureaucratic reforms (see chapter 7) include proposals to improve efficiency by adopting cost-benefit management and book keeping practices. More far-reaching is the privatisation of public services. Other reforms have tried to make public bureaucracies more responsive to citizens by involving them in the early stages of decision making.
- *Improving citizen participation* Citizens have been creative in inventing new forms of political participation and new ways of making their voice heard, including boycotts, demonstrations, sit-ins, civil disobedience and attracting the attention of the mass media (see chapter 8). Governments, for their part, have often responded by reforming laws relating to protest activity,

expanding opportunities to vote (the EP, neighbourhood councils, referendums) and to participate in public enquires and hearings. Various experiments with public opinion and participation are being conducted, including focus groups, citizen juries and interactive computer systems.

- *Strengthening the role of associations* Many governments now acknowledge NGOs and are willing to cooperate with them and support their activities, including their participation in decision making, especially at the local and community level (see chapter 9). Some governments are even attempting to 'unlock' policy communities and networks so they include a wider range of interests and organisations.

- *Strengthening the independence of mass media* Many governments are concerned about the concentration of the ownership and control of the mass media (see chapter 10) and are wrestling with ways of dealing with it. Some feel that the answer lies in allowing the 'old' and 'new' communication technologies to develop within an unregulated market, in the belief that they will form a highly diversified and competitive system. Other governments take the opposite view, maintaining or strengthening market and content regulation laws, including anti-cartel and cross-media ownership regulations and a wide variety of laws relating to such things as cigarette advertising and pornography.

- *Protecting and strengthening human rights* As we have seen, some democracies with multi-party elections are not particularly successful in protecting the rights of their citizens. They must guarantee the independence of their courts, but this is difficult because corrupt governments are unwilling to give up their power. NGOs such as Amnesty International try to mobilise opposition, and a range of institutions has been created to prosecute violations of human rights and empower citizens to take action against governments. These include the ECJ, the highest court of the European Union, and the ECHR, as well as special courts created by the UN to prosecute war criminals and to regulate conflicts between states.

- *Social security* Social security and welfare continue to be a central issue in democratic countries. Some argue that a healthy, educated and secure population is a precondition of both democracy and economic growth, and that in any case the state is morally obliged to create the conditions of civilised life for its citizens. They argue that a developed welfare and social security system is essential. Others, especially in the late twentieth century, argue that the best way of meeting the material and spiritual needs of citizens is to leave as much as possible to the 'invisible hand' of market economics, in the belief that this is the most efficient way of generating and distributing wealth and freedom. They argue that globalisation makes welfare states uncompetitive and that a return to laissez-faire economics is inevitable and efficient. The debate rages on.

Reforming democracies is not easy. Strong interests most generally try to protect their position and democratic reform is often entangled with a lot of

Briefing 17.1
The need for good governance

Political reforms, such as decentralising budgets and responsibilities for the delivery of basic services, put decision-making closer to the people and reinforce popular pressure for implementing the goals. Where decentralisation has worked – as in parts of Brazil, Jordan, Mozambique and the Indian states of Kerala, Madya Pradesh and West Bengal – it has brought significant improvements. It can lead to government services that respond faster to people's needs, expose corruption and reduce absenteeism.

But decentralisation is difficult. To succeed, it requires a capable central authority, committed and financially empowered local authorities and engaged citizens in a well-organised civil society. In Mozambique committed local authorities with financing authority increased vaccination coverage and prenatal consultations by 80 per cent, overcoming capacity constraints by contracting NGOs and private providers at the municipal level.

Recent experiences have also shown how social movements can lead to more participatory decision-making, as in the public monitoring of local budgets. In Porto Alegre, Brazil, public monitoring of local budgets has brought huge improvements in services. In 1989 just under half of city residents had access to safe water. Seven years later, nearly all did. Primary school enrolments also doubled during that time, and public transportation expanded to outlying areas. (*Human Development Report 2003* (New York: UN, 2004: 2); http://hdr.undp.org/reports/global/2003/pdf/hdr03.overview.pdf)

other complicated matters. This is because democracy is not above social and economic life; it is not something set apart from 'real' social existence. On the contrary, government and politics are an integral part of daily existence that help to mould and shape how we conduct our lives. Often it is not possible to change *social and economic patterns* without first changing *political patterns*. The suffragettes in the early twentieth century, for example, did not campaign for 'Votes for Women' because they saw the vote only as an end in itself, important though this was. They also knew that they could not change their social, legal and economic status without first gaining power in government. In this respect, improving government – that is, improving democratic government – seems to be the key to numerous other problems (see briefing 17.1).

■ The future

Although some of the optimism of the third wave of democratisation in the 1990s may have been exaggerated, it is clear that neither national states nor democracies are 'withering away' – at present, at any rate. For most people, the world has become a better place to live in as democracy spreads. Nevertheless, democratic principles constantly challenge the practice. Not only are the newest democracies somewhat fragile and underdeveloped by modern standards, but the best-developed ones continue to develop and improve as they push back the boundaries of democracy.

Can democracy spread and survive in a changing world? As always, prognosis is difficult and uncertain, and conclusions differ. Since democratic institutions are dependent upon a sovereign body to establish and maintain them, anything that undermines the continuity and stability of states seems to threaten democracy, and there seem to be a great many things that threaten both states and democracies at the present time. Nevertheless, we know that both the number of states and the number of democracies in the world has increased steadily over the past hundred years. There is no clear sign that this trend will not be continued in the near future.

We also know that democracy is unstable in many of the newest democracies, and that they can easily slip back into dictatorship and autocracy as has happened in the past. It is easier to establish free, multi-party elections in these countries than to guarantee freedom, human rights and government accountability, much less equality of opportunity and a decent quality of life. In the younger democracies, therefore, our studies should not be confined to elections, parties and formal decision making procedures, but broadened to encompass wider social and economic matters.

Democracy is certainly no paradise. And yet even modest success in replacing authoritarian, corrupt and abusive government with more democratic practices is desirable. As the UN concluded:

> When governments are corrupt, incompetent or unaccountable to their citizens, national economies falter. When income inequality is very high, rich people often control the political system and simply neglect poor people, forestalling broadly based development. Similarly, if governments fail to invest adequately in the health and education of their people, economic growth will eventually peter out because of an insufficient number of healthy, skilled workers. Without sound governance – in terms of economic policies, human rights, well-functioning institutions and democratic political participation – no country with low human development can expect long-term success in its development efforts or expanded support from donor countries. (UN, *The Millennium Development Compact 2003*, New York: UN 2004: 3)

◼ Summary

This chapter has dealt with scenarios for the future of the state. It argues that:

- The state is not 'withering away'. Conventional nations are still widely spread and new ones are establishing themselves, especially in large parts of east Asia and south America. The world's first supra-national state has appeared in Europe in the shape of the European Union. 'Proto-states' are found in several regions (Africa, Central Asia and eastern Europe), mainly after the collapse of larger states.
- Developments such as the concentration of commercial power, the rise of NGOs, globalisation, the changing nature of conflicts and the growth of international organisations all cast doubts on the state's claim to be the sole (or the most important) source of political power. The state persists, however, as the body with a monopoly of legitimate physical force.

- The power of some states has increased in some respects, but in other cases it is shared with other organisations, and in 'proto-states' some state power seems to have disappeared.
- Democracy is not fixed or static but a continuous and developing attempt to make government accountable and responsive to the needs of the people it governs. Reforming and developing, therefore, the democratic system is a regular aspect of democratic government.
- The number of democracies in the world is still rising, but some of the newest ones have problems protecting freedom and human rights. Organising multi-party elections seems to be less problematic.

Further reading

Various approaches to the changing role of the state are discussed by Susan Strange, *The Retreat of the State: The Diffusion of Power in the World Economy* (Cambridge: Cambridge University Press, 1996). Information about democracy in the world is provided by Freedom House (see website below) and in the UN's annual publication *Human Development Report* (see website below). A thought-provoking analyses of the rise of democracy that is mainly restricted to electoral procedures is presented by Fareed Zakaria, *The Future of Freedom: Illiberal Democracy at Home and Abroad* (New York: Norton, 2003). For a detailed account of the rise and decline of the state, see Martin van Creveld, *The Rise and Decline of the State* (Cambridge: Cambridge University Press, 1999). Georg Sørensen, *The Transformation of the State: Beyond the Myth of Retreat* (Basingstoke: Palgrave, 2004), examines the impact of globalisation on the modern state and a collection of readings on the topic is presented in T. V. Paul, G. John Ikenberry and John A. Hall (eds.), *The Nation-State in Question* (Princeton: Princeton University Press, 2003). See also Francis Fukuyama, *State Building: Governance and World Order in the Twenty-First Century* (London: Profile Books, 2004).

Websites

www.amnesty.org	Website of Amnesty International, the world's largest organisation campaigning for the international recognition of human rights.
www.curia.eu.int	Website of the ECJ with information about its operations and procedures.
www.echr.coe.int	Website of the ECHR with information about its operations and procedures.
www.freedomhouse.org	Provides information about democracy and human rights in each state of the world.
www.icj-cij.org	Website of the ICJ, the principal judicial organ of the UN, with information about its operations and procedures.
www.undp.org	Website of the UN Development Programme that offers extensive information on the relationship between development and democracy.

Projects

1. Make a list of five countries in the world that have improved their democracy since 1990, and another five that have slipped back. What are the main reasons for these changes? How likely is a change in democracy in these ten countries in the next decade?

2. What democratic improvements have been proposed in your country recently, and which of these have been realised? Present a systematic overview of the most important proposals according to their goals, means and people or groups they affect. Discuss the arguments for adopting or rejecting these proposals.

3. Why has it been so difficult to adopt a constitution for the European Union?

Glossary of key terms

Administration	A term with two meanings. Either (1) a term synonymous with government – e.g. the Bush administration, the Schröder administration or (2) a term synonymous with the management processes of bureaucracies – e.g. the administration of the state through bureaucratic agencies.
Affirmative action (also known as positive discrimination)	Policies designed to redress past discrimination. In this case, state bureaucracies may be required to increase recruitment of minority groups.
Agenda setting	The process by which a multiplicity of political problems and issues are continuously sorted according to the changing priority attached to them. In communication research, the theory claiming that the mass media may not exercise much influence over what we think, but can influence what we think about.
Alford index	A measure of class voting that calculates the difference between the proportion of working-class people voting for a left party, and the proportion of middle-class people doing the same. The higher the index, the greater the class voting.
Aligned groups	Pressure groups that ally themselves with a political party, the best examples being trade unions and left parties, and business organisations and right parties. Many groups try to maintain a non-aligned status if they can, because they want to work with whichever party is in power.
Authoritarian attitudes	A system or syndrome of attitudes based upon: prejudice, dogmatism, superstition, low tolerance for ambiguity, hostility to out-groups (anti-semitism and racism) and obedience to authority.
Bill	A formal proposal for a law put before a legislature but not yet accepted by it.
'Black economy'	The 'informal economy' in which goods and services are traded for cash, without bills, receipts, or financial records that would enable the authorities to levy taxes on them.

Bureaucracy	A rational, impersonal, rule-bound and hierarchical form of organisational structure set up to perform large-scale administrative tasks.
Cash transfers	A way to provide social security payments to citizens by giving them money. An alternative to cash benefits is the provision of goods and services.
Catch-all parties	Lacking a clear social basis, catch-all parties try to attract a broad range of supporters by advocating rather general policies.
Caucus	A small but loose-knit group of politicians (notables) who come together from time to time to make decisions about political matters.
Cause groups	Sometimes known as 'promotional groups' or 'attitude groups', cause groups are a type of pressure group that does not represent organised occupational interests, but promotes causes or ideas.
Centre–periphery cleavage	The political cleavage between the social and political forces responsible for creating centralised and modern nation-states, which usually became dominant, and other interests, usually on the periphery of the state, which resisted this process. Centre–periphery cleavages are often, but not always, geographical.
Charter of the United Nations	Founding treaty of the United Nations (UN) that defines the purposes of the UN and confers certain powers on it.
Checking and balancing power	*See* Separation of powers.
Civic culture	The term used by Almond and Verba to signify the balance of subject and participant political cultures that best supports democracy.
Civil service	The body of civilian officials (not members of the armed forces) employed by the state to work in government departments. In some countries, the term applies to all public officials (local government and teachers), but in most it includes only the officials of central government.
Civil society	That arena of social life outside the state and the family (i.e. mainly voluntary organisations and civic associations) that permits individuals to associate freely and independently of state regulation.
Class	Class is a form of social stratification that is determined by economic factors, notably the occupational hierarchy that broadly groups people into working-class (manual), middle-class (non-manual) and upper-class (wealthy property-owning) groups.

Class de-alignment	A process of decline in the class-based strength of attachment and sense of belonging to class-based political parties.
Cleavages	Cleavages are deep and persistent differences in society where (1) objective social differences (class, religion, race, language, or region) are aligned with (2) subjective awareness of these differences (different cultures, ideologies and orientations) and are (3) organised by political parties, groups, or movements. Cleavages are often the basis of political conflict.
Clientelism	A system of government and politics based on a relationship between patron and clients. Public sector jobs and contracts are distributed on the basis of personal and political contacts in return for political support.
Coalition	A set of parties that comes together to form a government. Coalition parties are usually represented in the cabinet, but sometimes one party takes all the cabinet posts with the support of a legislative coalition.
Cognitive mobilisation	The process by which increasing knowledge and understanding of the world helps to activate people to play a part in it.
Collective responsibility	The principle that decisions and policies of the cabinet or council are binding on all members who must support them in public in order to maintain the government's united front. What cabinet or council members say or believe in private is a different matter, but public disagreement should be followed by resignation from the government.
Conciliation	*See* Mediation.
Confederations	Organisations whose members give some powers to a higher body, while retaining their own autonomy and independence, including the right to leave the confederation.
Conglomerates	Single business organisations consisting of a number of different companies that operate in different economic fields.
Constitution	A constitution is a set of fundamental laws that determines what the central institutions and offices of the state are to be, their powers and duties, and how they relate to one another and to their citizens.
Content regulation	Regulation of the content of the media by public bodies in the public interest – e.g. to limit violence on TV, or ban cigarette adverts. The content regulation of news and current affairs programmes usually aims at accurate, balanced, and impartial political reporting, and fair access for the parties to the mass media.

Conventions	Unwritten rules that impose obligations on constitutional actors that are held to be binding, but not incorporated into law or reinforced by legal sanctions. (The term is also used to refer to meetings of political groups or parties – the Republican Party Convention, for example.)
Corporatism	A way of organising public policy making involving the close cooperation of major economic interests within a formal government apparatus that is capable of concerting the main economic groups so that they can jointly formulate and implement binding policies.
Corruption	The use of illegitimate means such as bribery, blackmail, or threats to influence or control the making of public decisions, or the secret use of public offices or resources for private purposes.
Country	Term usually used as a rather imprecise synonym or 'shorthand' for state or nation-state. It stresses the geographical location or territory of a state.
Cross-cutting cleavages	*See* Reinforcing and cross-cutting cleavages.
Cross-media ownership/Multi-media conglomeration	When the same person or company has financial interests in different branches of mass communication – e.g. when they own a newspaper and a TV channel, or a publishing house and TV network.
Decentralisation	Where some functions of the state are carried out by sub-central agencies that have a degree of discretion or autonomy from the central government.
'Declaration of the Rights of Man and of the Citizen'	The seventeen articles, describing the purpose of the state and the rights of individual citizens, proclaimed by the French National Assembly in August 1789. A similar list had been proclaimed in the USA thirteen years earlier, in 1776.
Delegated legislation	Law or decrees made by ministers, not by legislatures, though in accordance to powers granted to them by the legislative body.
Democratic deficit	A term used to convey the idea that the institutions of the European Union are not fully democratic, or as democratic as they should be. The criticism is often used to support suggestions that the power of the EP should be increased at the expense of the Commission and the Council of Ministers.
Democracy	A political system whose leaders are elected in competitive multi-party and multi-candidate processes in which opposition parties have a legitimate chance of attaining power or participating in power (Freedom House). Terms such as 'liberal democracy' are often used as synonyms for democracy.

Devolution	Where higher levels of government grant decision making powers to lower levels while maintaining their constitutionally subordinate status.
Direct election	Election by the electorate at large (popular election) rather than by an electoral college, the legislature, or another body.
Disproportionality	*See* Proportionality/Disproportionality.
Dominant one-party system	A party system in which one party dominates all the others. Dominant party systems are found in democratic countries with competitive parties. They must be distinguished from undemocratic one-party systems where only one party is allowed to operate freely.
Door-step response	The tendency of those with no opinion or information to respond to polls and surveys with the first thing that comes into their head, often something they think they are expected to say (sometimes known as 'non-opinion').
Dual systems	System of local government in unitary states in which local authorities have more independence than in fused systems but still operate under the general authority of central government.
Ecology	The relationships between organisms and their environment.
Electoral threshold	A way of discouraging small parties, by requiring them to get a given minimum percentage of votes or seats to be elected.
Empirical political theories	Theories that try to understand how the political world actually works and to explain why it works that way. Empirical theory is ultimately based upon evidence and argument that can, in principle, be tested and verified by political science.
Empirical statements	Factual statements about or explanations of the world. Empirical statements are not necessarily true or false, but they are amenable, in principle, to disproof and falsification (*see* normative statement).
'Episodic' groups	Groups that are not usually politically active but become so for a time when the need arises.
Essentially contestable concept	A concept that is inevitably the subject of endless dispute about their proper use (e.g. art, democracy, politics and a Christian life).
Etatism	Approaches to the relationships between state and society with a very strong emphasis on state power and an accompanying reduction of social and individual rights.
Executive	The branch of government mainly responsible for initiating government action, making and implementing public policy, and coordinating the activities of the state.

Externality	A cost or benefit that does not fall on those who are responsible for the decision or action that creates the externality, and which they do not take into account when they take the action.
False consciousness	The state of mind of the working class induced by the ruling class to conceal the real nature of capitalism and the real self-interests of the workers.
Federal states	Federal states combine a central authority (federal government) with a degree of constitutionally defined autonomy for sub-central territorial units of government (states, or regions, or provinces).
'Fire brigade' groups	Groups formed to fight a specific issue, and dissolved when it is over.
Framing	The theory that the way news stories are set up (framed) influences how audiences interpret them – e.g. the use of human interest stories to illustrate a social problem can deflect attention from government policies that help to cause the problem to the personal inadequacies of individuals who are the subjects of human interest.
Free-ride	To extract the benefits of other people's work without putting in any effort oneself. The free-rider problem is acute in collective action when some individuals benefit from a public good (clean air, for example, or public transport), though contributing little or nothing to it (continue to drive around in gas-guzzling car, not buying a ticket).
Fused systems	Systems of local government in unitary states in which officials appointed by central government directly supervise the work of local government and its elected officials.
General competence	The power of local government units to manage their own affairs, provided they observe the laws of the land and relatively few legally defined exceptions.
Gerrymandering	A form of electoral corruption in which electoral boundaries are drawn to favour a particular party or interest.
Globalisation	The growing interdependencies and interconnectedness of the world that are said to reduce the autonomy of individual states and the importance of boundaries between them.
Governance	The act of governing; that is, the total set of government's activities in each phase of the policy making process.
Government	A government executes the monopoly on the legitimate use of physical force within a state. Securing internal and external sovereignty of the state are major tasks of any government.

'Grand' coalitions	Oversized coalitions that include all parties or all the largest of them.
Gross Domestic Product (GDP)	The value of all final goods and services produced within a state in a given year. In order to compare the wealth of states the measure used is normally GDP *per capita*.
Hegemony	Originally a Marxist term, hegemony indicates a class that is so powerful that it does not have to rely upon force or power to maintain its rule because its values and attitudes have been accepted by all other classes. Often used now to mean all-powerful – since the collapse of the Soviet Union, the USA has become the 'hegemonic' world power, for example.
Human Development Index (HDI)	A UN index of national development that combines measures of life expectancy, educational attainment and wealth into one measure.
Human rights	The innate, inalienable and inviolable right of humans to free movement and self-determination in relation to the state. Such rights cannot be bestowed, granted, limited, bartered away, or sold away. Inalienable rights can be only secured or violated.
Hyper-pluralism	A state of affairs in which too many powerful groups make too many demands on government, causing overload and ungovernability.
Idealism	In political theory, the term 'idealism' refers to the theory that ideas have a life of their own and must be understood as the products of consciousness or spiritual ideals and values that are independent of material conditions. In international relations idealism refers to the view of politics that emphasises the role of ideas and morality as a determinant of the relations between states (*see* Materialism).
Ideal-type	An analytical construct that simplifies reality and picks out its most important features, to serve as a model that allows us to understand and compare the complexities of the real world. An ideal-type is neither a standard of perfection (as in 'an ideal husband') nor a statistical average, but a simplified, theoretical abstraction from the real world that helps us compare individual cases.
Ideologues	Those with an informed, broad, sophisticated and more or less consistent (systematic) view of the political world.
Ideology	A more or less systematic, well-developed and comprehensive set of ideas and beliefs about politics consisting of both (empirical) statements about what is, and (prescriptive) statements about what ought to be.

Immobilism	The state of being unable to move (immobilised) or in a political system of being unable to take decisions or implement policies.
Impeachment	To charge a public official, usually an elected politician, with improper conduct in office before a duly constituted tribunal, usually the main elected legislative body, prior to removing the official from office if they are found guilty. Not known much outside the USA, and not often used there.
Implementation	The process of applying policies and putting them into practice.
Incremental model	The theory that decisions are not usually based upon a rational or fundamental review of problems and solution, but upon small, marginal changes from existing policies.
'Insider' groups	Pressure groups with access to senior government officials, often recognised as the only legitimate representatives of particular interests and often formally incorporated into the official consultative bodies.
Interest aggregation	The process of sorting and sifting the great variety of political attitudes and opinions on any given political issues, so that it is reduced to a set of more simple and clear-cut 'packages' of opinion.
Interest articulation	The process of expressing political needs and demands in order to influence public policy.
Interest groups	Sometimes know as 'sectional groups', interest groups are a type of pressure group that represents occupational interests. The main types are business associations, professional associations and trade unions.
Interpellation	A parliamentary question addressed to government requiring a formal answer and often followed by discussion, and sometimes by a vote.
'Iron triangles'	The close, three-sided working relationship developed between (1) government departments and ministries, (2) pressure groups and (3) politicians, that make public policy in a given area.
Judicial activism	Judicial activism involves the courts taking a broad and active view of their role as interpreters of the constitution and reviewers of executive and legislative action.
Judicial review	The binding power of the courts to provide an authoritative interpretation of laws, including constitutional law, and to overturn executive or legislative actions they hold to be illegal or unconstitutional.
Judiciary	The branch of government mainly responsible for the authoritative interpretation of law and applying it to particular cases.

Knowledge gap	The gap between those with a good education and understanding of the world, which enables them to acquire knowledge and understanding at a faster rate than those with less education and understanding.
Labour productivity	The average production per labourer in a specific period (for instance, the average number of ballpoints produced per labourer in a ballpoint pen factory in one year).
Laissez-faire doctrines	The literal translation from the French is 'to let to do'. Laissez-faire is the principle of maximum freedom for the economic forces of the market, and minimum intervention from the state.
Legislation	Legislation is the body of laws that have been passed by the legislature. Legislating is thus the act of initiating, debating and passing such laws.
Legislative oversight	The role of the legislature that involves the scrutiny or supervision of other branches of government, especially the executive and the public bureaucracy.
Legislature	The branch of government mainly responsible for discussing and passing legislation, and keeping watch on the executive.
Legitimacy	The condition of being in accordance with the norms and values of the people. The 'legitimate use of power' refers to the use of power that is accepted because it is in accordance with the norms and values of the people it concerns.
Legitimation	The process of making something morally acceptable, proper or right in the eyes of the general public according to accepted standards and values.
Liberal democracy	The form of democracy that tries to combine the powers of democratic government with liberal values about the freedom of the individual.
Lobby	A popular term for pressure groups (based on the mistaken belief that pressure group representatives spend a lot of time in the 'lobbies' or ante-rooms of legislative chambers).
Low information rationality	Where citizens do not have a great deal of factual political information but have a broad enough grasp of the main issues to make up their mind about them, or else they take their cues about the issues from sources they trust (sometimes known as 'gut rationality').
Market regulation	The regulation of the media market by public bodies, often to avoid cross-media ownership, foreign control of important channels of national communication, or cases of market failure.

Mass society	A society without a plurality of organised social groups and interests, whose mass of isolated and uprooted individuals are not integrated into the community and who are therefore vulnerable to the appeals of extremist and anti-democratic elites.
Materialism	The theory that ideas are rooted in the material or physical conditions of life, as opposed to spiritual ideals and values which are constructs of the mind which can be independent of material and physical conditions (*see* Idealism).
Means testing	In contrast to public benefits that are universally available, means testing involves investigating a person's income and means of support to ensure that they cannot afford to pay for the service themselves. Means testing is often resented by welfare applicants and is politically controversial.
Mediamalaise	The attitudes of political cynicism, despair, apathy, distrust and disillusionment (among others) that some social scientists claim are caused by the mass media, especially TV.
Median voter	The median is the middle number in any distribution of numbers. The median voter is in the middle of the distribution with equal numbers of voters to the left and right. The support of the median voter is usually necessary to win an election.
Mediation	Attempt by a third party to reach an agreement between disputing parties by suggesting terms of settlement.
Meso-government	A middle level or tier of government between central and local authorities, and often known as state, regional, provincial or county government.
Military–industrial complex	The close and powerful alliance of government, business and military interests that is said by some to run capitalist societies.
Minimum winning coalition (MWC)	The smallest number of parties necessary for a majority of votes in parliament.
Minority government	A government or coalition that is smaller than a MWC.
Mixed economy	An economy that is neither wholly privately owned (a capitalist market economy), nor wholly publicly owned (a communist command economy), but a mixture of both.
Multi-member districts	*See* Single-member/Multi-member districts.
Multi-party systems	Where several or many main parties compete, often with the result that no single party has an overall majority.
Nation	*See* nation-state.

Nation-state	A state based on the acceptance of a common culture, a common history and a common fate, irrespective of whatever political, social and economic differences may exist between the members of the nation-state.
New Public Management (NPM)	New Public Management (NPM) refers to the reforms of the public sector in the 1980s and 1990s, based mainly on what were thought to be private sector practice and consisting mainly of privatisation, deregulation, business management techniques and 'marketisation'. Known also as 'reinventing government', it is said to have had the effect of 'hollowing out' the state.
New Social Movements	Loosely knit organisations ('networks of networks') that try to influence government policy on broad issues, including the environment, nuclear energy and nuclear weapons, economic development, peace, women and minorities.
Non-decision	The decision not to deal with an issue, perhaps not even to consider it.
Non-governmental organisation (NGO)	A non-governmental organisation (NGO) is a non-profit making, non-violent private organisation that is independent of government and seeks to influence or control government policy without actually seeking government office.
Normative political theories	Theories about how the world should be or ought to be. Normative theory is based upon philosophical arguments, and ultimately on subjective values and judgements. Sometimes it is known as prescriptive theory, political theory, or political philosophy.
Normative statements	Statement that are based upon faith, or contain a value judgement or an evaluation. Sometimes referred to as prescriptive, or evaluative statements. Normative statements are neither scientific nor unscientific, but non-scientific (*see* empirical statements).
Oligarchy	Government by a few.
Ombudsman	A state official appointed to receive complaints and investigate claims about maladministration (improper or unjust action) and to report their findings, usually to the legislature.
One-party systems	Government systems in which a single party forms the government.
Outcomes	The impacts, or effects, of outputs.
Outputs	The policy decisions as they are actually implemented.
'Outsider' groups	Groups with no access to top government officials.
'Oversized' (surplus majority) coalitions	A coalition that is larger than a MWC.

Parliamentary systems	Parliamentary systems are characterised by (1) a directly elected legislative body, (2) the fusion of executive and legislative institutions, (3) a collective and collegial executive that emerges out of the legislature and is responsible to it and (4) a separation of head of state and head of government.
Participatory democracy	That form of democracy in which citizens actively participate in government and political processes.
Partisan de-alignment	A process of decline in the strength of attachment and sense of belonging to the political parties.
Partisan re-alignment	A process in which social and economic groups show signs of a long-term change in their old party identifications in favour of new ones.
Party families	Groups of parties in different countries that have similar ideologies and party programmes.
Party identification (ID)	The stable and deep-rooted feeling of attachment to and support for a political party.
Party systems	The pattern of significant parties within a political system, especially their number and the party families represented.
Peak associations	See 'Umbrella' organisations.
People	Group of persons living together on the territory of a state whose common consciousness and identity usually form them into a collective entity.
Performance	Actual activities and results; how well government is doing or how successful it is in offering citizens what they prefer.
Pluralism	A situation where power is dispersed among many different groups and organisations that openly compete with one another in different political arenas.
Pluralist democracy	The theory of modern democracy arguing that political decisions are the outcome of the conflict and competition between many different groups and organisations representing many different interests.
Police	The branch of government employed to maintain civil order and to investigate breaches of the law.
Policy communities	Small, stable and consensual groupings of government officials and pressure group representatives that form around particular issue areas.
Policy networks	Compared with policy communities, policy networks are larger, looser, and more conflictual networks that gather around a particular policy area.
Political alienation	A feeling of detachment, estrangement, or critical distance from politics, often because the alienated feel there is something basically wrong with the political system.

Political behaviour	Term used to refer to all political activities of citizens as well as the attitudes and orientations relevant for these activities.
Political cleavage	A political division caused by the overlap of social differences (religion, race, language, class, culture, history) with ideological differences. Such cleavages are especially important if they coincide with territorial divisions.
Political culture	The pattern of attitudes, values and beliefs about politics, whether they are conscious or unconscious, explicit or implicit.
Political elite	The relatively small number of people at the top of a political system who exercise disproportionate influence or power over political decisions. If it exercises enough power in the system, it is a 'ruling elite'.
Political marginality	The condition of being on the fringes of politics, and therefore of having little influence.
Political orientation	A predisposition or propensity to view politics in a certain way.
Political parties	Organisations of politically like-minded people who seek political power and public office in order to realise their policies.
Political socialisation	The process by which individuals acquire their political values, attitudes and habits. Childhood socialisation is most important, but socialisation continues in adulthood as well.
Presidential systems	In presidential systems a directly elected president is the executive, with a limited term of office and a general responsibility for the affairs of state, who governs with a separate and independently elected legislature.
Pressure groups	Private and voluntary organisations that try to influence or control particular government policies but do not want to become the government or control all government policies.
Prevention	Attempt to hinder or deter delinquent behaviour.
Priming	The theory that the mass media can prime us to focus on certain things and in certain ways by highlighting some issues rather than others – e.g. focusing on foreign rather than domestic policy favours parties that are thought to be better at foreign policy than domestic policy.
Privatisation	The process of converting public services and amenities to private ones.
Productivity	*See also* Labour productivity.

Proportionality/ Disproportionality	A measure of the ratio of seats to votes. The more proportional the system, the closer the ratio of seats to votes. In the most proportional voting system a party getting 43 per cent of the votes should get 43 per cent of the seats, or close to this figure, since seats are not divisible.
Protest vote	Where citizens vote for a party not because they support it, but because they oppose other parties.
Provision of goods and services	A way to provide social security for citizens by offering them not money but specific facilities such as housing or job training. Cash transfers are an alternative to goods and services.
(Public) policy	Some general set of ideas or plans that has been officially agreed on and which is used as a basis for making decisions. A public policy is the long series of activities, decisions and actions carried out by officials of government in their attempts to solve problems that are thought to lie in the public or collective arena.
Public–private partnerships (PPPs)	Formal cooperations between government and private groups to obtain specific goals.
Public sector	That part of social, economic and political life that is not private but controlled or regulated by the state or its agencies.
Public service model	The system of organising radio and TV in which broadcasting licences are granted to public bodies, usually supported by public funds, for use in the public interest rather than for profit.
QUANGOs (Quasi-autonomous Non-Governmental Organisations)	Organisations that are partially or wholly funded by the government to perform public service functions but not under direct government control.
Realism	In international relations realism refers to the view of politics that emphasises the role of self-interest as a determinant of state policies and hence the importance of power in these relations. In realist theory states (and other actors such as business organisations) are presumed to act more or less rationally to promote their own interests.
Referendum	The submission of a public matter to direct popular vote. Sometimes known as a plebiscite.
Reinforcement theory (also known as minimal effects theory)	The theory that the mass media can only reflect and reinforce public opinion, not create or mould it.

Reinforcing and cross-cutting cleavages	Reinforcing cleavages are laid one on top of the other, making them more potent. Cross-cutting cleavages are laid across one another, thereby reducing their capacity to divide.
Representative democracy	That form of democracy in which citizens elect leaders who govern in their name.
Ruling elite	A political elite that is so powerful that it can make all the important decisions in government.
Salient	Something that is important, significant, or prominent in people's minds.
Semi-presidential system	Semi-presidential government consists of a directly elected president who is accountable to the electorate and a prime minister, who is appointed by the president from the elected legislature and accountable to it. The president and prime minister share executive power.
Separation of powers	The doctrine that political power should be divided among several bodies or officers of the state, often between bodies or officers performing different government functions, as a precaution against too much concentration of power.
Single-member/ Multi-member districts	Single-member districts have one representative each in parliament, while multi-member districts have two or more to make it easier to attain proportionality.
Social capital	The features of social organisations, such as trust, social norms and social networks, that improve social and governmental efficiency by encouraging cooperation and collective action.
Social expenditures	Social expenditures are the provision by public (and private) institutions of benefits to households and individuals in order to provide support during circumstances which adversely affect their welfare. This is the definition used by the OECD.
Social stratification	The hierarchical layering of society into socially unequal groups. It includes peasants and landowners, castes, classes and status groups.
Sociotropic voting	Deciding which party to vote for on the basis of general social or economic circumstances. The opposite is 'pocket-book voting' that is based on private interests of the voter.
Sovereignty	A state is sovereign when it holds the highest power and, in principle, can act with complete freedom and independence. Internal sovereignty means that, on its own territory, the state can act as it wishes and is independent of other institutions. External sovereignty refers to the fact that the state is seen as autonomous by other states.

Spectrum scarcity	The shortage of terrestrial broadcasting frequencies for radio and TV, which meant that there could be only a few channels.
Spin-doctors	Public relations specialists employed to put the best possible light on news about their clients. Often used in political life to imply attempts to manipulate the news.
State	An organisation that issues and enforces rules that are binding for the people living in a given territorially defined area.
Status	A form of social stratification determined by social prestige rather than economic factors or occupation. It is sometimes said that class is determined by how people make their money, status by how they spend it. Sometimes class and status are combined in the single measure of social and economic status.
Street-level bureaucrats	The bureaucrats who regularly come into contact and deal with the public.
Subjective or internal competence/efficacy	The extent to which ordinary citizens feel that they can make their views and actions count in the political system. The opposites of the term are 'powerlessness', 'inefficacy' or 'low competence'.
Sub-central/sub-national government	All levels of government below national/central government. Sub-national government covers everything below central government from community and neighbourhood government, through local government of all kinds, to the middle or meso-level of state, regional and provincial government.
Subsidiarity	The principle that decisions should be taken at the lowest possible level of government – that is, at the level closest to the people affected by the decisions. Usually the term subsidiarity is used in connection with the territorial decentralisation of government, but it is not limited to this form.
Suffrage	The right to vote. Hence 'suffragettes' were women who fought for the right of women to vote.
Supra-national government	Organisations in which countries pool their sovereignty on certain matters to allow joint decision-making.
System or external efficacy	The extent to which ordinary citizens feel that political leaders and institutions are responsive to their wishes.
Territory	Terrain or geographical area.
Terrorism	The use of violence (such as murder, torture, bombing, kidnapping, hijacking, violent resistance) to spread fear and horror for political aims. What some regard as terrorism is seen as 'freedom fighting' by others.

'Third wave' (of democracy)	Democratisation across the world is often divided into 'three waves'. The first, from the mid-nineteenth to the mid-twentieth century, saw between twenty-five and thirty states achieve a degree of democratic stability, depending on how 'democracy' is defined. The second, from about 1950 to 1975, was mainly the result of decolonisation. The third, from about 1975 to 2000, was mainly the result of the disintegration of the Soviet Union and the spread of democracy in Latin America and Asia.
Tri-partism	A looser and less centralised system of decision making than corporatism involving close government consultation – often with business and trade union organisations.
Two-party systems	Party systems in which two large parties dominate all the others.
'Umbrella'/organisations	Associations that coordinate the activity of their member organisations.
Unitary states	In unitary states the central government is the only sovereign body. It does not share *constitutional* authority with any sub-central units of government.
Values	Basic ethical priorities that constrain and give shape to individual attitudes and beliefs.
Volatility	The opposite of stability, volatility involves change in voting patterns from one election to another. Some voting studies refer to it as 'churning'.
Vote of confidence	A vote of confidence (or no confidence), to test whether the government of the day continues to have the majority support of members of the assembly. Its importance lies in the normal convention that governments losing a vote of confidence should resign.
Voting system	The arrangements by which votes are converted into seats on representative bodies.
Voting turnout	The number of citizens casting a valid vote expressed either as a percentage of those eligible to vote (adult citizens), or as a percentage of those on the electoral register.
Welfare states	Democracies that accept responsibility for the young and old, the sick and disabled and the unemployed and poor. Welfare states are characterised by resource redistribution policies.

Index of names

Index of subjects